Nadeem Hasnain

The Other Lucknow

An Ethnographic Portrait of a City of Undying Memories and Nostalgia

Vani Prakashan

Vani
Prakashan

4695, 21-A, Daryaganj, New Delhi 110 002
India
Branch
Ashok Rajpath, Patna 800 004
Phone : +91 11 23273167 Fax : +91 11 23275710

www.vaniprakashan.in
vaniprakashan@gmail.com
sales@vaniprakashan.in

In Association with

ESTD.-1986

Ayodhya Research Institute
presents

THE OTHER LUCKNOW
An Ethnographic Portait of a City of Undying Memories and Nostalgia
by Nadeem Hasnain

ISBN: 978-93-5229-420-6
Non-Fiction/Social Science

First Edition 2016
Second Edition 2017

Price : ₹ 795

(Based on a research project sponsored and funded by the Ayodhya Shodh Sansthan, an autonomous organization of the Department of Culture, Government of Uttar Pradesh)

Printed at S.K. Offset, Delhi-110 095 (India)

Vani Prakashan's signature motif is created by Artist Maqbool Fida Husain

लखनऊ

किसी नौजवान के जवान तरीके पर त्यौरियाँ चढ़ाए,
एक टूटी आराम कुर्सी पर
अधलेटे, अधमरे बूढ़े-सा खाँसता हुआ लखनऊ।
कॉफ़ी-हाउस, हज़रतगंज, अमीनाबाद और चौक तक,
चार तहज़ीबों में बँटा हुआ लखनऊ।

बिना बात बात-बात पर बहसें करते हुए
एक-दूसरे से ऊबे हुए मगर एक-दूसरे को सहते हुए
एक-दूसरे से बचते हुए पर एक-दूसरे से टकराते हुए
ग़म पीते हुए और ग़म खाते हुए
ज़िन्दगी के लिए तरसते कुछ मरे नौजवानों वाला लखनऊ।

नयी शामे-अवध
दस सेकेन्ड में समझाने-समझने वाली किसी बात को,
क़रीब दो घंटे की बहस के बाद समझा-समझाया।
अपनी सरपट दौड़ती अक़्ल को
किसी बे-अक़्ल की समझ के छकड़े में जोतकर
हज़रतगंज की सड़क पर दौड़ा-दौड़ाकर थकाया,
ख़्वाहिशों की जगह बहसों से काम चलाया,
और शामे-अवध को शामते अवध की तरह बिताया।

बाज़ार-जहाँ ज़रूरतों का दम घुटता है,
बाज़ार-जहाँ भीड़ का एक युग चलता है।
सड़कें-जिन पर जगह नहीं,
भागा भाग-जिसकी वजह नहीं,
महज़ एक बे-रौनक़ आना-जाना,
यह है-शहर का बिसातख़ाना।
किसी मुर्दा शानोशौकत की क़ब्र सा,
किसी बेवा के सब्र सा,

जर्जर गुम्बदों के ऊपर,
अवध की उदास शामों का शामियाना थामे,
किसी तवाइफ़ की ग़ज़ल सा,
हर आने वाला दिन किसी बीते हुए कल-सा
कमान-क़मर नवाब के झुके हुए, शरीफ़ आदाब-सा लखनऊ।
खण्डहरों में सिसकते किसी बेगम के शबाब-सा लखनऊ।
बारीक मलमल पर कढ़ी हुई बारीकियों की तरह,
इस शहर की कमज़ोर नफ़ासत,
नवाबी ज़माने की जवानी अदाओं में,
किसी मनचले को रिझाने के लिए,
क़व्वालियाँ गाती हुई नज़ाकत,
किसी मरीज़ की तरह नई ज़िन्दगी के लिए तरसता,
'सरशार' और 'मजाज़' का लखनऊ।
किसी शौक़ीन और हाय किसी बेनियाज़ का लखनऊ।
यही है क़िब्ला, हमारा और आपका लखनऊ।

–कुँवर नारायण

दामन को छोड़ती ही नहीं लखनऊ की ख़ाक
मिटना है आरज़ू इसी उजड़े दयार में

دامن کو چھوڑتی ہی نہی لکھنؤ کی خاک
مٹنا ہے آرزو اسی اجڑے دیار میں

*

इक लुत्फ़-ए-ख़ास दिल को तेरी आरज़ू से है
अल्लाह जाने कितनी कशिश लखनऊ में है

ایک لطف خاص دل کو تری آرزو سے ہے
اللہ جانے کتنی کشش لکھنؤ مے ہے

*

मुझ से सुबहोशाम शिकवा कर रहा है लखनऊ
देख तुझ में धीरे धीरे मर रहा है लखनऊ

مجھ سے سبحہ' شام شکوہ کر رہا ہے لکھنؤ
دیکہ تجھ میں دھیرے دھیرے مر رہا ہے لکھنؤ

*

Contents

Preface

Tehzeeb koi apni nazar me jachegi kya
Meri nigaah-e-shauq ne dekha hai Lucknow
(No other culture can impress me as I have seen Lucknow)

*

Mujh se subh-o-shaam shikwa kar raha hai Lucknow
Dekh tujh me dheere dheere mar raha hai Lucknow
(Lucknow is complaining to me day in and day out and lamenting that it is dying slowly)

These two Urdu couplets aptly express my inner feelings regarding Lucknow. From early childhood to becoming a senior citizen, I have made a fascinating journey in Lucknow spread over almost six decades. Though Lucknow has changed a lot over this period but the Lucknow of my childhood lingers in my memories. I had a good fortune in spending the formative years of my life in a typical, traditional 'Lucknawi' neighbourhood of Old Lucknow. Though not a native of the city (as my parents had their ancestral villages in Eastern Uttar Pradesh) my father chose Lucknow to settle down immediately after his retirement from government service in early 1950s and I fell in love with Lucknow and its culture. In the past forty years I have been teaching, researching and writing on different area of my discipline of social anthropology but I kept the dream of writing something on Lucknow alive.

Thus, Lucknow is not merely an academic work for me but also a part of my personal life and world. When I look at myself, I find that I am largely a product of the socio-cultural milieu of Lucknow. That is how this book came about. In a way, some parts of this book are like 'auto-ethnography'. To my mind only two cities of South Asia- Calcutta and Delhi, can compete with Lucknow in terms of nostalgia, undying memories and attention. This book should be taken as a humble tribute to Lucknow from an *aashiq* (lover).

My special thanks to Sandria Freitag, North Carolina State University, USA, Joel Lee, Max Planck Institute for Human Development, Germany, Syed Anwer Abbas, Lucknow, Akhilesh Dixit, Lucknow and Aseem Hasnain, Bridgewater State University, MA, USA for their special articles. When I invited them to write something on Lucknow for this book they readily agreed and sent their contributions within the deadline. All of them are lovers of Lucknow. Shamim

Akhtar 'Aarzoo' of Lucknow Society helped me in providing some photographs given in this book. I am grateful to him.

This book is the result of a research project fully funded by the Ayodhya Shodh Sansthan (an autonomous organization of the Department of Culture, Government of Uttar Pradesh). My sincerest thank to its director, Dr. Y P Singh who took keen interest in this project and did not allow the work to be bagged down because of financial constraints. My wife Nishaat deserves affectionate thanks for her patience and also freeing me from all domestic worries during the entire period of the research project andwriting this book. Moveover, She has also filled several gaps in this narration.

My entire research team has contributed in this project in a variety of ways and at different points of time. Akhilesh Dixit, Ashish Awasthi, Mahesh Chand Pal and Mashiyat Rizvi have not only collected valuable field data but also provided me with their write-ups making my task easier while Pooja Verma helped me with the analysis of the secondary data. My research students Sudhir Patel, Brijesh Pandey and Mauli Shukla came to my help whenever called and did some typing and corrections in the manuscript. I shall always be grateful to all of them.

Last but not the least I give my heart felt thanks to Mr. Arun Maheshwari, the publisher, who has taken personal interest in the entire process of production of this book. I am grateful to him.

30 August, 2015
Lucknow

Nadeem Hasnain
(nadeemhasnain@gmail.com)

Introduction

"Not Rome, not Athens, nor Constantinople, not any city I have ever seen appears to me so striking and so beautiful as this."

When these words were written by William Rusell, correspondent of The Times, in 1858, Lucknow was already in decline. In retaliation to the revolt in 1857, the British had already demolished and destroyed a number of buildings, roads and gardens and were in the process of reshaping Lucknow mainly for security reasons for any future eventuality. Had he seen Lucknow in 1855-56, he would have been dumb founded by all accounts. That is how Lucknow is remembered and continues to linger in the memories of many especially of the old elite.

There are few cities in the world that evoke the same nostalgia among its inhabitants, visitors and historians as Lucknow. Lucknow has been famous for its Urdu poets and poetry, *tehzeeb* especially *ganga –jamuni tehzeeb, adab-o-akhlaq*, kathak, muharrum, cousine and handicrafts. But this description is not completely free from over emphasis and stereotyping. Scholars have placed Lucknow as a space primarily constituted by coming together of Awadhi and Persian ways of meaning making, but open to influences form several other quarters. Lucknow, past and present, shows influence from the Kayastha groups who formed the backbone of the Nawabi and later, colonial bureaucracy, Kashimiri Brahmins, who served the Nawabs court, and various Shia and Sunni cleric- scholar-poet refugees from Delhi who came in search of patronage. Lucknow has also competed for the title of the 'Muslim city par excellence' with Delhi and Hyderabad and occupied a central place in the world for Shia Culture.

II

Most of the published scholarship on Lucknow is focused either on 1857 revolt, palace culture, monuments and the "traditional culture" of Lucknow. This fascination with the past is largely responsible for the neglect of various other aspects of Lucknow-its'social fabric (castes and communities), the subaltern and the marginalized sections of the society, problems and plight of the artisans, the vanishing skills, sectarian violence, the role of people from outside the state settling in Lucknow, virtual metamorphosis of Lucknow with of course, a number of continuities retained and a variety of other issues. Perhaps, Delhi and Calcutta are the only two cities on which more written than on Lucknow. The later writings on both these cities also dealt strongly with the present though retaining the nostalgia of a grand past.

The present study is an humble attempt to grapple with the present but not severeing ties with the past. I strongly believe that the wholesale loss of memory makes a city characterless. A little nostalgia must be there. It should not be a 'city of amnesia'. As Asad Zaidi (2015) rightly comments about Delhi, "The loss of memory is being compensated with manufactured nostalgia and consumerist solution- Heritage Walk, Heritage Talks, Heritage Food and Heritage Buildings. It becomes a burgeoning industry". Since more than 50% of the Lucknow city's population consists of people who have roots elsewhere and settled in Lucknow during the past 3-4 decades, they don't have any undying memories of Lucknow passed to them by the preceding generations. Thus ,Lucknow like Delhi is gradually turning into a characterless urban space.

Also, Lucknow is fast growing into a busy metropolis. It is witnessing a changing ethos from the city of gardens, literary salons, fairs and festivals to a place of shopping plazas and eateries, noisy traffic and congested roads.The chief reason for this population explosion and the consequent ramification is the fact that Lucknow is the capital of the most populous state of the country surrounded by a number of small towns. It is an important centre of education from primary to higher education and also a hub of medical facilities. It has also emerged as a major market where the fast expanding middle class is consuming 3-4 times more than it used to till 1970s or 80s. The net result of these developments is that the city is fast developing an impersonal life style, anonymity and alienation.

Every city has to pay a price for transition and Lucknow too is not an exception but it still retains some continuities. For instance shoppers flock the malls in large numbers but have not abandoned old markets such as Aminabad and Nakhas and continues with a leisurely pace of life in the midst of all amenities and comforts of big cities and those who are even the second generation Lucknowites get attracted to any thing from traditional Lucknow. On the contrary, many of the first generation settlers do not pick the refinement and sophistication of the traditional Lucknow. The rise of Awadhi and Bhojpuri colloquial on the campuses, bazaars and other public spaces prompt the persons nurtured in Lucknow culture to comment contemptuously, "the inevitable ruralization of urbanity".

If Lucknow, like any other city with a glorious and grand past, has to retain its character even in the midst of fast pace of modernization, it has to take some urgent steps to protect the heritage buildings being swallowed by urbanization. There has to be a closer association between the needs of the city and protection of heritage buildings and still, this could make for more vibrant urban neighbourhoods. Let Lucknow not degenerate into a city of cultural amnesia.

A Short Cultural History of Lucknow

In most of the earlier writings on the cultural history of Lucknow, the Nawabs, palace culture and the related issues figured prominently. Here, the cultural history has been dealt with from a slightly different perspective- a cultural history through Lucknow's cultural systems, colonial pressures, Shia-Sunni relations and the decline of Shia power and its resultant changes dealt with in a logical sequence. Post-independence Lucknow has also been given some space so that one may understand Lucknow now in continuities- freedom movement, creation of Pakistan and its' aftermath, advent of the Punjabi and Sindhi refugees and other peripheral issues.

1

A Short Cultural History of Lucknow

-Sandria Freitag

> *Outwardly the court of Lucknow became so magnificent that no other court could rival it and the town of Lucknow acquired great splendor. The money which Shuja ud Daula had spent on the army and on provision for war, Asaf ud Daula started to spend in satisfying his desire for voluptuous living and on the embellishment and comforts of the town. In a short time he had collected to himself all the pomp and splendor that could be found in the world. His one desire was to surpass the Nizam of Hyderabad and Tipu Sultan and his ambition was that the magnificence and grandeur of no court should equal that of his own.*
>
> -Abdul Halim Sharar,
>
> *'Lucknow : The Last Phase of an Oriental Culture'*

Introduction

If, as some people suggest, Lucknow 'suffers' from 'too much history' why should we begin with a description of the Nawabs and their impact on the city, even more with a quotation taken from a nostalgic look back at Nawabi Lucknow a half-century later? What this historic overview wants to suggest is that, however far the city may have moved from these beginnings, the inherited strategies that shaped Lucknow's cultural system so that its residents played (and still play) an active role in defining that system is fundamental to understanding life in this central place. At the heart of our narrative, then, lie the strategies inherent not only in the Nawabs' approach to their kingdom, but in the larger implications for contemporary India of what we call here, the (Mughal) Successor State modality of creating a cultural system that makes room for an inclusive polity shaped at least in part by the agency of its residents.

Sharar's chapter, from which this description of Lucknow comes, was originally published in installments from 1913 into the 1920s, in the Urdu literary journal *Dil Gudaz*, which Sharar founded and edited in Lucknow. Sharar's rendition of elite life in Nawabi Lucknow is based on his own experiences (1860-1926) or from first-hand oral sources. The chapter continues by listing the building program of Asaf ud Daula – including the Daulat Khana, Rumi Darvaza, along with 'his' Imambara and tomb – clearly making the case for the centrality of Asaf ud Daula (as well as the other Nawabs who followed him) to Lucknow's sense of itself. Asaf ud Daula, the fourth Nawab of Awadh, moved the capital city from Faizabad to Lucknow in 1775, and so had a clean slate on which to 'construct' both a cultural system and the urban built environments that conveyed this Successor State's identity. In contrast, for instance, to near-by Banaras (or Varanasi), Lucknow was a very different kind of city, designed to be a political capital for a different style of rule: the Nawabs were a Persian Shia Muslim dynasty, and used their Shi'ism to call out distinctive elements as markers of their cultural system, while also becoming known for their inclusiveness and even 'secular' characteristics of rule. At the same time, they could use their reliance on Persian to attract poets and other artists previously resident in Delhi to move to Lucknow as the Mughal Empire declined and its rich cultural production waned. Indeed, poetry became the most prominent marker of court culture in Lucknow, and enabled the new Successor State capital to lay claim to a preeminence Delhi could no longer contest.

Sharar wrote at the turn of the century, and rode a wave of nostalgia for that Nawabi cultural system that had dominated the city for the preceding century and a half. We might note two revealing aspects of his description: first, Sharar's language adopts the British tone of denigration (e.g., 'voluptuous', 'pomp'), which reflects the changing political system dominated by increased British power – something that Sharar not-so-implicitly condemns. Along with this changed context comes Sharar's acceptance of the characterizations and blame placed on the Nawabs by the British; initially this served as British justification for taking over direct rule in Awadh, but fifty years later the characterization stands unchallenged even in nostalgia. A second revealing aspect of the quotation, however, is the frame of reference Sharar presents: for the Nawabs (as for Sharar?), it is the other Successor States ruled by the Nizam of Hyderabad and Tipu Sultan of Mysore that the Nawab wants to "surpass". The neighboring Rohillas (the closest kingdom) are only worth mentioning because they are so uncivilized that everyone moves on quickly to Lucknow; the East India Company lands are, apparently, also too uncivilized to be considered. Moreover, the Mughals present neither the standard to measure against nor even an appropriate comparison, though the Lucknow court has been described by others as the zenith of late Mughal civilization.

These revealing contexts for Sharar's description of the city point our way to the argument that frames this brief treatment of Lucknow's history. As the capital of the (Mughal) Successor State of Awadh, Lucknow became the center of a new kind of rule and expectations for a cultural system that was distinctive both from what had gone before, and from what the encroachment of British/European 'modernism' represented. The most significant representation of this new mode was the Nawabi building program. As Sharar comments about Asaf ud Daula's buildings, they are "nothing like the Mughal Emperor's stone buildings… [they]

have a rare beauty and great dignity and distinction…[moreover, they] are in no way influenced by European architecture. In style they are purely Asiatic, without ostentation but with genuine splendor and dignity" (p. 47).

This helps us to see the importance of built environments for shaping a place, and for serving as the way that new claimants to civilizational significance may put their mark on the city (and beyond). The buildings thus helped to outline a set of practices and collective cultural expressions – characteristic patterns of Successor States that we may call a cultural system – that also implied a distinctive understanding of 'the public' and participation in it. That is, this cultural system's components point us to what was most valued in the urban place over time (for instance, other functions related to these key buildings) *and* served to tie the royal house to popular culture and the urban population. While the Nawabs' motivation was to demonstrate their authority and legitimacy through this strategy, it also made a space for popular as well as elite shaping of the new cultural system and its capital city.

Lucknow's Cultural System

As with all rulers – not least those with whom the Nawabs compared themselves – creating a local system with legitimacy depended on a janus-like function that situated these regional kingdoms in a distinctive way. On the one hand, they linked their authority to a relationship with the larger sources of rule represented by the Mughals (while trying to increase their distance and hence independence from this source). On the other hand, they located their legitimacy in part by connecting to what the local population valued, especially through activities staged in public spaces. A focus on public devotional activities enabled the implicit connection between local religious understandings of devotion and loyalty to the royal house. The strategy of facing two ways to claim authority and legitimacy, then, set up Successor States to create cultural systems that also possessed a crucial flexibility, enabling them to adjust as circumstances altered the larger context in which they operated (e.g. from Mughal to British rule, and then to independence in the mid-twentieth century). It also made space for adjustments to local changes of leadership and influence, and related claims to power, among the local populace.

Serving as patrons of a wide range of cultural activities, the Nawabs could underscore this implicit connection and, at the same time, direct these activities towards Shia narratives to put a distinctive stamp or (as modern parlance would have it) 'brand' on the resulting cultural system. In this way, they pursued the same strategies as the cited comparison Successor States as well as closer competitors, such as the Raja of Banaras (a comparison to which we will return). The central events of the Shia narrative, focused on the battle for leadership at Karbala during the month of Muharram, thus came to frame many of the public aspects of the Nawabs' cultural system, ranging from particular places in the urban fabric to the calendrical cycles that provide rhythm to the year. Other pivot points related to the dynasty itself, and its special role as patron and focus of the cosmopolitan, highly cultured court life of Lucknow.

One key site in the city was the dargah of Hazrat Abbas, step-brother and water carrier of Husain during the Karbala battle. Asaf ud Daulah established the shrine, apparently in the wake of a dream by "a poor man, Mirza Faqeera Beg" in which he was visited by Hazrat Abbas who directed him to a buried bronze alam in the popular Shia shape of a hand (that is, composed of five fingers and a palm). Concretizing the discovery, the Nawab ordered a dome to be built over the discovery site, and virtually every Nawab to follow added to the complex, building a two-storied gate, separate entrances for men and women, a silver *mimbar* (pulpit) and silver-foiled doors, and gilding the dome in gold. Popular appeal of the shrine can be measured not only by the practice that arose of bringing the alams paraded during Muharram to be blessed by the saint, but also the kitchen established by Malka Zamani (favorite queen of Naseer ud din Haider, 1827-37), set up to distribute free food to the poor. That popularity may also be measured by the fact that the dargah became headquarters for the city's sepoys when they rebelled against the British in 1857-58.

The propensity for processions, whether the mourning processions wending their city way during the ten days of Muharram observances, or royal processions, fundamentally shaped the layout of Nawabi Lucknow. As the processions either proceeded in boats down the river Gomti, or along a wide avenue paralleling the river, they made their way past the increasing number of significant buildings built by the Nawabs at least until Amjad Ali had Hazratganj constructed for that purpose. Each new royal-sponsored building punctuated the cityscape with palaces, imambaras, gates (most notably the Rumi Darwaza), mosques, even the Residency built to house the representative of the East India Company. Establishing the edges of this universe were Karbala grounds, to which the *tazias* were taken during Muharram processions for 'burials'. The purposes of these built environments help to convey the cultural system being established: imambaras represented not only the elaborate and highly illuminated buildings in which the permanent tazias were stored and displayed year-round, but their large, open rooms also hosted the crowds who attended *majalis* twice-daily to lament and hear sermons as well as installments each night of the Karbala story. (The concept of an imambara thus meant that not only the large and decorative buildings constructed by the court or city elite could be imambaras, but other citydwellers could devote a room in their house, no matter how modest, to this purpose as well. And as they served discrete audiences for the majalis, such gatherings could tell quite different versions of the Karbala story and so accommodate a wide range of participants and their understandings of the narrative). Imambaras also came to be the staging centers for poetry readings cum contests, marking the high status accorded to this literary form in Lucknow's cosmopolitan culture. Finally, imambaras could be built to serve not only these purposes but to serve as private tombs for wealthier families.

Taking such purposes altogether, the imambaras thus especially may reveal much to us about various associations attached to the families, neighborhoods and social groupings who shared distinct viewpoints, values, and responses to particular leaders, and who made up the social fabric of Lucknow.

Collective life, then, as expressed through processions and other public observances that underscored shared experiences, along with discrete gatherings that enabled differing understandings, fostered an inclusive cultural system. This was essential, since Shias were and remain a minority even in Lucknow, and the royal emphasis on Shi'ism gave it a particular and unusual bent (that is by using a minority culture often focused on martyrdom to express what was meant to be an inclusive and majoritarian cultural system). During the Nawabi period, inclusiveness took public-space expressions in which other residents participated in large numbers, often through particular kinds of alliances: e.g., Shias and Kayasths had affinities connected to executive and financial administration and cultural affinities; Sunnis, Baniyas and others dominated the economic life of the city. Lower-class/caste Hindus participated in the mourning culture as well, drawing parallels and seeing similarities through devotional practices as well as being situated within socio-economic interdependencies. One British observer, Emma Roberts, commented in 1835, for instance, that "A very large proportion of Hindoos go into mourning during the ten days of Mohurrum, clothing themselves in green garments, and assuming the guise of fakeers."

Among the many intriguing complexities of the Nawabs' cultural system is the particular contribution made by women, which was connected in part to the emphasis on Shi'ism and to the ability of a subculture to be shaped by them. Fashioned under the Nawabs, it continued long after the Nawabs had been removed from the city. For instance, the district gazetteer published in 1911 noted that two-thirds of those who identified themselves as Shi'as were women. Despite rulings by the Lucknow *mujtahids* against Sunni-Shi'a marriages, such marriages remained common, and the devotional culture of the women's quarter of a household could plausibly have perpetuated Shi'ism with relatively little interference from men. That many of the Muharram activities took place in gender-divided observances no doubt facilitated perpetuation of this devotional culture. Shi'ism was especially popular among courtesans, perhaps in part because it offered legal protection for them by recognizing temporary marriage (*mut'ah*). Also, in part, however, it undoubtedly related to the nature of the alternative culture created by these women, characterized by scholar Veena Oldenburg as "a style of non-confrontational resistance and packaged… not as a sporadic activity, but as a way of life."This was a way of life, we should note, based on economic independence as well as personalized religious devotionalism (often providing outlets for ostentatious display and patronage).

Different Karbala grounds also serve as markers for us of this complex cultural system and its impact on the changing map of Lucknow city. There were always multiple grounds, established for various reasons. But two in particular mark important moments in the history of the city. The main Karbala ground during the Nawabi period was located towards the eastern part of the city, but was closed down after the 1857-58 Uprising, as the British reshaped the city with roads designed to move troops easily throughout, and took over the area abutting that eastern location to form the Civil Lines where the British would live. (In the process of remaking the city they also took over the shopping district of Hazratganj to such an extent that it is usually identified as a British 'modern', consumer-oriented creation, with its origins under Amjad Ali Shah completely obscured.) The relocated Karbala grounds moved over to the southwestern part of the city, where they functioned as the 'main' grounds until Shia reformist activity underscored the very different styles of observance between Shias and Sunnis. As the largest karbala in the early twentieth century, this Talkatora Karbala ground was marked by a distinctive (and European-influenced) gateway, with 'Islamic' styled buildings inside: the large square is defined by a border of cells, while the square central building is set off on a raised platform meant to be the kerbala. This building has a gilt dome on top, and two towers. Graves fill the area between the kerbala and outer-wall cells. These grounds served not only as the destination for ('temporary') tazias that were to be 'buried,' but as the site of the culminating activities at the end of the ten days of observance.

Between 1906-08, however, the role of this particular karbala grounds became problematized. Tension grew out of changes experienced by both Sunni and Shia communities in Lucknow. For Sunnis, reformist efforts – led by the Ahl-i Hadis – had begun in the 1890s and came to be channeled against Shi'as not only in popular unrest on street corners (especially recitation of *char yari*, verses recited in favor of the first four caliphs and thus denying legitimacy to the leadership claims of the Prophet's family), but through two court cases as well. Shi'as, too, had undergone significant change in the latter part of the nineteenth century, marked by the emergence of a reforming and fairly aggressive new middle class component who emphasized differing personal behaviors as well as reworking of imambaras, where restoring existing buildings as well as constructing new versions of these community centers expressed claims by this middle-class group to leadership among Shi'as (see Jones in bibliography). Shia reformism, too, was brought to Lucknow in 1904 by a preacher from Rampur (the Rohilla kingdom), calling attention to practices seen as not specifically Shi'a but more in keeping with Sunni practices. These intra-community changes and resulting tensions then become routed through inter-sect conflicts (in a pattern parallel to what had happened in cities like Bareilly and Agra, where intra-community tensions became routed to Hindu-Muslim conflict instead). In 1904-08, then, Shi'as were reminded that the mourning elements of Muhurram were being undermined by the participation of large numbers of non-Shi'as, and especially lower-class Muslim artisans, in the observances. To ensure greater purity, new rules were issued for behavior and practices on the Karbala grounds, not least the discontinuation of shops, booths, and displays as well as games and entertainments on the Karbala grounds. Sunni protest against the imposition of these rules took the form of a petition to government that they be permitted to attend instead a new and barren Karbala ground set up at Kakori, which was approved. This separation of the Karbalas was a much more pronounced division by far than had been experienced in Lucknow before, and is a measure of a new divisiveness being introduced into what had been an integrative enactment in public spaces.

The Context of Successor States

Lucknow's role as capital city of the successor state of Awadh cannot be overstated in reckoning its significance. That the nawabs began as subimperial governors for the Mughal Emperors and, as the empire began to decline, claimed increasing independence is important not only for understanding Lucknow's self-perceptions, but also for its role in the region, since it came to represent the Mughal system there. At the same time, Lucknow's history demonstrates the larger process of devolution of power and political authority to those in a region; indeed, the regional cultures that emerged from this process still matter down to the present. Moreover, increasing urbanism in the eighteenth and nineteenth centuries resulted from shifting trade routes and new economic actors, along with pronounced commercialization: the role of cities expanded with these shifts in the political economy of north India. Examining Lucknow's role in this changing context, in turn, illuminates the larger processes determining how cities work, from the functions they perform within the larger world, and the way that urban places form a larger cognitive whole (not least, how residents used their identification as Lakhnawis to situate themselves in a larger world of similar urban places and people with parallel yet distinctive identities). In this respect, we have already seen how Lucknow/Awadh saw itself as superior not only to Rampur and even to Delhi, but strove to outshine Hyderabad and Mysore as well.

Perhaps most revealing for us, though, is how Lucknow could be compared to Banaras/Varanasi (or 'Benares' as the British knew it). The Raja of Banaras, in his turn, was supposed to serve as tax collector for Awadh, and did make a tax payment each year to the Nawabs. He, too, worked hard to establish and maintain independence from this supposed overlord, and to a large extent succeeded (not least because the Nawabs' reach outside of Lucknow became increasingly tenuous the greater the distance from the capital city). In this independent stance, the Raja's actions were important primarily because they served as a kind of comparison and goad to the Nawabs' own efforts: both were intent on establishing cultural systems that worked within similar (though not identical) regional contexts. That is, just as the Nawabs created an inclusive system in which popular values, especially around devotionalism and enactments in public could serve to connect people, so the Raja created new symbolic structures to express the Bhumihar Brahmin house of Narayan and its relationship with those it ruled. Both drew on the urban structures of *mohallas* (neighborhoods), occupational networks, *akharas* and the like to link a devotional-style state religion to the ruling house. In the case of Banaras, the Raja could present himself as a figure central to the cultural system's key events developed around Ramlila and thus in fundamental ways identified with the god-king Ram (while the Nawab could never figure at the center of the civic ritual of Muharram). These parallels led, not surprisingly, to a kind of cultural competition, in which Ramlila enactments expanded in the nineteenth century alongside the elaborations of Muharram nearby. The cities were also tied together in part by their differences in social composition: because Banaras lacked much in the way of upper-class Muslims, and this group occupied a relatively large social space as courtiers and others in Lucknow, the lower class Muslims of Banaras (most of whom were artisans otherwise tied to their upper caste Hindu 'paymasters') looked to Lakhnawi Muslims for leadership, advice and even a safety net not available in their own city.

Other key differences help to explain why the British, to a large extent, left Banaras to devise its own identity through the last part of the nineteenth and first half of the twentieth century. (The contrast here is instructive: the British took over 'direct rule' of the Banaras area much earlier, in the 1770s, and deprived the Raja of the title "Maharaja" until several decades later. Yet by the 1920s the British had begun using his partnership to counterbalance the nationalists; even before this, however, they actually did not intervene very directly in the Raja's administration of the area after the fiasco of their aborted imposition of a house tax in 1812-13.)

In contrast, British subterfuges in extracting ever-larger amounts of 'reparations' and taxes from Awadh, while ostensibly leaving the Nawabs in power, actually placed the Nawabs in such dire straits that they had to rely on exploitive revenue farmers and had very little room to maneuver in terms of 'ruling' until finally the British took over the kingdom in 1856 and sent the ruling family to Calcutta. That the Rajas of Banaras had established a set of mutually beneficial relationships with large landowners (Rajputs as well as their own caste of Bhumihars), along with the bankers and moneylenders of the city, also provides a revealing contrast with the position of the Nawabs in Awadh, whose position remained much more precarious in their Successor State, relying much more heavily on the courtier class in the city, and with only the thinnest alliances with the *taluqdars* or large landowners located in the mofussil. Despite these differences, what was shared was a reliance on cultural patronages a key element that underscored their authority in the creation of the two cultural systems. This was one of the strongest shared characteristics for Successor States in general. (Not least, it was one of the few avenues for rulers' actions left open as the British constrained them within the confines of "indirect rule").

Cultural patronage, then, as an important aspect for both Successor State systems, was tied both to the patronage extended by the ruler himself, as well as to the range of cultural activities supported by courtier and literati participation and encouragement. Virtually all successor states, for instance, supported particular literary forms that also helped to develop regional languages and created critical masses of works within literary genres (especially poetry and literary criticism). In Lucknow literary productions focused especially on poetry (enabling it to 'outdo' Delhi) and pre-eminently on *marsias* (the lamentations on the martyrdom of Husain's party), which were especially important because written in the vernacular and thus accessible to ordinary people when they heard them – in contrast with many other readings during Muharram observances, which were in Persian. Support of literary productions in Banaras related especially to those works read and produced by Brahmins, including Tulsidas' *Ramcharitmanas* (in the Ramnagar enactments, one of the three forms of tellings staged each day were the readings by Brahmins of the relevant parts of the 'Manas). These courts also had ateliers in their palaces for fine artists (painters, sculptors) and performers (musicians and dancers): their creations not only flattered the ruler and conveyed the stories of kings, gods, and key historical figures but provided material underpinnings to the cultural systems being developed. So too did the handicrafts of the region, which began to be consumed by the elite in each society: in Banaras this was marked especially by silk saris (the silk woven by Muslim weavers); in Lucknow it was chikan and other embroidery arts (involving zari); local craft production thus could be used to undergird the local identities of these cities.

Within this cultural system we might think of literary productions in two, related ways: they were not only performed (as poetry recitations in the imambaras) but also came to be published, drawing our attention to the important contribution made in Lucknow, as in North India more generally, through publication and the publishing industry that came to be based in Lucknow. Once again, these contributions relate to larger processes affecting popular participation in the Lakhnawi cultural system as in formation and influence of a 'public' in the region. Efforts to inform and shape public opinion drew on what one analyst has called "techniques of communication, debate and persuasion" emerging from Indian norms (long before they were influenced by western traditions: see CA Bayly in bibliography, especially chapter 5). These kinds of literary productions predated newspapers and public associations, expressing through handwritten media "the views of bazaar people and artisans" as well as the "Hindustani-writing literati", within the latter of which resided Indo-Islamic notables and officers of state, many of whom were Hindus, especially Kayasths, Kashmiri Brahmins and Khattris. In this way, (literary) cultural inclusiveness reached across caste and class boundaries and laid significant groundwork for what was to come, even after the removal of the Nawabs. That these networks of literati shared a common background in Indo-Persian and even Hindu classics, informed by 'cosmopolitanism' reinforced by 'intimate social relations', helps to explain the inclusiveness. Fundamental, too, were the special forms of literacy (connected to social propriety, notions of good rule) associated with Urdu-Hindustani, which in Bayly's terms had become a 'public tongue', a 'popular language spread by Sufi saints and Hindu devotees[, as well as] a language of the court and a discerning literati' (p. 193). This form of language was 'inclusive; it mirrored and even stimulated the rapid social mobility which was characteristic of post-Mughal [that is, Successor State-era] north India.' Bayly goes on to note that this inclusiveness enfolded ordinary artisans, people of the bazaars, and women within various cultural-production fields.

The publishing history of an Urdu *Ramayana*, written by the Kayasth (Munshi Jagannath Lal) 'Khushtar', suggests the patterns of contributions to the cultural system we want to capture here (see Robert Phillips in the bibliography). The first edition was written to be presented to Nawab Wajid Ali Shah in 1852. By 1860 – in the absence of the Nawabs– it had begun being published by Naval Kishor Press (NKP), the key enterprise in a new world of publishing in Lucknow. NKP issued sixteen editions up through 1924, all in Urdu script. Across those many editions, Phillips has tracked revealing shifts in the illustration program that reflect an increased sense of the author and publisher that they were publishing a Hindu classic important for both Kayasths and a larger Urdu-reading public within changing contexts, thus reflecting the wider world in which a publishing industry was being elaborated. That is, the illustrations in the Khushtar Ramayan moved from Lucknow locale-/Nawabi court-specific images to those shared and circulated in many different contexts that may be labeled 'pan-Indian' by 1924, Lucknow does not appear at all, and in fact many of the illustrations are not even specific to the version included in the Khushtar narrative, instead referencing well-known episodes of Ram's story that had *not* been included by Khushtar.

This expansion of reading audience and its knowledge of the larger, unbounded story of Ram tells us much about Naval Kishor Press, itself; this information is quite revealing for our interest in Lucknow's cultural system. Timing mattered: NKP's very success owed much to Lucknow's cultural profile, as well as to the chaotic circumstances following the 1857-58 Uprising (when most of the presses and printing businesses had either had their machinery destroyed or been forced to shut down), as well as the renewed importance of Lucknow when it was made a provincial capital after British takeover. Yet even more significant was Kishor's placement within the literati networks we have described. Although not a Kayasth himself, Naval Kishore drew on strong, often personally close relationships with Lucknow's substantial population of Kayasth literati who contributed their expertise to the Press as translators, compositors, and scribes. Indeed, Kishor's participation in widespread philanthropic efforts in the region (funding of hospitals; contributions and publicity for voluntary associations; strong fostering of educational efforts through contributions of books, publicity, and actual financial support) make clear the extent to which public-interest concerns repeatedly underscored the inclusive nature of the cultural system being reconfigured in the second half of the nineteenth century. At the same time, many of Kishor's actions also encouraged the development of new Hindu caste identity-narratives, as well as the Hindi Movement's efforts to raise Hindi vis-à-vis the Urdu-dominated literary realm.

Not least among these actions is the fact that Khushtar's version of the Ramayana was but one of several issued by NKP; indeed, within the much smaller publishing program NKP devoted to Hindi-devanagri script materials, it had "turned out over 50,000 copies" of Tulsidas' *Ramcharitmanas* by 1873 (see Stark in bibliography). As the late nineteenth century was marked by various groups working to forge new, higher-status identity-narratives (e.g. the Kayasths as Kshatriyas; the Dhursar-Bhargavas as Brahmins, et al), it was often Naval Kishor's publishing enterprises (both NKP and his newspaper *Avadh Akhbar*, the north Indian newspaper that was the most widely read Urdu daily there) who distributed these efforts.

In these ways the Successor States provided important intermittent historical 'moments' during which ideological identities could be created that bound them to their subjects and vice-versa. Not least important as a result of these functions was the ability developed in these places to both negotiate with the changes introduced by the British, and to utilize their cultural systems to withstand or adapt to deal with the impact of modern influences so that they made sense to city residents. What is especially salient about such Successor State cultural systems is that they provided a flexible (even ambiguous) frame that long outlived their originators. In Lucknow, that took a particularly striking form: where the ruling house had been from a minority within a minority, and yet had taken Shia traditions and adapted them to succeed as a powerful force at the apex of a socio-political hierarchy, the cultural system the dynasty designed was so flexible it could survive a decline in those fortunes, and the exile of the house itself. What remained behind was a mode of social inclusiveness that, while requiring important adjustments at key historical moments, nevertheless remained a powerful component of Lakhnawis' self-identity, as individuals and as constituent communities of an inclusive realm.

Lucknow's Cultural System and Changes under the British

As our earlier references to Lucknow's built environment have suggested, the changes in the physical fabric of the city reflected not only socio-economic changes taking place in the second half of the nineteenth century among the city's residents, but also the impact of direct British rule on this urban center. The insertion of Civil Lines for residences of the now-ascendant Britons, and recasting of the layout of the city through construction of broad streets down which the military might travel to put down unrest, were but two of the most obvious of these changes. Indeed, the residual strength of the Nawabi's cultural system may be even more impressive when we consider the kinds of changes introduced by the British. Where the Nawabi system had remained a bit tenuous in its reach into the countryside, for instance, the fact that the British forced the *taluqdars* to create city residences in Kaisarbagh shows us not only how the British tried to repurpose this initially magnificent Nawabi construction, but is even more revealing in terms of how the British "Oudh Policy" – centered on their bargain with these large landlords to keep the peace in return for buttressing their landlord-based power – ironically meant that the building blocks the Nawabs created for the city became even more important for identity-narratives, both individual and collective. Indeed, the Nawabi cultural system proved so powerfully attractive and adaptive, that the disappearance of the Nawabs from its midst merely provided more flexibility for those interested in turning its emphases to reflect their own importance in the narratives of the city, as new middle-class elites emerged and jockeyed for influence and status-recognition.

For instance, from the practice of a (court-shaped) Muslim lifestyle, many Kashmiri Pandits and Kayasths were 'among the first to enter English educational institutions. They continued their tradition of service by occupying large numbers of lower and middle bureaucratic positions in the colonial administration' (see Joshi in bibliography, especially pp 104-5). They took up, as well, professions in the law, journalism and literature: publishing through newspapers as well as books was, as noted earlier, an important extension of this reconfigured articulations of community identity-narratives. Their efforts to assert the middle-class 'right' to *speak* for 'the public' did not go unopposed. These new persona of literati ended up pitted against rural upwardly mobile peasantry (see Pinch in bibliography), even as they were lampooned by popular representations of them using highly Persianized Hindustani and putting on airs. Indeed, even participants in this emerging middle-class lamented their disempowerment and the limits on the changes they could effect within an arena subject to increasing British control.

Most dramatically – and in contrast to these re-interpretations of the Nawabs' cultural system undertaken by emerging middle class participants – we can see the British impact on the city through the competing narratives that came to characterize what the built environments of Lucknow represented. The Nawabi-built environments still anchored a sense of the city for most of its inhabitants, albeit reconstrued to fit the self-perceptions of various middle class groups emerging there, and visible to us not least through the refurbishment of certain key imambaras and the like by these new patrons. Other key structures took on another story entirely, one that signified British martyrs in the "Mutiny trail" traced through Lucknow, Delhi, and other key sites such as the riverside near Kanpur (for the massacre of women and children as they were supposedly being led to rescue by boats) that marked the British version of the 1857-58 uprising. Lucknow figured most dramatically in this narrative, with no site more central than the Residency. Indeed, photographs by Beato as well as lithographed sketches of a "ravaged" Residency were images featured regularly in British newspapers and illustrated weeklies to bring the conflict 'home' to British citizens. (These were reinforced by memorial plaques on British church walls of those who died in various regiments, as by mutiny memorial towers constructed in Indian sites, around whose bases were listed the officers and men who were killed in specific battles.)

By the 1870s, at least two competing understandings of Lucknow had emerged, one as the site of a continuing Successor-State styled cultural node (albeit with sub-narratives featuring different middle-class groups), and another as the premier site of the 1857 'Mutiny' and its British martyrs. Guidebooks created for British travelers to India depicted the "Mutiny Trail" most dramatically: Murray's Guide (in its eighth edition in 1911), for instance, devoted one page to the history of the Nawabs and almost sixteen pages to 'Mutiny' history, accompanied by a special map focused on the key spots figuring in the repeated battles for the city waged during 1857-58, with the Residency receiving the most intense attention. In fascinating contrast to Murray's is the guidebook created in 1874 by Abbas Ali, who served as both darogah of a Lucknow imambara and also a ("pensioned") municipal engineer of the Public Works Department, turned photographer ("under the Patronage of His Honor the Lieutenant Governor of the N.W. provinces and Oudh" as cited on the back of his carte de visite). So far as can be determined, this guidebook is the first to combine photographs with text and maps; called *The Lucknow Album*, it contains '50 photographic views of Lucknow and its environs'. As its introduction explains, it is aimed at *both* the touring audience of Britons *and* 'intelligent natives'. Accordingly, photographs include not only 'Mutiny' sites and Nawabi buildings, but bridges built by each (with an engineer's evaluations of the construction practices of each ruling entity). Most revealingly, it includes sites never before listed in guidebooks: sites that would have meaning for Indians, such as the shrine of Hazrat Abbas and the Talkatora Karbala grounds. He also included a number of kothis, buildings often originally built by the Nawabs and their courtiers, then taken over by high-ranking Britons as residences and, by the end of the century, beginning to be repurposed: in several cases, their functions shifted into buildings serving modern and economic purposes, such as the Railway Administration office and banks. Our argument would be that this guidebook's array of images represents the photographer's attempt to capture a third understanding of Lucknow – one that included 'traditional' buildings created by the Nawabs, sites significant to a larger and inclusive 'public' (including Muslims), *and* the buildings housing middle-class functions of a modernizing cultural system.

In support of this understanding of the nature of Lucknow's turn-of-the-century cultural system, we might note briefly two other collections of photographs produced by Abbas Ali. One was a reference work focused on the taluqdars and other elites of the area, with whom the Indian Civil Service staff would have to interact: *The Illustrated Album of the Rajas and Taluqdars of Oudh*. The other –*The Beauties of Lucknow*, with a text in Urdu – pictured actresses and courtesans of the city, still important figures in the perpetuation of the cultured life reflecting Nawabi style and values. Taken altogether, the audiences addressed by these three volumes suggest to us the layering of many understandings of the city and how their advocates contributed actively to Lucknow's changing cultural system emerging around the turn of the century. In the process, we can delineate the sinews of Lucknow's backbone, and its capacity to adjust to changing circumstances while retaining its cultural sense of its self and significance.

Twentieth Century Challenges and Lucknow's Cultural System

This polycentric use of public spaces and multiple narratives concerning what matters, affecting how the past and the present should be understood, are unique to Lucknow but, still, are akin to experiences in other urban centers over the turn of the twentieth century. For instance, the pattern marking inter-group conflict, especially that taking the form of politicized religious conflict (or 'communalism'), emerges from competition and conflict *within* one of the contending communities throughout cities of UP. These competitions usually were prompted by reformist efforts and their resistance by more traditionalist members of various cities – contestations that, we might note, necessarily affected they very understanding of who constituted the 'community' itself. They could also reflect the emergence of new claimants to informal leadership roles as socio-political and economic changes affected the standing of particular families in a locality. (For instance, conflict in Agra in the closing decades of the 19th century brought Sanatan Dharmists out to resist Arya Samaj initiatives, while new claimants to status and leadership among Hindus in Bareilly prompted them to deny the authority of old agreements around processions when Muharram and Ram Lila overlapped there.) These contestations tended to expand the ceremonial and leadership spaces occupied by the affected community, in turn impinging on what had been accepted delineations of respective zones occupied by that community and its "Other", usually Hindus and Muslims. That the cultural systems of these urban places are intimately connected to these reworkings of community definitions of identity is marked in large part by a new form one analyst has called 'public religion' which moves away from the detailed, specific practices that characterize particular sub-groups within that religious community (and which tended to pit them against one another), to emphasize what was shared as a big-picture.

At the same time, much attention is paid to elaborating and deepening the products of literary culture to underscore claims to cultural superiority. In Lucknow this meant that Kayasths and Kashmiri Brahmins, for instance, supported the Hindi Movement with its emphasis on the Nagri script, while Shia leaders, such as Munshi Ehtisham Ali (a rais and zamindar who was also a mill owner and member of the district board), led the anti-Nagari Resolution campaign of 1900, determined to resist this effort to replace Urdu. In many cities, this range of activity resulted in inter-community conflicts that ultimately led to a more reified set of expressions, along which conflict moved. In turn, these claims to public spaces and public-interest issues, as well as models for enacting protests, were taken up by the nationalist struggle in the decades leading through the 1920s, and were aided by better communication networks (newspapers and other artefacts of the publishing industry; railways for moving people as well as ideas and claims for public support), seizing on the potential of print capitalism to mobilize protesters. The Lucknow version of this process worked through the posting of placards, printing of collections of verses to be recited, publication of 'inflammatory' appeals, and the like. Meanwhile the stakes were raised repeatedly by the British emphasis on numbers as well as elaboration of new institutional contexts for the exercise of leadership and representation.

The overall pattern was similar throughout urban UP; what distinguished Lucknow from other cities was the way in which existing tensions became routed along conduits predominantly marked by Sunni-Shia conflict, rather than Hindu-Muslim.We can trace the specificities of Lucknow's circumstances beginning with the appearance of a Shia reformer, Maqbul Ahmad, who arrived from Rampur in 1904. His exhortations led to the systematic introduction of recitations designed to symbolize, through collective speech, the distinct doctrinal and historical position of the Shia community. Two forms of recitation were used: *tabarra* (a stylized abuse of the intervening three caliphs) and *bila fasl* (an assertion of the rightfulness of Ali's immediate succession upon the death of Muhammad). Sunnis retaliated with *char yari,* praise for the first four caliphs. Focused on such symbolic behavior, reformists also turned attention to practices in the observances during Muharram, attacking especially 'abuses' connected with the tenth-day *tazia* processions to Tal Katora Karbala. In anticipation of the Ashura of 1906, the reformers focused first on the 1905 *Chehlum* (the *tazia* procession held forty days *after* Ashura, the tenth of Muharram, and usually observed only by Shi'as). Leading Shias convinced the owners of land near Tal Katora to discontinue the booths, shops and displays that constituted the 'fair' traditionally held in conjunction with *tazia* processions. With the Collector's approval, they also published a list of rules to be followed by all those attending the karbala, which at this point affected Shias only.

These reforms (strengthened even to the extent of prohibiting games, entertainments, all shops, the chewing of pan, the smoking of tobacco, and swearing and jesting in the karbala compound) had a very different impact, however, when applied to the tenth of Muharram in 1906, when Hindus and Sunnis constituted the great majority of participants; the occasion had functioned in the past in a way quite different from *Chehlum.* Without going into additional detail of the events at this time, we can see that this conflict between 1904-06 had important legacies: the differences between Sunni and Shia understandings and behavior around the Muharram events were underscored – where previously the occasions could accommodate shared participation at least for the more public events – and new rituals (such as the recitations) were introduced to dramatize in public spaces these very differences. Perhaps the most immediate impact came through the decision by Sunnis to create a new karbala ground at the barren site of Karkori, so that the practices they associated with the Muharram observances could be continued. What had begun as intra-Shia negotiations had now clearly expanded to affect other

Lakhnawis as well, but were expressed particularly along the Sunni-Shia fault lines.

Besides the explicit recognition of different understandings of the occasion, this shift in venue accommodated other changes that had occurred by the turn of the century, including increasing prosperity among Sunnis – in contrast to the deepening impoverishment of *wasiqadars* (pensioners of the East India Company, along with ex-royal family members)– as well as the fact that Sunnis were more often living in areas to which the city had expanded, at a great distance from the Tal Katora site. These changes in socio-economic standing were reflected as well in the declining percentage of the population identifying itself as Shia: counted as 23% of Lucknow's population in 1881, by 1904 they represented only 14 percent; this decline was accompanied by an increase in the ratio of Muslims to the total population, which by 1916 had risen from 16 to 21 percent. Again, such altered numbers played out in a context in which British emphasis on numbers made the shifts that much more significant. And the changed circumstances for upwardly mobile Sunnis (marked, as well, by an increase in the number claiming the title "shaikh") as well as by increasingly aggressive lower-class Sunnis such as butchers and ekka drivers, also affected the relationships with non-Shias: wealthy Hindu merchants and professionally trained people (such as the Kayashs et al discussed earlier) had begun to dominate the local Municipal Board, whose actions were seen as discriminating against these Sunnis (or perhaps it would have been said, against "Muslims"). The old alliances were clearly fraying if not breaking down entirely, suggesting a fundamental reworking of Lucknow's cultural system.

The ritualized recitations of *tabarra* and *bila fasl* on street corners and other public venues thus became both a gauge of changing status within the city and a dramatically altered frame for participation in Muharram itself. The motif of martyrdom could now take on even greater salience, with such a motif of martyrdom most accurately linked to the declining status of Shias in the city. When the next great outburst of Sunni-Shia conflict emerged in the 1930s, then, these characteristics appeared to link directly the protests of the century's first decade with that of the 1930s. These similarities, however, may distract us from the very different circumstances in which this second big protest took place.

Even the compromise that ended the strife in 1906 (brought about by the "Piggott Committee" – appointed and operating on behalf of the government, although it included carefully selected representatives of all the interest groups – which forbade either community from reciting verses) was actually a measure of the changed position of Shias in Lucknow. From dominance, the community now had to operate under parity. And, as the state structures shifted towards majority rule, Shias experienced more tenuous support from the government than previously. When in 1935 and '36 Sunnis began reciting *char yari* (now called *madh-i sahba)* and Shias ultimately retaliated through *tabarra* curses, these public arena activities appeared to be a continuation of earlier protest modes. Significantly, however, these public recitations were not really aimed at the community of Others; in the changed and highly politicized context of the 1930s, both sets of protests were quite formally being staged *as attacks against the government.* (It is interesting that this shift is part of a larger phenomenon, as discussed below through the comparison with Jaipur. Whether 'government' was exercised by the British, a Maharaja, or an elected political party such as Congress, the shift from aiming protests at an Other community to the perceived shortfall of 'government' to protect minority interests has become a larger pattern in this period of change.)

That these ostensibly distinct targets could be used to comment on the inability of an unsympathetic harshstate to protect varied community interests is one important measure of the changed perceptions of public protest after numerous nationalist mobilizations. Mobilization, too, marked the changed circumstances by the 1930s: such protests now appealed far beyond the particular urban place in which they occurred. Indeed, what was most alarming to authorities was the daily arrival of 'batch' after 'batch' of protestors traveling to support fellow Shias by joining the expressions of civil disobedience. This ability to mobilize supporters far beyond the city's boundaries also tells us about larger patterns that situate Shia identity-narratives and mobilization within more general trends of rhetorical positioning of specific groups at odds with 'majority' values and/or in contestation for protection by the state.

Undoubtedly, experiences of staging the nationalist movement's myriad protests (joined during the early 1920s by the Khilafat Movement) had provided models for how public protests could be enacted. Even more important, these experiences had sharpened the perception that much of the problem between contending communities could be laid at the state's feet, though by now the 'state' was not so much British as it was Congress. Closer to the locality, the contestation reflected altered socio-political standing in the city, with the Sunnis now reaching beyond parity for its "right" to religious freedom to recite *madh-i sahba* – a right Sunnis had never previously been able to claim. In the very different nationalist-movement terrain of the mid-1930s, this right could be claimed especially because the Ahrars (from the Punjab), as a Muslim agitational group allied with Congress, could use their Muslim identity as a bargaining point with those in power. Although the procession for reciting Sunni verses on the Prophet's birthday was given a route far removed from most Shias, the action itself so incensed Shias around the country that huge numbers poured into town to recite *tabarra* in order to court arrest. The degree of coordination and mass mobilization took the Congress provincial government by surprise: in all more than fourteen thousand Shias were arrested during the long months of the protest.

Writ large, these protests underscore the importance of communication networks in expanding notions of what constituted 'public interest' and the significance of those issues when the call for action came to express, bodily and en mass, values understood to convey individual and collective identities. Both the ability to convey these issues, and the changing targets of protests organized to express them, bring within a single narrative the nationalist movement as well as various sub-groups' efforts to organize. How this worked becomes clear when we compare this Lucknow example with one from Jaipur at much the same time, where models and processes for protests had advanced beyond the parallels between Hindu-Muslim and Sunni-Shia conflicts we discussed earlier. Indeed, doubtless the closest parallel with Lucknow's 1930s unrest is that taking place in Jaipur, where the thwarted Muslim desire to enlarge access to their Jama Masjid located in the city center also became a cause for 'batches' of Muslim protesters to travel from out of town to join Jaipuris in protesting against a princely state. (Here, we have a suggestion that 'the state' has become an abstracted entity whose specifics are less important than the status of a self-perceived powerless minority. At the same time, the cultural system used by 'the state' to cement its relationship with a general public composed of many communities raised the stakes in resolving such contestations.) This was underscored, especially, when the local protesters eventually left town in large numbers, claiming the city was too inhospitable for them to live there, an accusation the ruler took much to heart.

This parallel may suggest to us that, in the face of a changing political system increasingly based on majority rule, minorities began to work to organize appeals that, first, would bring outsiders to their cities for protests and, second, could lead those feeling most disadvantaged to leave the city entirely. While in Jaipur those who gave up Jaipuri residence were eventually wooed back and won a resolution that gave them a wider staircase and hence greater access, while allowing the Jama Masjid to remain in the city center, this harbinger of alternative responses remained to haunt minorities as sub-continental British India moved toward new territorial resolutions. In particular, flexible cultural systems were faced with very new kinds of demands as Partition lines were delineated, and mass population shifts occurred.

Post-Independence Reworkings of the Cultural System

Recent scholars have focused on the implications for families of the imposition of boundary lines dividing British India into the two nation-states of India and Pakistan in 1947, with the massive transfers of population related to those lines (see Zamindar in bibliography). Outside of Delhi and Karachi, we still have too little systematic research to be able to grasp the impact of these dramatic changes, beyond likely statistics of death and family dislocations (not least, the fate of women in areas subject to population movements). We do not yet understand, especially, the experiences of particular cities, including Lucknow, and the extent to which we can generalize regarding larger patterns. From study of Delhi and Karachi, however, we do at least have glimmers of understanding of what was involved. Perhaps most important were three different phenomena: (1) many of those who migrated to the opposite nation-state did not understand that their move was a one-time, permanent decision; (2) the quite common pattern of having extended family distributed on both sides of what were now national borders – a distribution that had previously enhanced the socio-economic chances of the family – now worked against the family, both in terms of social mobility and in relation to the perceptions of the family by state as well as neighbors in each place; and (3) in the face of significant refugee populations in many cities, with a need to settle them in residential lodgings that only became available as a result of out-migrations, a family's hold and claim on property depended on vagaries no one could have calculated ahead of time. Not least of these was the frequent assumption that if the family were labeled the minority community in each state (ie 'Muslim' in India or 'Hindu' in Pakistan), their claims to property were dangerously jeopardized. Only with systematic study can these phenomena be traced for Lucknow, but we do have evidence that suggests several developments that necessarily altered the fit between the built environment and the cultural system whose outlines had served the city so well in the past.

For instance, certain famous examples may suggest the extremes of larger patterns, such as repurposing of imambaras and other significant buildings for goods storage and other prosaic (and ultimately detrimental) usages by newly arrived entrepreneurs after 1947. Only as the Archeological Survey has intervened for careful restoration do legal issues about repurposing, as well as the impact of encroaching shops and residences, seem to have been addressed. Moreover, this has addressed only a limited number of such sites, taking long years to be decided. Both the size and significant value of these properties have made their fate of great import, even without the symbolic and praxis issues embraced by Shias and others of Lucknow and beyond. In related issues, both the activism and intra-community tensions among Shia leaders involved in the Shia Waqf Board as it controls imambaras, karbalas and mosques (tension expressed through court cases, among other avenues) also reflect not only these older patterns of competition around community leadership, but also their significance for Shias in other parts of the subcontinent as well as abroad: Lucknow remains the central focus of Shia activity. Although scholars have yet to systematically analyze such evidence, it does suggest new demands and roles for the judicial system (and related issues regarding the contribution to be made by 'the rule of law' to a democracy with changing constituents' demands upon it). Moreover, the reconfiguration and exercise of power across Lucknow's population, most especially the influence and control by (predominantly Hindu) merchants, professionals and entrepreneurs, have placed new demands on both local and changing national cultural systems.

In this context, the prolonged court case and legislative follow-up regarding the holdings of the Raja of Mahmudabad, where the Government of India's seizure of 'evacuee properties' (which were then declared 'enemy properties' in the wake of the Indo-Pakistan War of 1965) set a pattern of making these properties available to others in Lucknow and elsewhere. The holdings of Raja Mohammad Amir Ahmed Khan have certainly been the most celebrated of these cases because of the scale involved; when the Raja migrated to Pakistan in 1962, he had left his son and heir, and his wife, behind in Lucknow, assuming they would continue as the property owners of these immense holdings. Even after September 2005, when the court case aimed at restoring the properties to the present raja was resolved in his favor by the Supreme Court of India, the Raja was unable to take up the massive holdings that had been declared 'enemy properties' in the 1960s and again through an ordinance passed by the Government to nullify the Supreme Court decision. Such steps were taken by the Government of India to prevent a substantial impact on government as well as private citizens: Mahmudabad's holdings included half of Hazratganj Market, as well as the bungalows occupied by the (BSP) state government's district magistrate, superintendent of police and chief medical officer in Sitapur (as well as holdings in Nainital and other locales beyond Lucknow). Mayawati's efforts to implement the Government's actions apparently included sealing of buildings and land to ensure that her government could gain possession of the buildings occupied by her officers. Only after Prime Minister Manmohan Singh intervened in 2010 were the holdings finally secured to the Mahmudabad Raja. Although the scale of these holdings make them unique, the larger processes of shifting property ownership and control to refugees and entrepreneurs – whether through direct ownership or through dramatically low rents that do not reflect property values – necessarily affected the close relationship between the values of Lucknow's cultural system and its use of built environments and other land usages, as well as its sense of inclusiveness.

The flip side of these developments has been that post-partition newcomers would contribute substantively to the reworked cultural system, as the availability of such properties provided opportunities to establish both residential and business roots. Not least among these has been the renowned bookseller, Ram Advani, whose shop became an intellectual center in Hazratganj, open to authors, students and public intellectuals alike (see Imtiaz Ahmed in bibliography).We do not want to overlook the point that in all of these shifts, the active participation by Lakhnawis as been responsible for reshaping both local and far-flung understandings of the cultural system of the city, and the nature of its inclusiveness.

Decades of these renegotiations and adjustments in the cultural system of the city have been moved now to very different footings by much more significant reconfigurations. These reconfigurations affect not only the built environment itself, but also new forms of voluntary associations (including NGOs) that have emerged to address contemporary problems as those are defined in Lucknow today. On the one hand, NGO work may be seen as a permutation of longstanding philanthropic impulses (such as those described in relation to Nival Kishor). On the other hand, these NGOs have espoused new values and issues, and also have become one of many new forms of leadership and, therefore, they provide sites of potential contestations as well. In this respect, these sites of agency continue to offer opportunities, as they did earlier, for participants to adjust the cultural-system's understandings to fit changing socio-economic and political contexts.

To capture these cultural-system shifts, we might begin with built environments.

As though taking up profound lessons from the Nawabi legacy in shaping this urban place, Mayawati's seven huge new parks and installations recognizing Dalit contributions have wrenched the map of Lucknow in very new directions, both literally and figuratively. With the exception of Parivartan Chowk, located within the city proper in the Kaiserbagh Historic District, these new built environments have pushed the city's outlines ever closer to the airport. As the real introduction to Lucknow for those arriving by air, Mayawati's memorial parks bring together a range of historical references of great import, from Buddhist stupas to Lutyens' reworking of new Delhi as the British capital in the early 20th century. (Indeed, Mayawati and her architect, Jay Kaktikar, have been referred to by more than one analyst as 'the new Lutyens'– a reference to the designer of British India's New Delhi capital city.) Moreover, the very presence of these large open spaces (in which Dalits are more than welcome – sometimes rather a contrast to other, older parts of Lucknow proper) and the increased value of properties in their vicinity has also lured those interested in expansion of the city to these once-outlying areas of the urban landscape. At the same time, fundamental power is communicated through the monumentality of the constructions, expensiveness of materials, visibility by way of their prominent locations,and accessibility of its messages (especially through statuary of the Buddha, Ambedkar, Kanshi Ram and Mayawati, along with larger-than-life size animals, not least the BSP's election-symbol elephants). Analysts see these architectural additions to the cityscape as examples of the 'reconstruction of memory' – a phenomenon we have seen already in the constant touchstone function of Nawabi buildings. We understand, therefore, the success that Mayawati's structures have achieved in their efforts to integrate the presence of Dalits into that exercise of 'memory' in the city (see Sinha and Kant in the bibliography). At the very least, Lucknow stands out now as the site of the only post-independence massive-scaled construction, enabling its designers to claim for it the recent ownership of a mantle previously worn easily by its Nawabi predecessors. Just as we could not understand the true impact of that Nawabi heritage without examining what has been done in repurposing and refurbishing those originary constructions, so we will not be able to gauge Mayawati's impact on the city's cultural system until we see what her successors do with this new material urban fabric. (One indicator may be the policies being pursued by the successor Samajwadi Party, which has drastically reduced its financial burden of maintaining the properties by cutting staff and renting out unused spaces for purposes never envisioned by the BSP. More time is needed for assessment of these actions, however.)

No doubt there are many other contemporary phenomena to gauge the shape and effectiveness of the Successor State-styled cultural system in its contemporary guise, at least some of which are discussed in the chapters that follow. We might focus briefly in conclusion on the distinctively late-20th century activity emerging in post-independence India from the 1950s on, those forms of civic-society enterprises supported through voluntary associations such as Non-Governmental Organizations (NGOs). This avenue towards social empowerment and uplift has been reshaping itself since NGOs first began to be widely established in the 1950s, and we can only suggest some of the innovative forms that have altered the cultural system characterizing Lucknow. Examples drawn from efforts to affect the well-being of women (often linked to children's well-being) may stand in for the much larger phenomenon. One especially interesting case study would be the Lucknow branch of the Self-Employed Women's Association which, like its parallels in other cities, has focused on women's work in the informal sector (particularly, in Lucknow, for Muslim and Scheduled Caste women). Especially interesting for us are its efforts to combine social empowerment for women with the preservation and perpetuation of the Nawabi art of *chikankari* (hand embroidery with patterns distinctive to Lucknow). SEWA's goal of freeing artisan women from middlemen has encompassed a wide range of educational and other training opportunities. That is, women attain both the literacy and numeracy needed to understand their contracts as well as acquiring the necessary embroidery skills, while management opportunities are afforded as they run SEWA themselves; new efforts involve schooling for their children as well. From a group of 31 women when the organization started in 1984, SEWA now involves more than 7,000 women.

Also part of civil-society efforts have been other kinds of associations interested in women's rights issues, to continue the focus suggested by the example of SEWA. Particularly focused on the "reintegration" of [Muslim] women into "public space", organizations like the first Indian Muslim Women's Movement, *Bharatiya Muslim Mahila Andolan,* established in 2007, constitute a particularly interesting example for us, given itsfocus on access to public spaces for Muslim women. As such, it also provides a very different emphasis than SEWA, given its religious rhetoric and argument that women have public persona as demonstrated during the originary period when Muhammad first organized the community. Sharing this rhetoric, the All India Muslim Women's Personal Law Board challenges interpretations of *hadith* that prevent women from becoming *qazi, mufti,* or *'alima* – thus incorporating public roles (as well as public spaces) as appropriate places for women.Although both of these organizations have been organized in the last decade, also at work in Lucknow is *Bazme Khawateen,* The Women's Club, established as early as 1934 and focused on a larger role for women in public and legal activities (see Tschalar in the bibliography). While these organizations differ in their approaches to how women's bodies should be deployed in public, they seem to agree that their shared goal is to push back against both the assumptions that the pure Muslim woman represents Islam on the one hand, or serves as a victim, on the other. In so doing, they all put together the *public* roles they defend for women and the *public spaces* in which women's identity may be enacted. These strategies bring us, in new and fascinating ways, back to the importance and fundamental accessibility of the built environments of Lucknow's cityscapes, and the efforts underway not only to change these material usages of such spaces, but the accompanying understandings that constitute the urban place's cultural system.

Conclusion

Returning to our thematic emphasis throughout, these developments after 1947 suggest both continuities and significant disjunctures in the history of Lucknow. Among the continuities is the self-perception of Lakhnawis that they all help shape, through their participation, the distinctive cultural system that marks them out from residents of other cities. That Lucknow is ever more tightly connected to other central places in the subcontinent and its larger global contexts also means, of course, that the fissiparous patterns that have so marked both the political and social history of India have affected developments in Lucknow as well. The impact of Hindutva as a political as well as social force cannot be denied. Alternatively, the ability of various marginalized groups to seize opportunities to shift the understandings of who and which values are incorporated into Lakhnawi identity has also made significant inroads into the place of such groups in society (following our one example of women in Lucknow). It has marked, as well and more dramatically than anywhere else in the subcontinent, the very space that marks out the city itself. 'Inclusiveness' of the Lakhnawi cultural system has broadened dramatically yet remains a fundamental and significant characteristic of place.

Foot Notes : Abdul Halim Sharar, *Lucknow: The Last Phase of an Oriental Culture* (transl and ed by E.S. Harcourt and Fakhir Hussain [London: Paul Elek,1975]), pp.45, 47. Originally published in installments from 1913 into the 1920s, in the Urdu literary journal *Dil Gudaz*, which Sharar founded and edited in Lucknow. Sharar's rendition of elite lifein Nawabi Lucknow is based on his own experiences (1860-1926) or from first-hand oral sources.

Bibliographic References

Ahmad, Imtiaz, "Through the Eye of a Street," in Violette Graff, ed, *Lucknow: Memories of a City* (Oxford University Press [New Delhi], 1997).

Bayly, C. A. *Empire and Information: Intelligence Gathering and Social Communication in India, 1780-1870* (Cambridge University Press, 1996).

Freitag, Sandria B. *Collective Action and Community: Public Arenas and the emergence of Communalism in North India* (University of California Press, 1989).

Jones, Justin, *Shi'a Islam in Colonial India: Religion, Community and Sectarianism* (Cambridge University Press, 2012).

Joshi, Sanjay. *Fractured Modernity: Making of a Middle Class in Colonial North India* (Oxford University Press, 2001), especially chapter three.

Oldenburg, Veena. "Lifestyle as Resistance: The Case of the Courtesans of Lucknow", *Feminist Studies,* 1990 (reprinted in Violette Graff, ed, *Lucknow: Memories of a City* (Oxford University Press [New Delhi], 1997).

——, *The Making of Colonial India, 1856-77,* (Princeton University Press, 1984 & Oxford University Press, Oxford Omnibus series, 1990).

Phillips, Robert. 'The Urdu-Language *KhushtarRamayan:* Verbal- and Visual-Narrative Repertoires and "Sense of Place" ' in *South Asia,* special issue on *'The VisualTurn",* vol. 37:3 (September 2014), pp. 454-473.

Pinch, William R. *Peasant and Monks in British India* (University of California Press, 1996).

Roberts, Emma, *Scenes and characteristics of Hindostan,* 3 volumes, (London: William H. Allen, 1835), 2:192-3.

SEWA, Lucknow: http://www.sewalucknow.org/home.php

Sharar, Abdul Halim, *Lucknow: The Last Phase of an Oriental Culture* (transl and ed by E. S. Harcourt and Fakhir Hussain [London: Paul Elek, 1975]), especially pp. 45, 47.

Sinha, Amita&Rajat Kant, "Mayawati and memorial parks in Lucknow, India: landscapes of empowerment" in *Studies in the History of gardens & Designed Landsapes: an International Quarterly,* vol. 35:1 (2015).

Stark, Ulrike, *An Empire of Books: The Naval Kishore Press and the Diffusion of the Printed Word in Colonial India* (Permanent Black, 2008).

Tschalar, mengia Hong, 'Muslim women's activists' growing visibility in *South Asia Multi-disciplinary Academic Journal(SAMAJ),*2015:11

Zamindar, VaziraFazila-Yacoobali, *The Long Partition and the Making of Modern South Asia: refugees, boundaries, histories* (Columbia University Prss, 2010).

Social Fabric

Under the umbrella of Lucknow's culture, diverse social groups exist- castes, occupational groups and religious minorities. The social demography of the city has largely been a neglected area in most of the earlier writings on Lucknow and thus conveying the impression that the social fabric of Lucknow is not full of diversities. Not only people of different districts of Uttar Pradesh have settled down in Lucknow but also from other states. Kashmiri Pundits, Bengalese, Punjabis and Sindhis, have also been described. The field research reveals that the Oriyas, Malyalese, Marathis, and Assamese too are now an important part of Lucknow's social fabric and have enriched the mosaic of human affairs in the city.

2

Social Fabric

Lucknow has never been a monolithic society in any sense of the term. Various castes and religious communities have adorned its social fabric and all these together have contributed to the 'Lucknowness' in a variety of ways. Significantly, when we browse through the Gazetteer of Oudh, William Crooks' multi-volume handbook of 'Castes and Tribes of Oudh and North-Western Provinces' and similar other ethnographic narrations of Oudh (Lucknow) and compare these with our primary data collected through fieldwork, we notice that several of these caste groups are missing. The reason may be migration, adoption of a new name and thus changing the identity, depopulation or any other reason. The multi-volume 'Communities in India' compiled and published by the 'Anthropological Survey of India' supports this contention. Following are brief descriptions of important Hindu and Muslim castes and religious groups living in Lucknow.

Hindu, Muslim Castes and Occupational Groups

Before proceeding further and to avoid any confusion regarding caste identities, it would be prudent to categorize the occupational groups/castes on the following lines:

1. Castes which are now entirely Muslim such as *Atishbaaz(*firework makers*)*, *Bhishti(water drawers)*, *Mirasi(*singers/bards*)*, *Qassab*(buchers*)*, etc.
2. Castes which have larger Muslim than Hindu sections such as *Darzi* (tailor), *Dhuniya* (cotton carder), *Manihaar* (bangle maker/seller), *Kunjra* (vegetable seller), *Rangrez* (clothe printer/dyer) etc.
3. Castes which have larger Hindu than Muslim sections such as *Dhobi* (washerman/Laundryman), *Nai* or *Hajjaam* (barber), *Kumhaar* (potter), *Teli* (oil presser), etc.

Thus except such castes /occupational groups, the others are either entirely Hindu or Muslim. Castes such as Ahir/Yadav, Baniya, Bhar, Brahmin, Bhumihar, Chamar/ Jatav, Dhanuk, Dom, Kalwar, Kayasth, Kewat, Khatri, Kurmi, Khatik, Lodh, Pasi, Rajput/ Thakur/ Kshatri, Teli etc. are Hindu castes living in Lucknow. On the other hand, Saiyed, Sheikh, Mughal, Pathan, Ghosi/Gaddi, Julaha/Momin

Ansar, Kunjra, Qasai/ Qassab, etc are Muslim castes.

Occupationally specialized castes have been a familiar feature of Hindu caste system whose influence has been all pervading and similar caste groups also emerged among the Muslims bearing almost all the features of Hindu caste system. With the passage of time, mechanization took over, technology changed and many of these castes either changed their occupation, declined, or languishing with the vestiges of the past. Only some of these, upgraded their technology, understood the market's mechanism, survived and flourishing. Following is a brief description of various Hindu and Muslim castes adorning the social fabric of Lucknow and the adjoining areas.

Brahman, traditionally, are priests and teachers, also known as Pandit, Purohit, Pujari, Shastri etc. Brahman is a varna category of Vedic period and also a caste. They have various endogamous groups namely Kanyakubja, Saryupareen, Chaube, Dikhit, Gaur, Joshi, Maha-Brahman, Sakaldwipi, Sanadh, Saraswati, Kashmiri Pandits etc. These groups are further divided into several clans or *gotras*. Among these groups Kanyakubja and Saryupareen are two most prominent ethnic Brahman groups of which various legends have been described. According to one such legend a section of Brahmans did not attend the *ashwamedha yajna* performed by Lord Ram. Those who attended the yajna were gifted land across the river Saryu thus they got the name Saryupareen while those who did not attend the yajna were named as Kanyakubja. The Kanyakubja consider themselves as the most superior group in the hierarchy of Brahmins. The Brahmans in Uttar Pradesh may also be divided into two broad sections: those of the plains and of the hilly areas. Kashmiri Pandits are recent migrants from Jammu and Kashmir belonging to the Saraswat Brahman group. They are a little distinguished from the other subgroups of Saraswat Brahman because of their inhabitation in the Himalayan regions in the past. The majority of the Brahman communities are engaged in government services followed by private services, business, trade and settled cultivation. A large number of Brahmans are employed in academics and teaching field. This community has also produced many poets and writers in the literary field. Though there is a decline in the traditional occupation of priesthood but still a significant part of this community is engaged in religious practices apart from their profession and they play a significant role in festivals and performance of rituals.

Dhobi is a caste of washermen having both Hindu and Muslim segments who take their name from the Hindi word 'dhona' or Sanskrit word 'dhav' both meaning 'to wash' . The Hindu Dhobis are also known as Rajak and they believe that they are migrants of Kannauj. The Hindu Dhobis have five endogamous groups namely Ajudhyabasi, Belwar, Kanaujia, Jaiswar and Megahiya. Besides being engaged to their traditional occupation of washing clothes they also indulge in cultivation. They have also taken up services, skilled and un-skilled labour and animal husbandry as additional occupations. The Muslim Dhobis are also known as *Baretha* and are believed that they were Hindus before they embraced Islam.

They belong to the Sheikh Muslim order. The Muslim Dhobis are mostly reliant on their traditional occupation of washing clothes while some have drifted into dry-cleaning, wage-labour, agriculture and government or private services. There are scholars, white collar employees, defense personnel and local leaders among them as well in this community. Among Hindus the Dhobis are regarded as an unclean caste and their social status is very low while the Muslim Dhobis enjoy a superior status than Bhangi and is regarded as a clean caste like Nai, Gaddi, Chikwa etc. (Ansari 1959). The Hindu Dhobis are notified as a Scheduled Caste.

Kalwar are a widespread community of manufacturers and traders of country liquour. They are also known as Kalar, Kallar, Sehore and Kallal. They use Batham, Gupta, Jaiswar, Jaiswal and Shaw as surnames. They place themselves under the Vaishya varna. Many of their families have migrated to urban centers in recent times. The traditional occupation of the Kalwars used to be manufacture and distilling of liquor as well as cultivation. Nowadays due to the restrictions on the manufacture and sale of liquor they have to take up varied occupations for the livelihood. They are mainly engaged in cultivation, business and trade. Those having land either cultivate themselves or give their land to the share croppers while others own shops selling edibles, grains and groceries. Highly educated among them are in government and private services and a few of them are engaged in manufacturing of liquour.

Tamboli/Barai are engaged in cultivation of *paan* (betel) leaves. The term 'Barai' is derived from the word *bari* meaning a hedge to enclose the saplings. Crooke (1896) distinguishes Barais with Tambolis stating that the former grows the plant, while the latter sells the leaves though the distinction doesn't work in Uttar Pradesh as the same community sells and grows betel leaves. The Barais in Uttar Pradesh are also called Baseeth in the countryside and Chaurasia or Tamboli in the cities. Barais have social divisions namely Chaurasiya, Katiyar, Nag, Jaiswar and Mahobia. They are worshippers of snakes and Nagpanchmi is a special festival for them. The Barais are still engaged in their traditional occupation of cultivating and selling betel leaves as they are encouraged by the government for horticulture and loans are also given to them. They also have small landholdings on which they grow betel leaves. Apart from it they are also engaged in agriculture. Their women help in plucking and arranging betel leaves. Now they are also taking to education and diversifying in occupation.

Bhar are a also known by the name of Rajbhar, they are followers of Shaiva Panth. According to a legend the ancestor King of the Bhars was a devotee of Lord Shiva and he used to carry the Shivalinga on his shoulders. Hence his descendants were known as Bhar Shiv. They are an endogamous community. The traditional occupation of the Bhars is agriculture. Many of them also work as agricultural labourers on others' farms. Higher communities like Brahman and Thakurs do not exchange food with them. Several of them are now working in different fields.

Ahir/ Yadav are a caste of cattle herders. They trace their descent to Lord

Krishna of Yadu lineage and traditionally assert their claim of being Yaduvansi; they use Yadav as surname. The Yadavs are one of the constituents of the wider Ahir community but often they are synonymously called as Ahir. The Yadav in Uttar Pradesh claim community identity without any subgroups, hierarchy and differentiation. There is continuation of extended families and they are strictly endogamous. Their women take part in all economic activities, rituals and religious sphere. The major economic source for them is land and they are progressive agriculturists. They have also taken up business, trade and industry as occupations and some of them are also in government and private services yet a large section of this community is engaged in agriculture and animal husbandry. Being agriculturalists and cattle-herders they maintain links with other communities.

Bhumihar are also known as Bhuinyar, Babhan, Zamindar Brahman and Grihasth Brahman. They are a community of landowners and agriculturists. They use Rai, Singh, Pandey, Thakur and Tiwari as titles. The primary occupation of most of the Bhumihaar is cultivation. Apart from agriculture they are engaged in business and government and private service. Many of them are also self-employed.

The term **Chamar** is derived from Sanskrit 'charma-kara' which means leather-worker. They generally place themselves as Shudras in the varna system. In Uttar Pradesh the Chamar are also known as Raidas. The Chamar women are engaged in agricultural operations and actively participate in social and religious spheres. They are traditionally landless and their occupation is mainly skin and hide work and agricultural labourer. According to the Anthropological Survey of India (1998) there has been a marked increase in the number of daily wage labourers. The educated among them are in government and private services and due to the constitutional safeguards and reservation their representation in the government services have increased substantially. Due to the emergence of political leadership among them there is a significant rise in the number of white collar employees among them. They are notified as a Scheduled Caste.

Kurmi are a large and widely distributed cultivating caste. Kurmis in Uttar Pradesh have several territorial groups namely Gangwar, Baiswar, Jaiswar, Katiyar and Sachan. They are a settled agricultural community having land as their primary economic resource. Besides, they also domesticate cows and buffaloes and make earning by animal husbandry. The educated among them prefer to enter in the government or private service than their traditional occupation of cultivation. There are a fair number of businessmen, engineers, lawyers and doctors in this community. They are progressive farmers availing benefits of all developmental schemes. The community also has writers, teachers, white-collar job holders, artists, journalists etc.

Lodha are an agricultural and labour caste seems to be recent immigrants from the direction of Bundelkhand. Lodha have two endogamous sub-divisions. They place themselves under the Kshatriya varna. The Lodha of Uttar Pradesh is an agricultural community and land is their main economic resource. Those who are landless are engaged in rearing cattle and serve as agricultural labour. Children often start working at an early age. They are skilled in the craft of making ropes which are used in making cots but they are engaged in rope making only in the seasons in which the required grass grows. Some of them are also engaged in business, service and self-employment. Only a few of them are in white collar jobs.

The caste **Mali** derives its name from the Sanskrit word '*malika*' which means 'a garland maker'. The majority of them are Hindu while a smaller section of Mali is Muslim. The Hindu Mali traces their descent from a garland-maker of Raja Kans at Mathura. Their traditional occupation is gardening and supplying flowers for Hindu worship. In Uttar Pradesh they are also known as Shrimali and Saini. The Mali are a combination of both landowning and landless people. Their traditional occupations are growing flowers and making garlands. Apart from growing flowers they are also engaged in preparing decorative headgears for bridegrooms and flower decorations on ceremonial occasions.

Bharbhunja/Bhujwa/Bhurji are traditionally a caste of grain-parchers. The name of this community is derived from the Sanskrit words 'bhrashtra' meaning 'a fry pan' and 'bharyaka' meaning 'the one who fries'. In Uttar Pradesh they are also called Bhuj, Bhujar, Gour, Bhuja or Kandu and are distributed all over the state. They are an endogamous community without any social divisions. They are placed in the Vaishya varna in the varna system. Their traditional occupation has been grain parching but nowadays they have also taken up varied occupations. The parchers used to receive a fixed proportion of the grains as wages which was generally one-fifth or two-fifth of the grain brought by the customer but in the city they charge in cash. Some of them are engaged in business or trade while some are in government and private services.

Khatri are a mercantile caste which traces its origin in Punjab. They claim to be Rajput and believe that the name of their community is a corrupt form of 'Kshatriya'. Widely distributed in north-western India they have emerged as a progressive and dynamic community. They use a variety of surnames. In Uttar Pradesh they are distributed in many districts. Kakkar, Kapur, Khanna, Lahauri, Mahendra, Arora, Mehra, Seth, Suri and Tandon are their sub-castes. The Khatris of Uttar Pradesh are mainly engaged in business and trade. They are a landless community since most of their land has passed to cultivators. This community has a significant number of doctors, engineers and advocates.

The name **Bania** is derived from the Sanskrit word 'vanik' which means trading. They trace their origin from Maharaja Agrasen. Majority of the Baniya groups place themselves as Vaishya under the varna system. They use titles like Aggarwal, Gupta, Lala, Seth, Vaish and Sahukar. There are six groups among them namely Bisa, Dasa, Saralia, Sarogi, Maheshwari and Oswal. The Baniya castes are traditionally engaged in business, trade and industry. They are also engaged in government and private services and self-employment.

Pasi are a community from Uttar Pradesh who trace their origin from Parashuram according to a Brahminical legend. They are also known by the name of Tarmali which means one who cultivates the palm trees. According to Russell and Hiralal (1961), the Pasis held a part of Oudh before it was conquered by Rajputs. They have several subgroups. They used to tend pigs and consume pig's flesh which was abominable to many. They are treated as a low caste by the Hindu society. Traditionally they are involved in cultivation and land is their main economic resource. Many of them have taken up other occupations like business, private and government service, labour and industrial labour. They are notified as Scheduled Caste.

Rajput/Thakur/Kshatri are traditionally known as warrior and land owning caste. They are believed to be rulers and protectors since the beginning of caste system in India. In Uttar Pradesh the Thakur are a large group speaking different dialects of Hindi and some amongst them also use Urdu. The Rajput or Thakur community is comprised of many branches and clans. Chauhan clan is more concentrated in Aita, Etawah, Agra and Awadh. In the Gazetteer of Oudh (1878) the Rajputs of Lucknow has been described as the most admirable, manly, frank and proud of his birth and lineage. Their main economic resource is land which was owned by the particular clan or lineage or family who developed it but nowadays individual ownership is prevalent. They are the largest landholders in Uttar Pradesh and are engaged in settled cultivation. They are also in different occupations like business, trade, industry, government and private service.

Kewat are a widely distributed community of boatmen, fishermen and cultivators. They are also known as Nishad and Mallah. The term 'Kewat' is derived from the Sanskrit word 'kaivarta' which means 'dweller of water'. There are several mythological legends connected to them which are narrated in epics like Ramayana and Mahabharata. The Kewats are famous for their bravery and they created troubles for British rulers in crossing rivers during the revolution of 1857, hence they were labeled as a criminal tribe by the British. In Uttar Pradesh they have ten subgroups or sub-castes. Water is the major natural resource of the Kewats as they own very little land. They are engaged in their traditional occupation of ferrying people across the rivers, transporting goods through waterways and fishing. They also indulge in cultivating vegetables and fruits like chestnuts on the riverbeds.

Sunar is a community of goldsmiths and silversmiths who used to specialize in money-lending, pawn breaking and general trade. They are also referred to as *Suvarnakar*. Their name is derived from the Sanskrit word '*suvarna*' and '*kara*' meaning the 'worker in gold'. There are various legends regarding their origin.

The traditional occupation of Sunar has been gold-smithy and their business used to be of making jewellery, money lending and pawn-broking. They were often accused of receiving and disposing stolen jewellery. The occupation of Sunar must be an ancient one as the deities were constantly portrayed in the Rigveda as wearing gold ornaments. Most of the Sunars are still engaged in the gold-smithy but many of them are finding it difficult to generate sufficient income from it. Hence many of them have averted to government and private service and some have taken up self-employment by becoming doctors, advocates, engineers and money-lenders and some others have engaged in the business by opening jewellery shops etc.

Halwai is a caste of confectioners and sweet makers who take their name from the word 'halwa' which is a sweetmeat made of flour, clarified butter, sugar and flavoured with saffron and nuts. The Halwai community comprises larger Hindu section than Muslims. The Hindu Halwai trace the origin of the term Halwai from 'Halwahi (ploughing)' which was the main occupation of the Vaisya. The Hindu Halwai have sub-castes like Kanaujia, Magahiya, Bantiria, Panchhainya, Madhesia, Purbia, Bhojpuria, Koranch, Maltaria etc. They use Gupta, Vaisya, Yagyaseni, Modanwal, Kanyakubja etc as their surnames. They place themselves under the Viashya varna in the varna system.

Muslim halwai are also known as Mithaiwale. They belong to the Sunni sect of Islam and place themselves as Sheikhs in the Muslim society. Urdu is their mother-tongue while they also speak Hindi. The Muslim Halwais are those who once belonged to the Vaishya groups and converted to Islam. They claim to belong to the Shaikh category of Muslims. They visit *pirs* and *mazaars*. They have traditional community councils or panchayats for dealing with issues like elopement, brawls, thefts and impertinent behaviour.

The traditional occupation of the Halwai has been sweet-making. Either they own their sweet shops or they work as skilled labourers in big and renowned sweet shops. Generally their shops are in markets and heavily populated localities. Some Halwais also act as caterers of pucca food during the marriages. In some Halwai families children help in the business arranging plates and cups, providing water to the customers, cleaning dishes etc. Nowadays they are also engaged in trade, business and service while some of them are doctors and engineers. In the rural area some of them have landholdings which are generally cultivated by the share-croppers. Being the major suppliers of sweets they play a specific role during the festivals, marriages, child-birth etc. and are respected for their social and ritual significance. Some of the Halwais have adopted modern manufacturing techniques and they have started producing packaged sweets in large quantities for wider supply. The Muslim Halwai are mostly landless and are mainly engaged in selling sweets, tobacco, wage labour and dyeing of clothes while some of them have taken up government and private service.

Lohar are a caste of the blacksmiths. The term 'lohar' is derived from the Sanskrit word 'lauhakara' which means 'a worker in iron'. Nowadays they address themselves as Vishwakarma. Some of the Lohars claim their descent from *Bhagwan* Manu. They are a widespread community of Uttar Pradesh. Most of them are Hindu but a small segment of Lohar is Muslim as well. The Muslim Lohar are known as Saifi.

Barhai are an occupational community of carpenters of which the majority are Hindus and only a small section of Muslims. They derive the name of their community from the Sanskrit word 'vardhika' meaning 'cutting'. They are mostly Hindu and use various surnames or titles like Sharma, Vishwakarma, Bharadwaj,

Mistry and Badhai. They worship Bhawani Devi as their family deity .They marry within their community but outside the gotra or clan. Divorce and remarriage are permissible.

The Muslim Barhai have two endogamous sub-divisions in Uttar Pradesh, the Desi or native and the Multani or immigrants from Multan. They, along with another artisan community of Muslim-ironsmiths, are also known as Saifi. They belong to the Sunni sect of Islam and their rituals and customs are similar to those of other Muslims of Lucknow.

The traditional occupation of the Barhai caste is carpentry which is believed to be an ancient one. Before the advent of industrialization the Barhais enjoyed the status of 'architect' or 'chief-engineer' in the villages and they used to provide sketches or blueprints to various other assisting communities for technical work. With the influence of industrialization more people from other castes started doing various technical works. Thus the inherited craftsmanship and skills of the Barhais are given less credit. Nowadays they have become a land-owning community who are mainly engaged in carpentry while agriculture has become their secondary occupation. As they do wood-work they are also skilled in wood carving and engraving. They are also employed in the fields of engineering and education, small-scale industrial manufacturing firms. Some of them also indulge in stone work and timber trade.

Teli are a community of oil makers and traders, in various commodities. The term Teli is derived from the Sanskrit word tailika or taila meaning the oil extracted from sesame or mustard seeds. The Teli of Uttar Pradesh have several subgroups. They use Gupta, Sahu, Rathor, etc. as surnames. Most of them place themselves under the Vaisya varna. They speak Awadhi and Hindi. The Teli have a small Muslim section also and they are an occupational caste. There are no social divisions among them. They belong to the Sunni sect. They visit the dargahs (tomb shrines) of Muslim saints and make offerings to Ghazi miyan. The tombs of Hazrat Nizamuddin, Dewa Sharif and Ajmer Sharif are their shrines. They are now mainly engaged in agriculture for livelihood but are also indulged in business of oil. Some work as unskilled labourer.

The traditional occupation of the Teli caste used to be oil pressing and growing oil seed which has now been given up due to the more efficient machine operated oil mills. In old times, they had their small oil mills known as *kolhu* or *ghana* having wooden expellers operated by oxen to extract edible oil from oil seeds like mustard and sesame. Nowadays most of them have taken to trade and agriculture on which they now largely depend. They have small grocery and general merchandise stores and their women also help in selling goods. Some of them have started working as *halwai*. Their main economic resource is land and many among them are engaged in animal husbandry. Those who are landless work as wage labourers in the villages.

Faqirs are a community of mendicants and beggars. The name Faqir is derived from the Arabic word *faqr* meaning 'poverty'. They trace their origin to Hazrat

Abu Bakr and Hazrat Ali, the first and the fourth Caliphs. They are also known by the names of Sain and Shah Alvi. They have two subdivisions namely *Ba Shara* referring to those who live according to the rules of Islam and the *Be Shara* to those who live without law.

They have several subgroups such as Zinda Shahi, Chishti, Qalandari etc. All of the subgroups belong to Sunni sect of Islam except the Zinda Shahi who are Shia. Among the Faqir hierarchy the Zinda Shahi are the followers of Sufi saint Zinda Shah. The term *zinda* in Urdu means alive and the Zinda Shahi believe that their spiritual guide is still alive. The Zinda Shahi use the title Shah. The Chishti are the followers of the famous Sufi saint Moinuddin Chisti. The Qalandari are followers of Qalander Shah. The Faqirs are a highly endogamous community. They wear loose black garment and carry rosary to offer prayers. They keep an emblem 'Panja' or a flag with them. They speak Urdu and regional dialects among them. They often believe in magico-religious treatment of maladies and Qalandars are believed to possess the expertise in this field.

The Faqirs' traditional occupation is begging. Some of them are nomadic while some beg within a small area. They used to get cooked food, clothes, grains etc during the holy month of Ramazan. Some of them live near cemeteries and tombs of the saints and depend upon the offerings of the visitors and some work as caretakers of mosques. At special occasions they are served food by the Muslim families. Nowadays most of them are giving up their hereditary occupation of begging and are turning up to wage labour and other occupations. A good number of them have become landholders and are engaged in agriculture, animal husbandry and poultry farming.

Qassab are an occupational caste of butchers and slaughterers, also known as *Kasai*, *Kasab* or *Bakr Qassab* and *Chikwa*. They derive the name of their community from the Arabic word 'qassab' which means 'to cut'. They claim their descent from the Arab settlers of the Quresh tribe of Prophet Mohammad. The Kasai use Qureshi as their surnames. They belong to the Sunni sect of Islam. In Uttar Pradesh they have two subgroups namely *Chhote* and *Bare Qasai*. The *Chhote Kasai* also known as *Chikwa* are engaged in selling goat meat and goat skin while the *Bare Kasai* deal in the big animals such as buffaloes, bullocks, etc. and in selling of beef, skin and hide. The *Chikwa* do not intermarry with *Kasai*. They are a strictly endogamous community. They also have a nationwide association named *Anjuman Quraish*. They are also invited on special and auspicious occasions like childbirth, marriages and festivals by some communities like Kayasth, Thakur and Bhumihar to slaughter animals for meat.

They are a landless community and are still associated with the slaughtering of animals. A section of the Kasai sells hides, intestines, lungs and bones which get them good money. Chikwas living in the villages sell animals in the towns. Most of them in towns have small shops or *gumtis* where they slaughter animals and sell meat whereas some work in big meat shops. Besides selling meats, they are also engaged in the sale and purchase of animals. Some of them are also engaged in agriculture and labour. This community also has doctors, engineers, advocates and teachers largely after taking advantage of reservation for OBCs.

Ghassal are often described as a microscopic community as they are concentrated only in Lucknow city of Uttar Pradesh. They derive the name of their community from the word 'ghusl' which means 'washing' which denotes their occupation of bathing corpses. According to Anthropological Survey of India (1998) they are a conglomerate of the Sayyad, Mughal and Pathan who have taken the job of bathing corpses for a livelihood and were at their peak during the regime of the Nawabs of Oudh but were later isolated because the stigma attached to their profession. It is known that the Shia Nawabs and nobles would not touch the dead bodies and hence some of the Sayyads took up the task of bathing the dead bodies. According to another belief they are the descendants of royal princes who took the profession of bathing corpses as they were disowned by the royal families because of their 'bad habits'.

This community now consists of only a handful. They are traditionally engaged in offering services at the funerals. They bathe corpses and accept alms, clothes, jewellery and footwear removed from the corpses in return. Since their income is uncertain and scanty they are forced to take up many other works. Many Ghassals have given up their traditional occupation due to low income and low social prestige attached to it. They are engaged in vending, selling fruits, fuel-wood and rickshaw-pulling. They are also engaged in crafts like taazia makng, chikan and zardozi embroidery.

Darzi is an occupational community of both Hindu and Muslim tailors. The name 'Darzi' is derived from the Persian word 'darz' meaning 'a seam'. They are also known as *Khaiyyat* meaning 'to sew'. In Uttar Pradesh the population of Muslim Darzi is far greater than Hindu Darzis. The Darzi of Uttar Pradesh use Idrisi as title and trace their origin from Hazrat Idris ,one of the prophets of Islam. It is believed that he was the original teacher who taught their ancestors the art of tailoring. The Muslim Darzi belongs to both Shia and Sunni sect of Islam though Shia Darzi are only a few. They speak Urdu The Hindu Darzi claim their descent from the Kshatriya, according to a legend narrated by Russel and Hiralal (1916) when Parshurama, the sixth incarnation of Vishnu was destroying the Kshatriya, two brothers hid themselves in a temple and were protected by the priest. The priest set one of the brothers to sew clothes for the idol and the other to dye the clothes. The descendants of the first brother became Darzi while of the latter were Chhipi.

The Hindu Darzi worships their tools like scissors, needles, sewing machine etc. before beginning their day's work. The Darzi are traditionally engaged in the tailoring business. They either work on their own or as an assistant under a master tailor. Some of them are now engaged in textile industries and some have started selling readymade clothes at their shops or at weekend markets. The profession of Darzi is poorly regarded and hence the educated among them prefer to join government and private services.

Manihar are a community of workers in glass and tin foils. According to Crooke (1896) the term 'manihar' is derived from the Sanskrit words 'mani' and 'kara' meaning 'workers in precious stone'. He further mentions that they specialize in making and applying the pewter foils which is used in the superior quality of bangles. The Manihar of Uttar Pradesh are also known as *Churihaar*. The Muslim Manihar claim descent from the first Caliph of Islam, Abu Bakr.

Earlier the Manihar did not use any surname but nowadays they have started using Siddiqui as their surname and claim to be Shaikhs. They place themselves at the middle of the social order in the Muslim society. They are an endogamous community. They have traditional caste panchayats to settle disputes and maintain social control. Most of the Manihars belong to the Sunni sect of Islam. They revere the shrine of Pir Sayyad Shaidan Shah Wali Naseh Pir which is in Fatehpur town. The Manihars play an important role during the festivals and the Hindu rituals as all married Hindu women wear bangles and they maintain a patron-client relationship with other communities in the rural areas. The Maniharin (wife of manihar) are often honoured by the Hindu women whenever bangles are traditionally worn during the ceremonies. She also gives an extra bangle to women as a token of blessing.

The traditional occupation of the Manihars is selling glass and lac bangles. They sell bangles by peddling, in the weekly markets, and some have established shops. While most of them are engaged in their traditional business of bangles, some have taken to tailoring and betel leaves selling as their subsidiary occupation.

Dhuniya are a caste of cotton carders and they derive their community name from the Hindi word 'dhunna' meaning 'to card'. There are some Hindu Dhuniyas too but the majority of them are Muslims. Dhuniyas are also known by the names of Behna, Naddaf, Dhuna, Sheikh Mansuri etc. The Muslim Dhunia claim their descent from Khwaja Mansur who is believed to be a Faqir who had power of working miracles. The Hindu Dhunyias claim a Rajput origin.

The Dhuniya belong to the Sunni sect of Islam and they visit local Pirs and mazaars in the area. Their sacred shrines are Ajmer Sharif, Dewa Sharif and Madaar Sharif. They believe that the saints act as intercessors and intermediaries for their prayers. Though they profess Islam, they follow a few Hindu customs and ceremonies too. The traditional occupation of the Dhuniya is cotton carding. They clean and make the cotton fluffy by using a traditional tool named *dhanuhi* and *muthi* or *dunki* which is a vibrating bow string. By using the tool the cotton is made soft and uniformly fluffy and at the same time dirt entangled in the fibers also falls out. The carded cotton is used for quilting and preparing mattresses and other bedding materials and is also ready to pass through spinner to make thread. The Dhuniya practice cotton-carding by going door to door to fill mattresses and quilts and have their own temporary shops as well. The occupation of cotton carding is seasonal and hence most of them now own lands and engage in cultivation as well in some rural areas. Some of them work as share-croppers and wage labourers while some are indulged in selling betel leaves, cotton cloth, leather goods, baskets etc and rickshaw pulling. The educated among them are also in government and private service.

Atishbaz are purely an occupational caste of the makers of fire-works also known as *barudgir* or *hawaigar*. The term atishbaz is derived from the Persian word '*atish*' meaning 'fire' and '*baz*' meaning 'to play'. They trace their origin from Iran and claim that their ancestors, who were experts in making gun powder and fireworks came along with the Mughals. In Uttar Pradesh they are spread in Lucknow and eastern districts like Mirzapur, Varanasi, Jaunpur, Azamgarh, Basti, Gorakhpur, Gonda etc. They are scheduled among the OBCs in Uttar Pradesh. They use Atishbaz as their title and sometimes refer themselves as Atishbaz Shaikh. They have no social division and differentiation among them.

The majority of Atishbaz community is landless and they are primarily engaged in selling and playing fireworks. The economic condition of Atishbaz is deteriorating due to limited and seasonal demand of their fireworks. Moreover, with the Chinese items invading the local markets, they are falling stiff completion. Hence many of them have turned to medium sized and small farmers and agricultural labourers in rural areas. Due to their occupation of playing fireworks they are professionally involved with both Hindu and Muslim communities. They display the fireworks in geometrical and graphic pattern. They offer their services during festivals and marriages. Their children are also engaged in the manufacture of fire-works. Due to lack of education the members of this community are not in good jobs.

Kumhar are a caste of potters who derive the name of their community from the Sanskrit word *kumbhakara* meaning 'makers of pots'. There are various legends regarding their origin. The Kumhars referring to their surname Prajapati claim to be descendants of Prajapati Daksha who was son of Brahma. Some of them connect their origin with the beginning of human civilization when man started making earthen pots. Most of them are Hindu and only a small segment of Kumhars are Muslim.

In Lucknow and adjoining areas, they are known as Kumbhar and Prajapati having subgroups namely Kanaujia, Baradiya, Chakbai, Gadhere, Atharia, Magahia, Duliwal etc. They are primarily engaged in making pots and toys from clay for livelihood. They claim that they were natives of Kannauj who migrated to other parts of Uttar Pradesh. They still have a traditional caste panchayat. But in the urban areas its influence is declining fast.

Though the traditional occupation of Kumhars is pottery but most of them have given it up and only a few are continuing with it. Nowadays, a few Kumhar own land and indulge in agriculture and some of them have taken up wage labour, cattle-grazing, masonry and other paid jobs. They are the suppliers of clay pots during the birth, marriage and death ceremonies and festivals. Some of the urban potters have started experimenting with new clay forms and are making decorative ethnic pottery according to the new and growing demands of the customers for the decoration of interiors. They have shifted to terracotta and colours instead of using traditional red clay for making pots and designs.

Kunjra is a caste of greengrocers who sell country vegetables and fruits and are also known as *sabz farosh*, *mewa farosh* or *sabzi farosh.* In Lucknow the caste usually deals in country vegetables and fruits are Kunjras, Kabaris or Kabarias. They are also referred to as Rayeen. They claim their descent from those inhabiting the Rayee Mountain. The term 'Kunjra' is derived from the Sanskrit word 'kunj' which means a bower. In Uttar Pradesh they have subdivisions namely Gorakhpuri, Jaiswar, Kolapuri, Purbia, Sarwaria, Uttaraha, Baghban, Kabaria and Tambakuwala. They are placed in the lower order of Muslim society and come under OBCs. The Kabaria group of Kunjra has become a distinct and endogamous community dealing in scrap. It is believed that they are converts who once belonged to Hindu Murao caste. They speak both Awadhi and Urdu.

The Kunjras are an urban based community and a substantial number of Kunjras own lands and are engaged in agriculture and growing vegetables. In the city they sell vegetables and fruits. Apart from their traditional occupation they are also indulged in business, trade, industry, service or are self-employed. This community also has scholars, white collar employees and political leaders at the regional level. The Kunjra women, apart from their household duties, indulge in selling the produce in the local markets to supplement the family income.

Rangrez are a Muslim caste of dyers who derive the name of their community from the Persian word 'Rangrez' which means 'dyer'. The Rangrez are mainly distributed in the states of Uttar Pradesh, Bihar, Madhya Pradesh, Delhi and Rajasthan. There are various opinions regarding their origin. Some believe that they came along with the army of Mohammad Ghori as washer-men and tailors. They speak Urdu and are also conversant in other local dialects. The Rangrez suffer from a low social status and they are ranked with Julahas and other low Muslim castes. Their income and property are also limited.

They are a landless community in U.P. who are mainly found in the urban and semi-urban areas. The traditional occupation of the Rangrez has been dyeing and printing beautiful designs on cotton fabric used for garments, sheets and quilts which has declined considerably. With the advent of cheap chemical dyes and machine made textiles the process of dyeing has become quite simple and the indigenous art of dyers has declined. Consequently only a small fraction of Rangrez are still engaged in the occupation of dyeing and printing and most of them have taken up laundry work, wage labour and rickshaw-pulling. Those who are still engaged in dyeing and printing, sell/ dry colours or dye new and old garments for the local customers. Some of them are also in government and private service and small business. Those who are self-employed are generally engaged in small laundry business, textiles, shops and labour.

Nanbai are a baker caste who also call themselves Rotiwala or Biskutwala. The name of this community is derived from the Persian word 'nan' meaning bread. They either sell English bread or cook dishes for customers. Some call them a purely occupational caste whose members may freely intermarry with other Muslims but it does not commonly happen. According to Ansari (1959) the caste of Nanbai is an offshoot of Bhatiyara. He adds that with the installation of railways travelling became easier and overnight lodging became unnecessary and gradually the inns (sarai) lost their significance. Thus most of the Bhatiyaras either opened food shops or took up the occupation of Nanbai. They are distributed in the areas where the Nawabs used to live i.e. Awadh.

They are an immigrant community believed to have evolved from the families of cooks of the Muslim rulers of North India. It is believed that their ancestors prepared and offered a delightful feast for their guardian saint and hence came to be known as Nanbais. In Lucknow they are mainly concentrated in the urban areas. They are an endogamous community belonging to the Sunni sect of Islam. They consider themselves under the Shaikh order of the Muslims.

The Nanbai are a landless community engaged in their traditional occupation of baking and cooking. They specialize in preparing Mughlai food. They also have expertise in baking fermented loaves and tandoori breads known as nan. Some of them have opened tea stalls. They are also indulged in business and some among them are working as rickshaw pullers while the educated ones among them are in white collar jobs.

Nau/Nai, the caste of barbers have larger Hindu segment than Muslims. They are also known by the names of Nau-Thakur and other names, while the Muslim Nai are known as Hajjam. Some believe that Nai, is a corrupt form of the Sanskrit word napika, or 'one who cleans nails'. It is also claimed by some that the term Nai is derived from the word 'nyay' meaning justice as Nais are considered to be good judges. According to a legend they were created by Lord Shiva from his navel to cut and clean the nails of his consort Parvati. According to another legend they have descended from a Kshatriya father and a Shudra mother.

They engage in services of a Brahman to perform all birth, marriage and death rites. The Nais have close interaction with other castes and communities and they are a social community as per the requirements of their occupation. Although they maintain patron-client relations with other communities yet their social status is quite low. The Muslim Nai or Hajjam trace their origin to Hazrat Suleman. They belong to the Sunni sect of Islam. They are placed in the middle order in the Muslim society. They play an important role in *Ashraf* marriage. They perform rituals and other duties during marriage ceremonies and other festivals and are rewarded by their clients in cash and kind. They work as match-makers, invitation distributors and also convey good and auspicious news.

The traditional occupation of the Nai is cutting hair, beard and nails, shaving, cleaning ears, extracting teeth, setting sprains right etc. and match-making. They used to carry auspicious messages and perform rituals in life-cycle ceremonies. Nai women worked as attendants at the birth of babies, and provide their services to the mothers and the newborn babies by giving massages and pedicures and manicures for which they were paid in cash and kind. The Nai women are also called for service to colour the feet of married women on festive occasions or during performing of life cycle ceremonies. They also sing folk songs during the ceremonies and celebrations accompanied by *dholak*, a musical instrument. Some of the Nais also indulge in cultivation and animal husbandry. The Hajjams are mostly engaged as barbers and some of them have indulged in settled cultivation. The Muslim Nai besides hair-cutting and shaving also performs the operation of circumcision.

Ghosi is a Muslim caste of herdsmen. The name of this community is derived from the word 'ghosh' meaning 'to shout' while herding the cattle. Crooke (ibid) mentions that they are converts like the Gaddi from the Ahir community. They belong to the Sunni sect of Islam. They use Urdu as mother tongue and also speak Hindi. They are further divided into several sub-divisions. As landless community they are engaged in their traditional occupation of rearing cows and buffaloes and selling milk. Some of them are also in government and private service. The Ghosi women are not involved in milching and are confined to household chores and making cow-dung cakes. They have seven area wise panchayats of which two are in Lucknow. The community also has advocates, doctors and engineers thanks to reservation in jobs for the OBCs.

Pathan are considered to have come either from Afghanistan or from Pashto speaking tribes of North–West Frontier province, now in Pakistan. They are a large population and widely distributed community and claim to be the descendants of migrants from Arabia. In Uttar Pradesh they are divided into several subgroups. The Pathans are mainly engaged in agriculture and business and land is their main economic resource. Most of the Pathans belong to the Sunni sect of Islam but some of them have also adopted the Shia faith. Owners and cultivators of the famous mangos from Malihabad tehsil of Lucknow are Pathans.

Bisati a community of vendors, hawkers and peddlers selling miscellaneous goods which derive its name from the word 'bisaat' meaning 'goods spread out for sale'. Crooke (ibid) describes them as a purely occupational caste of small peddler, hawker or huckster selling petty goods of European manufacture like needles, pins, tape, stationery, buttons, hardware etc. They are believed to be immigrants from Afghanistan. They are also known as Feriwala, Tikulihara, Manihar etc. In Uttar Pradesh they also live in Lucknow and belong to the Sunni sect of Islam. They use Beg, Hussain, Ansari, Siddiqui, Hashmi and Sheikh as their surnames. The majority of Bisatis in Lucknow are landless and they are engaged in their traditional occupation of vending goods door to door. They generally carry goods on their heads on a wooden tray and sometimes employ a servant. The goods they sell are generally buttons, bangles or cosmetics for women. A few of them own shops in markets. Some of them have also entered in government service.

Gaddi are basically a Muslim caste of cow-herders. They belong to the Sunni sect of Islam. They are perceived as a lowly placed community. They speak Urdu at home but they are also conversant in Hindi. Traditionally they are a combination of landowning and landless pastoral community. Most of them are engaged in dairy farming and those having land are indulged in settled cultivation. A few of them are also engaged in government and private service. Working as milkmen they have economic ties with most of the communities and they maintain patron-client and landlord-tenant relationship in rural areas. Very few of them are educated enough to get government jobs.

Bawarchi are an endogamous sub-group of the Kasai caste. They claim to be migrants from Iran and call themselves Quraishi in relation to a place named Quraish in Iran. This community is concentrated in Lucknow and especially in Husainganj, Chowk and Sadar areas. They do not have further sub-divisions among them. They are a community of professional cooks and most of them are engaged as cooks or assistant cooks at eating outlets, restaurants, hotels etc. They have expertise in cooking all kinds of dishes. Some of them also work on contract basis during feasts and festivals. Some of them are also engaged in business of tobacco. This community also has teachers and white collar employees.

Sayyad are like 'Muslim Brahmins'. The Sayyads are regarded to be descendants of the Prophet through the line of his daughter Fatima who was married to the fourth Caliph Ali. They hold the foremost position and rank highest among the Muslim classes. The Sayyad, which means 'prince' get respect from all Muslims and there is a tradition that a Sayyad in need must be helped in the form of present *(hadiyya)* instead of charity *(khairat* and *zakaat)*, without any degrading attitude attached to such help. In Uttar Pradesh they are found throughout the state. They speak Urdu amongst them while Hindi is used with the non-Muslims. Sayyad saints such as Chishti, Jalali, Qadiriya claim to be spiritual kins of the Prophet. The Sayyads of rural areas were zamindars and taluqdars who did not cultivate their lands themselves but entered into sharecropping with other groups while in the urban areas they were priests, men of letters, teachers, self-employed and in public-service. On one hand the Sayyad community has sacred specialists, maulvis and mujtahids who impart religious education and perform life-cycle rituals while on the other it has academicians, jurists, administrators, political leaders, governors etc. Most of the Sayyads happen to be Shia Muslims.

Julaha/Momin Ansar are a Muslim caste of weavers. The term 'Momin' is Arabic and means followers of Islamic theology. It is believed that they were Hindus who got converted to Islam but nowadays they claim to be descendants of Nabi Ayub Ansari who started the work of weaving. They use Ansari as their surname. They speak Urdu and Hindi. They do not have any social divisions among them but some are placed higher than the rest because of their economic, occupational and educational achievement. They are an endogamous community yet occasionally they also intermarry with those in the Shaikh category. They belong to the Sunni sect of Islam but some of them have also converted to Shiaism. The traditional occupation of the Julahas has been weaving, especially cotton cloth weaving, but due to the entry of the cheaper and machine-made textile it has made them trying other occupations. Their women and children also work on the *karghas* or handlooms. They are a landless community and those who are generally engaged in their traditional occupation are weaving coarse cotton cloths for bedspreads and rugs. Some of them are engaged in business and wage labour. This community owns a fair number of academicians. They are also in government services and the major chunk of Muslim OBCs come from this group.

Sheikh are a largely distributed community. The term Sheikh is Arabic word which means 'chief', 'elder' or 'a venerable old man'. The Sheikh rank second on the social scale among the Muslims after Sayyads. According to Ansari (1959), although the term Sheikh was used to denote pious spiritual guides during the early days of the Muslim conquest, today in India, it is used to denote a distinct group of people who are said to have descended from early Muslims of Mecca and Medina. Nowadays it has also been adopted by the converts from the Hindu population. In Uttar Pradesh the Sheikh includes both Sunnis as well as Shias. They speak Urdu and are also conversant with Hindi. Their traditional and primary occupation is cultivation. Besides they have adopted business, trade, weaving, government service, woodwork and masonry also as other sources of livelihood. This community has also scholars, teachers, advocates, doctors, engineers, businessmen and political leaders even at national level.

Mirasi are a community of singers and genealogists. The term Mirasi is derived from the Arabic word 'Miras' which means inheritance as they were the hereditary bards or minstrels. The Mirasi men are singers, musicians, story-tellers and genealogists whereas the Mirasin (Mirasi women) sing and dance but only in the presence of women. The section of Mirasi which converted to Shia faith were an integral part of the mourning recitation during Moharrum and specialized in *Soz* recitation, sometimes based on shastri sangeet. With the passage of time new generations of this group has been giving up their traditional occupation and now a very small number of them perform their traditional job.

Vajpayee Brahmins are a special and unique group of Brahmins deserving special mention. Though coming from Kanyakubj they are a Lucknow specific caste group and it is believed that wherever the vajpayees or bajpai may be living they trace their roots to Lucknow and within Lucknow to a particular mohalla, Chowk.

As the legend goes, around 1600 AD Emperor Akbar passed through Lucknow. A group of Kanyakubj Brahmins met him for financial support for performing 'Vajpeya Yaggya'. A sum of rupees one lakh was granted to them and the ritual was performed. The yagna has great vedic importance. This is usually performed on a large scale for a great purpose. As the legend goes when the Moghul King Humayun was defeated by Sher Shah Suri in 1540 at Chause Bihar, he alongwith his army had to make a hasty retreat to Agra passing through Lucknow. Desperate and short of food supply and money while halting at Lucknow, the headman of Bajpayees visited him and promised him help at this hour of need. He was given ten thousand coins, foodgrain and jaggery as *nazr* to him as they hold him for them. Humayun continuous to be their king. The king was overwhelmed with emotions and sense of gratitude. Perhaps, he must have told the young Akbar, his sun, about this help at a crucial time. That is how when he became the King, Akbar recognised this contribution and wanted to reciprocate.

Vajpayees/bajpais across the world have the same gotra and thus gotra exogamy becomes the norm which implies that marriages cannot be performed between Bajpais.

After this event this Kanyakubjiya Brahamin group inhabiting Chowk was called 'Vajpayee'. They are a small population and related with Lucknow though some people believe that they are originally from Bighapur, Unnao from where they came and settled. From literary figure Nand Dularey Vajpayee to former prime minister Atal Bihari Vajpayee, all the vajpayees claim to be belonging to Lucknow. They have made significant contribution to all spheres of life. It is said by some people that Vajpayees were not recruited in the armed forces because of their strong belief in untouchability and obsessive concern for maintaining ritual purity and thus goes the saying " chaar kannauji, nau chulha" (if there are four kannaujis at one place, the hearths would be nine). Some people describe them more 'Lucknawi' than even the Shias of Lucknow.

In present time a number of vajpayees have also moved to Ganeshganj and Ghalla mandi areas. Some prosperous Vajpayees have also constructed Dharmshalas and most of these are located in Charbagh and Ganeshganj. The hospital of municipal corporation at Ganeshganj is also built on the land donated by the Vajpayees.

Kayasthas

Historically speaking,the Shia Muslims,Kayasthas and Kashmiri Pandits have played the most important role in the development of modern Lucknow.

Kaysthas occupied the highest government offices serving as ministers and advisers during the Mughal Empire and holding important administrative positions during the British Raj and this continued to the modern times.

Their status in the *Varna* system has been a matter of dispute and controversy but irrespective of this aspect, there is hardly any sphere of life in which they have not contributed. The history of Nawabs of Awadh shall remain incomplete without their contribution. Since the Kayasthas have been very proficient in various government services, every ruler gave them important responsibilities. They had a knack in learning language of any ruler and his government. "When Emperor Akbar made Persian the official language, they learned it quickly with the result that they got entry into the Mughal Durbar and in all the provinces under the Mughals. They were appointed to such important posts as treasurer, Deewaan, prime minister and advisor." (Hemant Kumar, 2007).

Right from the begining of Nawab Dynasty since 1722, the Kayasthas got appointments in military and civil administration. When Nawab Asafuddaula moved the capital of Awadh from Faizabad to Lucknow he appointed a Kayasth as Diwaan and later prime minister. Raja Tikait Rai was a trusted minister in his regime. He not only served the Nawab very efficiently but also constructed new temples, *ghats*, tanks and even mosques and renovated a number of places of importance for the Hindus. Because of his donation and contribution he was declared as the royal *yajman* of Hanuman Garhi of Ayodhya.

After him a number of other Kayasthas served the administration during the Nawab's rule in different important posts. Raja Jhau Lal, Raja Gulab Rai, Munshi Hardayal, Trilok Chand Bakshi, Raja Jiya Lal, Jwala Prasad, Bal Krishna Bihari Lal and several others made important contributions not only in the administration but also in the construction of a number of religious and secular places of Hindus and Muslims especially of Shias. After the annexation of Awadh and the advent of British rule they immediately adapted themselves by learning English language and nuances of British administration. They quickly understood the judicial system and played very important role in the judiciary which continues to this day.

Whether it is medical field, judiciary and legal profession,higher education and research, journalism, literature or fine arts they have left a mark in all spheres of life. Needless to say, their contribution and representation in all these fields have been much higher than their population. Lucknow shall always be grateful for their contribution in the cultural life of the city. In Urdu poetry names such as Raja Nawal Rai 'Wafa', Khem Narain 'Rind' Luckhnawi, Jaswant Singh, Jiya Lal 'Gulshan', Shankar Dayal 'Farhat', Ram Sahay 'Tamanna', Dwarika Prasad 'Ufaq', Bisheshwar Prasad 'Munawwar', Krishna Bihari 'Noor' and so many others can never be forgotten. A number of roads, lanes, and institutions in Lucknow are known by the eminent Kayasthas.

Previously, *mohallas, tolas* and different types of other localities were exclusively inhabited by different castes or occupational groups. This was the extension of village life where different castes have been living in segregated quarters. The caste affiliation of old *mohallas* may still be seen. We knew that some *mohallas* like Ashrafabaad/Naubasta had a concentration of Kayasthas but well known Kayasthas like Hemant Kumar and Yogesh Praveen have added to our knowledge by identifying different old *mohallas* and new localities on the basis of the sub-castes of Kayastha population in Lucknow. Thus *mohallas* such as Saadatganj, Mashakganj, Birhana, Kundri Rakabganj etc. had Srivastava as the dominant population while Rakabganj, Subhan Nagar and Tazi Khana were brimimg with Nigams. Murghakhana and Terhi Bazar were the settlements of Bhatnagar, Thakurganj, Musahibganj had substantial population of Mathurs and Saxenas were in large numbers in Naubasta and Ashrafabad. Later when new areas came up some of which had substantial population of Kayasthas such as Chitragupta Nagar, Mahanagar, Janki Puram etc. Thus, an important demographic shift may be seen. Now, instead of sub-castes Kayasthas as a larger group may be seen in different now localities. Moreover, the present trend is the emergence of multi-caste localities and housing colonies and at the most the segregation, whenever it is there, is on the lines of religious affiliation such as a Hindu, Muslim (Shia or Sunni) or Sikh locality.

One thing that remains unchanged among the Kayasthas is their preference for service in the government, semi-government or private sector. Having a high level of education including professional education they hold respectable position. They also continue to have a knack for judiciary although some of them are also joining defense forces but rarely business/trade or agriculture.

Religious Minorities

For more than two hundred years, people of diverse religious faiths have been part of the social fabric of Lucknow- Hindus, Muslims (Shias, Sunnis, Khoja, Bohra, Ahmedia), Sikhs, Christians, including Anglo-Indians, Parsis, Budhists, and Jains. Among the Muslims, Isnaashari Shias (twelver Shias, the mainstream section) alongwith smaller groups such as Ismaili Khoja and Dawoodi Bohra, Sunnis alongwith the smaller group of Ahmedia/Qadiyani, have been the largest minorities followed by the Sikhs, Christians, Budhists, Jains and Parsis, in descending order, have been co-exiting in harmony. Except for Sunni-Shia violence, Lucknow has never experienced any religious/ sectarian violence and remained peaceful even during the frenzied days of partition in 1947 when almost the entire northern India was burning. This speaks volumes of the cultural environment of tolerance, accommodation and harmony nurtured with great care by the Shia Nawab rulers of Awadh. This is part of strong composite and 'shared culture' which has been the hallmark of Lucknow and the entire Awadh.

Anglo Indians, who were once in substantial numbers in Lucknow, evoke fond memories despite the fact that now only a handful of them remain in the city. It is true that few communities have been as consistently maligned as they are-victims of stereotype and myths. They are the people originating in India who have mixed Indian and British ancestry. Many have adapted to local communities, especially Indian Christians, and emigrated to UK, Australia, US and Canada. They formed a significant portion of the minority communities in India during the British rule. Their population in India was roughly 8 lakhs in 1947 and now it has declined to approximately 2 lakhs. Since Lucknow always had a tiny share of their population, this decline has also reflected on Lucknow.

Most of the **Anglo-Indians** lived in the localities adjoining Hazratganj such as Maqbara and Lawrence Terrace behind the Lucknow Club. Several of the men worked in Railways while the remaining worked as teachers in the Christian run schools, nurses and secretarial assistants in the government and private office. Most of them had little interaction with the other local people inviting disdain from the local population. The Railway Club near Charbagh Railway station, the Lucknow Cathedral in Hazratganj and Lucknow Club on Ashok Marg were their principal meeting places – gradually and gradually most of them emigrated to England, Canada or Australia and a handful of then remain in Lucknow. Thus their public visibility has declined sharply.

Indian Christians have a much better presence and visibility in Lucknow and integrated with the local population. The highly educated and better off are either professionals or work in the government offices and private jobs while others work as nurses and ward boys or waiters and cooks. Christian missions have always had a remarkable presence in the city since Nawabi times. It was largely because of highly tolerant attitude of the Nawabs who allowed and encouraged them to build churches and create a large number of educational, medical and cultural institutions. Educational institutions and hospitals run by the Christians have created strong goodwill among the people of the city and generations have come out from such schools and colleges and played important roles in the society and in nation building process. Hundreds of good quality schools have come up in Lucknow but the popularity of La Martinere, St. Francis, Loreto Convent, Mount Carmel and St. Agnes School has not declined.

Among the institutions of higher education IT College and Lucknow Christian College and hospitals such as Fatima Hospital evoke respect of not only Lucknowites but also of the people from outside Lucknow. Beautiful churches of different orders of Christianity could be matched only by the Imambadas and other monuments built by the Nawabs.

Like the Anglo-Indians, the population of **Parsi** community in Lucknow has also diminished substantially. In their case it is a worldwide phenomenon and if the trend continues they could become extinct. Among the hundred odd Parsis of Uttar Pradesh, the majority-forty-five odd live in Lucknow. There was a time till 1950s and 60s when at least one Parsi family could be found in many districts of Uttar Pradesh. I still remember from my childhood a Parsi gentleman having a grocery store in a small city of Ghazipur near Varanasi. By his physical appearance and language we the children looked at him with awe taking him for a *firangi* or *angrez* (Britisher). Among the 25 odd parsi families in Lucknow, fourteen live within the campus of Parsi Anjuman situated on Mirabai Marg in Hazratganj. Though tiny population, Parsi are known for their warmth and hospitality. Unfortunately, among the present generation of people in Lucknow the majority has no idea about the presence of the Parsis in Lucknow and knows the community only through some movies such as Pestonji or other characters portrayed in some other Hindi movies or their unique funerary practice of putting the dead body on a tower to be consumed by vultures. Let us hope that this community is saved from total extinction and continues to be an important component of Indian society.

Though one could find some **Sikh's** all the time in Lucknow but their sizeable presence was registered only after the partition of the country in 1947. In the aftermath of violence during those times large scale migration took place from the areas now in Pakistan and from North India to Pakistan. That is how thousands of Punjabis and Sindhis came to Lucknow as refugees and settled down. Though all of them were hardworking, the Sikhs were the most industrious and enterprising. Most of them had to begin from the scratch. The Sikhs are more visible among all the refugee groups mainly because of their appearance. The Sikhs may be seen in all spheres of life and now a very important part of the social fabric of Lucknow. Most of them are self employed-running small grocery shops to bicycle and cloth shops, restaurants, and virtually all categories and scales of business and trade. They have established a number of Gurudwaras whose doors are open to all and their generosity may be seen in big and small *langars* offering food to all on special occasions and various other forms of charity and humanitarian activities.

Budhists, Jains, Ismaili Khoja, Bohra and **Ahmadi** or **Qadiyani** are relatively much smaller groups in Lucknow especially Khoja, Bohra and Ahmedia. Though the presence of Budhists in Lucknow may be traced back to 1940s it became visible only from 1970s. The latest size of their population in Lucknow is around 8,000. There is a Bodhisattva Vibhar at La Touche Road (now Gautam Budha Marg) and another Budha Vihar at Resaldar Park, Lal Kuan. A grand Gautam Budha Park on the bank of River Gomti testifies to the growing popularity of the ideology and its followers. With the coming of Bahujan Samaj Party (BSP) rule a number of large statues of Budha were installed mainly the ones on VIP Road and Ambedkar Park. Significantly, the majority of Budhists comes from the scheduled castes who have been converting to Budhism in protest against the oppressive and discriminatory caste system. Budhism has given them confidence and self respect.

Among the minority Muslim groups mentioned may be made of **Ismaili Khoja, Dawoodi Bohras** and **Ahmedia/Qadiyani**. While the Khojas and the Bohras are sub-sects of Shia Muslims, Ahmedia or Qadiyani is a small Sunni group who are largely disowned by the mainstream Sunni Muslim society because of theological differences. They are accused of not having faith that Muhammad was the last Prophet of Islam which is an integral part of Islamic faith. The Khojas and Bohras in Lucknow, as in other parts of the country, are traders and businessmen and run shops selling all types of hardware, paint, mattresses etc and most of their shops and business establishments are located in Aminabad-Latouche Road area. The Bohras are immediately recognized by their special type of cap usually embroidered with silver or gold wires. Their mother tongue is usually Gujarati but they fluently speak the local languages-Hindi and Urdu. They, together, are only in hundreds yet their presence is felt in the market and business circles. Unfortunately, there is hardly any Jewish family left in Lucknow. A young researcher from a tribal group of mango growers of Malihabad and now teaching in a University maintains that the ethnic populations of Malihabad are descendants of a lost Jewish tribe. This claim has generated lot of heat, controversy and debate and many of the people of Malihabad feel offended by this claim. But the researcher maintains that his findings are based on scientific research.

Thus, one may infer that contrary to the popular perception Lucknow is not a monolithic society. Not only people of so many castes and religious groups but also people from outside Uttar Pradesh are today part of the social fabric of this unique city.

The World of the Shias

Lucknow occupies centrality in the Shia Culture of the world. The city may boast of being one of the two most important cities of Shia Culture in South Asia, Hyderabad being the second. Shia Culture and world view is reflected in the traditional culture of Lucknow. Though the Shias are now marginalized, economically and politically, Lucknow continues to occupy an important place in the Shia world especially in the context of *Azadaari* (Moharrum mourning rituals and practices).

3

The World of Shias

The Shia sect is one of the two major groups in the ranks of Islamic society. The word 'Shia' like Islam is an Arabic word which literally means a 'friend' or 'follower'. *The Oxford Encyclopedia of the Modern Islamic World* (1995) says that technically the term refers to those Muslims who derive their religious code and spiritual inspiration, after Prophet Muhammad, from Muhammad's descendants-the *ahlal-bayt.* The majority Sunni sect accepts it from the *Sahabah* (companions) of the Prophet. This is the pivotal point which distinguishes, despite unanimity on the fundamentals of Islam, the Shia from Sunni Islam. The Shias believe that the Prophet had declared Ali, his protégé, cousin, son-in-law, as his successor, the Sunnis dispute it and believe that in the absence of any explicit desire or declaration by the Prophet his successors, after his death, were elected by the community democratically taking into consideration the factors of loyalty and closeness to the Prophet and piety. Thus, his succession began as Caliphate and all the subsequent successors were Caliphs. Those followers of the Prophet who did not accept this arrangement were the 'friends, followers and partisans' of Ali. They and the future generations of Shias considered the Caliphs as usurpers and withdrew from the affairs of the state and devoted themselves to acquisition of knowledge and practice of religion as enunciated by the Prophet. Thus, the other group (always in minority) regarded Ali as their first Imam and promoted the institution and office of *Imamate* instead of Caliphate. The Caliphate always had political power. Though even Ali was unanimously chosen to succeed the third Caliph, the Shias continued to regard him as their Imam. Thus, the *Imamate* continued along family lines till the 12th Imam who, as believed by the Shias, went into hiding, when he was a child and shall reappear on the Day of Judgment to lead them to heaven.

Shias of Lucknow: After the assassination of Ali, his family and followers were put under great hardship for their religio-ideological stand and thus began the persecution. They took shelter here and there. Though the Shias kept coming to India but in trickle and with the passage of time the influx increased because they found shelter under the Hindu rulers and enjoyed full religious freedom. Even *Azadari* (mourning for the martyred Imam Husain) was patronised and adopted by a number of Hindu Rajas and Hindu masses. Significantly, all the Muslim invaders of India were non-Shias and so were the emperors who ruled India. Shiaism and the Shias flourished under the Moghul rule, except during the reign of Aurangzeb.

Awadhs' Shia Dynasty (1722-1858AD) is considered as golden period of Shiaism and the Shias in India as well as the composite Hindu-Muslim culture and syncretic traditions.

Shias of Lucknow have traditionally drawn their wealth from lands. After the Britishers crushed the uprising of 1857 and exiled the last Nawab as a punishment, they unleashed blood curdling vendetta against the people of Awadh especially the Shias. Most of them were dispossessed of their valuable assets and in the post-independence period the Zamindari Abolition Act of 1952 broke the backbone of Shia zamindars and all those who depended on them. As rightly pointed out by Gilles Verniers (2012), for Lucknows' rich Shias and the elite income generating activities were considered degrading and thus discouraged by the community. Having practically no experience in any sort of trade, turning to money making ventures proved difficult. Thus, proverbially, Zamindari Abolition was the last straw on the camel's back. Whatever little property remained, it was entangled in law suits and legal hurdles. That was the period of great social churning and this also marked the beginning of marginalization of Shias in state affairs and the ascendancy of Sunni Muslims in economic and political affairs. Almost all the occupational caste/groups were in Sunni fold, they were naturally the beneficiary of economic prosperity. The *wasiqadars* among the Shias drawing political pension from the East India Company and later the commitment having been honoured by the Government of India, were ruined because of division of amount with every generation (their pathetic condition has been described under a separate heading *Wasiqadars).* It was, perhaps, from 1970's that the Shias of Lucknow started showing some resurgence and the new generation tried to make adaptation to the changed socio-cultural, economic, and political situation. They were now reconciled that they were no more the privileged or 'ruling community'. Now most sections of the Shias had no problem in entering into those jobs their parents and grandparents considered 'demeaning' and 'degrading'.

Even during the tumultuous years of freedom movement and demand for Pakistan, Shias, Lucknow being the hub of Shia politics, made an important decision of going with India rejecting the demand for Pakistan. They had more faith in Mahatma Gandhi and Congress than the Muslim league and a Khoja Shia, Jinnah.

Population Distribution and Social Life in Lucknow: Muslims represent around 40% of Lucknows' population and out of this population of Muslims, Shias constitute approximately 30%-perhaps the highest percentage of Shias in any city of India. Though no census figures are available this should not be taken as a wild guess because a number of studies done on Lucknow-political, economic and socio- cultural, by and large agree with these estimates.

There are a number of mohallas in 'Old Lucknow' that are almost totally populated by the Shias. These mohallas are Kazmain, Dargah Hazrat Abbas, Kashmiri

Mohalla, Noorbaadi, Hasan Puria, Angoori Bagh, Buniyad Bagh, Muftiganj, Sheesh Mahal, Maqbara Alia Golaganj, Sarfarazganj, Raees Manzil, Mahtab Bagh Colony, Bazaza in Nakhas area that includes Gali Shah Chara, Ghazimandi, Aelia Colony, Peer Bukhara, Hata Mirza Ali Khan, Friends Colony, Jafariya Colony,Jhakkad Bagh, Zehra Colony,Muftiganj and may be some more. Besides the above mentioned mohallas there are several others where the Shias constitute 40-50% of the population. Such localities are Ali colony, Radhagram, Katra Abu Turab Khan, Haiderganj, Wazeerganj, Sajjad Bagh, Musahibganj, Thakurganj etc.

Though, by and large, Shias are city dwellers in Lucknow district,there are some villages and suburbs where the Shia households vary from 8-10 to 150-175. Such villages and *Qasbahs* are Bijnour, Amrai, Chandia Mau, Nagram, Chinhat, Rahimabad, Kakori, Bakshi Ka Talab and some others.

In some of these , the Shias used to be zamindars or later immigrants. Thus, we find that there is quite uneven distribution of the Shias in Lucknow.

Raphael Susewind, a German anthropologist, who has done a study of Lucknow in recent years, maintains that the Shia population in Lucknow has increased sharply as compared to other Muslims largely because of more migrants coming from small towns in Awadh who reach Lucknow than migrants who leave the city to go to Delhi and elsewhere. The reason for more migrants coming to Lucknow and settling down here is because of "Lucknow's strong public Shia Culture". Another reason behind the increase of Shia population is that they always choose to remain in their city while the Sunnis go outside to other cities for better employment and earnings.

Even a casual visitor may notice that the old Shia mohallas where majority of them live have been decaying and these may be described as 'Shia ghettoes' where the civic amenities are very poor, almost non-existent, bad sanitary condition, neglected garbage collection and poor electricity and water supplies. The more educated, upward climbing, enterprising Shias of the present generation move to other areas, organize themselves in cooperative housing societies, build good houses, have cars, develop their own roads, sanitary and draining system and keep generators to face the erratic power supply. Some such new housing colonies are Ali Colony, Friends Colony, Sarfarazganj etc. This is the new generation of Shias not burdened by the hangover of the feudal past. Other Shias of this socio-economic class move to either the state housing societies or private housing schemes and multi storied apartment complexes in areas such as Gomti Nagar, Indira Nagar, Aliganj and adjoining areas to live in mixed population localities. In such areas, they being a very small minority group, go for networking. Some enthusiastic ones among them maintain a register entering the names, addresses and contact numbers and invite each other for exclusive Shia gatherings such as *majlis*, *mehfil* etc. Since it is problematic to build new mosques, even small ones, outside the heavily populated Muslim areas, they go for small *imambadas* for their religious congregations and prefer to go to Asifi Masjid located within the Bada Imambara campus for Friday prayers. One such example is the construction of a small but elegant *Imambada* under the auspices of Husaini Educational and Cultural Society, opposite the army's housing complex Usman Enclave in Aliganj. Sometime back they began organizing even the collective Friday prayers in this hall. With the fast expanding Lucknow, Asifi Masjid seems to be quite far off from these newly established localities. Thus, most of them go to the old Lucknow only during the Moharrum's mourning programmes as almost all the important Imambadas and Karbalas are located there.

A heartening feature of their social life is the rapid educational and occupational mobility being achieved by them. The new generation of boys and girls are going to all new fields of education and economy specially their girls. At the same time religiosity among them has been increasing sharply after the rise of Ayotallah Khomeini of Iran. Yet, thankfully even the *hejab* (head scarf) wearing girls are marching forward on the path of technological and educational modernization. Business and trade have always been looked down upon among the Shias (except the minority Khoja and Bohra Shias who are traditional business men) including the Shias of Lucknow but the Shia youths in increasing numbers are entering into this field too especially tour and travel industry, computer software and even in construction business while their preference for government services and educational institutions still remain strong.

Wasiqadaar: *Wasiqa* is a unique practice or institution related with the descendants of the ruling Nawabs of Awadh. An Arabic word, *Wasiqa* literally means an arrangement based on a written agreement through which money is disbursed. Amir Hasan (1983) rightly opines that the story of Shia accendancy during the rule of the Nawabs would not be complete without a description of *Wasiqa* which helped to sustain Shia nobility and maintain Shia institutions even after the fall of Awadh. It is like a political pension paid to the descendants of Awadh rulers and some others under an arrangement entered into between the East India Company and some Nawab rulers. Those getting *wasiqa* are known as *Wasiqadaar*. Three categories of persons have been receiving the *wasiqa*. Among those enjoying entitlement to *wasiqa* are the descendants of the royal family, servants and other dependents. This endowment arrangement also covered maintenance of certain *imambadas*.

Some historians are of the view that the Nawabs were ever ready to give loans to the East India Company in order to buy peace with them. Bahu Begum was the first to execute a deed of deposit followed by Saadat Ali Khan and lastly by Mohammad Ali Shah in 1839. Taken together the loan amount exceeded Rs. 2 Crores. The *Wasiqa* is disbursed out of the interest accrued over the loan amount. Currently there are 909 *Wasiqadaars* drawing *Wasiqa* ranging from Rs. 1.01 per month to Rs. 569.99 per month. The meagerness of the *Wasiqa* amount may be explained through division after division of the amount with every generation.

Despite the ridiculously meagre amount the 'royal descendants' continue to collect *Wasiqa* from the state as it proves their royal ancestry. As per the records of *Wasiqa* office located in the picture Gallery, Husainabad there are also 11 Hindu *Wasiqadaars* -all Kashmiri Pundits who served the Nawabs in their administration.

Spending hundred rupees for claiming one rupee or even less sounds strange and ridiculous. But the fact of the matter is that it reinforces their identity and gives a sense of pride and nostalgia. The days of the month on which *wasiqa* is disbursed present poignant and pathetic scenes when one sees some *wasiqadaars* in old and tattered *sherwani* and a walking stick alighting from a *tonga* or rickshaw and takes to the stair leading to the *wasiqa* office.

The condition of many of the *wasiqadaars* is really miserable. Some of them even ply rickshaw or doing odd jobs to meet two ends meet. They are the ones who could not adapt themselves with the changing times and after selling all the valuables are left with nothing more to fall back upon and hence take to menial jobs and sulk with nostalgia of a glorious past.

Festivals

Though the Shias are known worldwide as the 'community of mourners' because of the all pervading *Azadaari* but it hardly means that their lives are devoid of festivities and merry making. Following are the exclusive festivals of the Shias of Lucknow, not shared by other Muslims. Several others are common to all the Muslims.

Nav Roz : It is primarily the festival of the Iranians and the Parsee or Zoroaster community in India also celebrates it by the same name, though in a little different way than the Shias. Parsees have migrated from Iran and the majority of the Shias trace their ancestry to Iran. Etymologically *Navroz* in Persian consists of two words *Nav* (meaning new) and *roz* (meaning day) and thus it is the first day of the year as per the Iranian calender. It is celebrated every year on 21st March. This is the day of great festivity among the Shias. They perform *Nazr* of Imam Ali and sprinkle Gulabjal/Kyora on each other. But in Awadh, Shias have adopted it like Holi and throw colour on each other. If somebody passes through any locality of the Shias one may get confused taking it as another Holi. As per the astrological predication in Shia *Jantari* (almaniac) the colour of the sweets and fruits as well as the exaltation are determined every year and the Shias perform *Nazr* accordingly.

According to the beliefs among the Shias, God created earth, brightened the sun, made the flowers bloom, and even the foundation of Kaaba was laid on this day as well as the creation of Adam by God. Because of all these reasons, it is a great occasion of festivities for them. Besides the *Nazr* on sweets and fruits, sumptuous food is also prepared, friends and relatives are invited and among some of them gift is exchanged too.

Eid-e-Ghadeer : This festival is celebrated on the 18th day of the month of zilhijja (Baqreed month), the last month as per the Islamic calendar. As per Shia faith this was the day when Prophet while returning from his last Hajj, declared Ali, his cousin and son-in law, as his successor before a large gathering of Muslims.

Since this event happened at a place called Ghadeer-e- Khum, they have named it as Eid-e-Ghadeer. The Shias of the entire world celebrate it by arranging *Mehfil* and *Milaad* (religious gatherings to celebrate the event), distribute sweets, illuminate their homes, Imambadas and mosques and exchange greetings. Many Shias also perform Nazr and throw feast on this occasion. The majority Sunni sect contests this claim and considers it as the fabrication of the event not backed by historical evidences.

Eid-e-Zehra: This marks the day as the end of the mourning period of two months and eight days related with the observance of the 'tragedy of Kerbala' in which their third Imam, Husain, was martyred along with his seventy two companions, including children, by the army of the then caliph Yazid at a place called Karbala in Iraq. Shias also believe that their 12th and the last Imam (believed to be in hiding for the past several centuries) was also crowned and declared successor to his father (the 11th Imam) who died on the previous day. Another reason assigned to this day is that their fourth Imam (the surviving son of martyred Husain) smiled for the first time after the 'tragedy of Kerbala' when he heard that devotees of Imam Husain had avenged his murder by killing the commander of the army, Umar Ibne Saad, who supervised the killings at Karbala.

For the Shias it is a day of great rejoicing. The black dress is discarded, their womenfolk purchase new bangles, wear red dress and prepare such dishes which are avoided during the days of mourning.

Madrasa and Seminaries

The ruling Nawabs of Awadh subscribed to the Shia faith and some of them were highly religious. They and a number of Shia taluqdars and zamindars contributed generously towards the establishment of a number of madarsas, Imambadas, mosques and seminaries. These places of religious importance had their glorious past but after the annexation of Awadh by the Britishers and decline of taluqdars and zamindars, especially after the zamindari abolition in the post independence period, the sources of funding dried up and most of these madrasas and seminaries are now fighting for their survival unlike the Sunni madrasas which are witnessing a boom.

Situated at the K.G. Medical College crossing there is an old desolate building with a huge lawn and this is **Sultan-ul-Madaaris**, a Shia Madrasa-theological school cum seminary of great historical importance. Literally meaning 'emperor of madrasas', it witnessed several ups and downs. Once a vibrant institution, after the loss of the royal and Shia elite's patronage and lack of interest among the Shia community in general, it is struggling to save its existence.

Equipped with a library containing rare books on Shia jurisprudence, theology, logic, history, etc. and a boarding house for outstation students, it has been continuing in one form or another since the days of Nawab Amjad Ali Shah, the ruler of Awadh, but it was formally founded in 1892 by the great Shia religious scholar Syed Abul Hasan Rizvi.

Madrasatul Waizeen, the 'madrasa of preachers' is yet another important religious institution of the Shias. Founded in 1919 by Raja of Mahmudabad, it is situated on Subhash Marg, the road just opposite KG Medical College leading to Rakabganj. The main objective of this institution was to train preachers of Shiaism and *zakirs* who could address *majlis* (mourning congregations) in an organized and impressive way. Immediately after its establishment, the Shia missionaries trained from this institution were sent to East Africa where a number of Shia sub-sects such as Agha Khani Khojas and Bohras, and the mainstream Shias i.e. *Isna ashari* Shias (the twelvers) had settled. Later, it became an institution for the training of *zakirs* only who addressed *Majlis* in various parts of India and abroad.

When virtually all the Shia religious institutions were dragging and struggling, a highly dynamic, imaginative and innovative religious scholar Late Maulana Ghulam Askari founded **Tanzeemul Makatib** in 1968. Located in Golaganj behind the Gulab Cinema Hall, its main objective was to create and maintain religious consciousness among the Shias and provide guidance in religious education along with modern-secular education to the younger generation of the community. Originally, the target set down by the founder was to open 1000 *maktab/madarsa* in different parts of India; it has already crossed this mark and running its branches in 17 states with some Shia population. Besides spreading literacy, it has also been spreading middle level education. Schools exclusively meant for young girls have also been opened under Khadijatul Kubra Schools.

It has its own publication house that publishes thousands of books, magazines and booklets in Urdu, Hindi and English. Besides imparting religious education and training Shia missionaries, *zakir* and *Pesh Imam* (one who leads *namaaz*/prayers), the **Tanzeemul Makatib** also supports the poor and the needy in a variety of ways such as financial support, health care and help for the poor and destitutes. Its founder's dreams are coming true because of untiring efforts of the present administration.

Jamia Nazimia, popularly called **Nazimia Madarsa** is one of the most prestigious and oldest centers of Shia Islamic education. Founded in 1890, it is located in a lane behind the Shia PG College (Arts Campus) on Victoria Street, Nakhas. It also imparts Hindi and English education and its syllabi for various stages include, beside Shia theology, geography, philosophy, science and now computer education. It maintains a hostel for outstation students and provides everything free of cost.

Shia Orphanage: Strongly believing in charity, especially care of the orphans without any financial resources for survival, the **All India Shia Yateem Khaana** was founded in 1912. The moving spirit behind this humanitarian venture was Moulana Aaqa Hasan Mujtahid. With a humble beginning with just two children, it was initially run in a dilapidated house in Gali Shah Chara, a lane on Victoria Street, Nakhas. By 1914 it had a huge, impressive building on Kazmain Road near Giridhari Singh Inter College, accommodating more than 200 children up to the age of eighteen years. Besides boarding and lodging, schooling was also arranged within the premises. With the dwindling number, it recently allowed even grown up boys and youths with little resource to live in the hostel and obtain higher education from elsewhere. Unfortunately, because of mismanagement and dwindling resources, it is decaying and it will be a great loss to the community.

Shia Post-Graduate College: The Shia community is one of the most educated communities in India. They have a very high rate of literacy, much higher than the national average or percentage. Being a 'religious minority within a minority' they always valued education because this was the only way to find a respectable place in the life of the nation. Since they were always persecuted in the world and this continues to this day because of their religious faith, they maintained their religious identity by creating a number of institutions of religious knowledge, but they also knew that it would not take them too far and hence always laid emphasis on secular, modern education too.

Shia College is now almost a century old and has become the largest college among all the colleges affiliated with the University of Lucknow. Its oval shaped emblem carries as its motto a statement of Prophet Muhammad- "I am the city of knowledge and Ali is its gate" (when translated from the Arabic to English). So, they owe their zest for knowledge, education and learning to Muhammad and Ali, their first Imam. With this in mind, the leaders of the community decided to have a college of modern education in 1915. However, the plan could not materialize at that time due to the restriction imposed by the State Government in view of the proposed unitary teaching cum residential University at Lucknow with Canning College as the nucleus. Thus, it had to make a humble beginning as a school in 1919, rising to the status of an Intermediate college in 1922 thanks to the generous donations from the former Nawabs, Taluqdars, and Shia masses. In the meanwhile the college was able to get a huge plot of land provided by the King Nasiruddin Haider's Karbala on Sitapur Road. When, in 1947, the University of Lucknow decided to permit the teaching of science outside the premises of Canning College, Shia College was one of the first three colleges of Lucknow which were found suitable for the purpose. Thus, the journey began with the teaching of science at the university level, made long and quick strides and now it can boast of all the major faculties- Science, Arts, Commerce, Law and the Computer Science and Management. Meanwhile ,another campus came up in old Lucknow at Nakhas, with facilities for girls going for higher education in science, arts, commerce and law. When the Lucknow University allowed the affiliated colleges to have post-graduate classes in select subjects, Shia College was one of the earliest to avail of this.

True to its commitment, this college has maintained its secular and non-partisan tradition and students and faculty of all castes and faiths have been part of this educational institution. The Shias take pride in the composite nature or their college.

Publishers and Book Sellers

Because of a very high rate of literacy and being a minority within a minority the Shias always had a zest for studying their religious literature along with the modern-secular literature. Some enterprising Shias entered into this field long back. Initially all this religious literature was being published in Urdu but during the last three decades or so, they have also adopted Hindi and English, mainly Hindi, to make it available to the present generation. **Nizami Press** may be considered as the 'flagship' agency in the publication of this religious literature.It was founded in 1830 with a humble beginning by the late Muhammad Jawwad. After his death his daughter and son in law took up this job and made it a premier agency for the publication of Shia religious literature. After Quran, *Tohfatul Awaam* is the largest selling and most important religious book for the Shias. It contains all the important *duaen* (prayers), methods for performing various rituals and a vast range of information. It comes very handy, especially for those Shias living in the areas where no religious authority may be there to guide them. Among the traditional Shia families, Quran and Tohfatul Awaam are the integral parts of the dowry or wedding gifts given to a girl. For the Past two decades the press has switched over to the offset printing and other latest technology. The Nizami Press has published thousands of books and booklets and their publications are always in demand wherever the Shias live in the world – USA, Europe, Africa and elsewhere. It is said that After Naval Kishore Press, Nizami Press has published the largest number of books in Urdu language. Their Shia Alminac (*Jantari*) is so popular that it may be found in virtually all Shia households.

Ahbab Publishers is the second biggest publisher of Shia religious literature. Established in 1957 in Golaganj area by the late Ansaar Husain, it began with the publication of books of Urdu literature but it switched over to mainly religious literature. In 1971 they started the publication of a Shia Islamic alminac and *Nahjul balagha* , in Urdu, the collection of the letters and sayings of Imam Ali. Thus, Quran, Tohfatual Awaam, and Nahjul Balagha, constitutes set of books most popular among the Shias. Its publications also reach all corners of the world wherever Urdu or Hindi speaking Shias reside.

Abbas Book Agency is the most popular book seller for Shia Islamic literature. Established in 1991 within the premises of Dargah Hazrat Abbas it began as a book selling shop, keeping books of other publishers. Since 1995 they also started publishing books and at the same time selling the books of others.

Moharrum and Azadaari

Husain tum nahi rahe,tumhara ghar nahi raha,
Magar tumhare baad zaalimo se dar nahi raha

(Husain! you did not survive nor your household , but after you, (we) are not scared of the tyrants)

No event in the history of Islam has so deeply stirred the emotions of Muslims as the massacre at Kerbala. Like the crucification of Christ, the *Shahadat* (martyrdom) of Imam Husain has lent a halo to Shiaism. The social, moral and political implications of the 'Tragedy of Karbala' immensely reflect themselves through glowing tributes paid to Husain by the scholars, rulers, and commoners of different communities, regions, faiths and schools of thought. Thus, this historical event has transcended the boundaries of religious communities and that is why the commemoration of this tragedy is not confined to the Shia Muslims but is shared by various sections and classes of Sunni Muslims, Hindus, Sikhs, Christians and even some tribal communities.

Aza (in Arabic) literally means 'mourning' or 'to mourn' and the practice is called *Azadaari*. For the Shia Muslims, it occupies a unique place in their religious-cultural life worldwide. As per the history, after the death of Prophet Mohammad his family members and descendants, the *ahle bait,* were put under great hardship. Not only them but all those who supported Ali as the legitimate successor of Muhammad were also oppressed by the Caliphs. Imam Husain, the third Imam of the Shias and a grand son of Muhammad, was under tremendous pressure by the then Caliph Yezid to declare his allegiance to the Caliph. Husain, his supporters and a large number of Muslims had no respect for him because of his way of life. They offered to leave the land under his rule and settle down elsewhere but it was not acceptable to the 'tyrant, oppressor, and debauch' Yezid. He sent his army to obtain oath of allegiance from him or bring his head. Thus, in the first week of Moharram (the first month of the Lunar Islamic Calendar) 680 AD, Husain, his family members, friends and supporters were confronted by the army and on the tenth day known as *Ashura* they were slaughtered including the six month old son of Husain. Since Husain stood for the principles of truth, honesty and justice, this event stirred the conscience of millions of people across nations and religions. Husain was regarded by many as dauntless standard bearer of freedom and justice, a non-violent-*satyagrahi* who also inspired Mahatma Gandhi. In India, besides the Shia Muslims in whose lives this event occupies a very important place, a large number of Sunni Muslims, Hindus and others also observe *Azadari* in one form or the other.

For many, this was an epic struggle between good and evil in which the good won despite losing the war. Today, one finds crores of people carrying the surname 'Husain' but nobody comes across a person with the name of Yezid. In the Indian context, it is like the epic struggle between Ram and Ravan.

Though the 'Tragedy of Kerbala' is commemorated throughout the world, *Azadaari* in Lucknow holds a special and unique place and known throughout the world. The Nawabs, rulers of Awadh, were Shias of Iranian origin and they were instrumental in elevating the observance of Moharrum Azadaari to heights unparalleled in the world.

With the sighting of moon for the month of Moharrum the entire Shia inhabited localities are drowned in mourning. As per tradition the Azadaari in Lucknow begins with the *Zarih* (the ornate wooden replica of Imam Husain's tomb at Karbala, Iraq) procession,a practice started by the Nawab rulers. The *imambadas* (public as well as private) are already decked for the mourning period. New *Tazias* (the replica of the tomb of Imam Husain made of bamboo and multi coloured paper), *Alams* (the replica of the flags of Husain) and other objects such as the small wooden cradle symbolizing the cradle of the six month old son of Husain, a small *mashk* (the leather casket used for carrying water) are kept ceremoniously in the *Azaakhana*/ Imambada. Shia women break their colourful bangles or put away the metal ones in their wardrobes to be taken out after the mourning period is over. The devout ones shun lip sticks, other cosmetics and jewellery during this period and wear either black clothes or white or green ones. Many males too take to black shirt or *kurta*. During the mourning period, most of the Shias don't watch movies, arrange feasts or celebrate birth days, marriage or any other festivity and merry making.

The mourning in Lucknow may be broadly divided into two categories-*Majlis* and *Alam* processions. While a *Majlis* is a congregation, big or small, in which the *Zaakir* (narrator), usually a Shia moulvi or preacher, addresses the gathering of mourners. In private Imambadas or within the homes he sits on a chair while the mourners squat on the white sheet of cloth or carpet. In larger gatherings in the public Imambadaas a wooden pulpit is always there covered with a black sheet of cloth. The zakir in the first part of the narration dwells on the nuances of the Quran, life of Prophet Muhammad and Islamic history, of course from the Shia point of view, while in the second part some aspect of the 'Tragedy of Karbala' or the personality of Husain and his relatives and companions is narrated in a highly emotional and melodramatic way and the mourners present there erupts into crying and inconsolable tears. Some start beating their heads in grief. After the *majlis* is over, a *Tabarruk* like *Prasad* is distributed which may be oven baked bread or *sheermal* (a special type of baked bread) or any other eatable but not sweets. The *zenani majlis* (majlis for women) are held separately usually within homes and addressed by a female *zakir* although the women also attend *mardaana majlis* (majlis for men) and sit at one corner or in the back rows,sometimes behind a curtain. With the days advancing towards *Ashura* (the tenth day, the day of martyrdom) the first part of the *majlis* gets shorter and shorter and from the seventh day (when food and water were denied to the camp of Husain) onwards the intensity of mourning touches the fringes of frenzied gestures of grief.

The second category of mourning rituals consists of mourning processions usually after sunset except the Shaahi Zari(royal zari procession began by the Nawabs) procession taken out before sunset. These Alam processions are carried out after the Majlis and terminates in one of the imambadas. Within the first nine days of Moharrum, the most important and popular processions are *Alam Fathe-e-Furat* (Alam of the conqueror of the river Euphrates taken out from the mosque located on the banks of River Gomti in memory of Abbas, a younger brother of Husain and leader/commander of the motley group of children, young boys and very old companions of Husain under siege of the ruler's army. Mourners carrying burning torches and beating their chests cover a distance of 2 kilometers in several hours for reaching the Imambada Ghufran Maab near Medical College where it terminates. The second big procession is taken out on the eve of *Ashura*. This is really a massive procession. It begins from the Imambada Nazim Sahab in Nakkhas and terminates at Kazmain near Mansoor Nagar covering a distance of 2-3 kms. The police and district-civil administration have to be on their toes for any eventuality.

During Ist to 9th Moharrum, besides *Majlises* and *Juloos* (processions) *Aag Ka Matam* (walking on fire) is also held in the compounds of Bada Imambara and Shah Najaf Imambara watched by thousands of mourners and non Muslim spectators. The climax of mourning is reached on the tenth day (*Ashura*) when thousands of Shia, Sunni and Hindu mourners take out their *Tazias* for burial. While most of the Shias go to Talkatora ki Karbala, barefooted, clad in black cloth, the Sunni devotees go to Phoolwali Karbala in Mahanagar, on Faizabad Road in procession beating drums and exhibting gimmicks. The point to be noted here is that the element of mourning and grief is missing here in most of the places and the occasion looks like a *mela* or fair. Hindu mourners and Taziadars prefer to go to where the Shias congregate. In the sea of Shia mournes in black, the Hindu mourners- men, women and children may be distinguished by their dress. No restriction is there on their cloth. Most of the women may be seen in Sari of different colours, wearing jewellery, and so are their menfolk and children in whatever way they wish to dress. Some of them also bring their small *tazias* for burial as well as perform rituals different from the Shia mourners. Some may be seen putting their children in the dug up pits (graves) for a while, sprinkle some clay over them and take them out. This is explained in terms of showing sense of gratitude and thanks giving to Imam Husain as his blessings gave kids to these parents who were not getting a kid despite of medical treatment. All along the route to Talkatora, the Shia mourners in groups carrying their *Tazia* and *Alam* pass noiselessly and the silence of grief gets broken only when an *Anjuman* (organized group of mourners) passes doing *Matam* with knives and small swords. The blood drenched mourners is such a gory sight that the weak hearted persons cannot watch it for long. The frenzied grief peaks when they reach the gate of the Talkatora Karbala where according to conservative estimate a crowd between 50-75 thousand is always there between 9 am to 2 pm after which everybody goes back to their homes silently and break the fast around 3 pm i.e. post-massacre, as it is recorded history that the last sacrifice that is of Imam Husain itself was over by that time. Thus, the slaughter of 72 persons had been committed. At around 8pm, a big congregation is held again- the last event of *Ashura,* named as *Majlis-e-Shaam-e-Ghareebaan* (the mourning congregation of the night) after the tragic event.

The Hindu mourners and devotees have formed an organization named 'Hindu Taziadaar Sevak Sangh' led by one Harish Dhanuk whose grandfather used to conduct Majlis in a small quarter known as Kishnu Khalifa Ka Imambada.

Another group popularly called as 'Husaini Brahmins' consists of Punjabi Mohiyal Brahmins, some of whom also participate in Moharrum mourning.

Marsiya, Nouha and Soz: In a typical Shia *majlis* ,beside the address of a *Zaakir, Marsiya, Nouha* and *Soz* or any of these is an added event preceding the address of the zaakir. *Marsiya* is an Arabic word meaning lamentation for a departed soul. It is in poetry form with all the nuances of Urdu poetry. The lyrical beauty becomes doubly impressive when recited with appropriate gestures. Lucknow's great master of *Marsiya*, Meer Anees made it an invaluable part of Urdu literature. Most of the amateur *Marsiyago (*reciters*)* recite his Marsiyas and some others who are themselves accomplished poets, present their own. *Soaz* or *Soz* in Persian means an elegiac poem composed to commemorate martyrdom. The expert reciters of *soz* used to compose this poetry on some *raag* of shastriya sangeet but this is a dying art. Some of the scholars and historians believe that the singers especially bards (*mirasi*) were encouraged to base the *soz* on a *raag* as the Nawabs, so fond of *Sangeet,* avoided music during the Moharrum mourning period but also did not want to miss it for a long time and thus even the narration of the tragedy/martyrdom was sought to be presented in a poignant style, but based on a *raag*. This is usually presented before the speech of the *zaakir*. While the *marsiya* and *soz* are dying arts, *Nouha* continues to be very popular. It is also lyrical elegy sung by a group of people with the beating and pounding of chest. Currently there are more than 100 *matami anjumans,* (groups doing *matam* with *nouha*) out which around 70 are active. These *anjumans* are invited by the organizer of a *majlis* to present some *nouhas*. During the mourning period night long *nouha* recitation by different *anjumans* is also organized by mourners called as *Shab Bedaari* (night long awakening or vigil).

Mourning beyond Ten Days : The intensity of mourning comes down after *ashura*. In the meantime *majlises* continue to be held privately at home or in public imambadas. The next big event is *Chehlum*, the 40th day after *ashura*, the day of martyrdom. A number of Shias do not take out their *tazias* for burial on the day of *ashura* though majority of them follow this tradition. Such devotees takeout their *tazias* for burial, *anjumans* take out their small processions reciting *nouha*, and some of them performing *Zanjeer Ka Maatam* (beating of their backs with a bunch of knives) or *Qama Ka Matam* (hitting their head with small swords) and move to the *Talkatora ki Karbala* where all their processions and *Maatam* terminates with a ritual performance.

As per practice the timing for the *ashura* and *chehlum* performances for the Shias and Sunnis are different for the convenience of police deployment although their Karbalas are located several kilometers from each other. It has been observed that in recent times these mourning rituals among the Sunnis have declined considerably because of high voltage campaign against it by the Sunni moulvis subscribing to the conservative and radical version of Islam known as *Wahaabi Islam* being promoted by Saudi Arabia. Those subscribing to the Wahaabi ideology consider *azadaari* and *taziadaari* as *biddat* i.e. innovation and idol worship and hence *haraam* (illegitimate,sin or prohibited).

After Chehlum the intensity of mourning further declines and *majlises*, *mersiakhwani*, *shab bedaari* continues to be held, but on smaller scale. However, a very significant change comes into the lives of the Shias. In between the first day of mourning (1st Moharrum) to the 40th day and even sometime earlier than the 1st Moharrum, hundreds of Shias pass away but their *Chaliswan*, the 40th day ritual for the deceased, is not held before the *Chaliswaan* i.e. *Chehlum* of the Imam (Husain). This is just to show that their personal grief is not important when compared to the Tragedy of Karbala. Thus, the *soyum* (third day ritual) of a deceased Shia is not performed before the *soyum* of the Imam i.e. 12th of Moharrum, the third after the martyrdom, and neither the *chaliswaan* of the deceased before the Chehlum of the Imam.

The period of mourning comes to an end after two months and eight days i.e. on 8th of the month of Rabiul Awwal (as per Islamic calendar). This day is marked by a massive procession of *Chup tazia*.(silent taazia, where the processionists move absolutely silently). The next day is the day of joy, celebrations and merry making. The Shia women take out their jewellery, cosmetics, and colorful dress (especially of red colour), cook a sumptuous meal, buy sweets and life comes back to normalcy. All the negotiated engagements, marriages etc may be performed from this day onwards with the only restriction of some particular dates when one of their eleven Imams died (the 12th is believed to be still alive and in hiding) or the death of Muhammad and his daughter Fatima. While fixing dates of marriage, engagement, house warming etc. the Shia *jantari* (almanac) is consulted to see that such dates do not coincide with any dates of mourning.

After the two month and eight days of mourning period the next event of high voltage mourning are the three days of the month of Ramzan- from 19th to the 21st, the days the murderous attack on Hazrat Ali, their first Imam and father of Husain, occurred and his death on the third day. This three day mourning is popularly called as *Shabein* or *Bistaikum*. After *ashura,* this is the most intense period of grief when no celebrations may be held.

This does not mean that the Shias alway remain in 'mourning mode'. During rest of the year they also celebrate the birthdays of Prophet Muhammad, his daughter Fatima and all the Imams. The Shias of Lucknow and other parts of world have kept the *Azadaari* alive against the threats to their life when living under some hostile Muslim ruler. That is why, as they assert, they do not make any compromises on this issue. When you talk to the Shias on this issue, they express a deep sense of indebtedness and gratitude to India and the Indians especially the majority Hindu community for never trying to curb *Azaadaari* unlike in many Sunni Muslim majority countries especially Saudi Arabia which has been continuing the severe curbs on the public performance of mourning.

A mourning kid peeping from behind

A Moharrum procession signifying the journey of Imam Husain to Karbala

Maatam on Fire by a young devotee

A Moharrum procession

The ceremonial horse of Husain

A mourning procession carrying the ceremonial coffin of Hazrat Ali

Female mourners in a Majlis

A mourner getting medical attention after the Maatam by Sword

Hindu female mourners of Imam Husain

Hindu mourners offering candles

A scene of Mersia recitation in a Majlis

A cleric addressing a Majlis in an Imambada

A young mourner of Husain after the Matam with knives

A Waseeqadaar receiving his monthly waseeqa

Mourners drenched in blood on the day of Ashura (martyrdom day)

Meer Anees

"Umr guzri hai isee dasht ki sayyahi mein,
Paanchvi pusht hai Shabbir Ki Maddaahi mein"

(Roaming in this forest (for words) spent life I mine, Praising Shabbir (Husain) fifth in progeny line)

Meer Babar Ali Anees (1802-1874 AD) popularly known as Meer Anees, through his *mersias* has played a crucially important role in the *azaadaari*, wherever it is performed, as the translations of his mersias are available in various languages. Yet, among the Urdu/Hindi knowing devotees of Imam Husain he occupies a unique place because of his depiction of the 'Tragedy of Karbala'. People of several generations grew up listening to and reciting his *mersias* in different styles and on different occasions shedding tears. Many Shias are firmly of the opinion that they cannot imagine the performance of *azadaari* without the *mersias* of Meer Anees.

Meer Anees had an amazing command over language and the style of poetry he is famous for. Born in Faizabad but lived and died in Lucknow, he spent a substantial part of his life during the most turbulent period of Awadh's history. When Awadh was annexed by the British colonialists he was persuaded to visit Azeemabad (now Patna), Hyderabad and Allahabad for patronage. It is said that in 1870 when he visited Hyderabad, he refused to be presented at the court of the then Nizam of Hyderabad who was a Sunni Muslim but a devotee of Imam Husain, and the Nizam himself had to go to a *majlis* where he was scheduled to recite his *mersias*. He was so proud as a 'servant of Imam Husain' that he did not care for the kings and rulers.

Moharram and Meer Anees have become synonymous in this part of the world. Not only his poetry, he was also a great performer who could mesmerise the audience with his language as well as style of presentation. Even Ghalib showered praise on him again and again for his poetry. His amazing language drew vocabulary from Arabic, Persian, Urdu, Hindi and Awadhi. He is unparalleled in whatever he described- nature, animals, human relations, loyalty and even war and weaponry. It is said that no other Urdu poet or writer has used the vocabulary as large as in his poetry and his style of recitation made his audience and readers feel as if they were present on the scene of action.

"Namak-e-khwaan-e-takallum hai fasaahat meri"

(My eloquence is the salt to the food of thought)

Mohallas, Mandis, Lanes, Roads and Markets

The urban public space of Lucknow has been unique in several senses and the advent of modern housing complexes, markets, malls and multiplexes could not eliminate this uniqueness. People of different castes and communities have been living in such a way that they got ample opportunities to share a lot between them thanks to the efforts of the Nawab rulers. The specialized and weekly markets still attract lakhs of people. Passing through the lanes and bylanes of old Lucknow takes one to a different world,exotic to many people.

4

Mohalla, Mandi, Lanes, Roads and Markets

Yeh mere koocha-o-baazaar samajhte nahee ab meri zubaan
Apne ghar me kabhi mehmaa na hua thaa,so hua.

(These lanes and markets now do not understand me, I was never a stronger in my own home, but now I am)

When any area or region is inhabited, settlements or *Mohallas* also come into existence. Most of the historical documents indicate that the origin of the present Lucknow (during modern times) may be traced back to the reign of Emperor Akbar. When Akbar divided the country in 1590AD into twelve provinces, Lucknow was chosen as the seat of *Subedar*. Shaikh Abdul Rahman was allotted a *Jaagir*. Around this time, Shah Meena Shah, a Sufi Saint also settled in Lucknow. It is popularly believed that the presence of such personalities attracted migrants from outside and thus the local population started increasing on a faster pace. His tomb is located at Nadan Mahal Road near Nakhas in old Lucknow. Veena Talwar Oldenburg (2007) writes that "Akbar liked the city and built several *mohallas* or neighborhoods south of the Chowk, the main bazaar of the city". Lucknow continued to grow gaining in palaces, gardens, and markets. Akbar gave special treatment to the Brahmins of this region, facilitating the establishment of mohallas such as Vajpayee Tola, Katari Tola, Sondhi Tola, etc. All these *mohallas* were established near Chowk and continue to be popular by the same names. "During the reign of Akbar, a French trader of horses constructed a complex of four houses near Chowk with his permission. After his departure the government took control of it and during the reign of Aurangzeb was given to an Islamic scholar Mulla Nizamuddin" (Mirza Jafar Husain ,1998)). With the passage of time the adjacent buildings became a part of this complex and known as Firangi Mahal that emerged as important centre of Islamic learning.

Thus, right from the reign of Akbar new *mohallas, tolas* and *bazaars* came to be established prominent among these are Mirza Mandi, Mahmood Nagar, Mansoor Nagar, Shah Ganj etc. However, after the capital of Awadh was shifted from Faizabad to Lucknow in 1775 the city got more grandeur and increased in size and population at a faster pace and this continued till the rule of the last Nawab

,Wajid Ali Shah after which it slowed for a while and after independence Lucknow emerged as a big urban centre, virtually becoming a metropolitan city. Significantly, Nawab Asafuddaula even after leaving Faizabad and settling down in Lucknow as the new capital, had a nostalgia for Faizabad and perhaps that is why a number of new Mohallas in Lucknow were named after the mohallas of Faizabad such as Amaani Ganj, Fateh Ganj, Rakab Ganj, Nakhas, Yahiyaganj, Bhawani Ganj, etc. After Asafuddaula, Saadat Ali Khan established mohallas such as Maqbool Ganj, Rastogi Tola, Daliganj, Saadat Ganj (after his name) etc. Nawab Naseeruddin Haider established Ganesh Ganj, Chand Ganj and Hazrat Ganj. By the time of Wajid Ali Shah almost the entire Lucknow of that time had been inhabited and his reign reached its zenith which declined only when he was deposed and exiled by the Britishers in 1856. Within a duration of 80 years (1775-1856) perhaps no other city of the world during this period, achieved this much expansion and grandeur as Lucknow in terms of opulence, architecture, and promotion of literature and fine arts.Though the Nawabs were themselves very fond of gardens and established many, the East India Company also established at least one in several cities coming under their jurisdiction that were popularly called as 'Company Bagh' like the one near Gol Darwaza in Chowk Area now being used as cricket field.

Besides the *mohallas* mentioned above and similar others, several *mohallas* were named on the basis of profession followed by the inhabitants such as Batashey Wali Gali, Dorwali Gali, Phool Waali Gali, Baan Wali Gali. This continued till the first quarter of 20th century when either some of these professions declined or under the pressure of population other people also began settling down in those quarters. Gradually, these lanes/*mohallas* remained only in namesake. By the early 19th century, in the *mohallas* around or near Chowk (the nerve centre of Lucknow) Hindu population had settled with the blessings of the Nawabs. Brahmins and Kayastha had their mohallas around Chowk and Ashrafabad while Kashmiri Pundits had settled down in Kashmiri Mohalla. In most of the remaining mohallas Hindu and Muslims were living in complete harmony. Historical records and gazetteers reveal that bulk of the then population was living in those areas which had very dense population.The later additions are Nishatganj, Lalbagh etc. which are now bursting with people are now older than 70-80 years.

Another important feature of these *mohallas* is that during the Nawabi period several *mohallas* were established on the names of women and several of these are named after Hindu women such as Bagh Padain, Bagh Kishna Maharajin, Rani Katra etc.A chronicler of Lucknow Yogesh Praveen adding a new dimension to the settlements of these mohallas tells us that when the Nawabs established new mohallas they ensured that,in order to promote harmony,Hindus and Muslims should live together or live in close proximity to each other.Thus,Ram Nagar was established with Husainabad,Katra Abuturab Khan with Raja Bazaar,Qasaibaara with Ganesh Ganj,Husain Ganj with Phool Bagh,Mehdi Ganj with Tikait Ganj and so on and so forth.

Roads and Lanes

During the early years of 20th century, Lucknow city could boast having just two roads – one was known as Mall Road which is now known as Mahatma Gandhi Marg and Victoria Street near Chowk, now called Tulsi Das Marg. Hazratganj was located on the then Mall Road. It catered primarily to the requirements of the Britishers – wines, canned food, toiletries, cakes and pastries etc. Only Britishers and Indian elite were the customers.

The other road Victoria Street was located in the heart of the city during those times. Perhaps, it is still the longest road in Lucknow stretching from Medical College at one end to the Talkatora at the other. Till the beginning of the 20th century this was the road which fulfilled all the necessities of Lucknow. The main vegetable market was also situated on this road. It has been widened several times to accommodate the rising population and vehicles. The well-known weekly Nakhas Market still continues on Sundays on this road.

The city has witnessed rapid expansion during the last six decades, hundreds of new roads have been built, dozens of new markets have emerged, housing complexes, apartments, shopping centres, malls and multiplexes have emerged but the charm of old Lucknow still continues.

The lanes and by lanes of Lucknow called *Galee/Koocha* presents a fascinating picture and takes you to another world so different from the present Lucknow. The old routes and pathways were built during the Nawabi era. Most of these were constructed in such a way that one could travel from one mohalla to another and thus one could cover almost the entire city of those times from one end to the other without coming on the main road. Several of these were wide enough to allow a horse cart to pass while most others could allow only a palanquin or pedestrians. The lanes related with occupational group were named after the occupations whose practitioners lived there like *Kanghiwaali Gali* (abode of comb makers). Several other lanes were named by the people as per their proximity to a particular *mohalla* such as Shahganj ki Gali, Katrawali Gali etc. In consonance with their literary taste and refinement such lanes that housed highly respectable persons were never called *Gali* but *Koocha* which almost means the same thing but connotes respect and reverence. Some such lanes are Koocha Meer Anees (where the great Urdu poet Mir Anees lived), Koocha Shah Chara (where the Sufi saint Shah Chara lived) etc. Mirza Jafar Husain (1981) who was a witness to the last phase of this era, while describing the characteristic features of old Lucknow between 1910, tells us of the beauty and cleanliness of these lanes. These were well lit though electricity was not there and kerosene lamps were installed on the poles maintained by the municipality of those times. There was no littering in the lanes. This author witnessed the remnants of this description in his childhood days in 1950s.

When the task of widening the roads and constructing new ones was taken up, hundreds of houses were demolished ruining thousands of people, mostly the poor.

Mandi

Mandi is a trading place of any commodity. When qualified it gives different meanings such as *subzi mandi* (trading in vegetables) or *ghalla mandi* (trading in food grains). These are wholesale markets meant for shop keepers who used to purchase various commodities from these mandis and sold these in retail to the local customers but now a number of people, in order to save some money, make their purchases from these for their own consumption. Initially two mandis were created – one in Daliganj (trans-gomti area) and the second in Saadatganj. A third mandi also emerged in Rakabganj during the same Nawabi period which had to be shifted to a nearby mohalla called Pandey Ganj, in the wake of constructing new roads and widening the older ones. *Mohalla* based shopkeepers attracted the local customers and street venders were in plenty to cater to the requirements of the locals.

Now the city boasts of having large *mandis* equipped with modern technology with lots of parking space for hundreds of trucks and the State Government manages these under a newly created department *Mandi Parishad.*

Markets

Baazaar is a general term used for markets not only in Lucknow but in many parts of India. It is a Persian word introduced and popularised by the Muslims and its origin in India may be traced to the advent of Muslims of Persian origin.

Before the advent of regular, modern markets these bazaars could be categorized into :

(i) A cluster of shops which were there in almost all the large *mohallas.* These were permanent shops and utilities could be procured from these in small quantities. Such clusters of shops are still there in several *mohallas.*

(ii) The second category comprises of those bazaars in which shops used to be established once in a week or a month. Here shopkeepers from other *mohallas* used to bring their merchandise. Such temporary markets were quite popular as a person of one *mohalla* used to get specialized items of different other *mohallas* at their door steps. Perhaps the weekly markets of the present time are an extension of such markets (weekly markets have been described later in this chapter).

(iii) In the third category comes those markets which used to be held on some special occasion mostly annually at a fixed place. These bazaars were very popular and attracted large crowds. Eid, Holi, Diwali, bathing festivals *(snans)* have been such occasions. A month long fair on the occasion of Kartik Purnima is still popular and held near Gomti River. Products of folk artists and craftsmen attract even affluent and highly sophisticated people of the city.

Among the specialized markets which continue to thrive even today are markets of Yahiyaganj specializing in brass and copper utensils, now largely replaced by stainless steel utensils, Daliganj market specializing in farm products especially agricultural implements.

Following is a list of well-known mohallas, lanes, roads, mandis and baazaars of Lucknow some of which have changed beyond recognition.

Lanes (Galiyan)

Batashey wali gali (Aminabad)
Ganney wali gali (Aminabad)
Dor wali gali (Chowk)
Marwari gali (Ganeshganj)
Pathar wali gali (Wazirganj)
Tapey wali gali (Kazmain)
Achuti gali (Pul Ghulam husain)
Kanghi wali gali (Nakhas)
Chaval wali gali (Nakhas)
Phool wali gali (Chowk)
Babboo wali gali (Daliganj)
Ghorey wali gali (Nakhas)
Gali Shah Chara (Victoria Street)
Baan wali gali (Chowk)
Gali Nishat ganj – from 1 to 7 lanes (Nishat ganj)

Tola

Bawarchi tola (Dyodhi Agha Mir)
Sondhi tola (Chowk)
Bhawani tola (Chowk)
Jhawai tola (Choupatiyan)
Rastogi tola (Raja bazaar)
Mallahi tola (Mashakganj)
Thawai tola (Raja bazaar)
Naalbandi tola (Dyodhi Agha Mir)

Katra

Katra Abu Turab Khan (Nakhas)
Katra Azambeg (Turiaganj)
Katra Khuda Yaar Khan (Saadatganj)

Mohalla

Kashmiri Mohalla
Jouhari Mohalla
Chobdari Mohalla
Dalali Mohalla
Beldari Mohalla

Mandi

Chik Mandi
Daal Mandi
Ghasiyari Mandi
Bheri Mandi
Mirza Mandi
Ghazi Mandi
Subzi Mandi, (Chowk, now shifted to Hardoi Road)
Subzi Mandi, Qaiserbagh

Kuan

Lal Kuan
Kankar Kuan
Bholanath ka Kuan
Chhachhi Kuan

Aabaad

Aminabad
Nazirabad
Husainabad
Hyderabad (old and new)

Khana

Murghkhana
Feelkhana
Zamboorkhana
Taazikhana
Baroodkhana
Farashkhana
Barfkhana
Rathkhana

Bagh

Chaarbagh
Alambagh
Qaiserbagh
Aishbagh
Banarsibagh
Khurshidbagh
Telibagh
Musabagh
Nazarbagh

Pul

Pul ghulam husain
Jhaoo Lal ka pul
Pucca pul

Darwaza/Phatak

Rumi darwaza
Akbari darwaza, Gole darwaza

Ahaata/haata

Ahaata Sungibeg
Ahaata Durga Prasad
Ahaata Sitara begum
Ahaata Matadin
Ahaata Sulemanqadar

Chowk

Lucknow has changed a lot during the last 5-6 decades. A number of new markets, shopping complexes and malls have emerged but the market called Chowk continues to attract despite the fact that even Chowk has changed a lot and lost its grandeur. In the Lucknow of yesteryears Chowk was like an institution where the entire culture of Lucknow could be seen at one place. Though Chowk was a normal road of about two furlong length– starting from Gol Darwaza at one end to Akbari Darwaza on the other,it had a fascinating history

This whole stretch of road could be covered in ten minute walk. This road/ lane had shops on both sides.

When one enters Chowk from Gole Darwaza, one is welcomed by Jewellery shops on both sides. This cluster of shop is popularly known as *Sarrafa.* Sometime back the *Sarrafa* used to be located on one side and the opposite side was occupied by the shops selling *Chikan, Zardozi* and *Kamdani* (all exquisite embroidery work) after which the polished articles with gold and silver plating occupied a small stretch. It culminates on huge ornate gate of Shahi Shafa Khana (the royal hospital) known as Darul Shafa. Here, the practitioners of Unani system of medicine, highly experienced *Hakeems* prescribed and distributed medicines free of cost. The hospital continued to function till 1960s. Just opposite to this Shafakhana, there was a compound which also housed a huge well known as Kaptan Ka Kuan. In this compound several shops of making and selling ornate finger rings are there. During evenings a number of venders used to sell their items around the well. A few yards more and you reach the mid or central point of Chowk. On the one side there were shops of ring stones, cuff lings etc. and on the other different varieties of silver and gold foil, tobacco, perfumed betelnuts etc. Beyond this point there were several shops selling different types of caps, items used in marriage ceremonies etc. Now we reach the last part of the road housing shops mainly of *kebabs, sheermal, mughlai* food, multi layered *balai* (extracted cream from milk settled in layers, a specialty of Lucknow) etc. Now the culmination point is reached and that is the other end of Chowk – Akbari Darwaza, a huge ornate gate under which beautiful clay toys, different types of *huqqa*, and a host of other things were sold. There were also some shops selling the locally made dyes and manufacturing units of silverfoil used to decorate various dishes.

Between the two gates, the upper stories of shops were the *Kothas* of *Tawaifs* – the courtesans and dancers. The courtesans were not ordinary prostitutes hawking sex. They were institution in themselves. They were trained in performing arts such as *Kathak* and Hindustani classical music as well as literature mainly *ghazal.* They were accepted as high class courtesans serving nobility only. They could be compared with the *geisha* tradition in Japan. They were so sophisticated and culturally refined that young men from the aristocratic families and other nobility were sent to their *Kotha* to learn etiquette and polished manners of those times. After the downfall of Nawabi rule in 1856, this institution declined. Though several of these *Kothas* survived the turmoil and political upheavals, gradually and gradually the dance (*mujra*) became secondary and used as a camaflouge for prostitution. Till about 1950s, or 1960s some *Kothas* survived in Chowk and the passerby could hear the sound of music and dance but even these faded away.

Weekly Markets

Weekly markets in Lucknow are not of recent origin. The more important factor is that even after the advent of modern, air-conditioned markets/shopping centers and malls, the attraction and popularity of weekly markets continue. Perhaps the main reason for this is the fact that such a vast variety of household goods at much cheaper prices, though not necessarily of high quality, is available to suit the purse and budget of all sections of the population. Since these markets are held on the footpath in front of closed shops, these are able to cut down the overhead charges.

One of the oldest weekly markets is held in Chinhat on Lucknow – Faizabad Road on Thursdays. Cultivators of nearby villages used to bring *chana* (gram) and other eatables to sell directly to the consumers hence the name Chinhat (chana means gram and *haat* is *bazaar* or market). Beginning from *chana haat* it became *Chanhat* and now *Chinhat.* Many people of adjoining villages still call it *Chanhat.*

The weekly market of Nishatganj held on Wednesdays is perhaps the most popular of such markets where even many persons from upper middle class and some from the richer sections also come to do shopping for the items usually not available in posh markets and malls or available at much higher prices. Other popular weekly markets are held at Alambagh and Sadar (near cantonment). The former is held on Tuesdays while the later on Sundays. In a recently conducted study done by the students of Indian Institute of Management, Lucknow, it was revealed that of the population of Trans-Gomti area every person visits this market at least once in a year. Seeing the popularity of this market, these students gave tips to the shopkeepers and street venders for enhancing their sale and profit. Because of heavy crowd of shoppers and encroachment on the roads by the shops thus creating traffic jams and other types of nuisance, several attempts were made by the civic authorities and the police to shift this market to a nearby area but it could never succeed and the authorities finally gave up. According to a conservative estimate business of 50-60 lakhs is transacted in this market every week. The business goes up beyond this estimate during the festival season of Holi, Diwali, Eid, and Bakrid.

Beside the usual household items one comes across a number of kiosks selling foodgrains and spices in Sadar market. This market is held near the Ram Leela Maidan and attracts the residents of Sadar, Purana Qila, Husainganj, Udaiganj, Cantonment and the adjoining areas. Though not as big as the market of Nishatganj, it caters to the requirements of the local people.

The weekly market of Alambagh is held on Tuesdays encompassing the area between Chander Nagar Gate and Alambagh crossing and beyond. Beside the other items of day to day use, one sees a number of shops selling clothes, toys, wooden items and cheap furniture. In recent years another weekly market has come up in Dobagga area on Thursdays attracting the resident of *mohallas* situated on both sides of Hardoi Road. It has not assumed the size of the older weekly markets yet but it is growing fast.

Nakhas Baazaar

This weekly market held on Sundays in Nakhas area located in Old Lucknow deserves special treatment in view of its historical importance. It is known for the old, used, and antique items for the past more than hundred years. Though local historians are not sure about its beginning but some of them tell that it began around 1859 – almost immediately after the British rulers resorted to destruction of buildings and persecuting people in revenge and retaliation for their participation in mutiny/first war of independence in 1857. During that period most of the inhabited mohallas were situated in Old Lucknow – Chowk, Saadatganj, Rastogitola, Raja Bazaar, Chaupatiyan, Gadhi Peer Khan, Turiaganj, Patanala, Jauhari Mohalla, Tehsinganj, Rakabganj, Moulviganj, Ashrafabad, etc. After the revolt was crushed, a number of families of elite class were reduced to penury and so were their servants and other dependents. They were faced with the problem of running the household. The lineage of the Nawabs found themselves in almost miserable condition. The pension (*wasiqa*) they were drawing from the British rulers was too meagre for a decent existence. First, they sold or mortgaged their jewellery to the money lenders and then, one by one, their valuables through their servants. That is how Nakhas Bazaar came into being. When the servants also left their masters to eke out a living for them and their families, members of the Nawab families and former aristocracy were left with no other option but to sell these valuables themselves directly to the traders. When the Nakhas Bazaar had taken its shape (though not sprawling and spread over quite a vast area as is now) the shop keepers used to open their shops around dawn time so that the ruined nawabs and the nobility were not to be embarrassed carrying bundles of utensils, cutlery etc. and be seen by public. Perhaps that is why the Nakhas Bazaar even today begins early in the morning (though not at dawn any more) as the remnant of the past. Unlike the present scenario only regular shops were there dealing with the used goods. Now most of the vendors do their business on foot paths and road side.

After perhaps, two or three decades, stocks of goods of antique value had almost exhausted and the proud owners had only a limited number of items left with them , new shops selling all sorts of used things – clothes, furniture, books, gramophone records etc. were added to the market.Thus the regular market (though much smaller than today's) was transformed into a weekly market. As mentioned in the gazetteer, Sunday was preferred being the weekly holiday, to the convenience of the Britishers so that they could visit the market and do shopping especially of goods of antique value. This market is still visited by a large number of people, many in search of old things of antique value, but by and large most of the market sells either cloth, readymade garments, old books, casettes, discarded electronic goods and similar other sundry goods. According to a conservative estimate business of around twelve lakhs is transacted on normal Sundays but this figure climbs astronomically during the festival season. With the passage of time this market grew in size and now occupies the road side of the entire Victoria Street and continues almost till Nadaan Mahal Road – a stretch of around two kilometers. Now it is a favourite destination of the poor and the economically weaker sections.

The description of Nakhas Bazaar shall remain incomplete without the **Chiriya Bazaar** (birds market). The history of Chiriya Bazaar is as old as that of Nakkhas market. Though a part of Nakhas market, it remains open throughout the week but come Sunday, it throbs with life with more variety and bird sellers. Once it used to be one of the favourite destinations of the Nawabs and others fond of keeping animals especially different types of birds but with the implementation of stringent Wild Life Protection Act, it has lost its sheen. What we find for sale today are pigeons, parrots, small birds like laal, hens, etc. When one probes one discovers that the bird sellers also deal with endangered species banned for hunting and sale. But this is not done openly and the transactions are conducted only through middlemen. It is popularly believed that some of the lower level employees of the wild life department connive in this illegal business. This market is also raided occasionally by the wild life officials but the business goes on though on a much reduced scale.

New Markets and Commercial Centres

Till the 1960s, Nakhas and Chowk in Old Lucknow and Aminabad and Hazratganj

Bird Market(Chidiya Bazaar) of Nakhaas

Weekly Nakhaas Market

A shop in Gadbadjhaala, Aminabad

beyond these continued as the main markets and commercial centers, though the later expanded with new shopping stores, restaurants and offices of the commercial establishments. After 1980s new markets appeared on Faizabad Road and Kanpur Road and inside the new housing schemes and colonies such as Bhootnath Market in Indira Nagar and a large market in Patrakar Puram in Gomtinagar. By the turn of the present century Aminabad became so crowded that it was difficult to walk smoothly and comfortably. A great number of new branches of virtually every bank appeared in the city and hundreds of ATMs could be seen everywhere.

Now appeared Malls and Multiplexes- a new phenomenon for Lucknowwalas. Currently there are six malls located in different parts of the city. Competing with these malls shop owners of Hazratganj opened the outlets of branded clothes and other merchandise of European and American companies, thus radically altering the demand and taste of the well to do and affluent sections of people. The tragic part of the story is that Chowk has been declining and except the Sarrafa and shops selling Chikan garments the remaining are virtually on the brink of extinction.

Hazratganj, 'Ganging' and Aminabad

Lucknow has expanded phenomenally during the last 50 years and now considered as one of the fastest growing cities of India. Many new markets, big and small, shopping complexes, Malls and Multiplexes have come up but the popularity and romance of Hazratganj and Aminabad especially of the former, has not waned. It still carries nostalgia for Lucknowites settled in all parts of the world. Thus, the

'Lucknow Diaspora', wherever it has made its home, compulsively visits it whenever they come to Lucknow. Not only this, they also pass this romance to their children who, when they grow up, visit it to see why their parents were so nostalgic about it.

As for as the history goes the idea of the present Hazratganj was conceived by the first Nawab of Awadh, Saadat Ali Khan in 1810AD. He created some European style buildings between the present District Magistrate's residences (Kothi Noor Baksh) to Raj Bhawan the Governor House (Kothi Hayaat Baksh). Later, Nawab Nasiruddin Haider concretized the idea and laid the foundation of a market. In 1842, it was named Hazratganj after the then Nawab, Amjad Ali Khan who carried the nickname 'Hazrat'. After the first war of Independence (mutiny) was crushed in 1857 the Britishers took vendetta and in retaliation demolished several buildings and at their place constructed building in European style and market not accessible to the native commoners.

Describing Hazratganj, the well known writer, Veena Talwar Oldenburg (2007) – a Lucknowite herself, writes that "at the heart of the city lies the Hazratganj, a market so glamorous, that it truly lived up to its name by creating desire (*hasrat*), (pun intended) in the heart of the Lucknowite who made it a prime destination for strolling, eating and shopping at the many splendid retail establishments that had sprung up." The way Lucknow has expanded in recent decades, Hazratganjs' location may not be described as *the heart of Lucknow* but it continues to be in the heart of Lucknawise.

When the newly emerging destinations were about to swallow Hazratganj as it continued to decay and declined – the landmark Mayfair Cinema and Kwality Restaurant, the band of Royal Café, BenBos, Filmistan and several others had passed into history, groups of Lucknowites – Lovers of Lucknow, Connect Lucknow, some others and individuals dedicated to its revival – unitedly campaigned for its revival in its 200th year i.e. in 2010. This was a citizens' initiative, perhaps first of its kind in the country, snowballed into a movement and the government of Mayawati stepped in to make this idea a reality.

The original makeover plan was designed by the country's well known architect Nasir Munjee and with some changes it was executed at a cost of more than rupees 30 crores. Encroachments on the road and big hoardings on the roof tops were removed, buildings were painted in a uniform cream and pink colour and sign boards in black and white gave it a new look. All the electricity poles with cobwebs of wires were removed and transferred to underground, beautiful Victorian style lamps on lamp posts were installed, benches on the pavements and fountains gave a new look and a modern multilevel parking was constructed where the fire station once stood. Thus, we have a revived and rejuvenated Hazratganj. Alas, its maintenance is poor and the indisciplined and arrogant among the citizenry refuse to go with the revived glory and continues with their old habits. The government has done its lot and now the lovers of Hazratganj have to strive to persuade the erring ones to develop respect for this place.

Ganjing is a word which has been continueing its popularity and acceptability for several generations. In whatever words the Lucknowites describe it, the best way to describe this in terms of romantic walks, leisurely strolling and carefree window shopping culminating in some coffee house or restaurant. I fondly remember my university days and my stern father's Interrogative comment whenever I entered home in late evenings – "Ganjing kar aaye? Bata kar to jaya karo." (Done Ganjing? At least inform us that you could be late). Strolling in the 'Lovers Lane' used to be the favourite pastime of the youths. From the Mulliks to the Jabbar's Coffee via Modern Novelties, there used to be 2-3 lanes of small shops. These are now gone but the 'Ganjing' goes on.

Compared to Hazratganj, Aminabad is a relatively neglected market but a number of people living around it, shopkeepers and traders have started demanding its revival and renovation on the lines of Hazratganj. For a large number of people visit to Aminabad Market in unavoidable and indispensible because of a big market of clothes, books and other sundry commodities despite its becoming so crowded that it is almost impossible to walk in it comfortably and without be jostling and colliding with somebody. Hazratganj was known as the market of the 'elite' while Aminabad was meant for middle class and commoners.

Going into history, Amjad Ali Shah (1842-47) was very interested in the expansion and development of the city. During his reign, his Prime Minister Amiruddaula created a new mohalla and named it Aminabad. Passing through the stage of thatched huts, *kuchcha-pucca* houses and witnessing political turmoil in the field, now a park, it evolved into a big market and an important commercial centre of the city. Near Nazirabad crossing there used to be a very popular tea house known as Abdullah Tea House where journalists used to gather after the night shift as it remained open virtually throughout the night and in the morning news paper hawkers even today sell news papers. On the other side where the Jagat Cinema is situated there is Chedi Lal Dharmshala and the famous Urdu book shop Danish Mahal. Jhandewala Park witnessed important political rallies where such stalwarts as Nehru and Subhash Chandra Bose had addressed the freedom fighters. Moving towards Ganeshganj, the unique Garbad Jhala Market where one gets anything and everything of utility. It consists of several lanes with shops selling crockery, hosiery, readymade garments, artificial jewellery, bangles etc. With the passage of time the number of shops and shoppers increased and so were vehicles. Now it is chaotic all the time but those addicted to this market keep coming.

The Subaltern and the Marginalized

Writers and Chroniclers of the Nawabi and Post-Nawabi era rarely took notice of those sections of the society who have also been playing important roles but remained ignored, socially excluded and marginalized. Here, an attempt has been made to portray the role and life of such sections, though briefly, some of whom have virtually become extinct or changed their profession beyond recognition or virtually fading out while the others are still there in substantial numbers but looked down upon by the larger society.Can the role of tonga/rickshaw drivers,brass band players,sanitation labour and host of others be ignored?

5

The Subaltern and the Marginalized

"Andherey me jo baithe hain nazar un par bhi kutch dalo, arey O roshnee waalon."

(O the people of light, throw a glance on them too who are sitting in a dark corner)

Kahaar

Though traditionally serving as drawers of water in villages and also towns where piped water was not there, with the passage of time, they have been transformed into a caste with the norm of endogamy. In Lucknow city they were known more as carriers of *doli* and *paalki* (palanquin). Here the more popular word for *doli* was *peenus* and there is *peenus waali gali* in Chowk area which was once inhabited by the Kahaars alongwith their *peenus.*

The *doli* and *paalki* were prevalent in Lucknow even before the Nawabi period and especially *doli* was used to carry women, sick and sometime children, from one place to the other. It was handy to use it in narrow lanes and bylanes as the convenient mode of transportation especially for women observing *purdah.* The ornate palanquin was used to carry the bride. From 1950s onwards the practice started declining and by the turn of the present century it is used rarely and sparingly by the wedding planners. Pavan Kashyap, the son of once well known Munna Kahaar of peenus waali gali tells that his six generations followed this profession. Now, he sells *makhan malai*, a delicacy of old Lucknow, at Gole Darwaza in Chowk area. He tells that most of the Kahaars have turned daily wage earners or indulge in self employment with low incomes such as roadside vendors. There are now hardly a dozen odd households of Kahaars in peenus wali gali. The Kahaars recall with nostalgia one of their ancestors Dhania Mehri, a close companion of Begums (ladies of Nawabi lineage) on whose name a small bridge on Haider Canal in Alamnagar still exists while a spacious mosque Dhania Mehri ki Masjid located in Moulvi Ganj carries her name. The Kahaars come under Other Backward Classes (OBCs) and those of them with some educational qualification have also entered into government jobs taking advantage of the reservation policy in employment.

Ekka/Tonga drivers

Once upon a time horse driven *Bagghi, Tum Tum, Tonga and Ekka* were the only means of transport on roads, and *doli* and *palki* in the lanes. After the Nawabi period these modes of transport started declining – first *Bagghi* and *Tumtum* went into oblivion and later *Tonga* and *Ekka* whose use is now confined only to some parts of old Lucknow. Horse cart is still being used to carry vegetables and fruits from the wholesale *mandis* to retailer shops.

While a Tonga has the arrangement of two long seats on the front and back with the provision of a hanging pedestal on which feet could be rested, an Ekka has only a sitting desk of almost equal length and breadth on which 3-4 people could sit with their feet hanging in the air. Both have canopies so that travelers are spared from the scorching sun or rain. A *Tonga* or *Ekka* was covered from all sides by a sheet of cloth used as curtain, if the travelers were *purdah* observing women. Such scenes may be observed even today but rarely. Till 1950s, there used to be more than a dozen *tonga* stands where one could see several t*ongas* parked in a row waiting for the passengers. With the advent of automobiles– public transport city buses, auto rickshaws, tempos etc. The slow moving horse driven *tonga* and *ekka* were largely replaced. Such *tonga* stands may be seen today only around the famous monuments in old Lucknow. The old covered *tonga/ekka* with a canopy has been replaced by horse driven open carts to transport vegetables, fruits and meat from the slaughter house and *mandis.*

The figures available with the municipal corporation reveal that presently there are around 450 *tonga* and *ekka* running in the city (it seems to be old information as one does not come across these frequently) but no figures are available about its number in the adjoining villages. The civic body had constructed a small pond of water and large utensils for putting fodder for the horses on every *tonga/ekka* stand but this facility has almost vanished and now only a couple of stands such as Daliganj/Hasan Ganj in Trans Gomti area may be seen as the remnants of the past.

The drivers of *tonga/ekka* are in miserable condition because of meager incomes. Maintenance of horses has become so expensive that it leaves only a meager amount as savings. With no provision of social security – insurance of horse or its owners, life insurance and health insurance – the *tonga/ekka* drivers/ owners are leaving this profession altogether.

Ragpickers and Scrap Dealers

Kabaadi is a popular, familiar, and house hold word being used in Lucknow for more than two centuries. While there has been specific *mohallas* named after a profession whose practitioners resided there, there has never been any particular locality as such for the *Kabaadis* and they may be seen scattered in different *mohallas.* But it is also true that those who buy and sell the scrap and botched material ,the scrap dealers, are concentrated in good numbers on Nadan Mahal Road, Yahiyaganj and

Alamnagar while the weekly market of Nakkhas is most popular for buying and selling of used and rejected goods.

The Kabaadis of Lucnow may be divided into two broad categories –in the first category comes those who roam on foot, bicycle and hand pushed *thela* and buy the *kabaad* on prompt payment. The bulk of this *kabaad* comes from old newspapers and magazines, items made of iron or plastic or rejected electronic goods. Most of such *Kabaadis* are merely collector of this *Kabaad* and after collection they carry the day's collection to a big *kabaadi* or scrap dealer and sell it with some margin of profit which is their earnings for the day.

In this category such mobile *kabadis* may also be added who exchange their stainless steel utensils with the used clothes in good condition – sari, shirt, pant, and silver/gold embroidered ladies garments such as *dupatta* (scarf), frocks, and *gharara* (loose skirt). Such used garments are then sold in the weekly markets. Many of such kabaadis are either local people or those who have migrated from such places as Gonda and Bahraich. Many of them have respectable earnings and may be leading a comfortable life.

The second category consists of rag pickers who roam about from dawn to dusk in search of saleable items in the heaps of public rubbish on the roadside. Till 1970s such rag pickers were few and mainly came from the poorest sections of the city or even from outside the city. However, from the 1980s or so a large number of people, mostly Bengali speaking, from Assam and West Bengal, majority of them being Muslims, descended in Lucknow. With the passage of time their numbers increased manifold and they are a familiar sight not in Lucknow but the whole of India except, perhaps, South India. It is alleged that several of them come from Bangladesh and that is why they are popularly described as 'Bangladeshis'. They are illiterate, unskilled, and poorest of the poor. These men and women, and even children as young as 10-12 years may be seen carrying a large bag and a wooden or iron stick probing the heaps of dirty garbage on the roadsides for anything saleable but mainly plastic – discarded and broken plastic *chappals* ,sandals and shoes, polythene bags, etc. Their usual destination is Aishbagh, Talkatora and some other localities where plastic granules or plastic goods are manufactured in small or large factories. Usually it fetches between fifteen to twenty rupees for a kilogram of plastic. Many of them have disclosed that on an average a person barely earns fifty rupees per day.

These rag pickers live in sub-human condition. The majority of them live on both sides of 23 kilometre long Haider Canal that carries a large amount of city's rubbish while the rest are scattered in the small and large slums of the city. Because of their acute poverty they are forced to live under extremely unhygienic conditions devoid of basic civic amenities. In several localities of the city their womenfolk provide their services as domestic aid.

The most tragic part of their plight is the barrage of harassment and humiliation they face day in and day out. Facing contemptuous scolding and reprimand by the people, they are exploited by the local goons and abused by the police including their girls being sexually abused. Those of their women who work as maid servant have to bear with all sorts of exploitation under the threat that they would be reported to the police as Bangladeshi infiltrators despite the fact that many of them are genuine Indian citizens coming from West Bengal and Assam and carrying all legal documents with them.

Kaanmailiya and Malishiya

Kaanmailiya has been a unique feature of Lucknow. Etymologically speaking *Kaan* means ear and *maila* is dirt. Thus a *Kaanmailiya* is one who cleans the ears by removing the wax and any other impurities from the ears. Their presence in Lucknow may be traced back to the Nawabi period. At a time when there were no ENT specialists, the *Kaanmailiya* developed the expertise of cleaning the ears with just a thin stick made of metal with a loop at the end entering into the interiors of the ears. First, they insert some drops of a particular oil and after waiting for some time they insert the metal stick and bring out the wax and dirt. They had to take extra precaution not to damage the ear diaphragm.

They tell that with the Nawabi era coming to an end resulting in loss of royal patronage they had to add an extra expertise to their skill in the form of massage of skull popularly called *champi*. Thus, it is now *Kaanmailiya* and *Maalishya* (masseur), two in one. Because of the diminishing popularity, the number of these practitioners has also been declining. Still, some of them may be seen even today in several parks especially in Jhandewale Park, Aminabad and GPO Park carrying small bottles of oil of several colours in a leather bag. Some of them may also be seen loitering in collectorate, lower courts and outside government offices in search of potential customers. After some bargaining they agree to extend their services for a fee ranging between 5 to 10 rupees for ear cleaning and the equal amount for hair massage. After loitering and roaming about for the whole day they earn between 120-150 rupees. The meager income has discouraged new entrants into this trade. Though their exact number is not available but some knowledgeable persons tell that their number has climbed down from hundreds to a few dozens. Perhaps, in a couple of decades, they will be found only in stories.

Saperey / Snake Charmers

Kyon naache sapera?

(Why the snake charmer is dancing?)

With the strict implementation of wild life regulations and loud advocacy by animal rights activists and organizations the number of *madaari* (animal handlers earning their livelihood by showing animals' antics especially monkeys and bears) had already declined substantially. The *saperey* (snake charmers) too are facing adverse times. Yet, their condition is a little better because of snakes carrying some religious legitimacy and sanctity.

A village called Bholukhera situated on Kanpur Road is known for the snake charmers. A population of around four thousands depends on the earning they get from snakes. It has been a hereditary profession for them continuing for several centuries. They have an amazing expertise of catching snakes from forests and dense foliage. They rear the snakes and earn their livelihood by displaying it to the village and city folks. Carrying a *been* (snake-charmer's flute) they roam around and attract people especially children by playing the instrument. The familiar sound of *been* is an announcement that some snake charmer is around and when some people have gathered they take out the snakes from the covered bamboo basket. After showing various tricks and movements of snakes they request the spectators to give some money. Since their children are socialized with snakes they too develop expertise of catching snakes at an early age. Even their kids are not scared of snakes.

Winters are lean season for them as the snakes retreat into deep shelters and go into hibernation. Whatever little they save gets consumed during this lean season and several of them have to take up odd unskilled jobs in the city to survive. The month of *saawan* (falling during rainy season) brings cheers for them as this coincides with the festival of *Nagpanchami* when the devout Hindus make offerings to the snakes especially to King Cobras and 'feed' milk to the the snakes. The fact remains that the snakes do not drink milk but hunts on insects and rats which is their usual food. During these days they may earn up to rupees five hundred per day while in the remaining months they earn barely hundred rupees. This increased income is further supplemented by easy availability of snakes as these reptiles come out of their hibernation and may be caught in abundance not only from jungles but also from several homes. After receiving calls from Municipal Corporation and individual households they search, locate, and catch the snake and also charge fee for this job. With the fast increasing urbanization their area of operation has been shrinking and many of them will have to look for other means of livelihood for their survival.

Slum Dwellers

Like any other big city of India, Lucknow too has its share of slums. With the increase in population, the number of slum dwellers has also been increasing at a fast pace. The biggest concentration of slum is found on both the banks of Haider Canal. It has ceased to be a canal and now reduced to a big drain or gutter that receives bulk of the city's rubbish and sewage. Here live lakhs of people, on both the banks, in small slums beginning from Rajaji Puram and traversing several localities of Lucknow it falls into Gomti River, the lifeline of the city. Several of these slums are known as Vijay Nagar, Shubham Nagar, Lakshmi Nagar, Mayawati Puram etc.

According to a report there are around six hundred slums within the municipal limits of Lucknow. Though the governmental agencies have enforced a ban on new slums in the city, the new immigrants have established new slums on vacant government land in Chinhat, Mohaan Road, Dubagge and Sitapur Road. This ever increasing migration to Lucknow takes place because of both the factors – 'Pushed out factors' and 'pulled into factors'. Impoverished people from Sitapur, Basti, Gonda, Bahraich and some other districts have been coming to Lucknow and settling down in search of better wages and living conditions. According to an estimate more than six lakh people are living in these slums. Many slum dwellers of Haider Canal have constructed pucca houses yet most of them continue to use open places for toilet. Though the well known private agency, Sulabh International runs more than two dozen toilets but many of the inhabitants of these slums are so poor that they cannot afford to pay even the small fee charged by the Sulabh toilets. Some MLAs have provided piped water and water tanks at some places out of their funds allotted to them but these have proved grossly insufficient.

The NGOs working among the slums tell that more than 80% of domestic help comes from the slums. Thus, women get jobs as maid servants while their menfolk earn livelihood as construction labour, rickshaw puller, rag picker and through other sundry jobs. It is tragic and ironical that the middle class and affluent people depend upon the labour and drudgery of these people but don't like them living anywhere near their localities. The local goons and police also extract their pound of flesh and fleece them on the charges of bootlegging, theft, gambling, prostitution etc.

Ghassal and Gorkun

Dabaa ke qabr me sub chal diye,dua na salaam,
Zaraa si der me kyaa ho gayaa zamaane ko.

(Every one left burying me in the grave without any blessings and salutation;the world has changed so quickly and rapidly)

Joined in a symbiotic relationship, these two groups provide crucially important service to the people but, perhaps, most socially excluded and marginalized.

A microscopic community on the verge of extinction,the *ghassaal* derives its name from the Arabic word *ghusl* meaning washing or bathing. They give the last bath to a dead body. It is popularly believed that this practice originated with the Shia Nawabs of Awadh and Shia nobles who would not touch the dead body. Unlike other Muslims, both the Shias and the Sunnis, of other parts of Uttar Pradesh or India the Shia nobility was wary, rather scared of touching the dead body of even their closest kin. While outside Lucknow, this job was always considered as good and an act of *sawaab* (good deed / piety) to give the last bath or even participating in this ritual; it was taken as the last service to the deceased. Even today, in several Shia households of pure Lucknowi people, a new exit is created by breaking a wall to take out the dead body not using the main entrance.

Under the circumstances described above the institution of *ghassaal* came into being. It requires two persons to give the ritual bath which takes around two hours after which a corpse is covered by *kafan* (white shroud) and the body is handed over to the relatives of the deceased. The body of males is bathed by male *ghassaals* and of females by the female *ghassaals*. Presently, there are four male *ghassals* (three Shias and one Sunni) and four female *ghassals* (all Sunnis) trained especially for this job. Significantly it is only the Shias who take the services of *ghassals*. The *ghassals* happily accept the clothes, ornaments, footwear, bed-sheet, blanket etc. removed from the corpses. Despite demand there are hardly new entrants into this job. Even those currently involved in this job are not happy due to low income and low social prestige attached to it. There have been two *Ghuslkhana* (bathing chambers) for several decades – one at Patanala near Chowk and the other at Malika Jahan ki Karbala at Aishbagh but now there is just one as the one at Patanala is no more functional as the *ghassaals* there have given up this job.

The supplementary service provider in the funeral of Muslims is *Gorkun* (grave digger). *Gor* in Arabic means grave and *kun* means to make or maker. The very name denotes their occupation. The *gorkun* are not specific to the Shias as their services are required by all the Muslims. Thus, they are available in more than a dozen grave yards of both Shias and Sunnis. Like the case of *ghassaals*, the *gorkun* too are not satisfied with their profession because of low income and low social prestige. Asked as to why they are continuing with this job, they replied that at least they do not starve. But one thing is for sure certain, neither the *ghassals* nor the *gorkun* are bringing in their children to this profession.

Eunuchs

The transgender, trans-sexual persons in South Asia are also described as eunuchs and their popular connotation is expressed in terms of *Hijra, Khwajasara, Kinnar, Chakka* etc. with several regional variations. The most popular term for such persons in Lucknow is *hijra* and they have been an integral part of the local society for several centuries.

The Nawabs of Awadh imitating several Mughal kings also recruited them since late 17th century in their courts and also for the ladies quarters of the palaces for the purpose of surveillance over the Begums and other women. Later, the *Khwajasara* won the confidence of the Nawabs to such an extent that they succeeded in getting important posts in the court and started influencing important decisions. One Tahseenullah became so powerful that he got a mosque constructed in his name and a mohalla was named after him known as Tahseenganj. Another powerful khwajasara Muqarim Shah established a whole *basti* Muqarim Nagar for his community which is located near Daliganj where a good number of them still live.

There used to be a fair or congregation of these people in Lucknow till 1994. The venue was on the back of *ramleela* ground in Aishbagh and the fair was known as Aloilc ka Mela. Hundreds of hijras used to participate in it in teams divided on the names of their gurus. The fair was usually held on the occasion of Nagpanchami. When the Lucknow Development Authority built a housing complex near the venue, people living in these houses objected to the obscenities in the fair and got it closed forever.

Though the community of hijras has undergone several changes during the last 3-4 centuries the *guru-shishya parampara* (teacher-pupil tradition) still continues. Names of such gurus still in vogue are Shankar Guru, Chanda Guru, Payal Guru etc. Today their main source of sustenance and livelihood is the *neg* (customary presents to be given on auspicious occasions like marriage, *moondan*, birth, etc.) they get from the patrons. In order to avoid any conflict or clash of interest they have divided the city for themselves. No group of *hijras* is supposed to encroach on other's locality or zone. Their groups descend on a household within their zone after getting information of a birth, marriage or construction of a new house. Initially, they used to accept whatever the patron willfully gave as gift or *neg* but later it degenerated into extortion. When this practice crossed all limits of nuisance the officials of the municipal corporation attempted an exercise of fixing this *neg*. Thus, the *neg* of marriage was fixed at Rs. 1100/- and birth of a child at Rs. 500/- but it was soon rejected by the hijras and they reverted to the old practice. Now they have extended this practice to constructing or buying a new house, opening of a shop or show room, *mundan* (the first ritual shaving of a child's hair), birthday and on somebody getting a job. One may also see their groups taking round of their zones on various festivals too.

Justifying the practice of extracting money they maintain that it is their only source of income but they also admit that their services are also sought by the land mafia in grabbing a land or house or for creating nuisance as pressure tactic. They also admit, and resent it, that some fake hijras have also joined this business. When interviewed, some of them have welcomed the judicial pronouncement on LGBT and demand that the government should extend the facility of loan for them and make some reservation in employment.

Bhaand and Naqqal

Perhaps there is no exact English translation of *Bhaand* but the nearest translation may be Jester cum clown while *Naqqal* is Mime doing mimicry. At a time when the means and sources of entertainment were limited such arts provided the much sought after relief from monotonous existence. According to Roshan Taqi(2014), no evidence of *Bhaand* and *Naqqal* is found in Lucknow before the Nawabi era. The Nawabs gave patronage and protection to these arts for the purpose of entertainment. It is said that the first group of *bhaand*s arrived in Lucknow on the occasion of the marriage of a son of Nawab Asafuddaula in 1795.

The earliest settlement of these Kashmiri *bhaand*s was noted in those localities where Kashmiri Pundits had settled, Mohalla Katra Bizen Baig, Peer Bukhara and Golaganj. Later most of the *bhands* moved to a new mohalla named Bhandotola which was specially established for them. After the First War of Independence in 1857, the Nawabi era came to an end, Awadh annexed and Nawab Wajid Ali Shah was exiled to Matiaburj, Calcutta. With this all types of entertainers – *Bhaand,*

Naqqal, Bahroopiya, and *Daastaango* went into oblivion after losing the royal patronage and the new rulers, the Britishers, did not encourage these arts. Now the b*haand*s fell into severe economic crisis. Though some of them got work in *Nautanki* an upward climbing art form during those days, and *mujra* dancers who utilised their services to provide entertainment to their patrons during breaks between two rounds of *mujra*. By early 1960s, even this avenue was lost as professional *mujra* came to an end

*Bhaandg*iri or *bharainchi* is now almost an extinct art form as hardly any member of this community earns his livelihood through it. Now many of them have taken to street vending, rickshaw pulling, and other petty jobs. The elderly persons among them still exhibit the last remnants of this art of entertainment which provides a glimpse of why this was once a lively form of entertainment and why the saying, gatherings without *Bhaand* are boring and colourless, was once true.

Brass Band Player

Begaani shaadi me Abdullah deewana…

(Why Abdullah is so excited in somebody elses' marriage)

One of the most familiar features of marriages in South Asia is the musical band accompanying the *baraat* (bridegrooms' wedding party) proceeding to bride's home or the venue of marriage. Though the *baraat* procession is accompanied also by fancy lights, fire work, and dance, the most fascinating part of this procession is the brass band.

In most of the cities of India one may find dozens of private brass bands. The character of brass band in Lucknow, or for that matter of the entire Awadh region, is different. Here, almost all of the brass bands are owned and manned by the Valmiki Caste, the erstwhile *safai karmchari* or sanitary labour. Except the bands maintained by the Provincial Armed Constabulary (PAC), Jail and Central Government, the entire business of brass bands is controlled by the Valmikis. The best known Soni Brass Band, Jai Bhagwan Brass Band, Bharat Brass Band, Hindustan Brass Band and dozens of such bands are not only owned by persons of this community but the majority of band players also come from them. Not only this, majority of cart pullers, sound system and mobile fancy lights arrangers also belong to this group. Those of them who are still engaged in scavenging or sanitation work get sufficient time of leisure to be a part of this business for enhancing their income.

Though brass bands are located in all parts of the city, three hubs have emerged in three localities – Daliganj in Trans-Gomti area, Naka and Alambagh where dozens of brass bands may be seen in clusters. The most important factor which has facilitated it is the clusters of tent houses and furniture providers being located in these areas. Thus, one may arrange the entire paraphernalia – tent houses arranging tents of all sizes and types, sofa sets, fancy and ordinary chairs, crockery, carpets and brass band – all at one place, though florists arranging for floral decoration of bridegroom's car and venue of the wedding and horses, buggies and palanquins are usually not located at one place but the tent house owners offer to arrange everything.

Music players in brass bands get remuneration as per their talent, expertise and experience. In smaller bands the *shehnai* (a large flute pipe) players get the highest while the cart pullers the lowest remuneration. In smaller bands every member gets at least Rs. 200/- per shift while in large and more reputed bands it may be a minimum of Rs. 500/- while the *shehnai* and trumpet players may be getting as much as Rs. 1500/- per shift. The demand for the brass bands varies from season to season. They are over busy during the marriage seasons locally known as *sahalak*-auspicious days and months calculated and decided by the Hindu astrologers/*pundits*. Such periods of the year may stretch upto 6-8 months every year. The practice of hiring brass bands is not popular among the Muslims. An important feature of these brass bands is that dozens of their bands are being run on cooperative basis.

About a dozen odd persons form a group, contribute to buy musical instruments, uniforms, other paraphernalia and take a shop on rent along with a telephone connection (now a cell phone) for running this business and divide the profit earned among themselves. During peak seasons some extra hands may be hired on the basis of daily wages. Most of the people hiring bands are so particular about it that they can't imagine a marriage without brass band and music.

Rickshaw Pullers

Passengers sitting with luggage on a cycle rickshaw being pulled and pedalled by a man, sometime old and emaciated, is a common sight on the roads and lanes of Lucknow. The cycle rickshaw is a modified tricycle used extensively as a mode of transport for carrying passengers and luggage. Once seen as a major technological advancement over the hand pulled cart, rickshaw presents a picture of human misery and drudgery. The cycle rickshaw was introduced in early 1940s and soon became a popular mode of transport for the local people especially from the low income groups.

Lucknow has around 5000 rickshaw pullers and the majority of them are not the owners of their rickshaws. In a landmark study, A.K. Singh (2012), in a working paper done for the Giri Institute of Development Studies, has come out with startling facts about the rickshaw pullers of the entire Uttar Pradesh, including Lucknow. The most important feature of this occupation is that the cycle rickshaws provide an instant livelihood to any able bodied person who otherwise has no job. If we look at the background of the rickshaw pullers of Lucknow, we find that they are mostly landless labourers who migrate to find some livelihood. Many of them are also seasonal migrants whose families are still based in their villages trying to eke out a meager livelihood from small and uneconomic landholdings. The rickshaw pullers plying rickshaws in lucknow are not coming from the nearby villages or suburbs only but may be coming from as far a distant district as Gonda, Bahraich and Basti in the hope of getting better wages.

These rural migrants, coming in search of a job, can hire a rickshaw within a day or two or even within hours of their arrival and start earning instantly saving them from starvation. Though usually a person hiring a rickshaw from the contractor or the owner is required to deposit some money as security deposit. But even this condition may be done away with if the new migrant is introduced by another rickshaw puller or any reliable person. The rental has to be paid either at the end of the day or on a weekly basis.

An average rickshaw puller earns between Rs. 3000-6000 a month and that is why many of them get trapped by the moneylenders. Pulling heavy load and undernourished, it takes a heavy toll on their health and many of them may be seen carrying lung related diseases. In order to save some money several rickshaw pullers may share a small room and cook meal themselves or eat in the road side eateries, yet several of them prefer to sleep on their rickshaws or on the road pavements to save some money. Being one of the most vulnerable sections of the society they lack access to basic amenities and social security in case of illness, accident or death.

Though the state government has been thinking of providing them improved pedal cycle rickshaw with speed gears and better suspension or a motor assisted pedal rickshaw with electronic switches that may allow the puller to use it according to his convenience and battery operated rickshaw to reduce or eliminate the drudgery but despite these proposals and efforts spread over several years only a few battery operated rickshaws may be seen on the roads. Perhaps, rickshaw pullers have never been the priority area of any government.

Pheriwaala

Lucknow's roaming venders/ hawkers/huckster/peddler popularly known as *Pheriwala* were once used to be epitome of Lucknow's language and culture. People of Lucknow could boast about them and claimed that the language and mannerism of their *pheriwala* were far better and refined than those of other places. I was fortunate to be an observer of the last phase of this aspect of Lucknow's society and culture during my school days in late 1950s and early 60s after which the original Lucknow's *pheriwale* faded out and gradually replaced by the migrants from other districts.

How can one forget a *Qulfi* seller taking rounds announcing his arrival by a loud voice saying "*Qulfi lijiye, na jaane kis ki mohabbat me ghul rahi hai*" (buy qulfi! don't know for whose love it is melting) or during summers venders selling *kakdi* (a type of cucumber,long and thin)attracted the potential buyers with a melodious slogan "*Laila ki Ungliyan, Majnoo ki pasliyan, lelo yeh kakdiyan*" (*Kakdi* as thin as Laila's finger and Majnu's ribs) for any tourists or guest coming from other places it was such a pleasant experience. Although this refinement and sophistication is now a thing of the past yet the last vestiges remain.

About fifteen years ago I happened to see a hawaker selling cucumbers on a cart. This was just the beginning of the season. I looked at the thin and small cucumbers with appreciation and asked its' price. The hawker demanded 3-4 times the normal cost and when I tried to bargain asking him to take reasonable amount of money, he made mc absolutely quite and speechless by saying "*huzoor abhi alladh batiya hai isliye ziyada qeemat hai*" (Mylord! It is innocent and young and has just entered adolescences and that is why it costs more). I was pleasantly surprised and paid him more than he was demanding.

The whole style and modus operandi of the hawkers and venders have changed drastically. Instead of carrying the commodity on head in a basket most of them have taken to *thela* (four wheel carriers) on which heavier load could be carried and also increasing the mobility. The literary and poetic invitations have given way to matter of factly announcements. In most of the cases the plight of the *pheriwala* is miserable. In severe winters, rains and scorching summers the poor *pheriwala* may be seen taking rounds on roads, lanes and by lanes walking all the time covering distances as long as twenty kilometers every day. Like other workers in the unorganized sector they don't have any social security. Although serving the people day after day, providing them their necessities on their doorsteps, theirs and their families and dependent's needs remain unfulfilled.

Sanitation Labour

Popularly known as *Mehtar*, *Bhangi* or *Valmiki* have always been socially excluded and marginalized though they have been giving such services to the society without which it could never have survived. Performing scavenging manually refers to the removal of human waste or excreta from such toilets not having a flush system. The job is performed using brooms and plates made of tin. The waste is piled into baskets and carried on heads or holding it with hands resting it on the back. Sometime this abominable burden may have to be carried to a designated place located several kilometers away from the latrines.

Though defying all cannons of human dignity this practice has been going on since times immemorial. Manual scavenging still survives in several parts of India not having proper sewage system. In Lucknow it is still in practice in the lanes and by lanes of the old city. However, the majority of them are now involved in removing garbage from the roads and lanes and sweeping the roads.

The *Valmikis* are a highly organized group and maintain strong kinship and *biradari* ties and have their own caste *panchayat*. According to a conservative estimate around one lakh of them live in Lucknow distributed in more than a dozen *mohallas* and *bastis*. Ambedkar Nagar in Talkatora, Lavkush Nagar in Indira Nagar and Bapu Nagar near KD Singh Babu Sports Stadium are some of their larger settlements. For many *Valmikis*, getting a regular job in the Lucknow Municipal Corporation is their most sought after objective where around four thousand of them are working as *safai karmchari.* (sanitation labour) and around the same number is working in government and private offices. A notable feature of their society is that women play an important role in their family economy.

Because of the stigma of untouchability they are forced to work in the sanitation sector. Only the educated among them, very small in number, get employment in various service sectors taking advantage of reservation meant for Scheduled Castes. Asserting their identity, Valmikis have established a Valmiki Temple near Niralanagar. Majority of them are Hindu while only a small percentage comes from Muslims. Popularly speaking, the Muslim scavengers are known as Hallal Khor or Lal Begi. The sanitation labour, whether Hindu or Muslim demonstrate a high degree of communal harmony and celebrate *Holi, Diwali* and *Moharrum* together. Though living on the margins and socially excluded, the *Valmikis* serve as a spine to the municipal services in Lucknow and elsewhere.

The Feast of Lal Beg : Dalit Religion 'Underground'

—Joel Lee

I was walking along the main *galī* (lane) of a Balmiki neighborhood by the northern bank of the Gomti when a fifty-year-old woman in a dark colored sari, sitting alone on a charpoy, gave me an impassive look, patted the empty space next to her, and said in a tone that would brook no refusal, "*baimho.*" Sit.

I sat. Soon we were joined by a woman of comparable age and an older, heavier woman wielding a bamboo staff freshly whittled, at one end, to a sharp point. This spear was soon to be thrust into a tightly ringed bundle of dried and split date palm fronds to make a *laggājhārū,* a long-handled broom. A short distance away sat old ShyamMehboob1 in his skullcap, sunning his arthritic knees in front of his house. None of the three women around me wore a *bindī, burqā, sindûr*, or other conventional markers of Hindu or Muslim femininity.

We spoke first of labor. The women told me to try to get them regularized, to convert their status in the municipal corporation from contract laborers to permanent employees. No one in their families, they explained, had a permanent position, and only permanent employees enjoyed any kind of security. I told them I had no influence at the municipality, and asked about their grown children, who theoretically ought to be providing for them at this stage. One woman had had eight, six of whom were alive. Do they live here, I asked, or have any moved away? She laughed at my question.

"They're all in England," said the woman next to me on the charpoy.

"They send her money from there," added the woman with the bamboo staff.

"Yes," concluded the first woman, "and my husband lives in Saudi!" The three laughed at their joke. In fact, all six of the woman's children live in the *bastī*, and all are involved in sanitation work.

Some young men wandered over and joined the conversation. It was autumn and various Hindu holidays were soon to occur, as was, this year, Muharram. There were also caste-specific sacred events upcoming: Valmiki Jayanti, the commemoration of the birth of Rishi Valmiki, was only two weeks away, and shortly thereafter would follow Jamghat, the day on which Lal Beg, historically, has been propitiated. Curious how my interlocutors might rank the importance of the various imminent festivals, I asked, "So, are there any *tyauhār*s [holidays, festivals] coming up?"

Immediately one of the young men replied, "Yes, Valmiki Jayanti!"

"When is it?"

"On the first."

"No, friend," interjected another young man, "It's on the eleventh."

"It's on the first of October," insisted the first.

"It's on the eleventh," repeated the second. "Check your calendar again."

While the young men argued the holiday's standing vis-à-vis the Gregorian calendar, I turned to the women, who had not yet said anything about holidays. "Diwali is coming," remarked the mother of six. The three women watched me expectantly, as though they were testing my knowledge of caste tradition.

"And the following day is... Jamghat, yes?" I asked.

The woman with the bamboo staff broke a slight smile. "Yes. On that day–" she then switched semiotic tracks from speech to gesture, moving her straightened right hand through the air as though it were a knife sawing flesh. The pantomime lasted several beats and appeared, as far as she was concerned, to complete the syntagmatic chain she had begun verbally. Then she added, "Cocks will be cut. Liquor will flow."

"In every home?" I asked.

The mother of six answered, "In every home. Cocks and liquor."

In the colonial period and probably well before, a large proportion of the sanitation labor castes – those Dalit castes that perform the vast majority of sanitation labor in South Asia – practiced a religious tradition that, in its liturgy, soteriology, and mythology, understood itself to be distinct from that of the Hindus, Muslims, and Sikhs. This tradition centered on the reverence of Lal Beg, also know as Bala Shah (or Bala Shah Nuri), a prophet (paighambar) or guru who secured admission of his followers into heaven (bihisht), and intervened in the world to improve the conditions of his people. His followers called themselves LalBegi, or in some placesShahi, and honored Lal Beg at their weddings and other life cycle rituals, as well as at an annual festival on the day after Diwali.

In the 1920s in Lahore and Delhi, sections among the LalBegis, encouraged by the Arya Samaj, began to call themselves Valmiki or Balmiki and to identify themselves as Hindu. Advocates of Hinduization claimed that the sanitation labor castes had a genealogical connection with Rishi Valmiki, author of the Ramayana; they repudiated Lal Beg as a Muslim saint, discouraged rites in his honor, andpromoted in their place a new set of religious observances related to Valmiki. The Hinduizing movement reached Lucknow only in the late 1940s, where it won Arya Samaj and Congress patronage – GovindBallabh Pant addressed the inaugural ValmikiJayanti celebration in 1950, Ghanshyamdas Birla funded Lucknow's first Valmiki temple in 1956 – and was accompanied by efforts to reduce alcohol consumption and increase education in the community. What ensued in the following decades was a generational struggle within the community in Lucknow, as many began to adopt Hindu names and practices, to abandon the *deg* for the *bhagaunā*, goat curry for *pûrī-sabzī*, burial for cremation, and Lal Beg for Valmiki, while others resented the assault on caste tradition and maintained the ways of their ancestors. For complicated reasons – including the restriction of state recognition of Scheduled Castes to people who "profess no religion other than the Hindu religion" (in effect, a legal incentive for Dalits with once-common LalBegi names like Farzana and Anwar to become Shanti and Shankar Valmiki in order to access crucial educational scholarships and housing entitlements) in the

Constitution (Scheduled Castes) Order of 1950 – the reformist camp has largely prevailed in resignifying the community as Hindus in a transhistorical sense, as descendants of Rishi Valmiki. In an inverse relationship to the proliferation of Valmiki statues and temples in the city, shrines of Lal Beg, recast by the proponents of Hinduizationas shameful signs of Muslim heritage, have been in many places either demolished or neglected –left to dissolve back into the earth from whence they came.When I arrived in Lucknow in 2011 to conduct research on the history of the sanitation labor castes, I was often told that the old LalBegi ways were a thing of the past; reform had purged the community of such "backward" practices and "superstition." Balmiki leaders assured me that "now nobody does it."

Yet others, like the women I described above, suggested otherwise. Their neighbor Gajendra, a recently retired fourth class employee, told me that the community continued to revere Lal Beg, but not openly. Rather, "we honor him *underground*."

Literally meaning "a dense mass, a crowd, multitude," Jamghat is a name for the day after the primary day of Diwali festivities. On Jamghat in Lucknow, the explosive sonic surround and sulfurous olfactory landscape of the weeks leading up to Diwali continue to prevail – it is another day of firecrackers – but the city's visual appearance is transformed by the widespread tradition, on this day more than others, of flying kites. Historically, asI knew from my research in the colonial archive, this day was also the traditional annual propitiation of Lal Beg. But given the conflicting messages I had heard, I did not know what to expect when the day arrived. Would blood and *bhāng* flow, as the woman with the bamboo staff foretold? Or, as the reformers insisted, would Jamghat in the Balmiki *bastīs* of Lucknow look the same as in the rest of the city: kite-flying and patākhe?

What follows are my notes from Jamghat in 2011.

Early in the morning I find the *bastī* more lively than usual, no doubt largely on account of this day being a holiday from municipal work (and many of the university and KGMC workers, as well as some of the private workers, have also taken leave for the day). The Valmiki temple is open but not busy. While I chat with the temple caretaker and his neighbors sitting on the stoop, a young woman enters the temple and conducts puja on her own. Self-service is the typical mode of worship at the Valmiki temple; there is no priest or pujari. I proceed to the back of the *bastī*. Children in the *galī* greet me with their usual effusive salutations, but today alongside "Namaste!" and "SalāmElekum!" they add, "Happy Diwali!" Jamghat does not have its own special verbal greeting.

In the very back of the *bastī*, just before the high brick wall that separates the Balmiki colony from the gardens and bungalows of awealthy neighborhood, sits the bastī's only remaining outdoor Lal Beg shrine. A few months ago it was easy to overlook – a small square of raised earth abutting the wall of Buggan's house, one of its five domes missing. Lately it has been moved and improved. The shrine now sits adjacent to Buggan's doorway, on a two-tiered, ziggurat-like, square platform of concrete, atop which rise the five domes. The structure is freshly whitewashed. A plastic incense holder sits at the ready on the first tier and nestled between the domes is a necklace of fresh marigolds. Buggan's teenage daughters have designed a *rangolī* of black, red and yellow on the ground next to the shrine, but already a few uncareful footsteps have blurred its powdery lines.

Buggan tells me I'm early. Born in 1958 and raised in his mother's village in Bara Banki, Buggan came to Lucknow with his parents when they sold their mules and small plot of land to work in the city as sweepers (his mother in the municipality, his father in a brewery). Buggan rebuilt the family shrine at their new home in the *bastī* using earth transported from the village original. Though Buggan's family maintains the shrine, it is available for everyone in the *bastī* to use – whether for Jamghat or for the propitiation of Lal Beg that remains, Buggan tells me, part of many weddings.

Not far away sits old Shyam Mehboob, Buggan's neighbor, the one man in the *bastī* who still routinely wears a skullcap. His sons invite me into their house for chai to pass the time before the sacrifices begin. Sukhdev, the younger son, offers an interpretation of the five domes of the Lal Beg shrine that I have not heard before; he suggests that they represent the five elements (*tattvas*) of ether, wind, fire, earth and water. "We can *speculate* that they are thus," cautioned Rajan, Sukhdev's more circumspect older brother, "but what they are, we do not know."

When I return to Buggan's house half an hour later, I find him in the *galī* chatting with a man who holds a rooster in one hand and a steel plate in the other. They tell me that the "cutter" (*kāmnewālā*), the man who will perform the sacrifice, is on his way. Hubert and Mauss designated this figure with the term *sacrificer*, whereas the person for whose benefit the sacrifice is conducted is denoted by *sacrifier* (in French, *sacrificiant*). Most people I have asked do not know the name of the sacrificer, but tell me that he is a Muslim who lives somewhere nearby. Buggan tells me his name is Taj; his next door neighbor thinks it is Sarfaraz.

The cutter is sighted coming down the main *galī*. A slim, clean-shaven man in his forties, thinning grey hair neatly combed, wearing a blue shirt and pressed trousers, his appearance strikes me as that of a minor bureaucrat on his day off. Except for the knife in his right hand. He walks energetically, almost jauntily, toward us, exchanges a few brief words with Buggan, and then sets about his work. Doffing his sandals, he takes from Buggan a polythene bag full of dirt, empties the dirt onto the concrete left of the shrine and shapes it into a mound with a depression at its center to receive the blood. Ignoring the plastic incense holder, he fills a small clay chai cup with dirt in which he will plant the incense sticks to come. He rolls up his sleeves.

The first sacrifice is Buggan's. Barefoot, Buggan and one of his daughters bring out from their house two stainless steel plates – one heaped with garlands of marigolds and a box of incense sticks, the other piled with *malīdā* (shredded *romī* mixed with sugar), sesame sweets, and an oil lamp fashioned out of dough – and a steel pitcher (*lomā*) full of sweetened water topped by a thick, leafy layer of *bhāng*. These they place before the Lal Beg shrine. The sacrificer, squatting, empties the box of incense sticks and lights the entire bundle. Buggan returns with a cock and squats next to the sacrificer, who waves the bundle of smoking incense over the bird and over the shrine several times. He then plants the incense in the soil-filled cup and places one of the marigold garlands over the cock's neck. With Buggan keeping the tense bird restrained, the sacrificer touches its beak to the closest of the five domes. He removes the garland. Then, his lips moving almost soundlessly, the sacrificer mumbles something – later he will explain that it is the *fātiha* – and blows a quick burst of air onto the cock's head.

Taking the bird from Buggan, the sacrificer pins its feet to the ground with one foot and secures its wings with his other knee. Pulling its head back, he applies the humble kitchen knife to the cock's neck in a sawing motion, holding the bird steady as it shivers and spasms and as its blood, after an initial spray against the whitewashed wall, flows into the depression in the pile of earth. A cup of chai appears before my face and I realize that Buggan's neighbor Ramesh is offering it to me, his arms extended over the crowd of women and children sitting around me watching the sacrifice. I thank him and start sipping. Buggan and the sacrificer remain silent and still as the life drains out of the bird.

An old rag picker

A kanmailiya attending to a client on a roadside

An old rickshaw puller pulling a traditional rickshaw

A traditional tonga

A group of brassband players

When the cock is truly dead, the sacrificer wipes the blood from his blade onto the nearest dome of the shrine, marking it a deep maroon, and hands the limp feathery mass back to Buggan, who takes it into his house. The next man in the queue steps forward with his plate, pitcher and cock. The procedure begins again.

By this time a queue of men and boys bearing birds – sacrifiers bearing victims – winds through much of the *galī*. There are girls, too, helping their fathers and brothers carry plates of *malīdā* and *lomās* of *bhāng*. At first women are present mostly as onlookers observing from *galī*-side *charpoys* and balconies, but before long Phulmati, a woman in her fifties, appears with a rooster under her arm. After Phulmati several women join the queue as bearers of sacrificial victims. Generally only one of the adults from a given household comes to perform the sacrifice, frequently accompanied by a child or children, who assist. Excepting the cutter and the victim, whose gender is fixed, the other participant roles in the sacrifice appear unstructured by gender: women offer cocks at the shrine in the same manner as men, girls and boys alike carry the slaughtered birds away.

The collective mood in the *galī* is cheerful, at times raucous. A cock escapes its captor and runs squawking about, prompting general laughter until it is again caught. In the space immediately encircling sacrifier, victim, and cutter, a degree of solemnity prevails; but even here, banalities periodically break through. Seeing a technical difficulty the sacrificer seems to be having, one person and then another comments loudly on the bluntness of his blade. An alternative is produced from a nearby household, then another. Before long four knives lie before the shrine. The cutter gives each of them a try and finally settles on one. The maroon array on the wall above the shrine grows.

With few variations, the sacrificer follows the same procedure for each client. There are, however, minor differences in what the latter brings. Some bring candles rather than incense, and one visibly poor man brings neither. A few people offer sherbet without *bhāng*. *Malīdā* is *de rigeur*, but other food offerings vary: sugar *batāūe*, puffed rice, sweets. Some clients place eleven rupees on the corner of the shrine, others twenty-one. The cutter periodically clears these donations off the shrine and puts them in his pocket.

The consumable offerings are treated as *prasād* and *tabarruk* usually are: a fraction is placed (*malīdā*) or spilled (sherbet) on the shrine and the rest is returned to the sacrifier to be distributed to the family at home.

I lose count after about a dozen sacrifices. It is nearing noon when there is a lull in the traffic. The cutter wipes off his original knife, slips on his flip-flops, and starts off for somewhere. I hasten to accompany him. He tells me, as we stride up the *galī*, that his name is Muhammad Yaqub, that he is Pathan by caste (I do not ask; he volunteers this information), that he has been doing this work for the Lal Begis (as he calls them) for several years, and that he would like to invite me to his home in a neighboring quarter to discuss it all at leisure after all the cutting business is over. At this moment we bump into the very client to whose house we are rushing; it seems that he has decided, despite his earlier arrangement with Yaqub, not to sacrifice at home but at Buggan's shrine, so with the client and his bird we retrace our steps and squat again at the shrine at the rear of the *bastī*. More clients arrive and it becomes apparent that Yaqub will be occupied here for quite some time still.

Friends in the servants' quarters of a large hospital have insisted that I spend at least part of Jamghat with them, so I take leave of Yaqub, Buggan and his neighbors. Departing the bastī I see that the rubbish depots are now covered by a blanket of bird feathers. Some residents are busily preparing the sacrificed birds for this evening's feast, while others – women and men – squat in circles gambling on a card game called *lakrī* ("wood"). I catch a tempo, cross the river, and quickly reach the edge of one of the old city's drains where the servants' quarters are located, and where a boy who recognizes me says *"Andar ho rahāhai! Jāie." It is going on inside! Proceed.*

It – and here the vagueness of the referent is typical, since almost no one denotes the cock sacrifice using words like *qurbān* or *bali*–is indeed going on. There are two public Lal Beg shrines in this colony, both in the back, far from the main road. The first, which abuts the front wall of a home much like Buggan's, has already seen a good deal of action, judging from the pool of blood at its base and the heaps of marigolds, roses, *malīdā, batāūe*, melted candles, blackened lamps and incense ash covering its five domes. Many of the morning's sacrifices took place there. Now, though, activity has shifted to the second shrine, at the base of a tree in a wide spot in the *galī*, where I meet my friend Rishi Kumar, a poet and retired hospital sweeper, who introduces me to the man who performs the sacrifices for this *bastī*. Aftab, also known as Lallan, squats next to the shrine wearing a checkered *lungī*, threadbare kurta and very thick spectacles. He is seventy or eighty years old, he tells me, and has been serving this function for the neighborhood since he was thirteen. He lives in a part of the old city "that is so interior you will never be able to find it," but has spent most of his working life as a roadside barber (*hajām*) at the gate of the dargah of Shah Meena Shah. Clients appear while we are chatting and Aftab resumes his work. His method differs from that of Yaqub; Aftab restricts his labor to handling the bird and cutting its throat, while the client is left to herself to waft the incense, garland the cock, light candles and so on. He also does not blow on the bird's head before killing it. For some clients, Aftab dips his thumb in the drained blood of the sacrificial victim and applies it, in the manner of *tilak*, to the clients' forehead. Though I offer no bird, Aftab spontaneously marks my brow with blood as well. It is warm and viscous. Trained to analyze the *meaning* of ritual, I almost start at its *tactility*.

Someone in a nearby house begins playing Hindi film music very loudly. Mahesh Balmiki, an Ambedkarite critic of Hinduism and "superstition" of all sorts who lives in the *bastī*, shows up and greets me warmly. I am surprised to see that he carries a rooster under his arm. He stands before the shrine, prays, gives the cock to Aftab to sacrifice, receives the blood *tilak*, and returns home with the carcass.

Another client, who is either drunk or stoned, complains in slurred speech when a jet of blood spurts onto his plate of *malīdā* and *batāūe*. Aftab points out that the client should not have placed the plate in the line of fire, as it were. The client grumblingly departs. The next sacrifier, a man dressed in garments of pure white, silently performs a complete prostration before the shrine.

The rites take on a somewhat different color in each *bastī*. In HasanGanj, the sacrificer is not an outsider to the community, but a Lal Begi/Balmiki man who has formally converted to Islam. Seeking to imbue the rites with pedagogical value for his caste fellows, he recites the *fātiha* over the victim not *sotto voce*, like Yaqub and Aftab, but audibly and clearly. In Ali Ganj, sacrifices are performed by a team of Muslim musicians – some call them Dafalis, others qawwals – who add their music to the proceedings. Asha, owner and caretaker of the only remaining outdoor Lal Beg shrine in that *bastī*, tells me that only two families sacrificed here in the morning, a dramatic decline from the previous year. It seems that most families in Ali Ganj now propitiate Lal Beg in the privacy of their homes, while some have stopped performing the rites altogether.

Everywhere, though, the day concludes with a feast. If blood flows in the morning, *bhāng* and liquor flow in the evening. Gambling circles grow, as do the sums exchanged. It is twilight when I encounter Kusmi, a widow who verbally adopted me as her son several months into my fieldwork, leaning on a motorcycle, talking with her neighbors. Her eyes pink with inebriation, she claps me on the shoulder and tells me to join a card game. The air is permeated with the aroma of cooking meat.

By chance I meet a friend, Gyan Akash, a leading figure in Balmiki politics at the municipality whose father was among the most ardent of the Hinduizing reformers. Not two days earlier, Gyan told me that there would be nothing to see on Jamghat; that his father and his colleagues had brought an end to the cult of Lal Beg in Lucknow, that "all of that is finished." Gyan is standing in his doorway, plucking the feathers from a freshly slaughtered cock. "We had the maulana cut it," he tells me. Recalling our conversation from two days ago, and looking at the confusion on my face, he laughs.

Note : [1] In accordance with the recommendations of human research ethics boards, I have changed personal names and names of neighborhoods in order to protect the identity of my interlocutors.

Landmarks

Every city, especially of great historical importance, has its own share of landmarks as part of its heritage. It may include a monument,a market, a library, a bookshop or any other thing which is so closely related with the city that many of the residents cannot imagine their city without these. Besides these,there may also be some objects that help the people to relate themselves with their city and at the same time keep the nostalgia alive. Some such landmarks have been chosen here for special treatment.

6

Landmarks

Coffee House

There are now dozens of restaurants serving coffee and exclusive coffee shops such as Barista or Cafe Coffee day but 'Coffee House' is only one which some Lucknowites call as 'India Coffee House'. Located in Hazratganj, the historic and iconic Coffee House has been a very important landmark during the last 7-8 decades. The Coffee House may be seen as an extension of the tradition of *Baithakbaazi* in Lucknow. Perhaps there is no equivalent term in English language which could exactly convey the nuance of *baaithakbaazi* and *addabaazi.* These are pastimes, prolonged sittings, discussing and gossiping. Kazim Hotel and Red Rose Hotel,two ordinary restaurants in Nakhas area, Abdullah Hotel and Kanchana in Aminabad area and BenBos Restaurant in Hazratganj have been the other places of *baithakbaazi* of intellectuals, poets, writers and politicians but the Coffee House had no parallel.

Established sometime in 1940s by the Coffee Board, it was along with other similar ventures of the Board in some other cities converted into a cooperative venture of its workers when the Coffee Board wound up all such outlets. Lucknow's Coffee House started running as cooperative since 1958. It is difficult to name all the prominent persons from different spheres of life who have been sitting here regularly but even a summarized list of celebrities may give one some idea of its importance. The very names such as Acharya Narendra Dev and Ram Manohar Lohia may create awe.

Among the literary figures, Amrit Lal Nagar, Yashpal, Bhagwati Charan Verma, and Majaaz are just a few names while among the politicians celebrities like Z A Ahmad, K M Ashraf, Firoze Gandhi, Chandra Shekhar, Narain Dutt Tewari, Veer Bahadur Singh, Sibte Razi, Janeshwar Misra, Lalji Tondon and many others have been regular visitors. Bishan Kapoor, Vidya Sagar Gupta, S M Jafar and several others have also been addicted to Coffee House. Among Urdu Literary figures, apart from Majaz, HayatUllah Ansari, Abid Suhail, Iqbal Majeed, Ram Lal, Satish Batra, Salaam Machlishehri and Bisheshar Pradip were regular *baithakbaaz.* A mix of very senior and relatively less senior intellectuals and literary figures such as Mudra

Rakshas, Ravindra Verma, Ramesh Dixit, Pradip Kapoor, Virendra Yadav, Rakesh, Shakil Siddiqi and others may still be seen here engrossed in serious discussions and so are politicians such as Amir Haidar, Ibne Hasan and several others.

Pradip Kapoor (2012) in his booklet on Coffee House tells that among prominent politicians, CB Gupta and Charan Singh never sat in Coffee House as thcy believed that the *baithakbaaz* of coffee House were involved in conspiracies against them. Passing through several closures and disputes, it still continues its journey but the old sheen is gone along with the old furniture and menu. Gradually and gradually it is turning into any other restaurant or coffee/ tea house but the nostalgia survives.

Amiruddaula Public Library

Like many crumbling monuments, scattered all around, are wailing, another rare heritage- Amiruddaula Public Library is crying for more care and protection Now

Amiruddaula Public Library

located in *Qaiser Bagh* amidst lush green trees in the backdrop of *Safed Baradari*, was established in 1882 and after being transferred several times, found a permanent place in 1921-its present building.

Named after Amirud Daula Saeedul Mulk of Mahmudabad it is an extra ordinary library. *Anjuman-e-Hind (Awadh),* the association of *Taluqdars* of *Awadh,* conceptualized the prized library way back in 1904. Maharaja Mahmudabad was the moving spirit behind a number of other intellectual centres including University of Lucknow. The Anjuman collectively and Mehmudabads individually donated huge amounts of money for the up keep and purchase of books. Their contributions may be seen in the book 'Tareekh-Anjuman-e-Hind-Awadh' written by Khan Bahadur Sheikh Siddique Ahmad who was the assistant secretary of the Anjuman.

Though, currently the library is in much better shape than before a lot more needs to be done. Because of neglect and poor up keep a number of books were lost. The great grandson of one of the founders of the library Raja Mohammad Amir Mohammad Khan, popularly known as Raja Mahmudabad, lamenting the poor health of the library due to its neglect by the state government wants this historical store house of rare manuscripts to be handed over to the Centre before it is completely lost.

Rare manuscripts in Sanskrit, Arabic Persian, Urdu, Hindi, Pali and Tibetan and Buddhist literature written on palm leaves are the treasured possession of this library and its contemporary literature collection attract even foreign scholars. Some of the manuscripts are as old as going back to the 17th century.

A new and prized possession was added to the library recently. In 2001, Rani Ram Kumar Bhargava, the then head of the family of the descendents of Late Pundit Naval Kishore made an offer of donating the entire collection of books in Arabic, Persian, Urdu, Sanskrit and Hindi published by Naval Kishore Press on the condition that the books and other material such as the old printing machine and other items are kept in a separate section of the library named after him. Finally, this arrangement could be done in October 2005. It was followed by the publication of the separate catalogue of these books with the grant given by the National Archive.

Amiruddaula Public Library is such a valuable store house of knowledge for the researchers that both the State as well as the Central government must do whatever they can to preserve this library. Otherwise like several other wailing ,crumbling landmarks, it may also be lost to us. And if it happens, it will be big big loss.

Bengali Club

There has been a strong presence of the Bengali Community in Lucknow. By the turn of the 21st century they may be described as the second or third largest community of Bengali speaking people in India outside West Bengal. They have enriched the Lucknow culture in a veriety of ways. Their landmark in Lucknow has been the Bengali Club located near Latouche Road. With the passage of time it has became a landmark of Lucknow too.

The Bengali Club was founded in 1892 and happens to be the oldest club in the city and the mother organization of the entire Bengali community of Lucknow. It had the privilege of honouring Netaji Subhash Chandra Bose in 1938. The Club is known for staging a member of plays, movies, lectures, social gatherings and above all Durga Puja. In 2014, celebration of Durga Puja completed 100 years since its inception. Though the golden period of Bengali Club is over, it is so much integrated with Lucknow and the local Bengali community that it is impossible to think of Bengalis of Lucknow without the Bengali club.

Karamat Button House

Lucknow has produced several imaginative and innovative persons who pioneered in a variety of arts and crafts. Could anybody think that as far back as 1920s a person could visualize a business in buttons? Late Ataullah Khan was such a person who had struck an idea specializing in a business which, though very crucial in clothing,was restricted to only a few places in India.He entered into this trade and made his small shop Karamat Button House a landmark in Lucknow.

In 1922, Nazirabad, in the Aminabad area, was a small market having only a few shops. An enterprising person opened a small shop dealing with sale of oil lamps and within a few years switched over to sale of buttons and threads mainly required by tailors. Gradually and gradually Karamat Button House added all other things required for stitching clothes yet their fame in buttons remains unparalleled. Beginning with army uniform buttons, it has now an amazing variety of buttons priced from 50 paise to more than 500 rupees per button. Though all these items are required throughout the year, their grandsons now running the shop ,are of the view that winters are their most profitable season. It is such a reliable and famous name that people come rushing from the other districts too, to get the buttons of desired type and colour. They also sell a variety of cuff links though its requirement is now confined to the elite class or connoisseurs. It is not possible for Lucknowites to talk of buttons and forget Karamat Button House.

Danish Mahal

This book shop catering to the requirements of book lovers in Urdu literature continues as a landmark at a time when most of the book shops keeping books in Urdu on a variety of subjects including literature have switched over to selling books on Islam and the related fields. Danish Mahal seems to be the last abode for the connoisseurs of Urdu literature-prose and poetry both. Very imaginatively named as Danish Mahal (place of wisdom) by its founder Late Naseem Ahmad in 1939, situated on the ground floor in the verandah of Zameer Mansion Opposite the Aminabad Park, comes as a pleasant surprise when one enters into it and finds the ambience so serene,peaceful and harmonious though surrounded by the humdrum and chaotic traffic from all sides caused mainly by the auto rickshaws.

Danish Mahal is not merely a book shop but a 'book adda' too. With a couple of sofa sets with a central table and some chairs kept neatly in the centre one can select the books from the glass shelves himself, sit down and browse before deciding which one to buy or not to buy at all. Two gentlemen sitting behind the counter, one being the son of the founder who has inherited the passion of his late father for Urdu books, not only sell the books but may also help you in case a book is out of print. During the life time of late Naseem Ahmad, one could see the gathering of the stalwarts of Urdu literature such as Masood Hasan Rizvi Adeeb, Ehtesham Husain, Jafar Ali Khan Asar, Raza Ansari of Firangi Mahal, Ali Abbas Husaini and novelists Ram Lal, Ratan Singh, Bisheshar Pradeep etc. Late Naseem Ahmad was a living encyclopedia of Urdu literature who could also help the researchers in a variety of ways. There used to be weekly literary meets and sometime it was difficult to find a place to sit.

It speaks of the passion of the successors of the late founder when they continued with this book shop instead of winding it up and opening a more profitable business in the most popular commercial hub of Lucknow. Almost every Urdu knowing person settled in Europe, USA or elsewhere does not miss the opportunity of visiting Danish Mahal even during a short visit to Lucknow. Every book lover of Urdu literature wishes and prays for the long life of this book shop which is like an institution at a time when the plight of Urdu language in Uttar Pradesh is far from rosy.

Ram Advani Book Seller

Like the legendry Danish Mahal, a haven for the book lovers of Urdu literature, Ram Advani Book Seller or RAB is a place for English books . Both are not ordinary bookshops in the usual sense of the term. These are institutions in themselves and for the connoisseur a source of joy. Situated in a quiet corner of now defunct Mayfair Cinema verandah with a simple sign board displaying 'Ram Advani Book Seller', one enters into a serene space in the hum drum of now very busy Hazratganj. When the glassdoor is closed behind you, you were welcomed, till some years ago, by a silver haired man with glasses and led to a book shelf where your desired book was resting. Now in his nineties he mostly sits in the inside cabin but always ready to come out to help and guide you. Ram Advani, an epitome of Lucknawi culture, comes from a family of book sellers, very unlike Sindhis who never considered book selling a very profitable venture. Initially housed in a corner in the Gandhi Ashram, it opened in 1948. After sometimes he had to move to the present location.

The Advanis had their shop in Lahore with branches in Rawalpindi and Nainital and later in Simla. His father and Seth Gyan Chand Thadani of Mayfair Cinema came to Lucknow in 1920s to explore a new world and that is how Lucknow became the home of legendry Ram Advani. Right from the beginning his bookshop specialized in Islam, Lucknow and Anthropology and that is why whoever having

The legendary Ram Advani
Picture courtesy-David Lelyveld, via CM Naim

any interest in any of these areas or religion and cultures in general has been a compulsive visitor to this bookshop. I met several famous anthropologists such as Harold Gould and made friends with several others such as Keith Hjorshoj of Cornell and Peter Vander Veer of Amsterdom. His wife, too, holds a masters degree in Anthropology from the University of Lucknow.

Ram Advani has always been choosy about which books to find a place in its show case irrespective of margin of profit. This along with his penchant for the rarest of the rare book makes it a unique bookshop.

P. S. *While this book was entering the process of printing, Ram Advani, the iconic bookseller, passed away on 9 March, 2016 at the age of 95. He was a lot more than merely a bookseller. As commented by many, what made him unique was that he allowed even the cash starved book lovers to browse-a concept unknown in Lucknow in 1950s and 60s. Needless to say, Ram Advani meant a lot to Lucknow. In his demise, Lucknow has lost an institution.*

Arts College

True to the spirit of makers of modern Lucknow this institution is yet another 'jewel in the Crown'. Popularly called as 'Arts college' it has made its journey from the College of Arts and Crafts to Lucknow College of Arts and Crafts and finally to the Faculty of Fine Arts in the University of Lucknow. Yet the Lucknowites continue to remember it simply as Arts College.

The history of Arts College is worth knowing. Established as the School of Industrial Design in 1892 at Wingfield Manzil near Banarsi Bagh area, presently Lucknow Zoo, moved to Aminabad, then to Baans Mandi and finally to its present building in 1909 on the University Road in the vicinity of the famous Islamic Seminary Nadwa and Lucknow University. Initially headed by the Britishers the emphasis was on western realism but after 1925 when several Indian stalwarts joined it, Indian Arts were also included in the curriculum. In the year 1975 the Arts College merged with the University of Lucknow as a constituent college. Not only diploma courses were converted into degree courses but there began a clear demarcation of under- graduate and post-graduate courses.

Painting, Applied Arts and Sculpture have been the strongest areas of Arts College. Fully equipped workshops of graphics, ceramics, photography, wood work, Iron and heavy metal work and computer graphics and studios for painting, sculpture and commercial art, along with a good library and museum make it a unique institution. In the recent decades AS Panwar, Mohammad Haneef, RS Bisht, Y N Verma and some others brought new laurels for this institution.

Bhatkhande Music College

Lucknow has always boasted of having a tradition of fine arts, poetry and other forms of literature. Located in the Qaiser Bagh area it has a glorious past. Established in 1926 as Marris College of Music, it witnessed a number of ups and downs. The renowned classical singer and musicologist Vishnu Narain Bhatkhande established it in 1926. The then education minister of the United Provinces, Rai Rajeshwar Bali, a connoisseur of music helped Bhatkhande in this venture and it was inaugurated by the then Governor of United Provinces William Marris and the music college was named after him as a mark of gratitude.

By the time the government of Uttar Pradesh took over the college in 1966, on the demand of music lovers, the college had already achieved fame nationally and internationally. After it was taken over by the state government, it was renamed as Bhatkhande Music College. In the year 2000, the Bhatkhande music college was declared as a deemed university and qualified for the much needed grants from the University Grants Commission. It became a complete music university when it included the teaching of Western Classical Music. The purists of Indian classical music did not like as they feared that its character as the exclusive college of traditional Indian music could get diluted and even be dominated by the western music in future. It has separate departments of Vocal (*Gaayan*), instrumental (*Vaadan*), dance, musiology and research and offers courses from diploma level to Ph.D. degree. Among the famous alumni produced by it are Pahari Sanyal, Talat Mahmood, Roshan, Begum Akhtar, Swati Mutakkar and others. Its current Vice Chancellor Shruti Sadolkar is herself an accomplished musician.

The presence of such an institution not only makes the government proud but also elevates the city in the eyes of the music lovers throughout the world.

Rifah-e-Aam Club

Literally meaning 'public good', Rifah-e-Aam Club is yet another heritage building and a landmark crying for preservation and restoration. Located near City Station, Golaganj on Jagat Narain Road, this building is of great historical importance. The Club was established sometime around 1860 when the members of the erstwhile royal family of Awadh and big taaluqdars and zamindars, recovering from the tremors of 1857, wanted a place for some recreation during the monotonous and depressing evenings as they were not allowed membership in the United Services Club at Chatar Manzil, an exclusive domain of the British.

Among other things the Club had a billiard and bridge room and a bar and later it also developed an indoor wooden badminton court that hosted a number of prestigious tournaments. The author is witness to badminton matches in 1960s and 1970s. It also had a small but rich library and reading room and often used for carrying out some charity work whenever exigencies emerged.

Rifah-e-Aam Club has been a witness to some great historical moments. During 1905 it served as a venue for meetings of Swadeshi Movement and also of Muslim League. The historical Lucknow Pact between the Indian National Congress and Muslim League was signed here in 1916. It is said that Mahatma Gandhi and Jawahar Lal Nehru met here for the first time. They, along with Gangadhar Tilak, met here on 15 October, 1920. Moreover, the historical founding session of Progressive Writers Association was held on its lawns in 1936. It was presided over by the great Urdu –Hindi writer Munshi Prem Chand. The entire galaxy of progressive poets and writers of Urdu, Hindi and other languages had assembled here. It was the beginning of a new type of literature and a protest against orthodoxy, religious fanaticism and capitalist system and its' evils.

Unfortunately, this unique building of great historical importance has fallen on the worst days of its' existence. It is so dilapidated that it may not survive heavy rains any more, the lawns have been encroached and private buses are being parked and as the night falls it comes under the control of anti-social and criminal elements. The 'heritage route' passes from its' vicinity with lots of properly maintained buildings with plaques narrating the eventful days and events and it will also attract a number of tourists. If the Government of Uttar Pradesh and Archaeological Survey of India do not take the desired steps, this heritage may be lost forever.

Local Fairs and Festivals

Besides other fairs and festivals being of Pan-Indian nature, Lucknow has several other fairs and festivals specific to the city. These add variety to the cultural life of Lucknow. Of such local festivals, Bada Mangal, celebrated on all the Tuesdays of the month of *Jeshtha*, is a unique local festival accompanied by fairs. This festival is dedicated to Hanuman and under the patronage of the Nawabs of Awadh it became the most important local festival representing Hindu-Muslim harmony. *Aathon Ka Mela* dedicated to Sheetla Maata is also a typically Lucknawi festival, as well as some others described in this chapter.

7

Local Fairs and Festivals

Yeh zindagi ke mele duniya me kum na honge, afsos hum na honge.
(All these fairs and festivals would be there but I wont' be there to see them)

Besides several regional and all India festivals Lucknow can boast also for some local fairs and festivals specific to the city. Some are more religious and less of cultural value while the others are more cultural than religious in nature. One thing that has been a hallmark of these occasions is active participation of all religious communities, yet another example of the composite culture described as *Ganga-Jamuni Tehzeeb*. Following are the brief descriptions of these local fairs and festivals.

Bada Mangal

Bada Mangal is most important and most popular among the local festivals. It is celebrated on every Tuesday falling in the month of *Jeshtha* of the Hindu Calender which usually coincides with May-June every year. *Bada Mangal* is devoted to Hanuman and celebrated on a very large scale. Though it is celebrated in all the Hanuman temples of the city but the main celebrations are held at the Naya Hanuman Mandir, followed by Purana Hanuman Mandir, both in the Aliganj area, Hanuman Mandir at Hanuman Setu opposite Lucknow University, and Hanuman Mandir at Chhachhi Kuan. Long ques of devotees may be seen beginning from the wee hours of Tuesday till the midnight. The devotees perform *darshan* and offer *prasad.*

During the last 2-3 decades the celebrations have proliferated and multiplied to such an extent that now 3-4 thousand *bhandaras.* (distribution of free food and beverages) are being held. Beginning with just *sharbat*, it diversified to *puri-subzi* and now lot of variety has been added. One may see noodles, ice cream, *laddoo* and several other eatables. At some points Muslims may also be seen distributing *sharbat.*

Those four or five Wednesday mornings (depending upon the astrological calculations) witness heaps and heaps of disposable plates, glasses and *pattals,* strewn over the entire city on virtually every cross road and in front of Hanuman temples. Some passionate devotees make a journey from their home to the Aliganj temple by rolling down the roads to seek blessing of Lord Hanuman for the fulfillment of their wishes or as a form of penance under the scorching summer heat of Lucknow.

The festival is also described as a symbol of Hindu-Muslim unity and harmony. Several legends are prevalent about the construction of the *Naya* and *Purana* Hanuman Mandir. According to one legend it was in 1718 when the queen Alia Begum of Nawab Shujauddaula discovered two statues of Hanuman during the construction for a regal building and got these installed and facilitated construction of what is now known as Purana Hanuman Mandir. Naming her son as 'Mirza Mangloo' after the deity she also started the tradition of a fair on Bada Mangal known as *Bade Mangal Ka Mela* in Aliganj.

Another legend is related with the wife of the Nawab Muhammad Ali Shah who got her child cured with the blessings of Lord Hanuman. Besides making offering to the temple she also arranged a fair on the suggestion of the priest as it could bring economic prosperity to the people, of this region. Since then the tradition of observing Bada Mangal is being followed along with a fair around the temple. Yogesh Pravin, a historian/chronicler of Lucknow, maintains that this Hanuman temple is the only temple in India with a crescent and star on its dome, and it was built as a mark of gratitude to the Nawabs who were also very benevolent towards the Hanuman temples and the Hanuman cult.

Ganga Snan Mela

The Ganga Snan Mela is one of the few local events that have continued for several hundred years without break. Even the nature of the *Mela* has not changed much over these years despite massive urbanization that has taken place over the last hundred years or so. Millions of devotees take a holy dip in Ganga on the day of Kartik Purnima but in Lucknow this day coincides with a fair of indigenous arts and crafts.

It is in fact a 'folk mela'. It is held over an area, near Gomti, spread over Bansmandi, Suraj Kund, and Moongphali Mandi, on the Nabiullah Road and extends right upto the City Station. Traditionally, it attracted predominantly lower class of neighbouring villages but gradually it started attracting the suave, urban middle and upper classes who look forward to this fair for 'ethnic items'. While it is organized on a Hindu festival a large number of shop keepers are Muslims coming from Kanpur, Lakhimpur, Saharanpur and other places. Clay toys, glass toys, pottery, wooden handicrafts, spices, a variety of eatables from *chaat* to *makhan/burf malai*, and house hold items of everyday use are available on much cheaper prices. Some of the shops continue for several days while many wind up and move away.

Chandrika Devi Ka Mela

Chandrika Devi Ka Mela is yet another local fair held around Maa Chandrika Devis's Temple situated in village Kathwara on Sitapur Road in Bakshi Ka Taalaab. This 300 years old temple is well known for the deity Chandrika Devi, a form of goddess

Durga. During the months of March and November coinciding with Amavasya and Navratri a huge *Mela* is held around the temple. Largely local in nature, people of all ages flock to it especially womenfolk for *tikuli-bindi*(pip), *sindoor*(vermillion), *choori*(bangles), *Jhumka*(ear rings), spices, herbs for various purposes, foodgrains, toys, utensils and other utility goods. Either fed up with their urban lives or in search of anything 'folk' or 'ethnic', hundreds of city people also flock to it and do shopping.

Aathon ka Mela

Aathon ka Mela is organized at the Sheetla Devi Temple. It is one of the oldest *devi* temples in Lucknow. The temple is situated in Mehdiganj Mohalla near Tikait Rai Ka Talaab at Talkatora Road. The temple witnesses each year the famous *Aathon ka Mela* held every year on the eight day of Holi. The fair is also known as *Sheetla Ashtami Mela.* Since Sheetla Ashtami is a local holiday and offices and schools are closed on this day, it attracts a large number of people who go for *darshan* of the devi first and then enjoy the fair. Lasting for two days it is visited by the newly wed couples in large numbers since it is a popular belief that visit to this temple is very auspicious for the newly weds.

Buddeshwar Ka Mela

Buddeshwar Ka Mela is held every year through the month of Saawan. It is related with the temple of the deity Buddeshwar Mahadav located on Mohaan Road. As per a legend Ram, Sita and Lakshman while going into *Vanwaas* stopped here on a wednesday and worshipped Lord Shiva and hence the temple is called Buddheswar Mahadev Temple.

The local administration organizes and supervises this fair spread over more than 2 kilometers around the temple. Besides all kinds of utility and fancy items it also provides lot of recreation especially for the rural folk in the form of cultural shows, swings, and rural sports.

It is worth mentioning that all the events described here had some role or patronage of the Nawabs of Awadh. Since several of the Nawab's close advisers, ministers and friends were Hindu they directly or through these Nawabs played an important role in the renovation or construction of this and several other temples. They were very fond of music and entertainment. They encouraged, helped and patronized such events as fairs and festivals adding lasting chapters of *Ganga-Jamuni Tehzeeb.*

Festivals of Non- Religious Nature

In the recent decades Lucknow has added some fairs and festivals of absolutely non-religious nature. This has added a new dimension to festivities providing opportunity to Lucknowites to express their creativity in a variety of ways adding a new flavour and spice to social life of the city.

Lucknow Festival

Lucknow Festival now called as 'Lucknow Mahotsava' began in 1975-76. The underlying idea behind it was to do something for the restoration and maintenance of Lucknow's culutre and tradition in a scenario when more than 60% of Lucknow's present population now consist of immmigrants from other districts of Uttar Pradesh and even from outside the state. It was also to provide to the new generation a glimpse of the glorious past for which Awadh was known throughout the world.

In the initial years Lucknow Festival presented a sparkling showcase of the arts, crafts, the wonderful cuisine and mannerism of Lucknow, the heart of Awadh. Colourful processions, traditional dramas, Kathak, various music forms of Lucknow gharana, ghazals and qawwalis, tonga race, kite flying etc. were the hallmarks of this festival. People, especially coming from outside, were fascinated.

With passage of time Lucknow Festival was transformed into 'Lucknow Mahotsava'. Though it continues to be held during November-December organized jointly by UP Tourism and Lucknow District Administration, the 'Lucknowness' got diluted.

Now you don't see a word in Urdu language not even on the entry gate of the venue. Craftsmen and venders from other districts and even from outside Uttar Pradesh are dominating the show. The popular participation decreases and the stranglehold of bureaucracy and officialdom are now complete. Gradually and gradually it is turning into yet another 'Sarkari Mela'.

Lucknow Book Fair

Lucknow Book Fair fulfills a long felt need of the book lovers of the city. Though National Book Fair is held every second year in Delhi with hundreds of publishers and distributers from India and other countries exhibiting and selling their publications, it was not possible for every book lover of Lucknow to visit it. When two agencies took up the task of organizing a book fair, now held every year on Moti Mahal Lawns, Lucknowites were delighted especially students and children. On the lines of the National Book Fair, it also organizes book release, interaction with authors, and recitation of poetry in Hindi and Urdu and discussions on the problems of publishing industry. Though not even a decade old these book fairs have received encouraging response from the readers. Sometimes an exclusive book fair of Urdu, though on a much smaller scale, is also held by some other agency.

Uttarayni Mela

Uttarayni Mela coinciding with Makar Sankranti, a fair is organized for a week portraying the cultural heritage of the Hills-Kumaon and Garhwal. Lakhs of people from the hills have been living in Lucknow for generations and the creation of a separate state of Uttarakhand could not change the social demography of Lucknow. Most of these people continued to live here not opting to settle down there despite the fact that many of them still have land and property there. In order to keep the *Pahadi Sanskriti* (hill's culture) alive they started the *Uttarayni Mela* under the auspices of Parvatiya Maha Parishad, Lucknow. In the first few years it was held in a park in Mahanagar but soon the space was cramped and it was moved to the river bank to accommodate the increasing number of people and shops. This fair showcases the food, herbs and spices, dress, folk song and dance-theatre of Uttarakhand. The Governments of Uttarakhand and Uttar Pradesh collaborate in organizing it. It provides an excellent opportunity for the local people to get introduced to *Pahaari* Culture.

Religious/Spiritual Centers

Lucknow is a multi-religious society and that is why its religious mosaic is adorned by a number of Temples, Gurudwaras, Churches, Mosques, Imambadaas, Karbalas, Mazaars and Maqbaraas. Several of these religious/spiritual centers exhibit the composite culture of Lucknow and add a fascinating variety of interface between different castes and religious groups.This chapter describes some of the lesser known temples and other religious centres.Religious institutions such as Nadwa and Firangi Mahal have also put Lucknow on the international map.

8

Religious/ Spiritual Centres

Temples

Surya Mandir

One of the ancient and the only Sun Temple of the state is believed to be almost 1100 years old which was constructed by Baba Ramdas. Situated next to Indira Gandhi Planetarium on the T joint of Nabiullah Road and Mahatma Ganndhi Marg near Daliganj crossing, this temple has a pond having medicinal importance and is believed to have its roots in Dvapar yug (the third age of the mythological Hindu world cycle, the period when Lord Krishna lived on this earth) occurred between Treta and Kalyug, the second and the fourth age of Hindu world cycle. As the legend goes the pond known as *Surya Kund* was created when Bhagwan Vishnu's chakra hit the ground so deep that water came up. Incidentally it's not out of the reference to quote here that the same legend is associated with the creation of Naimisharanya, an important Hindu pilgrimage centre in Sitapur district which is around 110 Km. away from this place.

During the regime of Nawab Asaf-ud-daula this pond and its *ghaats* (wharfs) were renovated. After ages, again this temple drew the attention of Bal Bramhchari Baba Shiv Shankar Ardhnarishwar Jangam whose efforts renovated and beautified it once again. Jangam Baba is said to be in deep meditation since 1980. People believe that by taking bath in this pond most of the sufferings and diseases are cured. Specially on Sundays devotees visit this temple to pay their obeisance to Lord Sun who is riding on a seven horse chariot. Shani and other devi-devtaas also find place with their small idols. Every year on 28th December *yagna*, *akhand ramayan* (the tradition of chanting the verses of Goswami Tulsi Das's Sri Ram Charit Manas from begining till the end without break) and a *bhandara* is organized here. A Neem and a Banyan tree embracing each other is another unique feature of this place and such spots are good for meditation as it is widely believed even in the Buddhism.

Mari Maata Mandir

Situated on the bank of river Gomti near Lal Pul which is also known as Pukka Pul and Nawabi Pul (bridge), this temple is considered to be one of the old temples of city. The name Mari Mata (dead goddess) has a myth behind its name. Lord Shiva was not invited in the *yagna* organized by his father in law Raja Daksh where all other gods and goddesses were duly invited. But as requested by his wife Sati the daughter of Raja Dakhsh ,Lord Shiva had gone there but he was insulted by Raja Daksh. Sati got upset with her father's behavior so much so that she immolated herself in *yagna* fire. Though considered dead, Sati who is a symbol of power In Hindu faith and belief is worshipped as Mari Mata (dead goddess) in this temple.

The temple is believed to have come into existence well before the construction of Pukka Pul and the Rajak (washer men) community is said to have got it constructed whose representatives still look after the temple. Initially the temple was limited to a platform where Mata ki Pindi (a round or oval shape piece of stone) was there for worship. Rajak and other dalit communities used to hold their panchyats here in which various social and related issues were discussed, sorted out, decisions made and the judgment pronounced. The money collected through fine as a punishment was utilized in the management and maintenance of the temple. In 1955 the UP Rajak Sudhar Samiti (washermen welfare committee) took up the task of its development through extension and construction. Presently, the triangular premise of around 8000 sq. feet has Mari Mata as its main deity along with other Hindu gods/goddesses like Durga, Kali, Bhairon Baba, Shanidev, Ram Darbar and Hanuman. Sant Gadge's statue is also there which is a clear indicator of its being predominantly Rajak community's (washer men) place of worship. Till 1955 only the dalit and backward community visited the temple but gradually all the communities started offering prayers and pooja in its premise. Maintained by the Mari Mata Utthan Samiti the temple is visited by people hailing from various faiths and beliefs.

Shiv Shakti Sai Mandir

Considered to be the first Sai temple of Uttar Pradesh this temple in Bada Chand Ganj is popularly known as Kapoorthala Sai Mandir. As an old Shiv temple is also housed in the same premises the temple is termed as Shiv Shakti Sai Mandir as well. Thursday is believed to be the most auspicious day and huge crowd of devotees visit the temple. Along with the regular activities throughout the year, a *shobha yatra* (procession in honour of Sai Baba) takes place where in a special palanquin devotees carry Sai Baba on their shoulders. This is an annual event taking place on 15th February every year culminating in a *bhandara* offering Prasad to all and sundry.

Gulacheen Mandir/Panch Mukhi Hanuman Temple

While going towards north from Kapoorthala crossing on Kursi Road, just before the right turn for Vikas Nagar, on the left, one can spot an imposing structure of a temple known as Gulacheen or Panch Mukhi Hanuman Temple. Surrounded by the woods a small idol of Lord Hanuman placed under a Gulacheen tree was worshipped and when a temple building came into existence it became popular as Gulacheen Temple. The idol of Lord Hanuman, which has five faces, is the main deity of this temple thus acquiring another name the Panch Mukhi Hanuman Mandir. Managed by Mahant Bhagwan Das one can also see Durga, Sai Baba, Ram-Janki-Lakshman, Radha-Krishna and a Shiva Lingum. Tuesday and Saturday draw large number of devotees. In the month of Jeth every Tuesday and on Kartik Poormina (full moon of the eighth month of Hindu calendar) bhandaras are organized to mark these auspicious occasions. The story behind the Panchmukhi Hanuman is that when he went to Paataal Lok (in Indian mythology there is a kingdom below the earth known as Paataal) and killed Ahiravan the king of Paatal Lok and the brother of Ravana to save Rama-Laxman he appeared with five faces representing five deities.

Raidas Mandir

'Jo mun changa to kathauti mein Ganga'

(If the soul is free of sin, water is as pious as Ganga even in a small bin).

Once on the kartik poormia i.e.full moon in Kartik the eighth month of the Hindu calendar also known as Ganga Snan (auspicious day for taking holy dip in Ganga] people going to bath in Ganga asked Sant Ravi Das to join. He was busy finishing the shoes he had to deliver in time he said, *Jo mun changa to kthauti mein Ganga.*' Raidas Mandir, adjacent to the railway tracks connecting Charbagh and Badshah Nagar now stands below the Raidas Mandir railway over bridge between IT crossing and Kapoorthala crossing. The temple was constructed by the cobbler community with their collective efforts in 1924 and is oldest among the three Raidas temples of Lucknow. Dedicated to Sant Ravi Das who was a disciple of Guru Ramanand and a contemporary of Kabir, this temple every year observes his birth anniversary by organizing bhandara and *shobha yatra* (eulogizing march). One can see the sketches of Guru Nanak Dev, Kabir and surprisingly Parashuram on the entrance with Ravi Das's big statue inside. The temple is presently looked after by Baba Tikai Das's widow Smt. Parvati who devoted his entire life to this temple. There is no trust or committee. The daily affairs are managed and taken care of with the rent received from the shops in temple building. On the first floor of the temple there is B.R. Ambedkar Hostel for Dalit students managed by the temple itself.

Mankamneshwar Temple

Situated in the Daliganj area on the bank of river Gomti this is one of the most important and ancient Shiva temple of Lucknow. Considerd to be 800-1000 year old Makameshwar Mandir, as it is popularly known, is visited by large number of devotees throughout the year. The *shiva ling* is believed to have been installed by the Thuthher (metal potters) community. The people of this community regularly visited Kudia Ghaat of Gomti and once they found a shiva ling during the bath. Scared and confused they left it there only and changed the ghaat for their daily chores. As the story goes Lord Shiva appeared in their dream and asked them to install the ling. The thuthhers followed the order and made a small temple which came to be known as thuthheron ka shiv mandir (Shiva temple of metal potters). Gradually, this shrine became quite popular among devotees for answering their prayes and fulfilling their manokamna (wishes) thus attaining the name Makameshwar Mandir.

Presently it's a grand temple thronged by huge number of people from all sects and communities especially on Mondays and particularly during the Sawan ke Somvar (Mondays in the month of Shravan, the fifth month of Hindu calendar), Maha Shivaratri and Nag Panchami. The small temples of Durga, Hanuman, Sita-Ram, Kali and Bhairav are also there within the premises of Mankameshwar Mandir. The most remarkable feature is a woman, mahant Divyagiri, being the head of the temple. The trust is continuously engaged in various social works and a library in the temple bears testimony to this approach.

Maha Saraswati Temple

This temple housing the goddess of knowledge and art Maata Saraswati was established by Swami Purushottam Nand at Shukla Ghat of river Gomti. Vasant Panchami, the fifth day of the second half of Magh (eleventh month of the Hindu calendar) is the most auspicious occasion when the pen is worshipped here along with other traditional pooja. On Kartik poornima (the full moon day of Kartik, the eighth month of Hindu calendar) Gangotsav (Ganga festival) is another important feature of this temple.

Shiva Temple - Mohanlalganj

Nineteen kilometers away from Lucknow towards south west this temple has derived its name Kashishwar Mahadev from Kashi Prasad, the person who is said to have constructed it in 1860. A peculiar example of Hindu architecture, this temple along with the Shivaling, a necessary feature for a Shiva temple, has a Nandi (ox, the carrier of Shiva) and eight *Shivalas* (house of Lord Shiva). Its top is decorated with Rudraksh. Like other Shiva temples every Monday and the Mondays falling during the month of Sawan, Nag Panchami and Shivaratri are the important occasions.

Kali Bari Temple

One hundred and fifty years old Kali Bari was established by Madhusudan Mukkhopadhyaya when "Ma Kali ordered him to erect her temple with the same looks and features as she appeared in his dream." Situated in narrow lanes of Ghasiyari Mandi locality on Cantonment Road,this temple is a very important center of worship among the Bengalis but people from various communities visit Kali Bari to offer their prayers. Kali Pooja, Durga Pooja and Vasant Panchami are the most auspicious festivals. Saturday is an important day when number of devotees increases many folds and once the prayers are answered they offer hibiscus flower and symbolically sacrifice Jack fruit, coco nut, sugarcane etc as sacrificing goat is no more in practice. Fish, brinjals and other dishes are cooked and offerd to Ma Kali as *bhog*.

Vaishno Devi Temple

The one and the only temple of Vaishno Devi in Lucknow, situated near UPSRTC bus stand in Qaiserbagh, came into existence in 1984 and is managed by Panch Dash Juna Akhada. The purpose of erecting this temple seems to felicitate and provide an opportunity to get blessings from the devi for those devotees who cannot make it to the Vaishno Devi shrine at Katra, Jammu. The idol of Kali, Durga and Lord Shiva are also there in the temple premise.

Hari Om Temple

Spread over an area of about 24,000 sq.feet, this temple predominantly belonging to the Sindhi community was initially established in a rented room as Har Mandir at Kasturba Narishala, Lalbagh during 1954. After two decades in 1974 it was shifted to its present building and was rechristened as Hari Om Mandir. Jhule Lal being the prime deity, other gods and goddesses like Kali, Ganesh, Hanuman, Radha-Krishn, Ram Darbar and Shiva are also present there to bless the devotees. A copy of Srimadbhagwat Geeta in Arabic script is placed besides Guru Granth Sahib. Open for various social, cultural and religious events this temple can be termed as a gift to Lucknow from the Sindhi Community.

Shani Dev Temple

Behind the Hotel Clarks Awadh on Rana Pratap Marg,some 40 years old temple of Shani Bhagwan at ancient Karonda Ghat is supposed to be the most invoked and rewarding Shani temple in Lucknow. The younger brother of Yamraj (god of death)he is considered as the supreme judge of the *Mrityu Lok* (the death planet). This temple was a deserted place and people hardly knew about it. It's a strange co-incidence that since the last 20-30 years, after the globalization and open market, this place has become very popular among the devotees especially the younger ones. Saturday, the day of Shani Bhagwan ,is most important when a big crowd visits and offers mustard oil to please the god and prayers for the removal of their miseries.

This is the temple where people mostly pray for minimizing or putting and end to their sufferings rather than asking for material or otherwise favours from Shani Maharaj. The gong bells are offered by the devotees as their obeisance and a long row of such bells can be seen here.

Jhulelal Temple

A small temple at Karunda Ghat of the river Gomati ,is also termed as Sindhi temple and Sindhi Ghat by the community. Sunday being the special day witnesses the worship of Jal Kalash (water pot) and Bahirana (the flame). The birth anniversary of Sant Jhulelal on the full moon day of Chaitra (first month of Hindu calendar) known as Chaetti- Chand is celebrated here on a grand scale

Buddheshwar Mahadev Temple

One of the most ancient worship place in Lucknow, this temple is believed to be as old as the Ramayan period.Situated on on Mohan Road and also called as Sita Vanvas Road in Alamnagar area in the west of Lucknow, this temple carries a very interesting story behind its existence. Sita, while going to Valmiki Ashram in the area presently known as Bithoor, travelled through this road. Laxman who was escorting Sita took a halt on this spot. This was Tuesday and next morning on Budhwar (Wednesday) he worshiped Lord Shiva thus acquiring the name Buddheshawar Mahadev popularly known as Buddhesura Temple. This is the only temple of Lord Shiva where Wednesday is considered as the most auspicious day for worship and prayers..

Chandrika Devi Temple

More than 300 year old, this temple in Kathwara village of Bakshi ka Talab is situated on the bank of river Gomati where the main deity is Mata Chandrika , no other than Ma Durga. It is believed that it was established by Laxman's younger son Chandraketu. It was some 250-300 years, when some villagers came here searching their lost buffalos in the forest and found the idols in form of *pindis.* They placed the idols on a rock and the temple came into the existence. Amavasya (the darkest night) is the most auspicious day for worship when huge number of devotees visits the shrine. Devotees place bricks and tie the red *chunaris* and bells to get their wishes fulfilled. Removal of bricks, untying the *chunaris* and bells is an indication that the wish has been fulfilled.

Old Hanuman Temple

Believed to have been constructed by Begum Aalia in Aliganj, the temple is a glaring example of communal harmony. One can see the crescent- moon on its dome. The large premise has several small temples of various gods and goddesses like Amba , Saraswati, Radha-Krishna, Sataya Narain, Ganesh and Sai Baba. Tuesday being the day of Hanuman attracts large crowd from the city and adjoining areas. In the month of Jeth (the third month of Hindu calendar coinciding with May-June the, all Tuesdays are special and known as Bada Mangal and attracts big crowds. On these days fairs are also arranged popularly called as Bada Mangal ka Mela.

New Hanuman Temple

The most sought after and famous Hanuman Temple of Lucknow, it is situated in Mahavir Purva locality of Aliganj near the Kapoorthala Crossing.As the legend goes it was constructed by the Nawab Mohammad Ali Shahs' wife Begum Rabia. She had no issue and requested Hanuman to bless her with a child and her prayer bore fruit. After she gave birth to a child Hanuman appeared in her dream and asked her to take out his idol buried under ground and make a temple. Complying with this order she got the said ground excavated and got the idol. The idol, placed on an elephant, was being brought towards Bada Imambara where the proposed temple was to be constructed on a nearby ground. But, as the legend goes, the elephant stopped at the spot where the present temple stands. All the efforts to move the elephant went in vain. A saint told the begum that Hanumanji is not willing to go on the other side of the Gomati, so she must construct a temple there only. That's how the new Hanuman Temple of Aliganj came into existence. Later, Raja Mahmudabad donated land surrounding the temple.

Venkateshwara Temple

While travelling through Lucknow-Kanpur Road towards south one can get into a pleasant surprise by a chanced glance on a temple with Suth Indian design and tone. Earlier the 25 year old temple was quite close from the city on Kanpur road but due to the lack of space it was shifted further to its present building in Banthara, a village on Lucknow-Kanpur Road, which was opened for public in November,2012. Owing its design to Tirupati Balaji temple temple it houses Sri Balaji, the incarnation of Lord Vishnu, who is also known as Sriniwas Balaji Venkatachelapati, the Lord freeing people of their sins. The gold and cash is offered to the deities along with the coronation from milk, curd and holy water of river Ganga. Kumbhabhishekam is observed every month in strict accordance with the planetary conjunctions.

The architectural beauty of this temple attracts all and sundry irrespective of their purpose of visit to this small but prominent center of South Indian religious sensibility.

Bhagwan Ayappa Temple

A symbol of faith for more than 10,000 South Indians, specially Keralites, of Lucknow the Ayappa Temple is situated in the posh and comparatively new locality of Gomti Nagar with the main deity being Bhagwan Ayappa, the son of Vishnu and Shiva. Ayappa Bhagwan was born to kill the demon Mahishi who enjoyed a boon that a person born out of man and woman's union could not kill him. This prompted Vishnu to acquire a woman's form to come in union with Lord Shiva consequently giving birth to a child known as Ayappa who killed the demon. Spread in an area of 20,000 sq. ft. this 30 year old religious place is also designed on South Indian temple architectural style.

Special pooja is performed on Saturdays while the Makar Jyoti worship is the auspicious occasion. All the rituals and rites of the temple are the same as observed in Sabrimala Temple of Kerala. Deepawali, Ram Naumi and some other North Indian religious festivals are also celebrated here with the same gaiety and galore. Idols of Lord Shiva, Durga, Bhadra Kali, Ram, Ganesh, Nag Devta (snake god), Hanuman and Nav Griha (the nine planets) are also there to bless the devotees. Excepting Durga all the idols are black reflecting the South Indian tradition of temple gods.

Sankat Mochan Hanuman Temple

Cosidered as the 'VIP Temple' of Lucknowow the new Sankat Mochan Hanuman temple is situated on the bank of river Gomati. Established by Baba Neem Karuri Trust this temple was thrown open for public on 26th January (one of the most important dates in the history of independent India), 1967 and every year temple celebrates its anniversary with great devotion, fun and fair. During the floods in 1960 the old Sankat Mochan Temple was destroyed but the idol of Hanuman remained intact. The devotees came together and constructed a small temple which is considered to be a *Siddh* (invoked) place. Being situated near Lucknow University this temple was visited by a large number of students. After the flood a dam was constructed to prevent the Gomati water to enter the city and the old temple got surrounded with water. A bridge was also being constructed but,as popular beliefs tells, the engineers and contractors were unable to raise it in spite of their continuous efforts. Then Baba Neem Karuri asked the contactor to construct a Hanuman Temple to get the blessings before raising the bridge. He very humbly complied with Baba's wish. Standing diagonally opposite the gate number one of Lucknow University, it is the most visited temple of Hanuman throughout the year especially on Tuesdays and Saturdays. Devotees offer *Besan ke Laddo* (laddos made of gram flour) as prasad and donate brass bells when their wishes are fulfilled. Alongwith prayers and offerings devotees write about their miseries and sufferings in letters to Lord Hanuman and believe that he reads them personally to solve their problems.. Sankat Mochan Hanuman Mandir has also a small temple of Ganesh and Baba Neem Karuri with a a huge idol of Shiva and a Homeopathy dispensary.

Lete Hanuman Mandir

One of the very few such temples in India, one among the three in UP (one at Sangam, Allahabad and the other in Agra) the temple of Lete Hanumanji (lying Hanuman) at Panchawati Ghat of river Gomati is believed to have been established by Baba Ram Prasad and Mauni Baba and was renovated in 1942.As per mythology, after saving Ram- Laxman from the demon Ahiravan, a tired Hanuman ji lied down to rest a while. This lying posture of Hanuman is the main feature of this temple. Here devotees offer vermilion as their gratitude to the Lord for granting their wishes.

Sandohan Devi Temple

As the legend goes,once a devotee saw DeviMa in his dream telling him about a *kund* (small pond) in Chaupatia locality in which her idol is lying. He did not believe it fully rather remained doubtful. During Navratri again the Devi appeared in his dream narrating the same. This prompted him to search the idol in the said *kund* and found it.. A large number of devotees are said to have gathered at the spot and thus the name Sandohan Devi (goddess killing all the doubts) was given to the idol and a temple was constructed at the same site. Twice a year during

Navratri the *charan darshan* (glimpse of devi's feet) of Sandohan Devi are open for devotees who come from all over India and abroad as well. The Samadhi of the devotee who saw *devi ma* in his dream and searched the idol in the *kund* are also there within the temple premises. The 700 year old temple is situated at Chaupatia Crossing near the tempo stand.

Koneshwar Mahadev Temple

As per the legend, this several thousand years old Shiva temple turned into ruins. A Shivalinga was spotted by the local people who renovated the temple and as per traditions put the Shiva linga in the center. But every morning it was found in the corner so was placed in the corner deriving its name as Koneshwar Mahadev Mandir. Situated at the Koneshwar crossing in Chowk area this temple is another important place for worshiping Lord Shiva. As per belief this shrine is very auspicious for marriage negotiations. Holi Milan Mela and Savan pooja (worship during the month of Sravan) are the most important celebrations of Koneshwar Mahadev temple.

Shri Badi Kali Ji Mandir

The 2000 year old temple was established by Adi Shankaracharya as per popular belief which claims to be the only temple where the idol of Mata Kali and Lord Vishnu are there in the same premises. Other deities like Nageshwar Shiv, Lord Jagannath (Krishna, Subhadra, Balram) and Ma Durga are also there in the temple.

During Navratri this place is overcrowded with the devotees from all over the country who, along with offering prayers enjoy the fair which is an inseparable part of Navratri celebrations. Devotees tie red *chunaris* and write their wish on a piece of paper known as *arzi* (application for favour and blessings) and give it to the priest who puts them up before Kali Ma. Situated in a narrow lane of Chowk, Badi Kali Temple is one of the prime centers of Hindu faith and belief in Lucknow.

Chhoti Kali Ji Temple

Chhoti Kali is another important religious place and can be reached through a narrow lane beside Khunkhunji building in Chowk. Kali's idol is said to have been found in a well 300 year ago by a devotee who erected a platform and placed the idol on it. Later, people came together and constructed a temple and named it Chhoti Kaliji ka Mandir as the older temple of Kali ji was already there. Navratri and the *mela* (fair) are the two most important occasions. *Aarti* performed with clove and camphor in this temple is believed to cure all eye ailments. The main entrance looks like an open mouth of a tiger and inside, Kali ma is sitting on eight lotus petals.

Shyam Temple

One of the famous temples of Lucknow, this one is situated at the bank of river Gomati on Birbal Sahni Marg. According to *Shyam Parivar*, the 800 year old temple was renovated in 1975. The main deity's roots can be traced to Mahabharata period.

A brave person, Shyambaba's original name is Barbarik. In order to test his devotion and commitment Lord Krishna asked him to offer his head and he did the same. Pleased with this,Krishna blessed him with his name 'Shyam'. As the legend goes, further Barbarik's head was found in Khatu, Rajasthan and he became famous as Khatu Shyam. Idols of Radha-Krishna and Hanuman are also there. Devotees from all over India and abroad throng the temple throughout the year specially during Janamashtami (Lord Krishna's birth celebrations). Coco nuts wrapped in red cloth, turmeric and rice are the main constituents in the offerings and once the *manokamna* (wish) are fulfilled the coco nut is unwrapped and distributed as *prasad.*

Ram Krishna Math

Established by Sri Ram Krishna Mission in Nirala Nagar, this *math* was inaugurated on 2nd February, 1987. Contrary to the popular belief of being a Bengali religious center this math is regularly visited by a large number of people from all over the world. An architectural delight and artistically designed, the *math* conducts regular Yoga training classes, runs a rich library, Vivekananda Hospital along with providing food and education to the underprivileged children. On the occasion of Swami Vivekananda's birth anniversary a national youth festival is organized every year on 12th January. Vasant Panchami also known as Saraswati Pooja is a very special occasion and observed with bhajan singing and distribution of prasad. On every Sunday people from all walks of life come here and participate in bhajan singing.

Maharshi Valmiki Temple

Among the Valmiki community the creator of Ramayan Maharshi Valmiki is worshiped as God. Lucknow's 60 year old Valmiki Temple at Valmiki Park in Paper Mill Colony,Nishaat Ganj, is considered as the oldest among all such temples which are a part of the community's settlements in different areas of the city and adjoining places. The idol depicts him as writing Ramayan. There is no regular or appointed priest and any one from the community can offer pooja. The birth anniversary of Maharshi Valmiki is the most important occasion when maha pooja and bhandara are organized besides taking out a *shobha yatra.* Members of the community also gather arround Valmiki's statute installed in 2001 at Parivartan Chowk. Plan to construct a grand Valmiki temple beside river Gomati at Birbal Sahani Marg is underway.

Batuk Bhairon Temple

Around 200 year old temple houses the idol of Batuk Bhairon (child Bhairon) which is believed to be more than 1000 year old. This temple is considered as an invoked place which was renovated by Raja of Balrampur. Sunday is special and the devotees come here to offer prayers and prasad in front of Baba Bhairon to put an end to their sufferings. The last Sunday of Bhadrapad (sixth month of Hindu calendar) colloquially known as Bhadon is the most important day when a mela takes place and devotees offer plenty of liquor to the deity which is distributed as prasd to all visitors. This Sunday is termed as *ghunghroo waali raat* (the night of anklets) as the training and vigorous practice in dance is taken up from this day only as per belief of various dancers specially Kathak. Several kathak dancers hailing from Lucknow and other places come here to perform on this occasion. The stalwarts of Lucknow kathak gharana are said to have learnt the basics of kathak and danced here with *gunghroos* tied in their anklets. Other than Kathak, Batuk Bhairon temple is equally important for performing arts and artists of various disciplines who come here to offer the prayers and prasad for their *mannat* (wish).Situated just behind Bindadin Ki Dyodhi (ancestral house of the doyens of Lucknow kathak gharana) near Jhau Lal ka Pul, Bhairon ji is also termed as *suron ke devta* (god of music). Anniversary of Baba Bhairon is observed on the *ashtami* (eighth day of fifteen day lunar cycle according to Hindu Panchang) during the Krishna Paksh (the darker half of the month) of Agrahyan (ninth month of Hindu calendar colloquially known as Agahan) when one can see a range of liquor from regular to world's best brands. The entire family of Lord Shiva, Hanuman ji, Kanya Kuwari, Ma Durga and Kali are also there to bless the visitors.

Shitla Mata Temple

An ancient temple in Mehdiganj locality of Lucknow is very close to the historical Tikait Rai ka Taalaab which belongs to the eldest Devi Mata Shitla among the nine sisters who are also adorning the temple with their presence. The temple is the most auspicious place for the newly wedded couples who frequent this place in large numbers. A fair known as Aathon ka Mela takes place on the eigth day of Holi which lasts for 24 hours. More than six hundred years old temple has been in ruins and after some time a businessman discovered the idol from the nearby pond and got it installed. It was later renovated by the Deewan of the Nawab, Raja Tikait Rai along with the pond known as Tikait Rai ka Talab. Priest of the temple, who is necessarily a woman, is appointed on monthly basis who should be either from a Brahmin or Saini family. The people from various religions come here and take away the holy water as it's believed to cure smallpox and chickenpox.

Arya Samaj Temples

These temples belong to the followers of Vaidik Hindu traditions. The most famous 133 year old main Arya Samaj temple of the city is situated in Ganesh Ganj which was raised by Pundit Ras Bihari Tewari with the help of other socially aware people. Other Arya Samaj temples are in Narahi, Dali Ganj, Alambagh, Rakab Ganj and Aliganj.

These temples are boon for those young lovers who wish to go for inter-caste marriage but are opposed by their families and relatives.

Other temples of various faith, communities and sects

1. Buddh Vihar Mandir – Risaldar Park
2. Bhagwan Sambhav Nath Digambar Jain Mandir – Daliganj

3. Bhuinyyan Devi Mandir – Ganesh Ganj
4. Bhuinyyan Devi mandir (*isht Devi* of the entire Village) – Ghazipur, Indira Nagar
5. Santoshi Mata Mandir – Ganesh Ganj
6. Santoshi Mata Mandir – Rani Katra, Chaupatiyan
7. Radha Krishn Mandir – Ganesh Ganj
8. Dakshin Mukhi Hanuman Mandir – Hazrat Ganj
9. Sri Balaji Mandir - Rajaji puram
10. Hanuman Mandir – Aminabad
11. Kapilnath Hanuman mandir – Cantonment
12. Nepali Mandir – Chowk
13. Tulsi Manas Mandir – Krishna Nagar
14. Kailash Puri Mandir – Birbal Sahani Marg
15. Mauni Baba Mandir – Alambagh
16. Durga Mandir – Near Bagh wali Masjid, Ganesh Ganj
17. Shani Dev Mandir – Birbal Sahani Marg
18. Chachhi Kuan Hanuman Mandir – Subhash Marg, behind Kothi Sabzposh
19. Kalyan Giri Mandir – Thakur Ganj, Hardoi Road
20. Bhoot Nath Mandir – Indira Nagar, Faizabad Road
21. Mansa Devi Mandir – Behind Kakkad Park, Chaupatian
22. Shri Banke Bihari Mandir – Bakshi Ka Talab
23. Bihari ji Mandir – Rastogi Tola, Raja Bazar
24. Dauji Mandir – Agha Meer ki Dyodhi, Raja Bazar, Subhash Marg
25. Sri Nath Mandir - Agha Meer ki Dyodhi, Raja Bazar, Subhash Marg
26. Dwarka Nath Mandir – Katari Tola, Chowk
27. Gokul Nath Mandir - Katari Tola, Chowk

Grudwaras

Gurudwara Naka Hinloda

Though all the religious places to every devotee is a center of faith and belief but few are more important than the rest. Gurudwara Sri Guru Singh Sabha, Naka Hindola between Naka and Baans Mandi crossing , which is 115 year old, is one such centre for Sikhs in particular and others in general. *Langar* open to all throughout the year is a special feature along with a dispensary, a small Sikh Visharad (art gallery/ museum) showcasing paintings of the martyrs and other exhibits pertaining to Sikh sect and their Gurus. The imposing entry gate and architectural beauty inside the gurudwara are very impressive. Guru Parva, the birth anniversary of Sikh gurus are the most important occasions. Nagar Kirtan takes place on the birth anniversary of the first guru Nanak Dev and the last guru Govind Singh with the celebrations on full scale through various social and religious activities. Anniversaries of other Gurus are also observed with much gaiety and fanfare. Recitation of *Guru Baani* and *bhajan* singing is a regular feature from 5 to 9 in the morning and 6 to 9 in the evening. Baishakhi festival is another time for big celebration when *raagi* (singers properly trained in music presenting Guru Vani) from Amritsar come here to perform in front of Guru Granth Sahib. The copies of Guru Granth Sahib arrive here from Amritsar and then sent to all other Gurudwaras of Lucknow and other places as well. The old copies from all over the state are gathered here and then sent back to Amritsar. The first *Ardas* (prayer) is for Ma Bhagwati, the second for Guru Nanak Dev Sahib and then for other Gurus, eleventh for Guru Granth Sahib and then for all the Martyrs. As per Sikh traditions Guru Granth Sahib is placed on a cushion over Bhanji Sahib (platform/ pedestal/table where Guru Granth Sahib is placed) under the tied *chandni* (a small cover created with a white cloth above the Bhanji Sahib) with fans.

Gurudwara Yahiya Ganj

This is another prime and historical Gurudwara enjoying a special status among the Sikhs enjoying privilege over the rest of Gurudwaras in Lucknow.. In the year 1670, Guru Tegh Bahadur Singh is said have stayed here for three days while returning from Patna. Guru Govind Singh had also stayed here for two months in 1672. All other festivals and traditions are the same as in Naka Gurudwara with a Sikh Visharad adorning the shrine. Parallel to Nadan Mahal Road this place of Sikh faith is situated in a narrow lane known as Yahiya Ganj famous for its wholesale market of metal pots, plastic and other utility goods ranging from socks and handkerchiefs to saris and blankets.

Gurudwaras in Chander Nagar, Nishatganj and Sangat Temple/Gurudwara in Khadra near Pakka Pul/Lal Pull (Harding Bridge) which is said to be there since Mughal Period are some other important centers of Sikh faith.

Ghaats

Kudia Ghat

One of the oldest ghaats (wharf/jetty) is named after Rishi Kaundilya who is said to have selected this place for his ashram. An old Shiva temple dated back to 1889 and a few small temples are there for the devotees who visit the ghaat for a dip in river Gomati. The ghaat is equally important for the tourism as it's quite close to the grand historical monuments of Nawabi era like Rumi Darwaza, Bada Imambada, Pukka Pul (Harding Bridge) and Hussainabad Clock Tower. In tune with Ganga Arti in Varanasi,Gomati Arti is performed here regularly at 7:00 PM with *deepdaan* (a bowl made of Palsh/Dhak leaves almost half filled with flowers and a lit up small piece of camphor placed on it are floated in the water). Dev Deepawali is special occasion for deepdaan when an array of flames reflecting in the water creates various spectacular designs.

Devraha Ghaat

Kartik Poornima (full moon day in the ninth month of Hindu calendar colloquially known as Katik and the occasion as Katki) is auspicious for Hindus when most of them ensure a holy dip in any of the pious rivers they can approach. Though in Lucknow devotees throng to various ghaats but Devraha ghaat is considered as most important for taking the holy dip on Kartik Poornima. Devraha Ghaat takes its name from Baba Devraha who established it and can be approached from Rana Prtap Marg behind Hotel Clarks Awadh.

Karounda Ghaat

Just beside Devraha ghaat adjacent to Chhatar Manzil, this ghaat is famous for Shani and Jhulelal temple. Sindhi community celebrates Chetti Chand, Sant Jhulelal's birth anniversary with other devotees offering prayers to small Shiva and Hanuman temple.

Shukla Ghaat

Another old ghaat of Lucknow situated near Patang Park was renovated by Rhini Devi Chunni Devi Trust. Ma Saraswati temple is the main attraction while Ganga Snan or Kartik Poornima witnesses huge crowd when people come here to take a holi dip in Adi Ganga, the mythological identity of river Gomati. Goma mai ki aarti and bhandara are also organized on the occasion.

Panchwati Ghaat

Famous for its *lete* (reclining/lying) Hanuman temple,this ghaat takes its name from Panchwati of Ramayan period where Sita lived in exile with Rama and Laxman. There was lot of vegetation and greenery surrounding this ghaat as Sita's Panchawati had vast flora around it.

Lallu Mal Ghaat

Almost one hundred year old ghaat is situated just beside the Daliganj Bridge on river Gomati. Kartik Poornima, Chhat Pooja, *pitra paksh* and Amavasya draw huge crowds on this ghaat. Well maintained ,Lallu Mal ghaat has verandas, shelves and a Dharmshaala where only Hindus can stay. Constructed by Lallu Mal Bhagwan Das Omar Vaishya this place is flanked by eighty year old Mahadev Narmadeshwar Temple on Kachcha Ghaat and Pahaadi Ghaat.

Visarjan Ghaat

Situated near Lucknow University the ghaat is mainly used for the immersion of Durga And Ganesha's idol after Durga Pooja and Ganesh Poojan and other regular occasions when worship is not considered fruitful and complete unless the idol of the deity is immersed. Chhat Pooja, Makar Sankranti and Kartik Poornima or Ganga Snan also draw big crowds. Lucknow Municipal Corporation has developed Jhulelal Park on the ghaat which has become the undeclared official place for all kinds of *dharnas*, protest, hunger strike, meetings and other such activities for voicing dissent.

Pipra Ghat

Considered as the old cremation ground of the city, it was situated on the other side of Gomati. Managed by the cantonment the present cremation ground came up in 1960. Scarcely 15-20 cremations are performed here during a month or two. A temple built in 1950 in honour of Bharat Mata is another feature.

Gulala Ghaat

Near Mohini Purwa, Thakurganj this ghat also known as Muktidham is another old place for the cremation and burial. Arrangement and availability of the material required to perform the last rites is available within the premises. An imposing gate at the entry, Mahakal, Shiva and Bhairon temples are there with an office of Lucknow Municipal Corporation.

Bhainsa Kund Ghaat

Known as Bhainsa Kund Dhaam the ghaat is situated between Gomti barrage crossing and Nishat Ganj Bridge near Balu Adda. As the story goes, male buffalos while fighting fell into a pond here giving the place its name while another version says that this area of Gomati bank was the grazing ground for buffalos giving its name. Some fifteen years ago the ghaat had scarce facilities but Sahara India Pariwar renovated it with all the necessary arrangements from fabricating the shades for cremation, place to sit and rest, drinking water, plantation and constructing the temples where bhajans are played. The ghaat has an electric crematorium also preferred by only a few. Persons working there observe, "Bijli wale mein ya to bahut garib jata hai ya wo bade admi jinke paas wakt ki bahut kami hai." (Electric crematorium is used either by very poor people or by those big (read rich and powerful) people who have no time). During rainy season demand for the electric cremation is increased substantially. Managed by Sahara India Pariwar, the ghaat has a municipal corporation office also for issuing necessary documents required for the death certificate.

Kala Kothi Ghat

Close to Kudia Ghaat this place is famous for its Shani Temple The twenty seven feet high temple has two and a half doors, small ventilators and windows, stands on seven and a half pillars with a pond measuring two and a half meter. Presently known as Kala the building near the Ghat was earlier famous as Qila Kothi was gifted to one Bhawani Mahara by the then Nawab. Music and dance performances were the regular feature of this place leading it to be known by its current name and subsequently the ghaat close to the building as Kala Kothi Ghat. Shiva Linga at the ghaat was established by the second chief minister of Uttar Pradesh Dr. Sampoornanad. Temples of Lord Hanuman, Kali ji and Kal Kuteshwar Mahadev are also there.

Chhat Mela Ghat

A part of Laxman Mela ground where Chhat Puja with two day *mela* is organized on the occasion has given this place its name. Chhat Puja festival is predominantly celebrated by the people hailing from eastern UP and Bihar. Situated on the road beside Gomati between the Nishat Ganj Bridge and Laxman Mela Police Post, this ground was the venue for Lucknow festival and various political activities but since 2008 administration has put a complete ban on all such happenings due to traffic and other administrative constraints.

Churches

The churches in Lucknow have added an important feature to the city's socio-cultural and religious life. Though there have never been large population of Christians in the city yet because of the British residency, cantonment and the highly tolerant attitude of Nawab rulers, a cultural environment was there which welcomed everybody with open arms.

There are now more than four dozen churches of different orders. History tells that the Christian faith came to Lucknow travelling through Tibet and Nepal. Moreover, "the Europeans had mercantile associations with Lucknow from the time of Akbar and Jahangir and a French trader had also built a mansion called 'Firangi Mahal' (Siddiqui, 2000)." However, there is no evidence of any church being built in Lucknow during the Mughal era. Claude Martin who settled in Lucknow and built in 1794 an impressive palace on the right bank of Gomti might have constructed a chapel in the vicinity, but it seems to have been destroyed in 1857. However, there are numerous churches of a later date, of historical and architectural importance. "Before 1857, Lucknow had only 2-3 churches which were located in Residency and Madion Cantonment and a chapel in the then Paadri Tola but all these were reduced to ruins and destroyed during the 1857 war of independence". (Naresh Singh,2014). Between 1858-60 the Sunday Service was held in Imambada Sibtainabad in Hazratganj and perhaps that is why the Christians, especially Anglo-Indians ,have been living in the houses around this Imambada.

The largest church is St. Joseph Cathedral just opposite the Mayfair Cinema, Hazratganj. The office of the catholic bishop is also located within the premises. The foundation of now spacious cathedral (at a place where the old St. Joseph Church was located) was laid in 1970 and this complex was completed in 1977. It looks a magnificent structure with a large prayer hall providing a thousand seats. It stands as a landmark in the heart of Lucknow.

The Christ Church is situated near Raj Bhawan (Governor House). It is also a very impressive structure, its doors and windows having Gothic arches. This beautiful church was built during the last decade of the nineteenth Century. The old Methodist Church situated in Lal Bagh is one of the oldest churches of Lucknow city. It was also built in the last quarter of the nineteenth century. Following are some of the churches among the important ones:

(i) All Saints New Garrison Church, Cantonment
(ii) Epiphamy Church, Lal Bagh
(iii) Central Methodist Church, Cantonment Road
(iv) Church of the Holy Redeemer, Mavaiyya
(v) Seventh Day Adventist Church, Vidhan Sabha Marg
(vi) Dua Ka Ghar, Mahanagar

Mosques. Imambada and Karbala

The skyline of Lucknow is dotted with numerous mosques, imambadas and karbalas and a number of scholars have published illustrated descriptions of these beautiful monuments. Although Lucknow can boast of some beautiful and grand mosques the city is known throughout the world for its Imambadas.

In the crowd of numerous mosques, three finds mention in any narration of mosques in Lucknow. **Asifi Masjid** build by Nawab Asaf-ud-Daula is so magnificent in its architecture that one wonders how such a monument could be erected in those times. Designed by the famous architect Kifayat Ullah, it was completed in 1794. This grand mosque is part of the Bada Imambada complex. Unfortunately it is not maintained properly and requires extensive restoration.

The second mosque is **Jama Masjid** situated near Chota Imambada and adjacent to the Unity Public School. This magnificent mosque was built by Nawab Muhammad Ali Shah during his reign between 1837-1842 AD. The third one is popularly known as **Teeley waali Masjid** because of its location on a mound *(teela)* on the bank of the River Gomti. A well known sufi saint of his time Shah Peer Muhammad lived on this mound and his **mazaar** is also there.

An important point that needs to be mentioned here is that in the Awadh region Sunni and Shia Muslims have separate mosques. While in the first two Shias offer prayers and the third is meant for the Sunnis. It is usually seen that wherever Shias are in good numbers they have their separate mosques and in those places where they are in a microscopic minority either they go to a Sunni mosque or offer *namaaz* at home. They don't feel comfortable in a Sunni mosque because of some variations of postures followed in the *namaaz*. After the ugly Shia-Sunni violence in 1969 the Shias have stopped going to a Sunni mosque because of apprehensions about their security and suspicions and prefer to offer *namaaz* at home if a Shia mosque is not available. During the last 2-3 decades the hostility among the Sunnis between the followers of Bareilvi School (popularly known as Bareilvi) and Deobandi School (popularly called as Deobandi) have sharpened to such an extent that many followers of these two schools prefer to offer prayers in mosques managed by these two schools respectively. The theological differences and interpretations have become so sharp that sometimes even close relatives, if adherents of these two different schools, may shun each other or avoid any matrimonial alliance.

During the days of the Nawabs, Lucknow was known for its gardens and imambadas and that is why many mohallas and localities are named after some garden such as Charbagh (where the main railway station is located), Qaiser Bagh, Lal Bagh, Khurseed Bagh, Nazar Bagh etc. Presently, there are hardly any gardens remain, swallowed by massive urbanization taken place during the last hundred years or so but several imambadas have survived.

During the Nawabi days virtually every mohalla had an Imambara or two but most of these were either damaged beyond repair or totally demolished during the first war of independence in 1857. In the Islamic architecture worldwide Imambadas hold the most important place after mosques and tombs. Imambada is a uniquely Indian word. Etymologically speaking it consists of two words-*Imam* meaning leader in Arabic (In the Shia parlance it refers to their most revered personalities after Prophet Muhammad and in the present context it refers to Imam Husain, their third Imam whose martyrdom is commemorated) and *baada* is a local word meaning abode and hence Imambada is 'abode of the Imam'. Thus, Imambada is the structure, in which the martyrdom of the Imam, his family members and companions is mourned.The the Imambadas may be of two types viz private and public.

A public Imambada, located at any public place, is open to all and anybody irrespective of caste and creed may enter into it and participate in the *majlis* (mourning address/congregation) and other mourning rituals while the private Imambadas are usually located within the four walls of the house which cannot be visited without the permission or invitation of the owner. Moharram mourning rituals are conducted in both types of the Imambadas. Many Shias of Lucknow maintain a private Imambada in his or her house if one can afford to spare one room for this purpose where a *tazia*, *alam* and other things are kept. Usually, an imambada, especially the spacious public ones, has three parts *shahnasheen* where **tazia, alam** or any other related object is kept for public viewing, outside the *shahnasheen* there is a covered corridor *(daalaan)* where the mourners sit on the ground over sheets of cloth or carpets, this may be followed by another corridor or just open space where the crowd of mourners could be accommodated if it is too large for the inner corridor. Outside the *shahnasheen* or the first corridor, a wooden *mimbar* (pulpit) is kept covered by black cloth on which the *Zaakir* (the speaker or one who addresses the *majlis)* sits on any of the stairs depending on the size of the crowd he/she is addressing.

In this brief description of the important imambadas, their grand architecture is being skipped as this has been described in many other previous publications on the imambadas. The grandeur and magnificence of the **Bada Imambada** is seen to be believed. Built by Nawab Asaf-ud-Daulah in 1784, it is a massive structure. Its main hall is 162 feet long and 54 feet wide. Regarded as an architectural marvel, it has a labyrinth called **bhool bhulaiyya.** Also known as Asifi Imambada on the name of its builder was the venue of *majlis* organized by the Nawabs and the

Shia aristocracy. Now it is a centre of attraction for the Indian as well as foreign tourists. Imambada Husainbad, popularly known as **Chota Imambada** was built by Muhammad Ali Shah between 1837-42. It is much smaller than the Bada Imambada and had a domed central hall. The ornate central hall still has beautiful Belgian Chandlers. The mosque in the complex is also reduced in size. It is a pity that such a wonderful building has been encroached from outside and not maintained properly by the Husainabad and Allied Trusts under whose supervision various Imambadas and other moments have been placed.

Imambada Shah Najaf is yet another magnificent building with hugely spacious lawns on all sides. It was built by Nawab Ghaziu-ud-Din Haider (1814-1827) on the banks of the river Gomti. Etymologically speaking the two words-*Shah* and *Najaf* have a definite meaning. While *Shah* refers to king, Najaf is a town in Iraq where the tomb of Imam Ali, the first and the most revered Imam of the Shias is located. Being the replica of the original tomb at Najaf it is out of reverence that it has been named as Shah Najaf. The road from Hazratganj leading to this Imambada is known as Shah Najaf Road.

There are Imambadas and Karbalas in Lucknow and elsewhere that were constructed as the exact replica of the tombs of their Imams located in Iraq and Iran. Thus, whenever and wherever the Shias got conducive environment, they erected such monuments as replica of the original buildings knowing well that they would never return to Iraq or Iran. Significantly, they also created the same ambience with sandy soil and palm or date trees. Look at Talkatora Ki Karbala. It is the replica of the tomb of Imam Husain, located in the town of Karbala in Iraq. Same is the case with a number of other monuments built in Lucknow during the reign of the Shia Nawabs. Following is a list of some important imambadas in Lucknow.

(i) Imambada Sibtainabad located in Hazratganj.
(ii) Imambada Qasim Ali Khan near Peer Bukhara in Chowk Area.
(iii) Imambada Zainul Abidin Khan in Chowk area near Kalicharan College.
(iv) Imambada Raja Jhaulal located in Thakurganj and built by Raja Jhaulal, the most important minister of Nawab Asafuddaula.
(v) Imambada Malika Zamania, Golaganj.
(vi) Imambada Mughal Saheb, Rustam Nagar.
(vii) Imambada Agha Baqar on Victoria Street, near KG Medical College.
(viii) Imambada Ghufran Maab, located near Imambada Agha Baqar.
(ix) Imambada Taqi Saheb, Chowk.
(x) Imambada Nazim Saheb, Victoria Street, Nakhas.

Karbalas

As already mentioned Karbala is a town in Iraq which is associated with the martyrdom of Imam Husain in 680 AD on the orders of the then Muslim Caliph Yazid. Later, a grand mausoleum was built on the grave of Imam Husain. In

South Asia, especially in India, Karbala has a definite and specific connotation. In order to commemorate the 'Tragedy of Karbala', the Shias built the replicas of the mausoleums in the centre of a piece of land around which *Tazias* are buried. In some Karbalas, part of the land is also used as cemetery. It all started from the fact that the great distance of India from Karbala and also the hostile regimes of Iraq (it is only after the overthrow of the Saddam Husain regime that the majority Shia population in Iraq got political power) acted as big hurdles for the very devout among the Shias of India to get buried near the mausoleum of Imam Husain or making frequent visits *(Ziyarat)* to the tomb.

This is the main reason behind Indian Shia's decision to establish local Karbalas. During the construction phase soil from Karbala was brought and sprinkled on the designated cemeteries. Every Moharram, thousands of *tazias* of various sizes are brought in small processions and buried at the designated place in the already dug pits of different sizes. Most of the *tazias* are brought for burial on the 10th of moharrum month, the day their hero was martyred.

Half a dozen karbalas have been built in Lucknow but the largest number of Tazias are buied in Talkatora Karbala near Rajajipuram. Beside a grand replica of the tomb of Imam Husain, some more *rouza* (mausoleums) have been added. In this huge and sprawling karbala not only tazias are buried but it also serves as a big cemetery for the burial of the deceased Shias. Apart from this, karbala, the others are as follows:

(i) Karbala Malika Jahan, Aishbagh
(ii) Karbala Nasiruddin Haider, Daliganj
(iii) Karbala Dayanutdaula, Kazmain.
(iv) Karbala Abbas Bagh, Hardoi Road
(v) Karbala Imdad Husain Khan, Rajajipuram
(vi) Karbala Munshi Fazal Husain, Bulaqi Ka Adda.
(vii) Karbala Misri Ki Baghia, Radhagram, Hardoi Road.

Mazaar and Maqbara

Chaar Yaaraan-e-nabi me 'Aasi',
Tabbiyat mujhe har yaar ki hai,
Talab-e-raahe-e-khuda me lekin
Pairwi Haider-e-Karraar Ki hai

These famous lines of 'Aasee' Ghazipuri summarize the popular practice of Sufism in Indian Sub-continent. It says that of four companions of the Prophet, I follow all the four (caliphs) but in seeking God, I follow Haider (Ali). Sufism or *Tasawwuf* (in Arabic) is defined as the inner mystical dimension of Islam. Practitioners of *Tasawwuf* are referred to as 'Sufis'. Sufi orders trace their precepts from Prophet Muhammad either through his cousin, son-in-law and the fourth caliph, Hazrat Ali (the first Imam of the Shias) or through his companion and friend Hazrat Abu Bakr (the first caliph after the Prophet.)

Some of the famous and popular mazaars of sufi saints are also situated in Lucknow and attract sections of Muslims and Hindus alike as these sufi saints always propagated humanism, peace and harmony. The deprived, marginalized and the weaker sections of the society found shelter and solace in the abode of the sufi saints. Most of the sufi saints here migrated from Iran when the ruling Shia Safvid Dyanasty of Iran did not kindly treat the philosophy of Sufism based on a particular way of seeking God. The mainstream Sunni Arabs were always skeptical about it and now the radical section of the Sunni Muslims treat Sufism and Sufi practices as 'unislamic'.

When the sufis migrated to India they found the local cultural environment very friendly and compatible. Moreover, it was also close to *Bhakti* movement in more than one ways. Among several of the sufis who migrated to India, some chose Lucknow as their abode *(aastaana).*

Perhaps, the oldest mazaar in Lucknow is of Hazrat Ibrahim Chisti. Mirza Jafar Husain (1981) writes that he was closely related with Khwaja Gharib Nawaz of Ajmer and came to Lucknow during the reign of Emperor Akbar. The most popular mazaar in Lucknow is of Shah Meena whose mazaar is located near KG Medical College and a road nearby is named after him. The mazaar of his grandfather Shah Qayaamuddin Abbasi is located on the campus of Medical College. As per the practice, a sufi saint is buried at the place where he dies. Significantly, the word 'death' is not used for the death of a sufi saint. Rather, they achieve *Visaal*, meaning meeting (God) and the annual *Urs* is held on this date and place.

It is believed that Saiyed Qayamuddin, popular as Khamman Pir, was among the earliest sufis settling down in Lucknow. His mazaar is located within the campus of Charbagh Railway Station and his *Urs* attracts thousands of people mainly Hindu devotees. Many people doing job in Railways believe that he is the presiding deity of this railway station and protects them, passengers and the trains, from any possible calamity.

Another early Sufi settler in Lucknow was Shah Pir Muhammad who, as many believe, was a contemporary of Shah Meena. He lived on a mound on the bank of Gomti River popularly known as Lakshman Teela. Because of this association it is also called Shah Peer Muhammad Ka Teela. On the same mound where his mazaar is located, the famous Teeley Wali Masjid was constructed later. The mazaar of Khwaja Muhammad Nabi Shah popularly called Dada Miyan is also quite popular among the devotees of the sufi saints. It is located in Sadar Bazaar, near Mall Avenue.

Besides several mazaars of lesser known sufi saints,a very unique mazaar also exists in Moosa Bagh ,on the outskirts of Lucknow on Hardoi Road.Moosa Bagh was built by Nawab Saadat Ali Khan in early 19th century where he used to camp for leisure and hunting.It lies in ruins but has become a centre of attraction for several neighbouring villages.In the midst of ruins a grave exists in which Captain Frederick Wale is buried who was killed during the 1857 revolt against the British.

The whitewashed tomb has an inscription that reads "Sacred to the memory of Capt.F.Wale,who raised and commanded the Ist Sikh Irregular Cavalry,killed in action on 21st March,1858". With the passage of time he was accepted as a saint and 'baba' backed by a number of orally transmitted stories.Many people of the neighbouring villages call him "Kaptaan Shah Baba","Gora Baba" and "Cigrette-Daaru waala Baba" and visit his 'mazaar' on Sundays and offer cigarettes and liquor to him. Quite a big gathering may be seen every year on Christmas as if this is his *'Urs'*,following the sufi tradition.Several people believe that that their wishes get fulfilled if they visit his mazaar and make offerings.

Maqbara

The word *Maqbara* refers to a *Qabr* (grave) or a tomb. While a mazaar is also a burial place or simply a tomb the nuances are different. While a tomb is simply a grave and does not necessarily carry element of reverence or devotion, a *mazaar* is revered by the devotees.

Beside the *mazaars* of the sufi saints, there are also a number of tombs of rulers and others exhibiting grandeur of architecture. Before the Nawabs took over and established their suzerainty over Awadh, the Sheikhs were the ruling clan in and around Lucknow. The maqbara of Shaikh Abdurrahman and some other Shaikhs are situated near Yahiyaganj and known as **Nadaan Mahal**. The dome of this maqbara was once very attractive because of its decoration with blue enamel but because of neglect, it is fading fast. **Maqbara Saadat Ali Khan** located in Qaiser Bagh area near Parivaritan Chowk and Begum Hazrat Mahal Park is a pair of grandiose maqbaras. The larger one is the maqbara of Saadat Ali Khan while in the other his wife Begum Khurshidzadi is buried. An imposing pair of buildings, these are built in a lush green grass land and its architecture is worth seeing. Another magnificent maqbara is known as **Maqbara Amjad Ali Shah** in the posh Hazratganj opposite Halvasiya Market. Simply called Maqbara it is also known as Sibtainabad Ka Imamabada because *majlis* (mourning congregation during moharram days) is also held here. Till about a decade back it was in possession of unauthorized persons who were running commercial activities from there till, because of agitation by the Shias, it was restored to them and the restoration work has been going on under expert supervision. Its' beautiful floral designs and paintings on the walls and ceilings are seen to be believed. The **Maqbara Aliya**, the burial place of mother of Nawab Saadat Ali Khan, located at Golaganj, Maqbara Ali Shah Kuli Khan situated in Noorbari, Kashimiri Mohalla and Maqbara Hakim Mehdi situated opposite the girls' college Taaleem Gaah-e-Niswan near City Station are some other notable maqbaras.

Firangi Mahal and Darul Uloom Nadwatul Ulema

Lucknow may take pride in claiming that education and research in Oriental Studies began from this city. Though Dewa, Jais, Gorakhpur and Banaras were also famous in promoting this field of knowledge but an institution such as Firangi Mahal was able to achieve fame and excellence which gained recognition beyond the country. Some scholars regard it as the first 'University' of oriental studies in the world. If we look into the history we find that by the time of Akbar, Lucknow had become a

A rare historical church

Durgah Hazrat Abbas, an important place for the Shias

Gora Kaptan Saheb ka Mazaar

Dariya waali Masjid on the bank of the River Gomti

Front view of Imambada Sibtainabad

Shah Najaf, replica of Hazrat Ali's tomb at Najaf (Iraq)

Interior of Sheeshe waali Masjid, a rare mosque with glass work all around

Shah Meena Ka Mazaar

Distribution of Prasad during Bada Mangal Festival

Hanuman Mandir of Aliganj

fairly developed centre of trade and commerce. Around this time, a French trader arrived and lived in the city with the permission of the Mughal administration. He specialized in the trade of horses and resided in a complex of a couple of big houses. The local people called his residence as *Firangi Mahal* (palace of the European/British). Some people say that it was during the period of Aurangzeb that some French businessmen came and stayed at this palatial building. Later, they left the place as their permit of residence could not be renewed.Enjoying the patronage of Auranzeb Mullah Nizamuddin founded a Madarsa here that became famous internationally. He developed a syllabus known as *Dars-e-Nizamia* that was unparalleled and remained unchallenged for years to come. It consisted of logic, philosophy, *fiqh* (Islamic jurisprudence), *hadees*, mathematics and a host of other fields of knowledge.

By the time Asafuddaula moved his capital to Lucknow, the teachers of Firangi Mahal had already achieved a high status in several Muslim countries and its alumni had spread far and wide in all parts of the sub-continent and teaching in institutions of learning and the Nawabs of Awadh, despite subscribing to the Shia sect, had great respect for Firangi Mahal and appointed many *ulema* of this institution to the exalted posts of *Qazi* and *Mufti*. The *ulema* of Firangi Mahal had a broad vision and free from narrow sectarian prejudices and that is why a number of Shia students were also coming to them and getting educated.

During the period of freedom movement a highly respected Islamic scholar of his time, Moulana Abdul Bari took active part in *Khilafat* Movement and then became a part of freedom struggle along with Mahatma Gandhi. The Maulana was a great visionary who knew that it was not good for the Indian Muslim to keep away from the mainstream politics. Mahatma Gandhi had also great respect for the ulema of Firangi Mahal and he also stayed for some time in Firangi Mahal. The Maulana accepted Mahatma Gandhi as the leader of Muslims too. The ulema of Firangi Mahal were charged to death by the British government for issuing a *Fatwa* of *Jihaad* against the Britishers. Inspired by the Maulana, a whole crop of nationalist Muslims emerged from this institution. Hayatullah Ansari, Mufti Raza Ansari, and some others were regarded as highly respected nationalist Muslims.

With the passage of time the Persian and Arabic languages declined in India and with this the educational institutions based on them. Firangi Mahal is no exception to it. It is a desolate place now and seen in the newspapers not for its scholarship and broad mindedness but political tug of war but there are still some scholars who stand for sectarian harmony and oppose the growing conservative tendencies in the matter of religion.

By the end of the 19th century a new school of thought emerged inspired by Sir Syed Ahmad Khan who exhorted the Muslims to 'adapt to westernization without compromising on religion'. During this period there emerged several ulema who were disgusted with the old system of education and that is how **Darul Uloom Nadwatul Ulema** popularly called **Nadwa College** came into existence and within a short period it gained acceptability among a large section of Sunni Muslims. It was founded at Kanpur in 1894. This institution was intended to be a modified version of Deoband. The founding fathers chose Lucknow to implement their ideas. Perhaps the reason may be that the Firangi Mahal had made the environment of Lucknow conducive to serious education, scholarship and research. The stewardship of Moulana Shibli Nomani helped it gain a position of eminence. He was able to attract persons from throughout the country interested in research in Islamic Studies as well as literature. Making its beginning from a humble place near Molviganj, it had moved to its present building on the bank of river Gomti near Lucknow University campus. Among the later leaders, Maulana Ali Mian Nadwi was instrumental in raising its stature at the international level and now students of not only different parts of India but also from abroad come to Nadwa to get education and do research.

Arts and Crafts

Historically, Lucknow has been an important centre of several exquisite and sophisticated arts and crafts. Its craftsmen have been known throughout the world. Some of these handicrafts fell victim to new technology as these could not keep pace with either the changing technology or tastes of the people. Even those craftsmen who are engaged in such handicrafts as Chikan and Zardozi that are so popular nationally and internationally live in abject poverty and deprivation. This social ugliness is usually ignored in the fascinating descriptions of these crafts.

9

Arts and Crafts

'Mumkin nahin ki kar sakoon main shukria ada,
Lekin shukarguzar hamesha rahoonga mai'

The couplet is an apt salutation to the *adab-o-aadab*, (mannerism and etiquettes) art, craft, and cuisine of Lucknow as the city has given and still provides so much to the people who live here, to the visitors and tourists as well that any expression will not serve enough to match the vast horizon of its culture which combines emotional warmth, courtesy, affection, sophistication and a fondness for gracious living. Combining the culture of two communities living together for centuries, sharing similar interests and speaking a common language has given birth to the world famous 'Lucknowi Tehzeeb' making many cultural traits and customary practices an inseparable part of Lucknow in particular and of Awadh in general.

Chikan Embroidery

Yeh Lucknow ki chikan,yeh zaree ki shaam-o-saher,
*Har ek taar me sau baar uljhe taar-e-*nazar

(Look at the chikan and the zardozi of Lucknow as if the vision gets entangled in every thread)

Chiken industry is one such sector where artisans have excelled in their art and contributed in a significant manner by providing subsistence to a large number of women and earning foreign exchange. A unique craft which involves delicate artistic embroidery work on various texturs of cloths like cotton, muslin, doriya, chiffon, silk, organdi, organza and others. Referred to as *chhatiis taanko ka khel* (game of 36 stitches) as there are thirty six types of stitches used for producing a vast range and variety of delicate artistic chikan work of which *bakhia*, *murri*, *tepchi, jaali, dhoompatti*, *hathkati*, *phanda, ulti bakhia*, *hathkati*, *chana patti*, *laung*, *dhaniya*, *pankhudi, kangan, zanjeera, keel* and *bijli*, arc most famous but presently *tepchi, bakhia, murri, jaali* shadow and *tappa* are much in use. Its origin is said to have taken place from the Persian word pronounced as *Chikaan* or *Chaakin* which means drapery or *Kashidakaari* (embroidery). Noorjehan, the wife of emperor Jehangir, is said to have introduced this work in India as she expressed her desire to replicate the minute designs and motifs on the walls and gates of palaces on the muslin garments as a designer product to be worn during summer. One of her attendants named Bismillah came to settle in Lucknow in Khadra locality near Harding Bridge (Pucca Pul) thus bringing this delicate art to the city of Nawabs. Khadra is considered to be the place of origin for chikan work in Lucknow which has become the most sought after embroidery work on cloths and garments during the last three centuries. Meethi Khichdi, a locality in Daliganj area, is another very important place for chikan work.

Passion and fashion for the rich and affluent, bread and butter for the poor, Chikan has been the most popular embroidery work among the women of Awadh. The Begums of Awadh are said to have learnt this work from their attendants which obviously came to an end after the fall of Awadh's Nawabi era. But for those who earned their livelihood with this art still continue to work day and night to make two ends meet. There are more than sixty thousand women chikan artisans working in and around the city. Though predominantly the chikan embroidery work is centralized among the women some males have also tried their hands who brought laurels to their names. Munne Mirza, Hassu Khan and Laddan were known for their specific work. Faiyyaz Khan was known as Ustad who became the first recipient of the national award for his micro fine chikan work in 1965. Hasan Mirza popularly known as Panke Babu won the national award for chikan work in 1970. He is credited with the invention of Anokhi Chikan work where stitches are done without crossing the needle from the cloth not leaving any trace of stitches on the other side of the cloth.

Far from any kind of pageantry the chikan work of Lucknow has represented a fine, simple and elegant craftsmanship but during the last four-five decades the introduction of broader motifs, coloured threads and the cloths other than fine cotton, though commercially successful, have 'polluted' the otherwise one of the finest arts of stitch work. The chikan embroidery work represents the trend of the period like when it was being produced during the Nawabi era, the fish pairs, peacocks, crowns, Persian letters, pigeons and other such motifs were preferred by the royalty and popular among the people as the central themes and designs. If we look at the traditional designs of chikan work which witnessed the minute and superfine embroidery is presently being almost replaced with broad and ordinary shapes which show some folk motifs also. Initially the chikan work was exclusive to the garments like kurtas, sari, shalwar suits with accessories like *dupalli topi* (caps) and hankies but later since the last few decades utility items like bed sheets, table covers, tray covers and others such cloths found a place in chikan work and became quite popular. Although this art is now being practiced in other parts of the country too but Lucknow remains the home of cikankari. The ever increasing demand for such utility cloths and the garments has paved the way for fake chikan work which is not only affecting the market for genuine chikan embroidery but bringing a bad name for this delicate and intricate art representing Lucknow's fine taste and aesthetics since centuries. Termed as *Doodhiya Kaliyan* (milky buds) for its initial choice of white the world famous chikan work of Lucknow mostly done by the women has never been fair to these artisans who, with their eyes and hand, stitch brightness on the garments for others can never afford to have one for them, not only live in the gloomy darkness of poverty but die unceremoniously.

Zardozi

Comparatively heavy and more elaborate work where a variety of gold threads, spangles, beads, seed pearls, wire and *gota* is used for embroidery is known as zardozi. The wedding dresses like saris, lehnga-choli, curtains, cushions, bags, animal trappings, purses, shoes, belts and coats are the main items which are decorated with this work.

It took its' origin from the Persian word *zardozi* which means embroidery with gold and silver threads on cloths. Though Agra and Varanasi are also known for such work but it is Lucknow where this craft has taken to heights during the Nawabi era when the minute and super fine designs and motifs were introduced to suit the artistic taste and elegance of Lucknow. *Kamdani*, *zari*, and *karchaub*, are some important embroidery works featuring in Zardozi. Along with the word Zardozi, *Aaree* is added to it and popularly speaking, these two are used together i.e. aaree-zardozi. It is said that the word *aari* has been coined and used in Lucknow only and derived from the way a cobbler stitches on leather. *Aaree* is done with thread and *kasabh* (thread covered with wire) while zardozi is done with wire, *teeki*, *motee* and other metallic things and called *maal ka kaam*. Since the job of aaree-zardozi is performed on a wooden frame unlike Chikan work done by holding the cloth in hand, it is also described as *karchoub*. Further, unlike Chikan work, Zardozi has always been the monopoly of males and now only a few women have taken to it in recent years. People still fondly remember the names of Ameer Husain of Khala Bazar, Taqi Husain from Balochpura, Haider Husain from Sheesh Mahal, Abdul Hai from Nakhas, Saleem Khan of Gadhi Peer Khan, Marghoob Bhai from Rustam Nagar and several other stalwarts and master craftsmen. Interestingly but significantly, there is almost a neat division among the workers of Chikan and Zardozi along sectarian lines. In Lucknow while the overwhelming majority of Chikan workers are Sunni Muslims, Zardozi workers come mostly from the Shia Muslims.

Up to 1970s, Zardozi work was confined to Lucknow but from 1980s it got lot of exposure in media adopted by several costume designers of Hindi film industry in Bombay. With the shooting up of its' demand, Zardozi crossed the borders of Lucknow for the first time and the first *Kaarkhana* (workshop) of Zardozi work opened in 1983 in Sandial, Hardoi district. Between 1980-2000, it was acknowledged as an industry. With this, a number of rural workers in the adjoining districts joined the work force presenting stiff competition to the Zari workers of Lucknow.

Bidri and Zarbuland

Though the Bidri work has its origin in a place called Bidar near Hyderabad, Andhra Pradesh, it has found exquisite expression in Lucknow. *Taarkashi, Tehnashin, Zarnashin* and *Aftabi* are some important features of Bidri work but Zarbuland is exclusively related to Lucknow. There is no authentic mention anywhere as to when this craft stepped first in the city but the initial work bearing the European style suggests that it may have began during the increasing influence of British and French on Awadh and its Nawabs. As Sayed Anwer Abbas(2011) mentions , the first recorded details of exclusive Zarbuland work of Lucknow are mentioned in the records of an exhibition held at Calcutta during 1883-1884. Craftsmen Hussain Ali, Mohammad Ali Beg, Bullan Beg, Mehdi Hussain and Mohammad Ali who belonged to the Mansoor Nagar, Sabzi Mandi and Pul Ghulam Hussain locality of Lucknow exhibited their Bidri work in the exhibition. The Bidri and Zarbuland silver work found expressions in *huqqa farshi*, jewel boxes, trays, bowls, cuff-links, cigarette cases and holders with other show pieces. State Museum, Lucknow, Indian Museum, Calcutta, Saalaar Jung Museum, Hyderabad and Bombay Museum house some of the best bric-a-brac of Lucknowi Zarbuland- Bidri work.

Supported by the then chief minister of UP Chandra Bhanu Gupta, Zila Udyog Vibhag had established a Bidri training center. It was run and managed by Mirza Nadir Beg who was a descendent of the same family of craftsmen who exhibited Bidri in the exhibition held at Calcutta during 1883-84 and then in 1903 wining silver medal for their work. Mirza Nadir Beg died in 1985 and his demise followed the closure of the training centre subsequently bringing an end for this world famous and much sought after exclusive craft of Lucknow.

Ivory and Bone Carving

An important centre of ivory and bone carving, Lucknow had extensively created objects like dagger hilts, plaques to adorn the sides of carriages and howdahs, chessmen, miniature figures, ear rings, necklace, broach and other items like combs, bangles and mirrors. Motifs of trees, leaves, creepers, flowers, birds and animals are the most common work along with some exclusive and intricate work like shirt pins, lamp shades, knives and tiny toys. Ivory work on furniture is another feature of this craft introduced by the British influence. Since the worldwide ban on ivory, craftsmen started carving on camel and buffalo bone with great skill. There are two styles of this craft. The *jaali* (lattice) work inspired by the Mughal architecture is carved extensively on jewellery boxes and table lamps. For jewellery, different shades of camel bone and even dyed pieces are often used. Carving in the round, comprising hunting and forest scenes complete with elephants, tigers, parrots, peacocks and flowering trees is done on thicker bones.

An Ivory and bone craft artist of Lucknow Abdul Salaam was awarded in an exhibition held at London during the second decade of the twentieth century. His ancestor Mohd. Wasim and his son Mohd. Naseem are still carrying the tradition who have been awarded by the State Government and in few other exhibitions for their exclusive work. Some years back Mohd. Naseem, in an interview, expressed his worries and pain for apathetic attitude towards this precious and rare craft. No one is interested in learning the craft. Even their own children are turning indifferent and opting for other professions to carry on with life and its daily struggles.

Kanghi (Comb) Making

There is a lane called Kanghi Wali Gali in Nakkhas where combs were made with cutting a wooden piece or a bone with a saw. Later this locality was re-christened as *Kanghi Tola.* These products were not just another utility item but also a piece of art engraved with beautiful designs and patterns. Much in demand before the plastic invasion, these combs were very popular throughout the northern India and in other parts of the country. During 1979-80 three families were reported to have continued with this craft but as on today there are hardly any takers leaving the Kanghi Tola devoid of kanghi making art with the only family still clinging to this skill and keeping it alive while once there used to be more than hundred craftsmen residing there. They were skilled in making combs from the horns of different animals especially buffaloes as these horns were always available in plenty. This art involves much skill. Lot of manual work is involved in washing and drying the horns, cutting and making teeth and sharpening these with tools. This art stands on virtually the brink of extinction due to availability of cheaper plastic combs and lack of encouragement and patronage by the governmental agencies.

Chandi ka Varq

Kise pata ki hum isi shaher mein rahte hain ya nahin? Chikan, Zardozi aur Khattati ki baat to kam zyaada ho hi jaati hai par hamare kaam ka kahin zikr hi naheen. (No one in this city has even a slightest idea that we are also a part of this city. The craft of chikan embroidery, zardozi and khattati(calligraphy) find place in some or the other way but we are totally neglected.) A small piece of silver placed between the hide and pounded with a wooden hammer create a unique mixed sound with wooden and metal tones. Usually, a small piece of 7.50 grams of silver yields 170 pieces of silver foil. It takes 3-4 hours of constant pounding to get this result. Chandi Ka Warq is used by all castes and communities and its demand increases during the festival seasons. Be it the bylanes of Chowk, Akbari Gate, Nakkhas, Raja Bazar or Gol Darwaza area, this sound is a perpetual part of the daily life of these craftsmen who are struggling hard to keep alive this art. Like the craftsmen of some other fading crafts of Lucknow, many of them have opted for some other business and those who are still into it and carrying the tradition have no plans to introduce their children in this profession. There are hardly 20-25 families who are making silver foil which is rolled over the sweets and used in garnishing the other delicacies in South Asian cuisine as well as *paan* and tobacco's *qimam goli.* Be it Javed Ahmad,

Shariq, Jameel or other silver leaf makers, all of them have in common their miseries, a will to get recognition, wish for the Government support and above all to save this unique and famous art of Lucknow.

Clay Toys

Hum se tum dil ki tamannaon ka sauda na karo,
Hum to mittee ke khilono se bahel jaate hain.

(Do not bargain with me on hearts' desires as I may be deceived by the toys of clay)

Some 65-70 years old Kanahiya Lal who still pursues his traditional family craft and profession of clay toy making says with a deep sigh, '*Aap hi bataaiye, jis kaam mein barkat na ho, fayeda bahut kam ho, us kaam mein hamare bachche kaise dilchaspi leing? Aur hum bhi yahi chahte hain ki hamare bachche padh likh kar koi aur kaam ya naukri karein jisse unki zindgi thodi sahooliyat se chale*' (You only tell, the profession/craft which is not growing, accrues very little profit, how can our next generation be interested in it. We also wish them to study and join some other profession or job so that their lives run with a little ease.)Living in a small house cum shop in Kallu Pahelwan Ka Haata in Kandaha Tikaitganj locality of Khajua area near Nadan Mahal Road, he complains about the middle men, government apathy and lack of any formal training center and says, '*yahi haal raha to mitti ke phal, khilaune aur moortiyan banaane ka ye kaam 20-25 baras mein katam ho jayega.*' (If such conditions prevail this craft of making clay fruits, toys and idols will not last more than 20-25 years.)

The craft of clay toys making in Lucknow is said to have existed well before the Nawabi era but reached its zenith during this period and maintained its sheen well after the annexation of Awadh by the British till the seventh-eighth decade of twentieth century. Taking its origin from the various soils found in different mounds/hillocks mainly on Hardoi Road, it was originally the profession of Prajapati community which over a period of time was joined by several other castes and communities. Kaala Pahaad, Dussehri and Sigrauri villages, Kharja Nalah and other ponds in nearby villages are the main source of the raw material. Though all kinds of clay toys and idols are produced here Kandaha Tikait Ganj is predominantly known for its clay fruits which look so real and speak volumes of the craftsmanship of these artists. It is said that during Nawabi era this practice of clay fruits emerged as a fun during the lavish feasts and festivals hosted by the Nawabs. The real and the clay fruits were placed side by side for the guests to play the prank and most of the time guests were trapped by picking the clay fruit. Lakdmandi in Saadatganj area where idols of Laxmi-Ganesh and other gods-goddesses are the main feature is another very important centre for the clay toys. If we see the geography of these areas both the localities are close to the Hardoi Road which has been the main source for the clay and specially the black clay. Items created by these craftsmen include the bhangda dance, dashavtar, desi naach, king-queen, bheel set, kitchen set, gwalin, buddha-buddhi, servant set (traditional 12 servants of the British), jack fruit, brinjal, water melon, orange, apple, banana, lion, frog, crocodile and other items on demand. Women of the household are equally involved in the process no wonder adding more beauty, softness and better nuances to the end product. The demand for these toys and idols increases many fold during Deepawali season which lasts for two months and then as clay crafter Azad says, *' diwali ke bad das mahine zindgi chalana bahut mushkil ho jata hai. Aise mein doosre kaam bhi karne padte hain jinmein dil nahin lagta magar kya karein, bachchon ko padhana hai unka pet bhi bharna hai. Sarkar bhi hamari sudh nahin leti, Cheen ki sarkar apne yahan ke khilauno ko sab jagah bhejti hai magar yahan ki sarkar kuchh nhain karti, khair; chalna to hai hi kya kiya jaye.'* (it becomes very difficult to manage the rest of ten months after Diwali. We have no option but to do other odd jobs which have no charm for us but what to do, have to ensure the education of the children, feed them. Chinese government is so supportive and sends its products everywhere but our government is so indifferent, any way; one has to keep the life going.) But he has not given up, *' dekhiye Chinese maal to fast food hai, asli desi khana to hamare hi khilaune hai, log pooja mein ab bhi mitti ki hi moortiyan rakhte hain.* (Look, Chinese goods is just like fast food, the real and native food is our own clay toys, people still prefer to place our clay toys on auspicious occasions and worships.) Bibi Ganj, Kharehi, Yaseen Nagar, Muazzam Nagar and Shekhpur are some other localities which have joined this profession later. There are some who have got their wards admitted in Arts College and other such centers to equip them with the formal training and technical know how so that they may continue with the family tradition on a larger and better scale and market their products directly without getting trapped by the middle men, government apathy and other such hurdles faced by them and the earlier generations. But for the annual art and craft exhibitions organized by the state and central governments there are no avenues where they can exhibit and market their products. Allotment of stalls in such exhibitions is another story of corruption and malpractice of which many of them don't wish to or cannot become a part.

Though there are mixed feelings among the craftsmen about the future of this centuries old craft of making clay toys, it is rapidly losing its'grip and seems to be moving towards extinction .

Tazia Making

Dil magar bahelta hai Karbala ki yaadon mein....

Sultan-ul-Madaris, a Shia madarsa situated at the KG Medical College Crossing in old Lucknow where famous progressive poet Kafi Azmi was sent by his family to study Islamic Shia Theology but his revolutionary soul prompted him to flee away and pursue his dreams of a socialist India, turns into a center for tazia seekers during the Muharram.

Replica of the mausoleum of Imam Hussain, a symbol of resistance against the evil, taziadari in Lucknow is believed to have been started by the nawabs of Awadh who introduced beauty, aesthetics and perfection so much so that the art of tazia making emerged as another shining feather on the world famous craft canvas of Lucknow. A derivative of the word 'aza' which means mourning the tradition of *taziadari* is attributed to Timur who invaded India during the fag end of fourteenth century AD. As it was not possible to take his army to the annual trip to Karbala in Iraq he ordered to create a replica of the shrine coated with *Khak-e-shifa* the soil of Karbala which was specially brought from Iraq on his order.

This replica is supposed to be the first tazia made on Indian subcontinent. Later the practice of taziadari gained momentum with Mughal kings making it a far reaching tradition through regional courts. Numerous local traditions of tazia making have emerged over the centuries which vary is shapes and sizes according to the region can be classified in various class and categories like silver/ metal, wooden and bamboo- colored paper decorated with small toys, flags and other embellishments. For the rich tazias of green-glass with brass mouldings, ivory, sandalwood, cedar or wrought silver and for poor it's of the talc and paper. Although some were originally made of precious materials for royal and wealthy patrons, to be housed permanently, the majority of tazias are of kind of disposable sacred art which are buried at the culmination of tazia procession. Such disposable structures are the predominant feature on the popular level today. Materials used to build tazias include wood and bamboo for the frame and paper, tin foil, mica and glass for the ornamental exterior.

Accomplished and the world famous craftsmanship of tazia making of Lucknow has seen the peaks, faced the challenges of time since last 175 years is presently fighting for a decent survival. All that glitters is a tazia, as artisans writhe in debt to keep the tradition alive.

A faint smile on her wrinkled face exhibits her sense of achievement in the days of mourning. The smile braves the hard fact that Akhtar Jahan has taken a loan of Rs 50,000 to keep up the generations old tradition. That she will have to pay back Rs 20,000 as interest against the loan doesn't bother her.

Putting the mundane challenges of survival aside, the 60-year-old woman makes tazias (tableaux) during Muharram, a custom started by the nawabs of Awadh. "I help people fulfill their pledge. My reward is their appreciation and good wishes," she said. But the future of this craftsmanship may not be as bright as the glittering tazias of different shapes, sizes and heights lined up for sale at Sultanul Madaris, during Muharram. Like Jahan, most of the tazia makers are trapped in the clutches of private money lenders.

Sarkar Mirza, another tazia maker, tells us why. "Tazia making is a time consuming job that begins about six months before the Islamic month of Muharram. But buyers come only when the month starts. Most of us are small-time artisans employed usually as zardozi workers, having limited means. So, the challenge of input cost always stares at us," said Mirza, adding that he borrowed Rs 45,000 for the inputs.

Mohd Wahid, an elderly tazia maker, who was supervising for many of his counterparts at Sultanul Madaris, said time had come to give some assistance and patronage to tazia makers. "I wonder if the next generation has the patience needed to turn coloured sheets of paper into interesting motifs and design a tazia. They would be discouraged to take the tradition further if they have to go to a money lender to gather money for the material," he stated.

But what makes an ordinary embroidery artist walk the extra mile to keep a tradition alive? In answer, Nawaz Haider said making tazia has become an important part of his life. "I grew up seeing my father and grandfather making tazias. While their deft hands shaped the tazia, their minds were engaged in convincing us that we have to take this tradition forward," he said. Another tazia maker Hasan Raza added that tazia making was an art dedicated to Imam Husain who sacrificed his life in the battle of Karbala.

A Shia scholar Maulana Sayed Saif Abbas Naqvi says, "Artisans would continue to make tazias till azadaars (mourners) demand." Informing that the tradition of making tazias in Lucknow ,is about 175 years old, he said, "It is believed that tazia processions were unique to Lucknow and spread to other places from here." Interestingly the tazias are not part of Moharrum mourning in Hyderabad, the second largest centre of Moharrum observance in South Asia after Lucknow. In Hyderabad, only Alams are kept in *Ashurkhanas* and carried in procession on the days of *Ashura* and *Chehlum.*

Plight of the Artisans

Khushiyan dete dete aksar khud gham me mar jaate hain,
Resham bunne waale keede resham me mar jaate hain.
(Those generating happiness, many a times, die with sorrow.
This is the fate of silk worms who die in the web of silk)

These lines of Urdu poet Khushbir Singh 'Shaad' so appropriately portrays the plight of the artisans of Lucknow-Chikan and Zardozi embroiders, *Chandi ka warq* (silver foil) makers and virtually the craftsmen of all the handicrafts in Lucknow. With the multifarious craft specialties Lucknow has been a shopper's delight and at the same time it has also brought international recognition to the trade and the craftsmen but mere recognition of the talent of some master craftsmen and women becomes ironical in the face of exploitation and deprivation of the practitioners.

In the lanes and bylanes of old Lucknow and the sub-urban areas one comes across family after family, mohalla after mohalla 'embroidering dreams' with the subtle movement of their fingers. **chikankari** got the 'geographical indication' in recent years and this aroused the hope of the embroiders, mostly women, that the international branding would bring some cheer to their lives by ensuring fair remuneration and better living condition. Unfortunately, their plight did not change and they continue to get virtually subsistence wages when their art fetches lakhs

Workers ingrossed in Kaamdaani embroidery

Intricate Kaamdaani work

Zardozi embroidery

A Chandi ka Warq (silver foil) maker

Some artefacts carved on bone

Bone carver in the midst of his products

Knife and scissor sharpening

and lakhs of rupees. By working on more and more intricate and delicate designs and patterns their fingers get numb, eyes become weak and vision blurred in the insufficient and dingy light, the spine may not cooperate beyond fifties and what do they get in return? On an average the remuneration per month varies between Rs. 500-3000/= only. Then who grabs the proverbial lion's share? Of course the middle men, traders and shopkeepers.

The chikan workers would be much better off if they get direct access to the market but the vicious cycle of exploitation has been invincible to them. With no savings many of them get trapped by the private moneylenders and their miseries are further accentuated. Despite all the promises by the State Government and various governmental agencies there is no provision of institutional finance for them, no credit facilities, no medical insurance and no subsidies. Some schemes have been floated but exist only on paper. It is shocking to know that the government has no record of the number chikan workers engaged in this craft in Lucknow and adjoining districts. The workers bitterly complain that the selfish and clever designers take their embroidery and after minor cuts and designs, sell the products and mint money but they continue to languish within their vicious cycle of deprivation and exploitation.

After chikankari, **Zardozi** has received national and international recognition and attention. Even outside India, Sarees and other dresses with Zardozi embroidery is quite popular- from the middle class to the affluent elites, movie stars and fashion designers, fetching very high prices. Like chikan workers, one of the reasons for their exploitation has been their reluctance to go beyond the four walls of their homes or mohallas. Most of the Zardozi workers have continued to languish while only some successfully carved their path and through untiring efforts became big *karkhanadar* (workshop owners).

The demands of this craft, like chikankari is such that requires constant sitting and stretching on the floor and doing embroidery on a piece of cloth fixed tight from all sides between a wooden frame resting on its four legs. Several senior workers of Lucknow city complain bitterly about the role of their counterparts living in villages. Zardozi workers have to face 4-6 lean months every year during which they get hardly any work to do and they have to fall back upon their meager savings or forced to borrow from moneylenders. The rural artisans have the advantage of having some mango orchards or mint crop or earning some money from such rural employment schemes as MNREGA and thus able to ward off the total penury and are able to survive. Thus, they can afford to work against lower wages which is to the advantage of the traders. Hence, the urban craftsmen have to compete with them and forced to accept whatever wages are offered to them. Within this shoe string budget they pay the fee of their school going children, bear medical expenses and other contingencies. Many a times they have to request the clerics and generous members of the community to help them with such Islamic charities like *Zakaat.*

Some zardozi workers disclose that because of lack of unity among them, they have to engage in cut throat competition among themselves and offer lower and lower prices for their product to the advantage of the traders and shopkeepers. One can imagine their miserable plight by the fact that even presently an average zardozi worker earns wages as low as hundred rupees a day for an eight hours job and that is why they demand that minimum wages on the lines of MNREGA should be fixed for them along with the provisions of social security such as life insurance, medical insurance, pension, help for the aged workers etc. The most unfortunate part of the story is a marked tendency of distortion in productivity gains, that is, rising share of profits of the organizers and falling proportion of wages of the workers even while the industry remains labour intensive. It is certainly in handicrafts like chikan, zardozi, wood carving and others.

Unlike the chikan and zardozi workers who are in thousands the makers of **Chandi ka Warq** (silver foil) and **Tazia Makers** have now been reduced to a few dozens. Besides Lucknow silver foil making is also done in Kanpur, Varanasi and Moradabad. In Lucknow the number of *Warq* making families are now barely twenty five and they too are waging a grim battle for the survival of their art. They resent that their plight is never highlighted by the media while chikan and zardozi are always able to grab attention. Several of them swear that they would never introduce their children to this art that promises only starvation. **Tazia making** is also a very intricate art involving a high degree of skill and expertise. The demand for this craft is largely confined only to the two months of Moharrum mourning days and specially to the first ten days but the work starts 4-6 months before the advent of Moharrum. Thus, it involves investments whose returns come after a few months. Moreover, since the sales of tazias are limited to only a few weeks, it cannot be a full time job and hence most of the *tazia* makers are *zardozi* workers having limited means. Most of the *tazia* makers are Shias who are emotionally involved with the mourning practices because of their religious faith. They maintain that they would not leave it despite incurring debts and meager returns.

Vanishing Skills

With the changing technology, demand and tastes of the people, a number of skills which made Lucknow proud are dying and stand on the verge of extinction. For instance the art of dying clothes, *rafoogari* (darning), *kitaabat/khushnaweesi* (calligraphy) and several others had reached their zenith during the Nawabi era and known far and wide are gasping for breadth. Such interesting skills as Urdu *muamma*(crossword puzzle based on references from books) giving idea about the literary taste of the people are also dying.

10

Vanishing Skills

Rangrez (Dyers)

Hamri na maano rangrejwa se poocho......
(Don't trust me, ask the dyer)

The art of dyeing is not a new one in Lucknow but it developed and touched new heights during the Nawabi period especially during the reign of Wajid Ali Shah. Madhu Trivedi (2010) digging from different sources writes that the Nawabs, keen to improve this art, invited skilled dyers from different places to Awadh.

The dyers were known as Rangrez and (*rang* meaning colour and *rez* is competence) were mostly Muslims. Sometimes, they were also called *neelgar* perhaps because of the reason that many of them dyed fabrics with indigo. Almost all the dyes in use were produced locally. Later, European dyes were introduced. As per a legend some of the dyers excelled in this art to such as extent that they could dye both sides of a *dupatta* in different colours. The dyers used to do brisk business during certain months and occasions. For instance, during the month of Saawan there used to be in great demand for light green *(dhaani)* saree while during the mourning months of Moharram dyeing clothes in black and, to a lesser extent, green was the usual practice.

Perhaps, Lucknow is the only city in India in which an exclusive mohalla in Husainabad was created for the dyers and they were settled there. Since large quantities of water were required in the process of dyeing this settlement was located on the bank of the river Gomti. After the end of the Nawabi era and the connoisseurs of colour falling on the days of penury and with the advent of machines the dyers lost a major share of the market. Now one hardly comes across independent dyers. Whosoever continues in this business work for some laundries and most of them earn their livelihood through washing clothes. It never happened before as a *rangrez* look down upon washing clothes and this was the profession of *dhobi* (washerman), a different caste altogether. Like several others, dyeing in Lucknow is also a 'dying' art.

Rafoogar

Any skilled person doing darning is called *rafoogar.* The root word is *rafoo* meaning to mend anything torn or damaged and this skill is known as *rafoogari.* It is an ancient art to mend a minor damage to an expensive dress which may not be discarded or thrown away because of a minor scratch.

Until 1960s or 1970s *rafoogars* could be seen in virtually all markets, laundries and drycleaners but with the passage of time their number has been dwindling. Now a days there are just 20-25 *rafoogars* left in the field. Though this skill is not community specific yet it is seen that most of the darners in Lucknow came from the Muslim community. Explaining the skill, Reyazuddin Quraishi, an experienced rafoogar, discloses that *rafoo* may be performed on any type of clothes but darning on cotton clothes is more difficult and labourious than doing it on woolen clothes. For this purpose the thread is taken out from the same clothe so that the darned portion is perfectly matched and may not be noticed easily. The real expertise in this skill is acknowledged only when one is not able to indicate the darned area of the cloth. The darning is done sitting either on a wooden *chowki* or simply on the floor and its explanation as given by the *rafoogars* is that the required 'balance' of the needle is achieved best while sitting like this.

Those in the business reveal that though they continue to get some work throughout the year but the demand increases during winters because of the damage done to woolen clothes by the silver fish and other insects and pests. One experienced *rafoogar* disclosed that one may earn Rs. 200-300 per day except during winters when their earnings may climb up to Rs. 400-500 per day. One of the reasons behind this fast vanishing skill is that the work is very delicate, intricate and time consuming but the income is not commensurate with the skill and time involved.

Ittar/Attar Making

If one enters Chowk Bazaar from the side of Gol Darwaza and walks around two furlongs one is hit by a pleasant and exotic fragrance emanating from the shops selling *Ittar.* An Arabic word, *Ittar* stands for natural perfume oil obtained through steam distillation, distilled naturally. Herb, flowers and fragrant woods are the raw materials used in the manufacture of *Ittar.*

It is popularly believed and maintained by the *Ittar* traders, that *Ittar* achieved mass popularity during the Mughal period. The elite and connoisseurs used to keep the ittar in ornate tiny crystalcut bottles called *Ittardaan.* Even today the last remaining old shops in Chowk area exhibit the beautiful glass *Ittardaans* in show cases but the *Ittar* is sold in small, ordinary glass bottles.

The hundred percent pure *ittar* is free of alcohol and chemicals and that is why its perfume last much longer than the alcohol based scents. Another difference is with regard to its application. While the *ittar* is applied directly to the skin on the inner side of the wrist or on the back of the earlobe, the alcohol based perfumes are considered harmful if applied directly on the skin. Though the *ittar* comes in more than three dozen fragrances, the more popular ones are *khas, gulab, shamamatul ambar, kevda, mogra* and *mushkambar*. Those fond of Ittar, even today, know which fragrance to use in which season. For instance in summers, *khas* is considered best for its soothing, cool fragrance. It is tragic that *Ittar* is fast fading out and the younger generation has taken to chemical, alcohol based scents and deodorants and there is every possibility that it may soon become a thing of the past in Lucknow.

Jarrah

The *Jarrah* of Lucknow were once very important persons for the local population. An Arabic language word, *Jarrah* has been derived from the word *Jarahat* meaning wounds and *Jarrah* is one who takes care of wounds and injuries. In the popular parlance, it refers to what we understand from the English word Surgeon. Among the Urdu speaking people a *Jarrah* is an orthopedist, physiotherapist and surgeon, all in one.

Before the doctors- the practitioners of modern systems of medicine, surgery and orthopedics took over, the *Jarrahs* were in great demand. In Lucknow, they could be seen having roaring practice but gradually the people started reposing faith in modern surgeons and physotherapists and this system of medical care declined and is now confined only to the uneducated and economically weaker sections of the society. Though their job of minor surgery and bone setting and mending declined substantially, their expertise in performing *Khatna* (circumcision) continues to provide them a large Muslim clientele. Though not compulsory or religiously enjoined this is one practice which is being followed all over the Muslim world. Only a few Muslim take their male kids to the modern hospitals for circumcision and the rest continues to take the services of an experienced *Jarrah*. Sometime even the surgeon of a modern hospital advises a worried father to get the circumcision performed by a *Jarrah* who may be performing this surgery several times a week while the surgeon of a modern hospital may be performing it only occasionally. After the *Khatna* has been performed the *Jarrah* visits his client at home a couple of times to examine the progress of healing. Beside his fee he also gets some gifts in cash or kind.

Several clinics/shops of the *Jarrahs* may still be seen in old Lucknow especially near Raja Bazar, Jhawai Tola, Nakhas and Aminabad. A *Jarrah* in his clinic also does bone setting, adjusts joint dislocations and performs physiotherapy. Most of the times they tend to fractures without applying any plaster. They do not require an x-ray plate to make diagnosis. Their dexterous fingers may spot the fracture and set it right and then applies a paste, bamboo stick and bandage. The job is over within minutes. The patient is handed over some oil for massage or paste prepared in the system of Unani medicine. Let us see how long the institution of *Jarrahi* is able to survive against the modern system of surgery and physiotherapy.

Calligraphy

Lucknow has also been known as a prominent centre of calligraphy. Muslims have always deemed calligraphy, the art of beautiful writing, the noblest of the arts as it was closely associated with Islam and Quran. Writing in Arabic script was a hallmark of Islamic civilization. *Khush nawees* is the word used for writing beautifully in Arabic, Persian or Urdu. Etymologically speaking, *Khush* stands for good or beautiful and *nawees* means writer. Those who used to copy any written material were known as *Kaatib* and the skill is known as *kitabat*. Generally speaking *kitaabat* is used for the skill of writing. The art of calligraphy is also known as *khattati* and there are several styles of calligraphy such as *kufi*, *nastaleeq* etc.

With the advent of Industrial Revolution in Europe in 18th century when the new printing technology was invented and used the art of writing books declined radically as it was cumbersome and time consuming. In India, Arabic, Persian and Urdu printing was taken up through litho printing press which required the services of calligraphers. Thus, a number of calligraphers got jobs in newspapers and publishing houses. Till the time when computer typing took over, the entire newspaper in Urdu was hand composed by the calligraphers.

As already mentioned, Lucknow has been a well known centre of calligraphy but as Syed Anwer Abbas (2011) writes, there are no definite records to show when exactly calligraphy began in Lucknow but a very old evidence of calligraphy may be seen on the stone on the entrance of the tomb of the 16th century sufi saint, Ibrahim Chisti. During the Nawabi period we find mention of such names as the famous calligrapher Mir Ata Husain 'Tehseen'. With decline of the Mughal Empire, a number of calligraphers of Delhi migrated to Lucknow and settled down. The Nawab rulers were appreciative of their skills and utilized their services in official work. During the reign of the last Nawab, Wajid Ali Shah, there were two famous calligraphers by the name of Amirullah Tasleem and Munshi Haadi Ali 'Ashk' attached to the royal court. After the end of the Nawabi rule, they accepted the job at Naval Kishore Press that was printing newspapers, magazines and books through litho press. Since Naval Kishore Press was the biggest press of its time, it required the services of dozens of calligraphers, some of them were Hindus who were new entrants in this field. Some of the best specimen of calligraphy may be seen in various monuments such as Chota Imambara, Talkatora Karbala, Imambada Sibtainabad and others where walls and ceilings are decorated with beautiful calligraphy.

Some of the most prominent calligraphers of 20th century are Sheikh Tajuddin 'Ishrat', Qari Muhammad Aleem, Syed Najmul Hasan, Asif Mirza, Syed Hasan Naqvi 'Hadaf' Ijtihadi, and Moulvi Agha Mehdi. By the turn of the 21st century almost all the Urdu newspapers had adopted computer typing and offset printing and the art of calligraphy has become endangered as it is now difficult to earn a livelihood through calligraphy. Calligraphy in Urdu is now, mostly, required for

A Rafoogar (darner) doing his job

A Rangrez (dyer) in the process of dying a cloth

An Ittar shop displaying some rare cutglass containers

A kanghi (comb) maker working on the horns of buffalo

Giving finishing touches to a kanghi

A Jarrah treating his client for a dislocated bone

inscription on grave stone, or name of a building or writing on banners made on cloth. With the rapid decline of calligraphy in general, a beautiful art form of it- *Tughra,* also suffered the same fate. It is calligraphy done in different forms and shapes. Such as circular, oval, floral (such as flowers, leaves, bouquet, plants, peacock, horse etc.). Some of the better known last calligraphers still clinging to this art are Hashim Akthar Naqvi, Azeem Haider Jafri, Agha Mohd. Hasan and Asad Jafar Zaidi.

Urdu Muamma

Before the advent of cross word puzzle in English and Hindi *Shabd Paheli* (word puzzle), *Muamma* in Urdu language had already made a mark probably in seventeenth century. The sophisticated elite and wealthy people in Lucknow indulged in chess along with Urdu *muamma* while the middle class had also added it in their scheme of recreation and pastime. As the present organizers of Urdu *muamma* tell us, award in cash for the winners was not the idea in the initial period. Moreover, the elite looked down upon cash payments but its' popularity continued to grow among the middle classes.

Literally meaning enigma/riddle/puzzle, the *muamma* after making its beginning in the *Nawabi* and feudal environment of Lucknow spread rapidly to the nearby cities. During the reign of the Nawabs, *Darbaari Muamma*, sponsored from the courts and palaces had also a parallel competition sponsored by the *zamindars* and wealthy people. Some of the oldest *muammabaaz* (experts in *muamma*) tell that right from its beginning the result of *muamma* had always been declared on the Thursdays. Once costing a meager two paisa, the *muamma* proforma now costs between 2-5 rupees and the winners get awards of ten to fifty times of the cost of these proformas.

Till the 1960s, centers of the *muamma* were distributed almost the entire city but now a days it is confined to only some mohallas such as Nakhas and Moulviganj. On Thursdays the agents carry the filled in *muamma* forms and return with the amount of money to be given to the real stake holders. It is said that the wealthy elite class used to give money to the winners from their own pockets as gesture of appreciation for the expertise and skill of the winners but later it took the form of lottery which prevails now. The source of money for these awards comes from the sale of *muamma* proforma and it is distributed among the organizer, winners and the commission agents.

The *muamma* is prepared with the help of highly knowledgeable people of Urdu literature and either printed or photocopied and sold to the customers. Interestingly, even today some interested persons still come to Lucknow on Thursdays from Barabanki, Faizabad and as distant places as Tanda, Bahraich Gonda and Balrampur. It is said that the most addicted *muamma* players reside in mohallas such as Kandhari Bazaar, Ghous Nagar, Raja Bazaar, Chowk, Nakhas and Choupatiya.

With the decline of Urdu language and advent of several other means of recreation and pastime the popularity of *muamma* has been shrinking rapidly and may pass into oblivion with the passing away of the present generation of *muamma* lovers.

Ghadisaaz

It is said that wrist watch was invented in 1868 by a Swiss. Before that, people carried the watch in pockets tied with chains. Thus, the fashion of having wrist watches picked up after the World War I. The watches and hanging clocks were based on the principle of winding and unwinding. The ornate clocks of various types were also in vogue and a rich collection of such clocks may be seen in Saalaar Jung Museum of Hyderabad.

Lucknow could boast of having legendry watch and clock mechanics and repairers. Till 1970s one could get a familiar sight of a man with a rounded lenses stuck to one eye stooping low over a watch set on a glass stand moving his fingers with great dexterity on a road side watch and clock shop. Several of them had achieved legendry fame for their skill. With the advent of quartz watch in 1969 and its growing popularity since 1970s the earlier generation of watch repairers started going into oblivion. The reason was obvious. The digital, quartz watch was based on a different technology and the watch repairers were not conversant with it. Several of them, who could invest in watch business, opened the watch shops or converted their repairing shop into a watch, time piece and wall clock shop if it was located in or near a market or on a road side. With this a new generation of watch mechanics emerged conversant and trained in the new technology. The legendry Sadiq mechanic and members of his tribe are now living in the memory of older generations or find mention in the history of this skill.

The revival of the defunct clock towers in big cities demanded the quest for the last remaining knowledgeable mechanics of this art. The ongoing repair of the famous Clock Tower of Husainabad is a case in point. The 230 feet high Clock Tower was built in 1782 by the Nawab Nasiruddin as a mark of arrival of Sir George Cooper Brat, the first lieutenant Governor of North Western Province of Agra and Awadh. It is said that the famous clock maker of the British Empire, James William Benson was specially called for it and it cost a whopping one and a half lakh rupees at that time. Its needle, indicator of the hour, is six feet long and the minute indicator is as long as eight feet. The tourism department of Uttar Pradesh and the Husainabad Trust together has taken up the task of getting it repaired. The famous clock mechanic Ehtesham of Bareilly has been commissioned for this purpose and the Clock Tower may regain its past glory in a couple of months from now.

Hakeem and Vaid

Hakeems and *Vaids* have been an integral part of life in Lucknow especially *hakeems* were better known. While the hakeems are the practitioners of *Unani* system of medicine, *vaids* treat people with Ayurvedic system of medicine. Unani refers to a tradition of Greeko-Arabic medicine based on the teachings of Greek physicians developed into an elaborate medical system in the middle ages by the Arab and

Persian physicians. Historically speaking, Unani medicine arrived in India around 13th century during the period of Delhi Sultanate but flourished under Mughal rule.

Unani system of medicine, also known as *Ilm-e-tib,* presently has its centre in Jhawai Tola in Chowk-Chaupatia area. It's an important part of the Indo-Muslim medical tradition. Previously, persons from the so called nobility had a knack for *tib* and adding 'Hakeem' before one's name was a matter of pride and *ilm-e-tib* was part of the syllabus in their education. Mirza Jafar Husain (1981) writes that the higher caste persons had an inclination towards it as it could easily be a source of income because every 'noble man' used to maintain a *hakeem.* Such hakeems also had their *matab* (clinic) in their respective mohallas with the result that virtually every mohalla had at best one hakeem. It was not merely a source of livelihood but was also considered as a job that pleased God. Most of the hakeems did not have dispensing facility and their prescribed medicines could be prepared only by an *Attar* (dispenser of Unani medicine) who were many. Nawab Nasiruddin Haider established two hospitals – one in Chowk and the other at Turiaganj (Victoria Ganj) near Nakhas. Both are still there but the one at Chowk called Dar-ul-Shafa is now in Shambles and in very bad shape.

Lucknow had legendry hakeems who were believed to have miraculous power of treatment. There was one Hakeem Patti who treated his patients only with *patti* (leaves) of different plants. Another was known as Hakeem *Lasoda* who treated his patients with *Lasoda* leaves and fruits. Later, there were such famous Hakeems as Hakeem Kamaluddin, Hakeem Shamsuddin, Hakeem Meeran Sahab, Hakeem Saheb Aalam and Hakeem Munne Agha. None of them were related with Jhawai Tola and had their *matab* where the students were also taught *tib.* When the individual *matabs* and 'study circles' declined and faded away an organized college of medicine came into existence in Jhawai Tola named *Takmeel-ul-Tib* and its founder was the famous Hakeem Abdul Azeez on whose name the road in the Chaupatiya area is named. This college saved *Ilm-e-tib* from total extinction and has been producing hundreds of *Hakeems.* This Unani College was established in 1902. It has now been taken over by the Government and called Government Takmil-ul-Tibb College and Hospital, Lucknow and affiliated to the Kanpur University and managed by the Directorate of Medical Education and Training, U.P. Despite the declining popularity of the Unani system of medicine, many people continue to go to Hakeems, Vaids and *Jarrahs.*

Ayurvedic medicine is a system of traditional Hindu medicine evolved within the Indian sub-continent. In an age when a section of people look at Ayurvedic system as pseudo science, its popularity has been growing after a declining fortune. Even today a well known *Vaidya,* Daya Ram Awasthi aged 92 years treats his patients in Baan wali Gali, in Chowk area. In the Talkatora area, another well known Vaidya Chandrabali Dube had started his manufacturing unit for Ayurvedic medicines. Among the popular *vaidya* one finds ND Misra treating his patients in his clinic at Aminabad, Turiaganj, and Jalalpur. Among the younger ones many people talk of Vaidya Ashok Kumar Bhagat, UK Verma and some others. With the establishment of an Ayurvedic Medical College in the year 1948, the Ayurvedic education got a boost. Now located at Turiaganj, the State Ayurvedic College and Hospital comes under the Faculty of Ayurveda University of Lucknow, but under the administrative control of Director, Ayurveda and Secretary, Medical Education, U.P.

The popularity of Ayurveda has been rising in recent years because of high pressure advertising of its products and growing patronage of the government but not many people go to a vaid. Presently, there are big companies in Lucknow such as Tansukh and Meghdoot, manufacturing Ayurvedic medicines. Unfortunately most of the Ayurvedic and Unani practitioners do not depend solely on their respective systems of medicine and prefer to prescribe allopathic medicine.

Cuisine and Culinary Art

The sumptuous Lucknawi cuisine is famous all over the world and remains a gourmet's delight. Not only the *dastarkhwan* of the elite but the food consumed by the commoners has several commonalities though not in terms of quality. Though several of the once famous dishes are no more available as their recipes have faded away with their cooks, but whatever remains is also a delight to the taste buds. Significantly, some of these items are so affordable that even the economically weaker sections may consume these occasionally.

11

Cuisine and Culinary Art

Cuisine

Clothing, cuisine, customs and etiquettes reflect an important part of the culture of a society and its aesthetic growth over the centuries and Lucknow is a place where not only the traditional arts and crafts reached great heights but also the simple vocations like cooking developed to the level of an art leaving the hosts and the guests mesmerized with the taste and the presentation.

The *dastarkhwan* of Lucknow (of course of the elite and affluents) has always been a combination of taste, class and the novelty where traditional dishes and the innovative delicacies were served together. Under the royal patronage the culinary skills scaled the ultimate heights where *bawarchis* and *rakaabdars* of Awadh with their expertise in blending the spices and serving styles achieved a high degree of finesse in cooking and laying a plethora of food and delicacies. Being the favourite pastime for the nobility of Awadh, experiments and the innovations in the art of cooking gave birth to a number of new dishes and recipes. Lucknow *dastarkhwan* would not be considered complete without *Korma* (braised meat in thick gravy), *Saalan* (a gravy dish of meat or vegetable), *Keema*(minced meat), *Kababs* (pounced meat roasted or fried over a charcoal fire), *Pasanda* (fried slivers of very tender meat in gravy), *Pulao* or risotto, a rice dish. Vegetarian dishes like *Bhujia*(cooked vegetables without curry),*Daal* (pulses), *Paneer pasanda,Shahi Paneer, Paneer Do Piyaza* and other varieties are also an inseparable part of the Awadhi cuisine.

The *Mutanjan, Safeda, Yakhni Pulao, Moti Pulao, Noor Pulao, Coco Pulao, Gulzar Pulao, Chameli Pulao, Nau Ratan Pulao, Korma Pulao, Korma, Keema Kofta, Mutton Do pyaza, Qaliya, Nahari- Kulcha, Roti, Khamiri roti, Naan, Sheermaal, Warqi Paratha, Taaftaans, Rumali roti, Baqarkhani roti, Gosht ki tali Arviyan, Panch ghuiyan Biryani, Dal Sultani, Kakori Kabab, Shami Kabab, Boti Kabab, Patili ke Kabab, Ghutwan Kabab, Seekha Kabab, Murg Musallam, Zami Doz, Muzafar, , Sheerbiiranj ke Khawanche, Ananr ki Mithai, Malai Paan, Lab-e-Mashooq* popularly known as *Malai Makkhan* (whipped cream flavored with saffron), *Naan Jalebi, Dussehri and Safeda mangoes, Shahi Tukda, Kulfi Faluda-* the list in unending. The richness of Awadhi cuisine is not just restricted to variety but the ingredients used in creating such potpourri also play an important role. *Dum* style of cooking is a result of such innovations where the food is cooked over a sim fire.

The history of Lucknow cuisine can be traced from the last days of Nawab Shuja-ud-Daula when Hasan Raza Kahan alias Mirza Hasnu from a reputed family of Delhi was *munatzim* (manager) of his *Bawarchikhaana*(kitchen) who appointed Maulvi Fazl-e-Alam of Safipur, Unnao, as the *naib muntazim* (assistant manager). Fazl-e-Alam regularly served *Khasa* (royal food) on different platters at the *dyodhi* of Nawab from his *bawarchikhana* where, it is said, an amount of seven lakhs and twenty thousand rupees were spent annually on food. Shuja-ud-Daula used to have food with his wife Bahu Begam. Every day the *khasa* was served from six different *bawarchikhanas* so one can imagine the total expenditure on the gastatory desires of the Nawabs. Asif-ud-Daula shifted the capital of Awadh from Faizabad to Lucknow but the *bawarchikhanas* and ever increasing variety of dishes added more and more bawarchis and rakaabdars learning and showing their culinary skills. The variety mixed with fun has been another interesting part of Lucknawi Dastarkhwan where the taste buds were augmented by the rib tickling anecdotes and stories. This included the most interesting part of their talent when these rakaabdaars used to give different shapes and sizes to one dish. There is an interesting anecdote when Prince Mirza Asman Qadr of Delhi visited Lucknow. At a dinner hosted by Nawab Wajid Ali Shah a dish of *Murabba* (a dessert of stewed or baked fruits) was served which looked to be very fine and tasty. Allured by the appearance Mirza Asman took a bite only to find that it was mutton korma which was given the shape of murabba. Wajid Ali Shah when invited at a feast hosted by Mirza Asman Qadr took every care not to get deceived by any dish where a variety of delicacies were laid on the dastarkhwan but to his surprise every dish was made of sugar, even the utensils. There are hundreds of such incidents where the mastery over cooking and decorating a large variety of the dishes and delicacies has given birth to many anecdotes which are still told and have created history in Awadhi cuisine mostly during the nawabi era.

The sumptuous Lucknowi dastarkhwan is famous all over the world and remains a gourmet's delight with Tundey and Sakhawat ke Kabab, Idris ki Biriyani, Shahid's stew, Rahim's Kulcha Nahari, Halua Sohan, Jalebi, Imarti Malai, Radhey Lal, Chhappan Bhog, Mithai waala, Ram Asrey and Prem ki Mithai, Prakash ki Kulfi and other vegetarian dishes prepared with pulses, paneer and seasonal vegetables.

The *bawarchis*(cooks) of Lucknow excelled in a variety of food and even today some of the descendants of these expert cooks are a source of culinary delight.A whole mohalla was exclusively reserved for them and was called Bawarchi Tola which still exists.One of the unique features of Lucknow's culinary art has been the utensils used by the cooks.Even today the utensils are either of copper or iron. Several types of *kebabs* are prepared on a large pan known as *maahitava*.The big *degh* is made of copper and used for cooking large quantities of *biryaani,qorma* and curried preparations.Among the traditional families ,on special occasions,*dastarkhwan* are laid on *durees*(rug or carpet) and *chaandni*(white sheets).

Lucknawi Chaat is another mouth watering platter sought after to satiate the taste buds of all and sundry be it a Lucknowite, visitor or a tourist.

Spring and Summer special – *Kulfi Faluda*, Dussehri and Safeda mangoes, Chaand Patti, Laiyya Patti, Chuski Baraf.

Autumn and Winter variety – *Tahri, Lab-e-Mashooq* or *Malai Makkhan*, *Revdi Gulab, Nimona* (a gravy dish with grinded peas or green grams with potato), *Til ke laddo, Ramdane ki Patti*, *Budhia ke Baal* or *Budhiya ka kata* (during Melas).

Rainy season – *Andarse ki goli*, *Khoya Patti.*

Makhkhan Malaayi. Reori and Gajak

Makhkhan Malaayi of Lucknow is famous all over the world for its taste and experience.Prepared and sold only during five months of winters, it developed during the Nawabi days to provide a feeling of summers during the winters.A product of milk,stirred and beaten intricately adding sugar ,keoda etc. for taste this highly fluffy dessert is an speciality of Lucknow.Thae makers of *makhkhan malaayi* reside mostly in village Shaikhpura near Khinni Chauraha on Mohaan Road,Thakur Ganj,and Newaaz Ganj and many of them happen to be Brahmins. Most of them switch over to Qulfi making during the summers.The helping hands may be taken from elsewhere but the manufacturers of *makhkhan malaayi* are the natives of Lucknow.

A paanwaala offering paan on a ceremonial occasion

Like the *makhkhan malaayi*,the *reori* and *gajak* of Lucknow are also very popular and famous.These are also consumed during the winters though available in restricted quantity throughout the year.Very sweet , based on either sugar or jaggery with a fair sprinkling of sesame seeds,*keoda*,and *gulabjal*,it is considered an ideal dessert during the winters.*Gajak* is much more sophisticated in preparation than the *reori* as the process of making it is very delicate and time consuming.The production units of these Lucknawi desserts are mostly confined in the localities of Charbagh,Pandariba,Malviya Nagar,Moti Nagar,Saadat Ganj,Mashak Ganj,Bashirat Ganj and Aminabad.

Lucknawi Paan

Paan kahta hai ki main sookh ke mar jaoonga
Ai lab-e-yaar agar tu ne na chooma mujhko.
(Paan says that I would die thirsty if the lips of my lover do not kiss me)

Its hard rather impossible to think of a begum of Awadh without a *Paandaan*, a very decorative box of gold, silver or other metal in various shapes and sizes containing beetle leaves, *chuna* (lime paste), *kattha* (catechu), *supari* (betel nut), illaichi (cardamom), *laung* (clove), *kiwam* (fragrant tobacco paste), *Mushki Tambaku* (tobaccos with a range of fragrance) of various kinds and many other varieties of ingredients used in the preparation of paan. *Tawaanai ke nuskhe* (male potency enhancing prescriptions/formulae) and other aphrodisiacs were also an important part of a nawabi paandaan.

Even today offering *Paan* (betel leaf) is another important feature of famous Lucknowi *mehman nawaazi* (hospitality). It existed much before the Nawabi era as in Hindu culture *paan* is considered to be an auspicious leaf and is an inseparable part of all the religious, social and family celebrations. This symbol of love and the ultimate honour reached its zenith during the Nawabs of Awadh where no feast was complete without paan and the tradition goes on. This heart shaped leaf laced and filled with different fillings is also considered as a very delicate and refined expression of romance.

During the Nawabi era *paan* leaves were placed on an inverted earthen pitcher and their arteries were chiseled with a special knife so that the lips and the tongues of those delicate begums are not hurt. From palaces to courtesans' courts and from auspicious ocassions to temple territories, paan has enjoyed an important place and despite the current invasion of *paan masala/gutkha* pouches it continues to enjoy immense popularity.The event managers of Lucknow have revived some old and traditional practices specially in arranging marriage feasts.You go to any marriage of persons from middle class upwards and you will find a raised,decorated platform where two or more paanwaalas sitting in ceremonial dresses offering a variety of paan and *huqqa* to the guests and while leaving,after relishing the rich food, most of the guests including the non-regular paan chewers picking a paan or two for 'the road' back home.

Popular Eating Places/Khaan Paan ke Adde

Though Lucknow may not boast to have a 'food galee' such as the ones in Indore,Ahmedabad and Bombay but a large number of people throng to particular shops or restaurants, or '*adde*' to satisfy their taste buds.The influence of Iranian and Turkish cooks is obvious on the traditional non-vegetarian food and breads.Breads such as *khamiri* (tandoori) *roti*,*sheermaal*,*naan* of different types,*baaqar khaani*,*rumaali roti* etc. provide a connoisseur a wide range of options.Perhaps,Lucknow is one of the very few places in South Asia where a whole lane is dedicated to the *naanbai*(bakers of bread) and this is located near Akbari Gate in Chowk area.

Among the most popular addas for non-vegetarian food are the famous 175 years old shop of Raheem known for *Qulcha-Nahaari*.It is located near Akbari Gate. The famous Tunde Kebabi is is also there.Though they have opened their outlets in Aliganj and Aminabad to cater to a larger clientale,the loyalists especially those settled outside India prefer to go to the original one because of nostalgia attached to it.*Biryan*i of Idrees,*Roghan Josh* and *Haandi Gosht* of Dastarkhwaan and Aalamgir restaurants also attract large number of people

Though Lucknow may be more famous for its'non-vegetarian food this does not mean that vegetarians don't have any thing worthwhile to eat.*Khasta*,*Puri*,*Kachori* of Ratti Lal,Radhey Lal, Tewari and Durga Khasta Bhandar are some of the popular food joints.Lucnow is also known for its' *Chaat* but the sweets of Ram Asrey and Radhey Lal and now comparatively younger Chappan Bhog are famous far and wide..The *Qulfi-Faluda* of Lucknow is also very popular .From the next day of Holi the Qulfi shops open and windup before Diwali.Among the dozens of shops,Dayal Singh' and Prakash qulfi attract the largest number of people.

Music, Singing and Dance

The Nawabs of Awadh were great connoisseurs and patrons of fine arts and under their patronage music- both instrumental and vocal, singing and dance especially *kathak* flourished. During the reign of Nawab Wajid Ali Shah these arts reached great heights as he was himself an accomplished singer, actor and dancer. This legacy continues in Lucknow and the city has several centers of music and dance and many of the artists have gained recognition and popularity nationally and internationally and have made Lucknow proud.

12

Music, Singing and Dance

Akhilesh Dixit

The legend has it....
"*Allah Nabiji Karam Ki Boondein Barsa Deeje*
Karam Ki boondein Meher Ke Badal
Begi Mere Piya Se Mila Deeje."

As the last grand master of Lucknow Gharana of vocal music Ustad Khursheed Ali Khan sang his favorite *khayal* in raga *Nat Malhar* the rain started pouring in.

Lucknawi tradition of vocal music has its origin in *Qawwal Bachcha* Gharana which had its roots in Lucknow well before the advent of nawabi era. In 1724 when Mohammad Amin Naishapuri Sa'adat Khan Burhan-ul-Mulk was appointed naib- subedar of Awadh by Muhammad Shah, the king of Hindustan, Lucknow was much under the influence of Sheikhs and Pathans. The soil of Awadh was already rich with performing and fine arts, literature and music. Bilgram had produced many poets and the musicians as well. Madala Nayak during the regime of Shahjehan rose to the fame and was repeatedly offered to join the royal court but he declined. Meer Abdul Wahid Bilgrami was another famous laureate during Aurangzeb's rule that possessed good knowledge of music as well.

The tradition of singing qawwali at the Sufi shrines was a regular practice. With the decline of Delhi Raj musicians got attracted towards Awadh during the time of Nawab Shuja-ud-daula and after his death his son Nawab Asaf-ud-daula shifted the capital of Awadh from Faizabad to Lucknow. This can be termed as the most important period for the establishment of one of the finest school of musical traditions later to be known as the Lucknow gharana of vocal music credited with the *khayal* gayaki, *thumri* and *tappa*. Niyamat Khan Sadarang a great *veena* maestro was highly respected musician in the imperial court of Mohammad Shah Rangeele. He was continuously irked with a tradition through which, despite being a master veena player, he had to sit behind the *dhrupad* singer as a *sangatkar* (accompanist). Once he refused to perform *jugalbandi* (duet) with a sarangi player as he considered it against the dignity of a veena player of *Seiniya* gharana to play a duet with a sarangiya (sarangi player). The infuriated king expelled him from the court with an order to leave Delhi. This, as it is believed, brought Niyamat Khan to Lucknow where he lived in hiding. During those days he evolved the *khayal* style of singing and trained two talented young boys Bahadur and Dulle as his disciples. These two boys hailing from a poor *dhrupad* singer family who died early were trained by Niyamat Khan Sadarang in new style of singing created by him. Bahadur and Dulle later known as Miyan brothers became accomplished and immensely popular exponents of *khayal gayaki*; the new style of singing which emerged as a prime jewel in the crown of Lucknow's musical traditions and made Sadarang immortal in the history of Hindustani classical music crossing all the national and international boundaries. This popularity created a huge repertoire of *khayal* compositions and a number of musicians and composers joined in. Sa darang's sons and disciples Adarang and Maharang, Manarang and Harrang are the few very important names in this style of singing. If we straight away come to the *khayal* composers of nineteenth and twentieth century the list is so long that it's not possible to quote all.

The roots of *Qawwal Bachcha* gharana also known as Lucnow Gharana can be traced through famous qawwal Ghulam Rasool whose great grand-sons Shakkar Khan and Makhkhan Khan became very famous in the art of *khayal* gayaki. Bade Mohammad Khan and Naththan Peerbux sons of Shakkar and Makhkhan khan respectively emerged as the best *khaya*l exponents of their time.

During the regime of Nawab Wajid Ali Shah the music of *Qawwal Bachche* gharana witnessed great change in public taste with the growing popularity of *dadra, thumri, ghazal* and other forms which had the faster tempo with an undercurrent of flattery. Resultantly the serious exponents of *khayal* gayki migrated to Gwalior where they got royal patronage and encouraging atmosphere to flourish their art. The emigration of these talented and accomplished *khayal* singers Lucknow gharana lost its sheen and glory while *Gwalior* gharana emerged as the center of *khayal* gayaki so much so that it is widely considered to be the inventor of this form of classical singing. The exponents of Lucknow gharana gradually lost their distinguished identity by merging into other gharanas or schools mainly Jaipur and Gwalior.

> *' Zarre zarre mein hain yaan gauhar-e- yakta tahe khaak,*
> *Dafn hoga na kahin itna khazaana hargiz.'*

(Every particle here contains rare and unparalleled pearls; there would not be any richer treasure anywhere else).

As the famous music composer Naushad Ali, a great composer of Hindustani film industry in one of his articles in *Naya Daur* by quoting this couplet by Maulana Haali observes that though this couplet was composed on the loot, demolition and destruction of Delhi it is equally true for those great music exponents of Lucnow whose art has either been buried or cremated with them. Unfortunately the great musical treasure of Lucknow could not be preserved as it is in case of *Gwalior* and *Kirana* gharana.

Inheriting the rich musical tradition of Ustad Pyara Khan, Ustad Haider Khan and Ustad Sahet Khan who were descendents of Tansen, Ustad Sadiq Ali Khan, the master of *druvapada, dhamar, tappa, tarana* and *thumri* was the most outstanding and versatile exponent of *Qawwal Bachbe* gharana. During his time Ustad Sadiq Ali not only enriched the *Thumri* with grace and beauty the other singing forms like *sozkhwani, marsia, masnawi* and *qawwali* received great respect. Sadiq Ali trained his cousin Khurshed Ali, whom he later adopted as his son and the musical heir. Ustad Sadiq Ali Khan sahib was teacher of Nawab Wajid Ali Shah and sensing the growing popularity of *thumri* he introduced and refined *bandish ki thumri* with slow tempo. His favorite disciple Khursheed Ali Khan like his ustad mastered the unique and typical genres of Lucknow *soz, marsia* and *kalam* under the guidance and training of Syed Meer Ali of Lucknow. Khursheed Ali saheb trained his son Iqbal Ali Khan (1901-1980) and his grand-daughter Sikandar Jehan in music. His grand-son Momin Ali Khan preferred Mumbai film industry to carry on his family tradition of music. Sikandar Jehan was a great sozkhwan and her daughter Nafees Jehan who lives in Mufti Ganj still carries on with the *Sozkhwani* during Moharram. Sikandar Jehan initiated many of her disciples in *sozkhwani*.

Sozkhwani

One of the most important features of Lucknow's vocal traditions, *sozkhwani* has two different stories regarding its origin. During the mourning period of Moharram any kind of entertainment was not allowed leaving all the musicians and singer of that time without work and no earnings. On the other hand for Nawabs of Awadh who were fond of music it was difficult to stay without listening to the maestros. Thus the poetry of *Ahl-e-Bait* became the literature of musical presentation from the first day of the month of Moharram till the *Imam ka teeja* i.e. the twelfth day of Moharrum. This served both the Nawabs and the artists in their respective requirements. It is said that during the regime of Ghaziuddin Haider the *sozkhwani* rose to the heights and became an important part of Awadh's musical treasure and tradition.

Another version regarding the evolution of *sozkhwani* narrates that there was a gentleman known as Syed Sa'dat Rizvi. As it is believed he was Barah Imamon Ki Aulad (a Twelver Shia), and could introduce some changes in otherwise strict disciple of Islamic teaching. He was fond of music but due to the prohibition of music in Islam he could not learn or listen it. Hence he invented the idea of singing religious songs or the poetry of *Ahl-e-Bait* in respect of Hazrat Ali. (This gave birth to a practice where *marsias* were sung in musical fashion to be known as *sozkhwani*. It does not seem important to debate on the authenticity of these two versions as *sozkhwani* enjoyed a respectable place among all the great exponents of Lucknow tradition of singing).

'*Bigda gavaiya sozkhwan* (incompetent singer becomes sozkhwan).' This was a saying among the Ustads as according to them a singer who could not perform up to the standard of classical singing used to take shelter in *sozkhwani* where the literature was the only operative factor and not music to charge or emotionally move the audience. But there were exceptions too. As Mirza Rajab Ali Beg mentions in his book *Fasan-e-Ajayab* ' ,*marsiago* Meer Ali sahib has invented such a new style of *marsia* presentation that even the sky has bestowed blessings upon him by calling him Ustad.' Meer Ali *sozkhwan* finds place in another book *Kashaf-ul-Hakayak* by Imdad Imam. This poetry of *Ahl-e-Bait* was presented in the form of *Bund* (a set of six lines), *Rubai* (four lines) and *Qata (four lines)* were composed in various *ragas* considering the time of the event during the battle of Karbala. As Sha'd Azimabadi writes that when Meer Ali *sozkhwan* presented Meer Zamir's *marsia* '*Sapediye subah ka jab ran mein aashkaar hua*' in *raga Bhairvi* hundreds of listeners got unconscious and its impact remained the same for many years to come. Meer Zameer has described the morning scene in his *marsia* before coming to the main theme and the *raga bhairvi*, according to the Hindustani classical music, is sung in the morning. There are many such examples where *sozkhwans* of Lucnow excelled in their art of presenting *marsia, nauha, salam* and other form of poetry in the glory of Imam Hussein

Even today the *marsias*, *nauhas* and *salam* are heard during the month of Moharram but those musical connotations are almost missing from the *sozkhwani* as most of the presentations fall under the *Tahtul lafz marsia* (rendering in prose form) from the *mimber* (an elevated seat like pulpit). Hadi Raza saheb is considered to be the last sozkhwan of Lucknow's musical tradition who lives in Muftiganj. Similarly Nafees Jehan the grand-daughter of Ustad Iqbal Hussein Khan and daughter of Sikandar Jehan *sozkhwan*, living in Muftiganj area is also carrying on the tradition. Working with UP Sangeet Natak Academy, Gomti Nagar, Lucknow, Shahnawaz Khan is another *sozkhwan* who was trained by Nafees Jehan and is trying hard to keep the art alive for the last 30 years with Hadi Raza sahib.

Tabla Tradition of Lucknow

Once Ustad Sudhar Khan of Delhi court during a muqabla mehfil (competition concert) could not outperform the other pakhawaj player known as Bhagwandas. Not happy with this he broke his pakhawaj into two pieces inventing a new percussion pair tabla later to become the most popular instrument for solo performances and accompaniment as well.

Sudhar Khan's grand-sons Ustad Modu Khan and Ustad Bakhshu Khan are said to have come to Lucknow where they met *kathak* and pakhawaj experts of that time. As the Delhi style of tabla playing applied only two fingers it became difficult for them to match the *tatkar of kathak*, *bols of pakhawaj* and other light classical renditions. This prompted them to introduce certain changes by combining the forceful *pakhawah bols* with the graceful and delicate *bols of kathak* using rest of the fingers in their playing style to produce the desired resonance and the energy. This synthesis gave birth to Lucknow gharana of tabla. Another version says that these two grand-sons of Ustad Sudhar Khan were invited to join the royal court as musician by Nawab Azmat Jung Bahadur. Habib Raza another talented musician of Lucknow who was settled in Calcutta says that Modu Khan and his brother Zahid Khan came to Lucknow after leaving Jhajhar court and joined the royal court of Nawab Nasiruddin Haider. Nawab gifted them a *kothi* (a big house) in *Chowk* and were known as *kothiwals*. From Modu Khan there is a chain of well known tabla exponents which includes Ghulam Hussain Khan, Chuttan Khan, Akbar Hussain Khan, Sa'dat Ali Khan, Raza Hussain Khan and so on. Bakhshu Khan, as Habib Raza khan says, came to Lucknow during Nawab Asaf-ud-Daulah and from him we can trace another highly talented line of tabla experts including Mammu Khan, Mohammad Khan, Munne Khan, Nadir Hussain, Khalifa Abid Hussain, Kahlifa Wajid Hussain and his highly talented son who added many dimensions to the tabla gharana of Lucknow, Kahlifa Afaq Hussain who worked with AIR, Lucknow, UP Sangeet Natak Academy and Television till his demise in February 1990. His elder son Ustad Ilamas Hussain is working with Doordarshan Lucknow while younger one Iliyas Hussain is also carrying on with the family traditions. However, all the versions agree on one point that Modu and Bakhshu Khan were the founders of Lucknow gharana which was also known as *Kothiwal* gharana in its earlier stage.

Lucknow gharana is credited with the creation of Banaras and Farukkhabad gharanas of tabla. Ustad Modu Khan's disciple Pt. Ram Sahay established Banaras gharana. Haji Vilayat Khan, who was the originator of Farukkhabadi style of playing, got married to the daughter of Ustad Bakhshu Khan. He received many *qaydas* (composition of tabla beats) of Lucknow gharana as dowry. Finding such a treasure he created Farukkhabad gharana. Ustad Ahmad Jaan Thirakua was also a disciple of Ustad Munir Khan. Munir Khan was trained under the apt guidance of Haji Vilayat Khan's son Ustad Husain Khan. Though Ustad Ahmad Jaan Thirakua worked as the head of tabla department of Bhatkhande College of Hindustani Music and had very close affinity with Lucknow he belonged to Farukkhabad gharana of tabla contrary to a wider belief that he was from *Lucknow* gharana.

Sitar Tradition

Other than vocal and tabla Lucknow has a very rich tradition of sitar and sarod players. In 1775 when Asaf-ud-daula shifted the capital of Awadh from Faizabad to Lucknow, many these artists from various places came to Lucknow. Rabab player Basat Khan, Pyar Khan, Sarod player Niyamatullah Khan, Sitar exponent Raza Khan and beenkaar (veena player) Mohammad Hussain Khan are few to name. Ustad Raza Khan is credited for the creation of *Raza Khani gat* which is said to have come into the existence to please the nawabs and amirs who were losing interest in slow and serious style of *Masit Khani gat*. This migration popularized the classical instrumental music in Lucknow in bringing forth many families and new gharans of instrumental music as well like Barkat Ali Sanwalia's Faruukhabad gharana, Ustad Mohammad Hussain Khan's Lucknow gharana which later branched out through Ustad Abdul Ghani Khan and Ustad Yusuf Khan. Other than these gharanas there are many masters like Ghulam Mohammad Khan, Nabi Bakhsh Deredar, Sajjad Mohammad Khan, Qutub-ud-daula, Nawab Hashmat Jung, Panna Lal Bajpeyi, Vaid Arjun Das, Babu Ishwari Prasad, Chunne Khan, Nawab Ali Naqi Khan, Ustad Rahmat Hussain Khan, Banwari Lal Srivastav and many others who have contributed not only through their performances and training but also by continuous efforts to develop various styles in sitar playing. Ustad Mohammad Khan wh initiated Lucknow gharana of sitar also known as Dulhe Khan's gharana was born in Lucknow. His father Ustad Dulhe Khan was an apt *Druvpad*, *Hori*, *Sadra* and *Khayal* singer. Mohammad Khan used to perform in royal court and other selected mehfils (musical sittings) mostly at Thakur Nawab Ali's place. He adopted his nephew Rahmat Hussain Khan and trained him in sitar, *been* (veena) and singing also. Since Rahmat Khan was a beenkaar he never played sitar in any mehfil but trained many of his disciples like D.N. Sanyal, Bashir Khan, Rahmat Hussain Khan and Tulu Dutta who has been a teacher in Shashi Bhushan Inter College. This tradition of sitar and beenkari where learning the intricacies of vocal music was a pre condition for all the disciples was carried forward by other great masters like Ustad Raza Hussain Khan, Baqar Khan and Ustad Khalifa Ahmad Hussain Khan. He also trained many tawaifs (courtesans) like Ali Khursheed Alla Rakkhi, Badi and Chhoti Mushtari Bai, Qamar Jahan and the Salma of Mohammdi. He was invited to join Bhatkhande College of Hindustani Music by Thakur Nawab Ali Rai, Umanath Bali and Pt. Vishnu Narayan Bhatkhande where he worked for many years other than training atists like Bisimilla Khan, Iqbal Khan, Ayodhya Prasad, Amjad Khan, Ahmad Khan to name few. His only son Ustad Rahmt Khan, a fantastic sitar player, has introduced many *gats* to suit the *thumri* style of playing. Vimal Misra, Pawla Sarkar, Gauri Shankar, Spana Bhattacharya, Bhola Nath, Suraj Narain Lal, Vimla Kanoongo and Bal Krishna Nayar are among his major disciples. Born in 1941 at Lucknow Ustad Basharat Khan is another name worth special mention who was trained by his grand father Khalifa Mohammad Hussain Khan. He worked with AIR Lucknow for almost 20 years from 1952 to 1972. His main disciples were Gopal Chakroboroty, Suhasini and Bhuwan Mohini Nigam. Ustad Tajammul Khan can be termed as the last torch bearer of the sitar tradition of Lucknow who had worked as sitar lecturer with Bhatkhandey College, later to become principal of the college.

Presently, Lucknow, once a center of art and the artists, doesn't have much to boast in tune with its more than two and a half century old musical heritage. With the demise of the last representative Ustad Khursheed Ali Khan in 1950, whose style was a perfect blend of old and new Lucknow gharana put an end to the great tradition of *Qawwal Bachche* gharana. His life span of almost one century saw many changing and challenging times through the decline of Awadh, India's first freedom struggle, British onslaught, western industrialization and finally the Indian independence. This was the most crucial phase of Indian history.

Though there were many accomplished *khayal* composer who lived in Lucknow or were associated with the Bhatkhandey College of Hindustani Music but by the 1950, the year when Ustad Rasheed Ali Khan died, independent India had already entered into the modern times with its own broadcasting policies with All India Radio being the most important medium of spreading the cultural values and changing idioms of musical expressions. That was the time when AIR played a very important role in striking a balance between the old school of *khayal*, *thumri*, *dadra*, *tappa*, *ghazal* and *bhajan* singing with the emerging trend of light music where *raga* based melodies began to assimilate the western chord based style in compositions. AIR Lucknow can be termed as one of the pioneers in this new emerging trend. Evergreen but gradually fading style of Begum Akhtar was being coupled with this new style in recordings and in performances as well.

There were regular music concerts in Lucknow organized by AIR and other voluntary and government agencies like Uttar Dakshin Cultural Organization, Lucknow Mahotsav organizing committee and many others during the last four decades of twentieth century. Lucknow radio produced many composers like Vinod Chatterji, Gora Sen, Altaf Hussain, Manohar Swaroop and Kailash Srivastava with their subtle but very effective tunes still showing tones and shades of Lucknowi tradition. Famous singer Anup Jalota, a product of Bhatkhande College also shot to fame through his *bhajans*. Eighties, nineties and the first decade of twenty first century has gone through a sea change in music scenario of Lucknow when composer like H. Vasant, Hem Singh, Uttam Chatterji and Ravi Nagar brought about the new style of synthesis through western, Indian classical and folk music in their work.

Ravi Nagar deserves special mention for his contribution in theatre music with his musical presentations of progressive and modern Hindi, Urdu and free verse poetry where he crafted some new dimensions of interpreting the text through musical notes. His compositions for solo, group and dance drama in kathak are the perfect blend of traditional and modern themes. Sadly he breathed his last on 21st April, 2012 at the age of 49 after fighting cancer for almost two years. A true progressive human and an artist par excellence he was a poet of musical notes, a restless soul in search of new dialogues between the text and the tones.

The musical canvas of Lucknow is so vast and versatile and has been discussed by many authors, scholars and artists through various writings where conflicting opinions can also be seen at times but one aspect where all of them agree is the gradual decline of such a rich tradition.

Lucknow Gharana of Kathak Dance

Kathak and Lucknow are intimately intertwined with each other, thus creating a popular perception that *Kathak* originated in Lucknow. Though there are various opinions among the scholars regarding its place of origin but it's a well know fact that the art of *Kathak* dance reached its ultimate glory in Lucknow.

Kathak has been derived from its root word *Katha* meaning story thus it means a story teller, '*Katha kahe so Kathik kahave* (one who narrates a story with actions is a kathak performer). These artists who were accomplished story tellers presented *Pauranik* (from Puranas) themes through song recitation and acting conveying didactic messages to the masses. This tradition of story tellers can be traced from the mythological references of Lava and Kush the twin sons of Lord Ram who narrated the verses from *Valmiki Ramayan* in the royal court of Rama. These two boys from Awadh, possibly, can be termed as the earliest known *kathiks* as all the story tellers in the region were called Kushi-Lava.

The history of *kathak* dance takes its seeds from Chulbula village of Handia tehsil in Allahabad where, as the legend goes, Lord Krishna appeared in *Kathik* Ishwari Prasad Misra's dream and blessed him with the gift of dance and asked him to propagate and promote this religious dance. He is said to be the first *Kathak* performer to leave Handia to settle down in Lucknow. Ishwari Prasad, inspired by Lord Krishna's blessings wrote a book and trained his three sons Adguji, Khadguji and Tularamji in the art of dance which he had named '*Natvari dance*'. Khadguji and Tularam donned the saffron robes to become *sadhus* (saints) while Adguji trained his sons Prakashji, Dayalji and Harilalji. These brothers are said to have taken the art of this religious dance to the court of Shuja-ud-Daula and Asif-ud-daula and with their patronage this dance form from temples entered into the royal courts creating 'Darbari Kathak' getting its specific identity as ' the *kathak* style of Lucknow' later to be known as 'Kalka-Bindadin Gharana' and finally Kathak Gharana of Lucknow .

There is no evidence of any classical dance form or stylized dance until the arrival of Nawab-wazid in Awadh. The migration of various artists from Delhi to Lucknow included a considerable number of these dancers making Lucknow a great melting pot of different arts and the artists. During the reign of Shuja-ud-Daula artists which included dancers, singers, musicians and courtesans came to Awadh and settled in Lucknow in 1775 when Asaf-ud-daula shifted his capital from Faizabad to Lucknow.

Though *Kathak* dance originated in temples and Hindu surroundings it flourished during the reign of Shia Nawabs and kings of Awadh. There may be many reasons for these Kathak dancers to get attracted to the royal courts to exhibit their talent expecting rewards in the form of employment, cash and kind and for this these Gaud Brahmin Kathaks had to change the emphasis of performance from devotional and spiritual stories to romantic themes which were pre-dominant feature in all art forms inside the royal courts. Lord Krishna, the Natvar Nagar, being an ultimate icon of love and romance, these dancers combined the two themes with ease. Muslim courtesans who were expert singers and expressive dancers followed them with their own style of performance and the combination of the two, male dancers' *nritya* (body movement) and the courtesans' *bhav* (expressions) emerged as a distinct new style of *kathak*.

From the early days of *kathak* in royal courts until the reign of the last king of Awadh Wajid Ali Shah in 1847 *kathak* was performed by the male dancers. King got hundreds of girls trained in his *Parikhana* for the portrayal of amative dalliances with grace and feminine allure. Lucknow *kathak* style must have evolved as a distinct form during the time of Wajid Ali Shah but the *Kathak* as of the present time owes its existence and style to the combined creative genius and talent of Kalka-Bindadin, sons of Durga Prasad and the grand sons of Prakash ji whose son Thakur Prasad is said to have achieved the position of Wajid Ali Shah's guru and was given a seat of honour at par with the king's throne.

Kalka-Binda ki deodhi, the family residence of *Kathak* giants of Lucknow gharana near Jhaulaal ka Pul, Gwin Road is a place of pilgrimage for the students, scholars and the *kathak* lovers. Bindadin had created more than 1500 *thumris* of which many are lost but a large number of these *thumris* have been preserved through generations and are still an inseparable part of almost every *kathak* performance. His brother Kalka Prasad, another genius of Lukhnow *kathak* gharana had three sons Achchhan Maharaj, Lachchhu Maharaj and Shambhu Maharaj who diversified this art of dance to many directions including films during the 20th century.

Achchhan Maharaj's son Brij Mohan Misra popularly known as Birju Maharaj has created many ballets and dance-dramas with modern and innovative themes. The roots of these ballets and dance dramas can be traced to Wajid Ali Shah's *Rahas* which was inspired by the *Raslila* of Brij. For many years he served as guru and the director of Kathak Kendra, New Delhi and presently lives in Kolkata still serving the art with his creative genius and decades of experience.

Shambhu Maharaj, known for his gestures, postures and expressions in his dance performance was a good vocalist, could play harmonium and tabla with ease. He had two sons Ram Mohan Misra and Krishna Mohan Misra. Both are highly talented dancers performing across the globe.

Baijnath Prasad alias Lachchuu Mahraj, who had no progeny, is known for his control over the *bhavas* (expressions) is said to have maintained a balance between the traditional *kathak* and modern taste through his ballets and films along with bestowing the art with his talented disciples. He has been dance director and choreographer in many Hindustani films such as Mahal, Mughal-e-Azam, Pakeeza, Teesri Kasam, Ye Raat Phir Na Ayegi, Char Dil Char Raahen, Mujhe Jeene Do and so many other films. He left Bombay in 1973 to become the director of much awaited Kathak Kendra, Lucknow where he devoted the last five years of his life imparting the dance training to his famous disciples such as Kapila Raj, Kum Kum Dhar, Kum Kum Adarsh, Malavika Sarkar and Shashi Bharadwaj. His ballets became the most popular presentations of Kathak Kendra which still produces a number of ballets with modern and progressive themes.

Guru Vikram Singhe who came to Lucknow from Sri Lanka and became disciple of Achchhan Maharaj was another great *kathak* exponent who was appointed as *guru* of Lucknow Kathak Kendra till his death teaching the intricacies of Lucknow kathak gaharana to many of his disciples.

The Kathak Kendra, Lucknow was initially housed in the Qaiser bagh complex is presently situated at the Uttar Pradesh Sangeet Natak Akademy building, Gomti Nagar.

The art of *kathak* making its journey from temples to royal courts of Awadh has reached across the globe and is one of the most popular classical dance making new leaps with the artists like Veronica Azan, Shashwati Sen, Bhaswati Misra, Arjun Misra, Surendra Saikia, Manjari Chaturvedi, Manisha Misra, Anuj Misra and so many young and energetic kathak dancers who are either direct descendents or the disciples of Lucknow Kathak Gharana.

Musical Instrument Shops

Lucknow has been a seat of music learning ranging from classical to semi classical and light music. Be it tabla, vocal, sitar, sarangi, sarod , pakhawaj, harmonium and so on. Some of the masters of folk music had also chosen this city of culture as their center of activity to spread their knowledge among the disciples through folk singing, dholak and harmonium along with other percussions. This scenario brought many musical shops where one could see various musical instruments displayed in a harmonious manner attracting even the most non-musical passerby. The famous *Allan Saheb & Sons* at Latouche Road (now Gautam Buddh Marg) bears testimony

Mirasins (female bards) singing with dhol

to the rich tradition which boasted of the perfect pinnacle between the artists and the shop owners. Famous music composer Naushad was a regular visitor and used to spend hours together discussing various aspects of the innovative ways to bring betterment in the sounds and tone of the instruments during the process of making. Same is with *Melody Mart*, another shop at Safed Masjid Wali Dhaal, adjoining the cycle market and Latouche Road. Till the end of nineteen eighties and early nineties every evening witnessed a nice gathering of well known musicians having a chit-chat with Mohd. Hussain sahib, the owner of Melody Mart and Idris Bhai who was highly respected master expert of tuning the harmonium. Mahfooz bhai of Allan Saheb & Sons had also commanded the same respect from the artists and the shop owner. Farzand bhai at Allan Saheb's shop was another master craftsman of tabla. Artists had to wait for weeks together to get their instruments repaired. Mahfooz died many years ago and Idris bhai during the last few years of his life took to the piano tuning during Christmas days which fetched him some money. Some two years back he also decided to exit the stage. There were many such masters who suffered at the advent of 'market', post-modernity and consumer culture which ensured that the younger generation should not be bothered about its roots and culture rather get sunk into the marshy lands of westernization.

Earlier *Ustads* (teachers) guided about the quality and make of the instruments and for the disciples it was the final world. At present neither there are such ustads, but for very few, nor the dedicated students. Fake gurus are increasing day by day who not only charge hefty amounts for the so called training but ensure their commission from the shops they refer to buy the instruments.

Now the scene is entirely different. Number of shops has increased but the sale of traditional Indian instruments has gone to its lowest level as there are very few who opt to learn Indian classical music. Shop owners have put all their efforts to continue with the same but are now compelled to look for other alternatives. On the other hand the show rooms, as the modern outlets of western instruments like guitar, synthesizer, key boards etc. are doing a flourishing business.

Ram Leela, Qawwali, Daastaangoi and Theatre

True to their secular nature the Nawabs also patronized Ram Leela and that is why it emerged as a symbol of communal harmony. Muslims have been playing an important role in several of these Ram Leelas and continue to be involved in its' enactment *Qawwali* at the *mazaars* of the Sufi saints continue to attract the devotees from several communities while several other Qawwals have decided to cater to the popular taste of the masses and made qawwali a vehicle of romance,*shabaab* and *sharaab*. The art of storytelling *(daastaangoi)* declined with the advent of several other new forms of entertainment is being revived again while Lucknow is witnessing a resurgence of theatre.

13

Ramleela, Qawwali, Daastaangoi and Theatre

Ramleela

Ram jharokhe baith kar sub ka mujra lein
(Ram accepts salutations of the devotees sitting at the window)

The history of Ram Leela in Lucknow is old, unique and fascinating. Though it had begun in the reign of Nawab Saadat Ali Khan (1797-1814AD) and he also participated in it, a lasting and permanent place for its enactment was given by Nawab Nasiruddin Haider (1827-1837AD). Thus the first 'Ram Leela Maidan' was established in Aishbagh. Since then Ram Leela has been enacted every year on this place without a break. Ram Leela of Raniganj, Dugaawan is also more than hundred years old and so is the case of Ram Leela of Mausamganj in Daliganj. Even Ram Leela of Chowk has completed a century in 2011. In the rural areas of Lucknow, the Ram Leela at Bakshi Ka Talaab is said to be the oldest where the major characters were played by the Muslims.

Aish Bagh area present a unique example of the Nawab's generosity, liberalism, open mindedness and sense of justice. They donated large chunks of land to the three major communities- Hindus, Sunni Muslims and Shia Muslims- where the present Ram Leela Maidan, Eidgah and Malika Jahan Ki Karbala stand. This represents a 'sacred complex'. The local historians tell that financial help for the Ram Leela of AishBagh used to come from the government treasury and the Nawabs used to be present there to encourage the actors.

The Ram Leela of Chinhat is also unique in the sense that all the characters are played by children under the age of 14 years. The elders take the responsibility of stage decoration and dress. The district administration has a record of 53 Ram Leelas being enacted within the boundaries of Lucknow. Beside the old Ram Leelas, some new ones have made their debut especially in big housing colonies that have come up during the last 20-30 years such as in Aliganj and Rajajipuram. Another important feature of all these Ram Leelas is the fact that the skeleton of Ravan as well as the fire crackers are made and supplied by the Muslim craftsmen.

Looking at the mass popularity of the Ram Leela, the 'Market' has also entered into it. Some multinational companies have also started sponsoring the selected ones such as the Ram Leela of Aish Bagh is now being sponsored by the producers of

Coca Cola. They plan to introduce new technological features to the enactment but in the process there is every possibility of getting the spirit diluted and the whole show being transformed into another stage show based on technological innovations.

Qawwali

Because of the advent of a number of sufi saints and the presence of their *mazaars,* the cultural environment of Lucknow and areas around it was conducive for the development of a particular form of singing – sufi devotional poetry known as *Qawwali.* Described from the root word *Qaul* meaning utterance, a *Qawwal* is someone who often repeats or sings it. The roots of Qawwali may be traced back to 8th century Persia (todays' Iran and Afghanistan) but in South Asia Amir Khusro Dehelvi who belonged to the Chisti order of sufis was instrumental in its mass popularity. He created a beautiful fashion of Persian and Indian musical tradition. The formal name used for a session of Qawwali is *Mehfil-e-Sama.* A popular form of Qawwali begins with *Hamd* (praise) of Allah followed by *Naat* which is praise of Prophet Muhammad, then comes *Manqabat* (characteristic features) of Hazrat Ali and later of the sufi saints. Significantly, of the four major orders (*silsilah*) of the sufis, three derive inspiration from Imam Ali while the *naqshbandi* are inspired by Hazrat Abubakr, the first caliph.

Dewa Sharif adjacent to Lucknow played an important role in the promotion of sufiana qawwali in this part of India followed by Shah Meena Mazaar, the most popular *mazaar* in Lucknow. Qawwalis are sung on every thursday in all the minor and major mazaars. However, the best is reserved on the occasion of annual *Urs.* Beside the factor of conducive circumstances and effort of the followers of sufism, development of music also played very important role. It gave rise to various *Raga* which were sung on different occasions. Various musical instruments brought by the Muslims to India help the Qawwali to be more appealing and attractive. It is said that the 'Lucknow Gharana of Qawwali Singing' started with the famous Qawwal Ghulam Rasool who was influenced by Amir Khusro. Some of his followers migrated to Gwalior and created a new Gharana.

The notable *qawwals* of Lucknow from the seventeenth century to the present are Akhtar Husain, Aghghan Kakorvi, Mohd. Umar , Moharram Ali Khan, Haider Baksh, Ashraf Ali, Inamullah Warsi, Chandan Warsi, Niyamat, Dilkash and Patrick (a Christian Qawwal).

With Qawwali becoming more and more popular it was brought to the stage performances and also to Hindi/Urdu movies. It required changes in the content as well as style. Yet, some of the Qawwalis in such films as 'Barsaat ki Raat' are outstanding and a connoisseur's delight. At the same time vulgarity and lumpenization have also entered into it through Jawabi Qawwali (when two sides of males and females) compete with each other. Obviously, this is nothing to do with the 'Lucknow Gharana of Qawwali'.

Daastaangoi

Daastaangoi is another art form on which Lucknow once boasted, declined and faded away and now again being revived. *daastaan* (in Persian) means story and *goya* means to speak or tell, thus, *daastaangoi* was a form of story telling which originated in pre-Islamic Arabia and when Islam made its eastward journey, it moved to Iran and then to Delhi in India. In the 18th century it was a part of Indian mutiny of 1857 enthusing the freedom fighters and transmitting its message, reached Lucknow when several *daastaango* (story tellers) moved to Lucknow and other parts of Awadh. Unlike its elitist nature elsewhere, it gained popularity in Lucknow among all classes of people. The story tellers performed in private gathering as well as at public platform. "It became so popular among the opium addicts that they made listening to stories and important element of their gatherings. The prolonged intoxication and prolonged stories narrated by the professional story tellers was mostly combined. Each *afeem khaana* (opium den) had its own story teller to entertain the clients, whereas among the rich, every house hold, used to appoint a *daastaango* as a member of its staff (Ghaus Ansari, 1993).

Mahmood Farooqui(2012) tells that the early story tellers told tales of magic, war and adventure and borrowed freely from other stories such as the Arabian Nights, story tellers such as Rumi and storytelling traditions such as the Panchtantra. The 14th century Persian story tellers started focusing on the life and adventure of Amir Humza, the paternal uncle of Prophet Muhammad. The Indian stream of *Daastaangoi* added story telling elements such as *aiyyari* (trickery) to these tales. *Daastaangoi* continued through oral transmission till 1850 when Munshi Nawal Kishore, the pioneering publisher in Arabic, Persian and Urdu published a few stories in Persian after which the entire Daastaan-e-Amir Hamza was published in 46 volumes.

Describing the prevalence of *daastaangoi* in Lucknow, Pandit Ratan Nath 'Sarshaar' wrote at one place that it was difficult to find a place other than Lucknow where the *daastaans* were so much popular. Perhaps the main reason of the promotion of *daastaangoi* during the period of the Nawabi Awadh was that the King as well as the elite did not exercise much power. They did not have the courage to face the hard realities of life and they wanted to drown themselves in an imaginary world of fantasy. Gradually and gradually, *daastaangoi* faded out and with the death of the last story teller in 1928, the art saw its end.

Inspired by the famous Urdu critic Shamsur Rahman Farooqi, his talented nephew Mahmood Farooqi took the task of reviving it but in a different format. He assembled an equally dedicated team which included Darain Shahidi, Dan Husain, Ankit Chaddha and a couple of others. They added new themes and made it realistic. They organized sessions on Partition, on Saadat Hasan Manto, even on Kabeer. In 2014 two story tellers trained by him, Ankit Chaddha and Himanshu Vaipayee performed *daastan* on the famous Urdu poet Majaaz organized by a local, innovative organization, *Bewajah*. In June 2015 Himanshu Vajpayee presented the story of mangoes and it place in Urdu literature.

There is a strong reason to believe that the way the revived art of *daastaangoi* is increasing its popularity, it can definitely compete with the other forms of entertainment.

Theatre in Lucknow

-Akhilesh Dixit

Lucknow has been a fertile ground for various fine arts and during the Nawabi rule virtually every field of fine arts flourished. As for the other performing arts, theatre has also been an inseparable part of Lucknow's cultural world. Yet, this art form never enjoyed the royal patronage of that level as the music, poetry and dance did. The second king of Awadh Naseeruddin Haider was an amazing person and a great patron of fine arts. He did encourage such activities titled *Jalsa* but these were performed inside the palace for sheer entertainment. Common people couldn't even think of watching such performances and were entertained by the folk theatre where the dance and music was the dominating factor with nominal elements of drama. During the time of Wajid Ali Shah some dramatic and theatrical activities were patronized by the royal court named as Shahi Stage. 'Radha Kanhaiyyia Rahes' was one of the prominent performances of the Shahi Stage. Though Agha Hasan Amanat's *Indarsabha* during the Wajid Ali Shah's regime is generally considered as the first theatre performance in Lucknow open for general public when several fairs which used to take place inside the four gates of Qaiserbagh were thrown open for the general public. This was a turning point and for the art lovers, drama became a passion as much as many well known Urdu poets started writing dramas. Amanat's *Indersabha* created a way for many other plays and these performances were known as *Sabha* which sounds more of a people's place replacing the word *Jalsa* gradually giving way to the rise of Parsi theatre in Lucknow.

British annexation of Awadh in 1857 put all the cultural activities at halt for almost 20 years but progressive theatre activists firmly believe that theatre is not just an entertainment but a medium to create the awareness about socio-economic, political, cultural and other relevant problems and follow the dictum firmly, 'to break all the shackles of slavery..stage a play… a play… and..another play.' *Neel Darpan* was staged by national theatre Kolkata somewhere in March 1875 at Chhatar Manazil. Enraged by the anti-British content of the play, the then English district magistrate and British sepoys climbed the stage during the performance and stopped the play. The group was deported from Lucknow. This incident became the cornerstone for enactment of Dramatic Performances Act 1876. During the British period folk theatre based on mythological and romantic themes was regularly performed at Dilaram ki Baradari in Chaupatiyan locality. Having a tradition of drama which can be traced from Dilaram ki Baradari to some localities near Buland Bagh where temporary arrangements were made for the performances attracting thousands of spectators bears testimony to Lucknow's common man's keen interest in theatre. During the First World War the emphasis of the dramas shifted toward social, political and nationalistic themes leaving the fantasy, romance and mythological stories behind.

During the end of nineteenth century and especially in the first half of the twentieth century a big diaspora of creative and literary Bengali *bhadra lok* arrived in Lucknow and enriched the entire cultural horizon of the city with their talents.

This was the time when Atul Krishna Singh came to city and started his theatre activities along with other creative enthusiasts in the field and soon these theatre performances became very popular. Realizing this growing popularity Atul Krishna started Bengali Club at his residence and then in Sundar Bagh in a rented house where Durga Pooja was also celebrated. The plays were staged at Mewalal ka Hata in Maqboolganj under gas light. Modelhouse was another venue where the plays were presented. Actors like Vireshwar Chattopadhyaya, Suren Roy, Naresh Chandra Ghosh and Krishadhan Chattopadhyaya who were later joined by the famous theatre personality Dwijendra Nath Sanyal went on carving space on the stage during their performances. Atul Krishna's dream for a permanent place for such activities was realized when in 1914 the building of Bengali Club was erected but Atul Krisha died soon after that. The challenge to live up to the motto ' show must go on' along with the management of two separate organizations,The Bengali Club and The Young Men's Association, was difficult to deal with. By this time Atul Prasad Sen, a contemporary prominent citizen, had already settled in Lucknow who initiated the idea of merging the two organizations and in 1929, with the efforts of many respected Bengalis emerged a new organization to be known as 'Bengali Club and Young Men's Association'. Later an auditorium inside the Bengali Club premises- Atul Natya Mandir, was dedicated to his memory which ensured regular theatre activities. Bengali club situated on Shivaji Marg, the then Hewett Road, became the hub of all kinds of religious, cultural, social and sports activities among the Bengali community and still has the same reputation. Bengalis attach serious importance to the theatre and from the mid thirties Lucknow saw regular theatre activities through various organizations like Friends

Performance of daastaangoee

Union Club, Railway Recreation Club, Independent Club and the Sarvjonin Pooja Committee of Vidyant College which brought forth many talented theatre artists, technicians, light designers, stage craftmen and design experts. Many railway personnel transferred to Lucknow during early forties were inclined towards art and literature and founded Uttar Bharat Mahamilan Sangh, Samanvay, Shaitya Chakra and Abhiyantriki performing regular theatre. Uttar Bharat Mahamilan Sangh presented a play at Cathedral Hall, *Nuton Yahudi* during 1952 where the women from their families also performed. The play was performed in Hindi in addition to Bangla version. This was a protest against the elite Bengali Club's opposition to the women performing on stage. This performance revolutionized the entire scenario and raised the level of exuberance among the young, progressive minds who fought against this rigid approach in theatre, finally got their due and the iron gate of orthodoxy was thrown open when Atul Natya Manch of Bengali Club was made available, though with reluctance and opposition from some hard core orthodox members, and the play *Babu Moshay* having female actors too was staged. Now these young activists created an organization Shobhuj Shongho under the leadership of Robin Mitra which provided a new horizon to the Bangla theatre by presenting the plays like Sankranti, Pathik, Kaler Jatra and such other progressive plays which finally brought Bengali Club's orthodoxy to an end. Atul Natyamanch at Bengali Club witnessed Guru Dev Rabindranath Tagore's Plays, *Gora* and *Rokto Korobi* presented by the Group Theatre. An annual Bengali theatre competition, running almost for two months, is organized at Bengali Club in the fond memory of Praksh Chandra Ghosh, an intense and fine actor who died in 1962.

Around Second World War the world was changing rapidly in terms of social-economic and political terms. Dr Rashid Jahaan a medical practitioner,emerged and was one of the founders of Progressive Writers Association and IPTA both in 1936 and 1943, respectively, at Lucknow. She had already penned the play *Parde ke Peechhe* in 1931 and was published in 'Angarey'. The play was banned by the British government to satisfy the fundamentalists. Later IPTA continued under the leadership of Amrit Lal Nagar who directed the famous play Idgaah in 1953,an adaptation of Premchand's story of the same title. The play was not allowed to be performed without prior permission and scrutiny of the play under the Dramatic Performance Act, 1876, but Amrit Lal Nagar, Razia Sajjad Zaheer, Babu Lal Verma and Shiv Narain Mehrotra fearlessly performed the play and were prosecuted. However, Justice Anand Narain Mulla ordered the Act to be null and void making UP the first state to be free from the draconian Act. There were some theatre personalities from 1947 to 1970 like Bishan Kapoor, Kunwar Kalyan Singh, Sant Ram,Vishwnath Mishra, Amjad Ali, Jeet Jardhari to name a few. Theatre Art Workshop (TAW) by Raj Bisaria established in 1965, was a major breakthrough underlining the importance of theatre training and education. The effort of Raj Bisaria for theatre training resulted in the establishment of Bhartendu Natya Academy (BNA) in 1975. Meanwhile Darpan in 1961, Meghdoot in 1974, Sanket and a few other groups came into existence with the help of KB Chandra,

BN Shargha, Shashank Bahuguna and other theatre activists.

Kunwar Kalyan Singh, Raj Bisaria, Vilayat Jafri, Sidharth Pakrasi, Atam Jeet Singh, Surya Mohan Kulshreshtha, Anil Rastogi, Urmil Kumar Thapaliyal, Swadesh Bandhu, Hare Krishna Arora, P.D. Verma, Vijay Vastav, Vimal Bannerji, Vijay Bannerji, Jugal Kishore, Chandra Mohan, Ravi Nagar and KN Kakkar played very important role in the growth of Lucknow theatre. Pramod Bala, Krishna Misra, Vijay Naresh, Mridula Bhardwaj, Veda Rakesh, Chitra Mohan, Krishna Jafari, Sandhya Deep, Manju Gupta and some other female artists have contributed tirelessly towards the Lucknow Theatre. Later, IPTA was reorganized in 1987 and continues to work. Other organizations like Yayaver, Manchkriti, Darpan and few other groups are there with serious work but last one and half decade has witnessed rapid mushrooming of the so called theatre groups. Most of these groups depend on the grants from the Ministry of Human Resource Development and other such State and Central government agencies. This practice has got nothing to do with the serious theatre but mainly to avail the grants. The competition between such groups is tough and the quality and content are not up to the mark.

The Bollywood Connection

One of the lesser known facts about Lucknow is its old link with Bombay's film industry. Way back in 1926 a highly technologically advanced film studio had been established here with sophisticated equipments and arrangements for indoor as well as outdoor shooting. Around a dozen feature films were also produced here. This studio was able to attract talent from various fields- direction, acting, singing, photography, script and song writing etc. Many of these artists, writers and poets joined the film industry in Bombay. Lucknow also occupies an important place in Bombay film industry in several other ways.

14

The Bollywood Connection

Lucknow has always figured prominently in Bombay's movie world right from the days when talkies replaced silent movies. Lucknow and Bombay's movies world have fascinated each other to the extent that a full fledged film studio was established in Lucknow in 1926 on Vidhan Sabha Marg. It was named Ideal Studio which was later renamed as Kailash Studio. It was the result of a joint effort by some Zamindars and Rajas mainly Raja Saheb Mauravan, Raja Saheb Oel, Alipur State, Ausanganj State. Even at that time the studio was equipped with all the necessary paraphernalia-projection theatre, lab, rubber flooring and a grand outdoor studio. Here several films were produced such as Chor, Bebus, Dulhan and some others. It closed down in 1950 as a result of the sudden demise of the owner.

One of the earliest cinema halls in Lucknow was Pearl Theatre, renamed as Royal Theatre and then Mehra Talkies opened in early 1930s. As the chroniclers and film journalists tell, there was no provision of ads, promos or songs/music during the interval. Hence, in order to engage the spectators some musicians used to give live performances during the intervening period. The famous music director Naushad, a native of Lucknow, used to play tabla for a remuneration of four annas. A number of legendry personalities of Bombay's film world have made Lucknow proud because of their contributions in different fields of Hindi/Urdu cinema.

Right from the days of talkies dialogues and songs were largely in Urdu with a fair sprinkling of Hindi words. Thus, a refined and sophisticated language of the cinema was developed and in many films the mannerism and etiquette of the characters reflected Lucknow's linguistic culture as many of the dialogue writers were from Lucknow and groomed in the same culture. Not only in the so called, 'Muslim social films' but in several others too Lucknow's sherwani, chikan kurta-pyjama, churidar and gharara used to be the attire.

In various areas of film making artists, writers, poets, cameramen, makeup men contributed significantly to the Bombay's cinema. Such eminent dancers of Kathak as Pandit Thakur Prasad, Pandit Durga Prasad, Kalika Maharaj, Bindadin Maharaj, Achchan Maharaj, Lachchu Maharaj, Shambhu Maharaj and Birju Maharaj taught and trained several film stars as Kathak used to be the popular dance form in films those days.

Several eminent Hindi and Urdu writers and poets contributed with their pen. Wajahat Mirza was the writer of Mother India, Ganga Jamuna, Mughal-e-Azam and several other films; KP Saxena wrote Jodha Akbar, Lagaan and some other films; Ali Raza wrote many films; Achla Nagar wrote Nikah, Akhir Kyon and others; writer of Ready and No Problem, Ikram Akhtar also belonged to Lucknow and so many others from the city wrote the story, dialogues and screenplay of hundreds of film made in Bombay.

Agha Hashr Kashmiri, the legendary playwright from Lucknow wrote the songs in films such as Devdas in 1930s. Hasan Kamaal, the well known Urdu journalist and poet wrote the songs of several films including Nikah and Tawaif and the song "Dil ke arma aansuon me bah gai" became a big hit. Yogesh wrote the popular songs of films like Anand and Mili. Before the present crop of poets, many poets of yesteryears such as Muzaffar Lucknawi, Nafees Lucknawi, Jalal Malihabadi, Suroor Lucknawi and some others gave memorable songs to Bombay's films. Among the singers, who can forget the contribution of the famous Talat Mehmood whose silken voice continues to attract even the present generations of lovers of quality songs and ghazals. Begum Akhtar too, acted and sung in some films before returning to Lucknow.

Among the directors, Muzaffar Ali has made the Lucknowites proud by giving an immortal film Umrao Jaan and directing some other meaningful and serious films such as Gaman and Anjuman. Atul Tewari has been an assistant to the legendry Shyam Benegal and also wrote some films recently. While Shaad Ali, the son of Muzaffar Ali, directed the popular film Bunty and Bubbly. Roshan Abbas a promising producer-director also comes from Lucknow. Among the better known actors Bina Rai, the famous heroin and the character-actor Kumar (Mijjan) were also from Lucknow. The list will be too long to be enumerated and many names have been left out but even this brief description is sufficient to give some idea about the nature and extent of the contribution made by the personalities from Lucknow to the Bombay's Hindi-Urdu Cinema world.

The contribution of U.P. Film Journalists Association (UPFJA) and the moving spirit behind it, Ram Krishna, also cannot be forgotten. Founded in 1963, the UPFJA began an annual award giving ceremony which provided the film buffs of Lucknow an opportunity to see their favourite film stars, writers, poets and directors from close quarters and interact with them at a time when film shooting in Lucknow was rare. It was to be a prestigious award and most of the awardees were bearing their own expenses on travelling and staying in hotels and did not charge any fee. From this platform such well known film personalities as Prithvi Raj Kapoor, Raj Kapoor, Shammi Kapoor, Dev Anand, Vijay Anand, Suchitra Sen, Rakhi, Pran, Utpal Dutt, Raahi Massom Raza and many others were honoured with award.

Lucknow, its cultural ambience, cuisine and historical monuments have been attracting and fascinating the directors. A number of scenes were shot in so many movies but some films were based totally on Lucknow. Most notable among them are Shashi Kapoor's Junoon, Muzaffar Ali's Umrao Jaan, and Satyajit Ray's Shatranj Ke Khiladi. Recently, the film Ya Rab was also based on Lucknow. During recent years so many films have been shot in Lucknow that it is difficult to keep track of these or compile a list. The present government in Uttar Pradesh is launching some ambitious schemes for reviving film making in Lucknow and if the efforts succeed, Lucknow may emerge as the second most important centre of Hindi/Urdu film making after Mumbai.

Urdu in Lucknow

Though the Deccan, Delhi and Lucknow together are very important in any narration about Urdu language and literature, Lucknow occupies a unique place in poetry and journalism. During the Nawabi era almost all the important poets from Delhi except Ghalib had left for Lucknow and lived here. Moreover, because of the establishment of Munshi Nawal Kishore Press in 1859, Urdu publishing including Urdu journalism got such a boost that all other centers of Urdu were left behind. Urdu's decline in Lucknow began from the first quarter of 20th century and reached a precarious stage in the post-Independence period yet because of Urdu poetry, it continues to survive.

15

Urdu in Lucknow

Daawa zubaan ka Lucknow waalon ke saamne?
Izhaar-e-boo-i-mushk ghezaalon ke saamne ?

(To claim mastery over (urdu) language before the people of Lucknow is to talk of musk scent before musk deer)

Urdu Poetry

There has been a long standing debate regarding the two schools of Urdu poetry, Delhi and Lucknow, described as *Dabistaan-e-Delhi* and *Dabistaan-e-Lucknow*. A number of literary critics including the living legend Shamsur Rehman Faruqi questioning the very classification, debunk the 'two school theory'. Does Lucknow possess its' own style? While it is largely accepted that before the arrival of Delhis' poets Lucknows' ghazals were characterized by sensual, flashy and very particular about words and not ideas and thoughts and thus it was like *Ustaadi* and word craft. The Delhis' poetry was truer to Persian literary tradition, straight forward and emphasizing mystical concerns. However, the 'Lucknowness' and 'Delhiness' seems more socio-political in nature than in terms of literary nuances.

With the decline of Mughal empire, a number of poets and practitioners of fine arts began thronging to Lucknow while several others left for Hyderabad and Azeemabad (Patna). Thus, Delhis' loss was Lucknows' gain. Scholars are of the view that before the advent of Nawabi rule, Lucknow had hardly any literary tradition in Urdu prose as well as poetry. It was because of the illustrious ulema of Firangi Mahal that Lucknow emerged as a major centre of scholarship in Arabic, Persian, and Islamic Studies. Although Urdu poetry was born in the Deccan, it attained growth and development in Delhi. With the decline of political power, the later Mughals also lost wealth and were in no position to extend patronage to fine arts and literature. A number of states under the Mughal rule including Lucknow flourished and rolled in wealth. The poverty stricken poets who once had spurned invitation from the Nawabs of Awadh now were willing to migrate. The great poet Sauda left Delhi and came to Faizabad and when the capital of Awadh was shifted to Lucknow he moved and settled here. He was followed by several others notable among them were

Meer Hasan, Qalandar Baksh 'Jurrat', Insha allah Khan 'Insha', 'Mushafi' and others. Perhaps, Mirza Ghalib was the only one among the greats who stayed back and never left Delhi to settle down and get buried elsewhere.

Thus, we find that Lucknow became the favorite destination of prominent poets of Delhi and they played a very important role in the development of Urdu poetry in Lucknow. 'Naasikh' is usually described as the first important Lucknawi poet not connected to Delhi. He was and 'Ustaad' and had a big following of pupils. 'Aatish' was another major poet of 'Lucknow School'. Among the illustrious pupils of 'Aatish' were Daya Shankar 'Naseem', Mirza 'Shauq' and Mohammad Khan 'Rind'. 'Mushafi' was also a great poet and often described as founding father of *Marsiya* writing in Lucknow.

Some of the most important poets of Lucknow, whether originally from Lucknow or migrant from Delhi or elsewhere, are Meer Taqi 'Meer', Mirza Rafi 'Sauda' Meer Anees, Mirza Dabeer, Insha allah Khan 'Insha' , Meer Hasan, 'Mushafi', 'Aatish', 'Nasikh', Daya Shanker 'Naseem', Mirza 'Shauq', Amir Meenai, Ratan Nath Sarshaar, Naubat Rai 'Nazar', 'Safi', 'Azeez', 'Asar', 'Zareef', 'Aarzoo', Brij Narain Chakbast, Behzad, 'Josh', 'Yaas' Yagaana, Majaz, Anand Narain Mulla, Waali Aasi, Krishna Bihari 'Noor' and others. The list excludes the living poets.

Ghazal has been the most popular form of Urdu poetry in Lucknow and elsewhere and most of the poets were *ghazalgo* or ghazals' poets. Ghazal is a unique form of Urdu poetry, a blend of rhyme and rhythm, a collection of compressed and capsule thoughts conveyed through a medium of metaphors and imagery, delicate, sensitive, and sometimes sensuous. Ghazal is perhaps the best mirror of the 'Urdu Culture'. The poets of purely Lucknow origin were more conscious about the language and style while those coming from Delhi laid emphasis on introspection, emotion and mystical dimensions. Moreover, unlike Delhi, *Mushairas* that popularized the ghazal immensely were not largely confined to the palace but held everywhere, in public places, in open fields, in fairs and festivals and on so many occasions. This was also instrumental in making ghazal more 'peoplecentric' as we witnessed when the poets coming from the Progressive Movement composed their ghazals reflecting the problems being faced by the masses.

Masnavi is yet another form of Urdu poetry. It is a long narrative poem,that may be stretched to hundreds of pages, usually based on love and composed in the style of *Qissagoi* (story telling). The more important masnavis composed by Lucknows' poets are *masnavi sahr-ul-Bayaan* by Meer Hasan, *Gulzar-e-Naseem* by Daya Shankar 'Naseem', and *Zehr-e-Ishq* by Mirza 'Shauq'.

Marsiya is also an important form of Urdu poetry in Lucknow. These are elegies composed on the tragic events at Karbala. Though Marsiyas are the narration of a tragedy, poets like Mir Anees and Mirza Dabeer raised this form of poetry to such heights of literary excellence that the Urdu poetry shall always be proud of it. In the hands of these marsiya poets especially Anees and Dabeer, marsiya became practically a form of epic. This is largely an offshoot of Shia impact on

Lucknows' Urdu poetry. *Salaam* and *Nauha* (dirge) are shorter poems on the same theme-martyrdom of Imam Husain at Karbala. These forms of Urdu poetry are usually recited during the Moharrum mourning days or in a *majlis* (mourning congregation) or other occasions.

Among the relatively minor forms of poetry in Lucknow have *Rekhti* and *fuhashiyaat*. *Rekhti* refers to the poetry composed by the male poets in feminine gender, portraying females' sentiments. It is a dead art now as the last poet of Rekhti passed away recently. A section of people, especially the nobility, was also fond of vulgar and obscene poetry composed in a literary language. Obviously, such recitals could not be held at public places and hence described as 'underground mushaira' organised behind closed doors where unprintable poetry was recited. Among the acknowledged poets of this form of poetry were Chirkin, Jaan Sahab and others. Omitting the more vulgar parts, the collection of the poet Chirkin was published recently. Moreover, astray verses were always composed sometime by reputed poets who shared this type of poetry with their intimate friends only.

Thus, the Urdu literary culture in Lucknow had several shades but with the advent of Progressive Movement and after the inaugural session of Progressive Writers Association in 1936, a new type of ghazal emerged that was not confined to the theme of romance and mysticism only. *Nazm* also made its debut. It is a form of poetry with no fixed rhyme or meter but focused on a particular idea or theme unlike *ghazal* whose every *sher* may convey a different idea. The ghazal has achieved countrywide popularity today largely because of *mushairas* and its rendering by great singers. Begum Akhtar and Talat Mehmood were the most outstanding ghazal singers from Lucknow. First, the gramophone records and then audio cassettes, CDs and DVDs have played an important role in popularizing the ghazals.

Some of the most outstanding poets in Lucknow after independence are 'Dil' Lucknawi, Umar Ansari, 'Saalik' Lucknawi, Fazal Naqvi, Waali Aasi, Krishna Bihari 'Noor', Irfan Siddiqi, Saghar Khayyami and then the disciples of 'Waali' Aasi namely Khushbir Singh 'Shaad', Bharat Bhushan Pant and Munnawwar Rana. Of these poets Munnawwar Rana has achieved phenomenal popularity largely because of his simple language, outstanding skill of recitation in mushairas and availability of his poetry in Devnagri script while 'Shaad' and 'Pant' excel in deep thoughts and philosophical tone and tenor appreciated by the more serious readers and audience and connoisseurs of Urdu poetry. Of the younger and upcoming poets, Tariq Qamar, Abhishek Shukla and Manish Shukla are very promising and compose serious poetry. Significantly, after the earlier non-Muslim poets of Lucknow having faded away from the scene, a new crop of such poets are knocking at the doors of popularity among the lovers of Urdu poetry.

Rekhti in Lucknow

Saiyed Anwer Abbas

Indian poets have been depicting *shringar* and *riti-kala* in their love poetry since early days. Maithili and Sanskrit poets like Vidyapati (1352-1448) and Bihari (1595-1664) have depicted females confiding with their *Sakhi* (female friends) of their illicit romance, amorous relationships, seductions, longing for their lover, clandestine meeting and mating, apart from the exchange of notes for other common items of female interest such as clothes, jewellery and grooming. Interestingly, influenced by such Indian classical form of love poetry, somewhat similar form of poetry also appears to be there in Urdu and Persian. It is called 'Rekhti'.

Rekhti as a term is derived from 'Rekhta', a lyrical form wherein the male poet makes an exclamation of his romantic feelings and makes a direct or indirect declaration of love for his beloved and pines with longing for her. In Rekhti , the male poet incorporates certain very specific words that are only used by women to address each other. The poetry contains such phrases and exclamations that are mostly used by women folk. In Rekhti, the couplets are mostly composed in first person of speech to present a female conveying an observation to another female, who is a childhood mate, close friend or neighbour or a group of domesticated women that live in her vicinity.

Hashmi (d.1697), a poet and Sufi saint of Bijapur, also popularly known as Miran Shah, is considered to be the earliest poet who used this form of composition in Deccani Urdu. It was then called 'Zenani ghazal' (Female Poetry). Hashmi Bijapuri referred to it as 'Oyee ki Boli'.

Rekhti in India, has its roots in the royal courts of late 15th century Deccan at Gulbarga, Bidar, Bijapur and Golconda (Hyderabad). Lutfi, a poet of the Bahmani kingdom around 1489, is beleived to be the earliest poet who composed in this feminine form of poetry in Persian. One of the Sultans of Bijapur, Ali Adil Shah II (1638-1672) who was himself a poet, besides encouraging poets in his Court to compose Rekhti also composed it himself. Between 1489 and 1849 at least 27 poets in Deccan, who were all males, find mention for presenting compositions in the Rekhti form of feminine poetry.

Rekhti proceeded from Deccan to North India and reached Delhi in the 18th century. Thereafter, the decline of the Mughal empire deprciated patronage to poets and many of them migrated to other states for livelihood. A good number of these poets also migrated to Faizabad which was then the capital of the Nawabs of Awadh (Oudh). Alongwith other forms of prosody, the poets brought Rekhti to Faizabad. Later, when the poets shifted to Lucknow with the Court of Nawab Asaf-ud-daulah when he designated it as his new capital in 1775, Rekhti also came along with them and settled at Lucknow.It became a source of private entertainment for the Nawabs and their courtiers. We have two famous poets of Delhi named Saadat Yaar Khan 'Rangeen'(d.1835) and Insha-allah Khan 'Insha' (d.1818) who were attached to the Court of Nawab Asaf-ud-daulah at Lucknow. Both were well-known for their unusual composition of Rekhti besides their compositions of the other usual forms of Urdu poetry that were in vogue. Rangeen bragged about himself being the inventor of Rekhti and even mocked Insha, his rival in this form of poetry, saying:

Rekhti kahni, aji, Rangeen ka ye eijaad hai
Munh chidhaata hai, muva Insha jiya, kis vaaste

However, later research in Rekhti has proved Rangeen's claim to be false and incorrect.

Feminine colloquy is the main ingredient of Rekhti. It had the flavour and spice of the speech of females with words and phrases selectively used by Begums and their intimate female companions and personal attendants in the *zenana* of the Nawabi palaces and the *Dyodhis* (households) of the aristocracy. Light hearted exclamations, witty phrases, literary idioms, sarcastic remarks, ridicule, scorn, pun, innuendo and rhetoric are presented in Rekhti in their basic feminine colour to depict the various shades of womens'emotions in Rekhti. Rekhti was involved and concerned with each and everything of interest to women that excited their curiosity. Be it grooming, dressing, jewellery, toiletry, beauty treatment, fashion, amusement, celebrations, festivals, fairs, ceremonies, superstitions, religious observances, family life, marriage , pregnancy, child birth, small pleasures and sorrows and the drudgery that was part of a woman's life. But all this was presented by male poets garnished with light hearted humour and innocent sarcasm and served before the audience which happened to be male. Rarely did Rekhti come in the reach of women. Its entry was barred in the women's quarters. There was no such ban for men and Rekhti was enjoyed by men alone. The atmosphere during poetic sessions of Rekhti was often so charged with lewdness that men would mimic and imitate the actual manner of speech and behaviour of women. Rekhti poets often chose to adopt female names for their *takhallus* (pen-name)and consequently we find pen names such as Nisbat, Naubahaar, Ismat, Hidayatan, Nazuk, Shabnam, Begum, belonging to Rekhti poets.

Mir Ali 'Jaan Saheb'(1810-1886) ,a poet who resided at Rustam nagar in Lucknow for a major part of his life, dared to be different in society by openly declaring himself being a poet of Rekhti. He further went to astonish his audience (at Rekhti sessions) arriving heavily dressed and made up like a Begum of some Royal household. Some other poets are also believed to have followed his example.

Amongst the earlier Rekhti poets of Lucknow, we have Syed Ahsan "Makhlooq', Mir Ahmad Ali 'Nisbat', Amjad Ali Khan 'Ismat', Mir Hussain Ali 'Aafaaq', Abid Mirza 'Begum',Nuktachin, Naazuk, and Yakrang. Other poets associated with Lucknow include Syed Mohammed Mohsin 'Raunaq', Jamiat Ali Khan'Suraiya',Kallan Khan 'Bechain',Nisar Hussain Khan 'Shaida',Sheikh Mohaammed 'Baqa', 'Ranjoor' Azimabadi, Bahadur and Hazeen.

Interstingly, names of two female Rekhti poets of Lucknow also find mention. One is that of a *kaneez* (female attendant) of Mirza Sulaiman Shikoh (the Mughal Prince from Delhi),having the pen-name 'Zaleel'. The other is Rashk Mahal, one of the many wives of King Wajid Ali Shah, who used the pen-name of 'Begum' for her compositions. There is no information about their participation and recitation in any Rekhti session and it is presumed that if their compositions were ever recited there, it was some one else who rendered them on their behalf.

Often frivolous or bawdy Rekhti verses were sometimes laced with a licentious invitation of romantic liaison, lust and passion. Rekhti had the audacity of using 'double entendre' - i.e. words which had a double meaning, one of which was intentionally placed to express the repressed passion of women or indirectly related to lesbian tendencies and coitus. This provided its critics a ready excuse for declaring Rekhti obscene and vulgar and strictly disallowing it to sneak into the women quarters where young girls and women resided.

Rekhti was never accepted in society as a respectable form of literature. It was never considered as something normal and respectful and its recitation was considered disgraceful. It was shameful to relate to Rekhti in public as it was believed to be unsophisicated, licentitious, obscene and vulgar. Many poets fearing disrespect and disrepute resorted to its composition with an alternative *takhallus* (pen-name), one that was different from their usual one with which they were recognised by the audience in in the *mushaira* (poetic gathering).

Post Independence when human rights and gender equality came to be recognised for both men and women alike, Rekhti also got an opportunity to come out of its underground confines and reach to the world outside.

In fact, it was a poet born at Lucknow in 1922, Syed Sajid Ali Rizvi'Sajni', popularly known as Sajid 'Sajni' Lakhnavi who spearheaded Rekhti for making a pronounced dent in society and using this feminine poetry for improving the condition of women, particularly the Muslim women of the middle class or those poor that lived in the ghettos. Sajid had started composing couplets in the usual manner of Urdu poetry when he was just an adolescent, studying in class nine. He adopted his first name 'Sajid' as his pen name. Despite guidance and encouragement from an accomplished poet Bekhud Mohani in his youth, Sajid was not satisfied with what he composed. He shifted to Bhopal in 1946 for making a living, and continued composing ghazals at leisure and reciting them at poetic gatherings. Around 1953 he happened to meet Takhallus Bhopali, a writer and poet who used humour for light hearted presentations and satire particularly directed towards issues concerning women. Takhallus Bhopali was intending to publish a magazine titled *Bhopal Punch* and asked Sajid to contribute for it. Sajid who was disenchanted with his usual form of ghazals decided to change his form and compose in the Rekhti style. As he was now going to relate to the problems of common women, he adopted 'Sajni' (female companion) as his new pen name. His Rekhti which was mostly concerned with women in the present day society as home-maker and bread earner as well soon became very popular because Rekhti could now easily reach the female members of the society without restriction. He was soon a familiar name in Bhopal, Lucknow and elsewhere and was applauded for highlighting the problems of women and directing constructive social change and reform towards progress in a positive direction. Two of Sajid 'Sajni'Lakhnavi's Rekhti collections titled Raqeeban(1983) and Nigodiyaat(1987) have been published.

One of the most most hard hitting, ironical yet popular couplet of Sajid 'Sajni' Lakhnavi depicts a woman's ire protesting against divorce:

Talaaq de to rahe ho, ataab-o-qahr ke saath
mera shabaab bhi lauto do mere mehr ke saath

(You utter 'divorce' in a fit of anger and wrath, then do consider giving back and returning the youthful years of my youth alongwith the 'mehr' (alimony) that you pay).

Alas, this crusader poet did not live to witness the positive change and response provided to Rekhti, its being treated respectfully as a responsible and useful social tool in a society which earlier despised it. Sajid 'Sajni' Lakhnavi expired on August 16, 1989 after a brief illness at Bhopal.

Besides citing Syed Sajid Ali Rizvi 'Sajni', as a Lucknow poet of Rekhti in the 20th century, Urdu scholar Kazim Ali Khan has also cited poets named Baquir Hussain 'Rangeen', Habib Parvez 'Nazneen', Mister and Aadil. Ayaz Ahmad in his introduction to Kuliyaat-e-Rekhti (collection of Rekhti) quotes Aslam Mahmud (known for his rare collection of books in his personal library at Lucknow) for adding the name of another Rekhti poet of Lucknow named Hidayat. His sole collection of Rekhti is entered in the catologue of books of the Lucknow University Library, but sadly, it is not traceable and appears to be lost.

Some examples of Rekhti poetry are as follows:

Saadat Yar Khan 'Rangeen'

Bheja hai got ka ye dupatta, che khush,
Aur aap odh baithi hain malmal ki odhni

(So unfair that in these hot season, you send me a heavy ornate stole to cover myself, and for your own wear you choose one of light muslin).

Kal Mughlani ne si de ke marodi angiya
Ho gayi tang pichhaon se nigodi angiya

(Yesterday the saemstress has twisted my bra while stitching it in such a way that it is now tight at the back and hurts)

Theek kuchh gaat pe ye hai nahin Bi Mughlani
Tang is se bhi zara keejyo thodi angiya

(These bra cups are sliding off my breasts, Dear seamstress; you need to reduce them a bit more, to fit)

Inshaullah Khan 'Insha'

Marduva mujhse kahe hai "Chalo aaraam karen"
Jisko aaraam wo samjhe hai wo aaraam ho nauj

(He invites me to come, lie and relax, am I so simple as not to know what this 'relaxation' means to him and what it will do to me.)

Hathon se tere mai to, kambakht aajiz aayi
Jo kaam hai nigoda, tera, so halbali ka

(I am so disgusted with the work that you rush to do with your hands, actually you spoil all that you do in haste.)

Dhar mukut Insha ke sar, kahe "Jai Kanaihya Lal ki"
Ban, khadi ho Radhika, jo khelti Holi hai tu

(Adorning Insha's head with a crown , you utter "Hail, Kanaihya Lal" with joy and stand prepared like Radhika to drown Insha in colour in celebration of Holi)

Mir Yaar Ali 'Jaan Saheb'

Chupke rahne me tha haraam wo kaam
Ek do bolon se halaal hua

(This couplet mocks marriage ceremony that turns coitus into a legalised act, which otherwise is considered to be illicit)

Bholi na samajh mujhko, sunta hai Jaan Saheb
Aisi nahin hun nanhi, aaon jo daon me tere

(Dont think I am simple, Jaan Saheb, someone innocent enough to be tricked to fall into your trap.)

Habib 'Nazneen'

Doob kar nikla hai, qismat ka sitara, Baji,
Mai duhaaji hoon magar wo hai kunwara, Baji

(My lucky stars are here again, Oh dear elder sister, for I am twice married yet my groom is still a virgin)

Duble patle hi sahi mere doolha bhai
Ho mubarak tumhe tinke ka sahara Baji

(Dear sister, Do not bother if my brother in-law, your husband is so slim and thin, be glad for it, "the thin reed that floats is good enough to save someone from drowning" is an old adage)

Sajid 'Sajni' Lakhnavi

(Note: In comparision to other Rekhti poets, more aspects of Sajni's Rekhti poetry are being presented here)

Jise bhi dekho mujhe ghoorta hai ai Baji
Mera shabaab mere waste azaab hua

(I find every one ogling at me, O brother's wife, this blossoming to youth is infact a source of trouble for me)

Ho jism par libas jo achchha dikhai de,
Parde ki cheez kyon pas-e-purdah dikhai de
Sajni , is slacks ke, kapdon se, aayi baaz
Jisko pahen ke, har koi, nanga dikhai de

(The garment that one wears should look nice, not exposing those parts of ones body which are supposed to remain under cover and hidden; Sajini, I abhor clothes like the 'slacks', which even when they have been worn, make the wearer appear nude/naked)

Wo mujhse roz padosan ki baat karte hain
Kuchh isme daal me kaala dikhai deta hai

(Every day he, my husband keeps mentioning the neighbour woman which I find to be queer with something being fishy therein, a matter of concern for me)

Wo jo hona tha huva, raat gayi baat gayi,

Chaar aankhen to karo, nazren milao Sajni

(Whatever was expected, has already occurred, The night has passed, so has the act; Do not blush, just face me now and look into my eyes Sajni)

Maine jis simt chhaha, chalaya unhe,
Unki kashti ki mai nakhuda ho gayi

(I took him to proceed in whichever direction I wished since I had the rudder of his boat in my hands)

Phir bhi kamzor si ek sinf use kahte hain,
Jab ki aabaad hue sare gharane, hum se

(Strange that people keep referring us as 'the weaker sex', forgetful of the fact that all populace that is in this world, owes its existence to us)

Saas nandon ne wo diye taane,
Do ghadi mai jo unke ghar me rahi

(My in-laws, husband's mother and sisters bickered and cast aspersions for the time that I was alone with him)

Ja ke qaziyaat mai le loongi usi roz talaq
Marduva mera, zara, saut ke ghar jaye to

(I will immediately go to the Qazi's office and seek divorce. How dare my husband go to the other woman)

Wo doosri ke saath the mai doosre ke saath
Ankhen hui jo chaar to, sharma ke reh gaye

(He was with the other woman and I was with some other man, Peevishly, we faced each other, redfaced with shame)

Pi kar sharaab aaye the,Bhabhi,wo raat ko
Shaitan jaagta raha, insaan so gaya

(O Bhabhi, my brother's wife, he arrived last night heavily drunk; the devil within him was out throughout the night, while the good human being in him lay inert, asleep)

Jab tak ada na ho gayi bachchi ke farz se
Jaise ki mere paon me bedi padi rahi

(Till I was bound with the duty of getting my daughter married, I had this notion that my feet were chained)

'Yaas' Yagaana Changezi

Takra ke dekhen tum kya ho hum kya,
Jeete to jeete haare to haare.

(Let us clash and fight to know who is superior;
do not come whether I win or lose)

Perhaps this *sher* of Yagaana aptly describes his personality. True to his name he was 'Yagaana' – the one and the only one, unique. His life was tumultuous and end tragic.

Born as Mirza Wajid Husain in 1884 in Azeemabad, now Patna, he selected his pen name as 'Yaas' meaning despair. Initially, he described himself as 'Yaas' Azeemabadi but later became Yagaana Lucknawi when he settled in Lucknow. An enigmatic personality, he developed contempt for Ghalib and enjoyed when described as *Ghalib Shikan* (Ghalib basher/demolisher). He consistently attacked Ghalib's iconic status and consequently earned the hostility of millions of the great poets' fans and his contemporaries alike.

Yaas Yagaana Changezi

Spending sometime in Calcutta and then Lahore and Hyderabad doing different jobs, he finally settled in Lucknow and lived in a small house in Taape wali Gali near Kazmain in Old Lucknow.

He was an outstanding poet with a new melody, strength and style in his poetry. But his egocentricity and self indulgence crossed all the limits and as a result damaged his poetry, name and personality. When he settled in Lucknow in 1930s his contemporaries in Lucknow were some well known poets of high stature such as Aarzoo, Aziz, Safi, and Saquib who held Ghalib in high esteem. This provoked Yagaana to attack them too and consequently earned their hostility as well as Urdu poetry lovers of Lucknow. He became a *persona non grata* and people stopped inviting him to Mushairas. The indifference, neglect and later contempt from the people and literary circles of Lucknow made him more rigid, stubborn and maverick. He developed a knack for stinging his friends and foes alike with the result that he was totally isolated. Though he had to leave Lucknow for some time in search of employment but his attitude did not change. It was no more confined to polemics but degenerated into mudslinging.

After returning to Lucknow, he had decided to spend rest of his life in this city though he was economically hard pressed. An ugly incident occurred on 31 March, 1953 which not only broke him but was absolutely not in conformity with the refinement and sophistication of Lucknowites. He wrote a private letter to Niyaz Fatehpuri, an eminent literary figure of his time, whom be considered a friend. In a lighter vein Yagaana shared some of his thoughts with him which were, perhaps, derogatory to the Prophet Muhammed. Niyaz Fatehpuri, committing an impropriety, forwarded the letter to Moulana Abdul Majid Daryabadi, a prominent Sunni Islamic scholar who was provoked and hurt and wrote a protest note in his weekly magazine *Sidq-e-Jadeed*. Besides condemning the tone, tenor, and content of the letter he also exhorted the Shias to 'handle' him (as Yagaana happened to be a Shia). *Sarfaraaz* the Urdu organ of Shia Conference also published a protest note against Yagaana. Within a few days a group of rowdy and and anti-social elements, consisting largely of Shias, attacked 'Yagaanas' house, looted his belongings, blackened his face and forced him to wear a garland of shoes and ride a donkey in a procession. Some of the aged persons of Old Lucknow tell that Mufti Raza Ansari of Firangi Mahal and Pandit Anand Narain Mulla, two of his friends and eminent personalities of Lucknow, were instrumental in rescuing him with the help of the police and he was sheltered in Nakhas police station. He left the house where it all happened and after living for sometime in the house of Prof. Masood Hasan Rizvi, well known Urdu literary figure, moved to a congested and dilapidated house in mohalla Shah Ganj near Nakhas Crossing. Mirza Jafar Husain (ibid) writes that he died a lonely man in this house on 4 February, 1956. Mufti Ahmed Ali led his funeral prayer. Only six persons formed his funeral procession and he was hurriedly buried in Karbala Munshi Fazal Husain located in Nakhas area to avoid any further ugly incident:

True to some of his verses:

Zindagi me to woh mehfil se utha dete the
Dekhein ab mar gai par kaun uthata hai mujhe,
Nang-e-mehfil mera zindah, mera murdah bhaari,
Kaun uthaata hai mujhe, kaun bithaata hi mujhe.

Watan ko chor kar jis sar zamee se dil lagaaya tha,
Wohi ab khoon ke pyasi huee hai karbala ho kar.

[Having left the motherland (Patna), gave heart to the place (Lucknow) which has now become thirsty of my blood like Karbala]

After sometime, his daughter came from Pune and got his grave cemented with a stone epitaph. Tragically, along with his other belonging his unpublished collection of poetry that was composed after 1934 was also lost.

Yagaana was an important poet of Urdu. His individuality, style and diction put him in a class of his own but his eccentricity and maverick behaviour proved his undoing. Restraint was alien to his personality and he paid the price by resorting to self-destruction.

Majaaz

The first decade after independence witnessed the end, in tragic circumstances, of

The poet Majaaz on a postage stamp

two outstanding and brilliant Urdu Poets with unusual personalities-first, of Yaas Yagaana Changezi and the second was Majaaz. The former left the world in 1956 and the later in 1955. Though Yagaana was much senior to Majaaz in age, both had a strong streak of self destruction.

Majaaz, born as Asrarul Haq on 19 October 1911, in an affluent Zamindar family of Rudauli (Barabanki), was destined to become Majaaz-one of the greatest poets of modern Urdu poetry. He rose to become a prominent poet of romance and revolution. Brought up in a literary atmosphere, he started writing poems-both ghazal and nazm while studying in Aligarh Muslim University. The popular *taraana* (anthem) of this University was penned by him:

Yeh mera chaman hai mera chaman mai apne chaman ka bulbul hoon

[This is my garden, mine and I am the bard (nightingale) of this garden]

His popularity among his fans at the University especially among the female students was seen to be believed. His contemporaries vouched that there was a mad scramble among his female fans to keep his photograph under the pillow while sleeping so that Majaaz came to their dreams. Later he worked for sometime in All India Radio and edited its' journal, 'Aawaaz'.

By this time he had already been attracted and inspired by *Taraqqi Pasand Tehrik* (progressive writers' movement). A fine and justice loving human being that he was, he hated inequality and the glaring contrast between the rich and the poor and was opposed to capitalist system. Though never been a member of the Communist Party, his best and closest friends were all known communists- Faiz Ahmed Faiz, Ali Sardar Jafri, Makhdoom Mohiuddin and others. His progressive views were obvious:

Zamane se aagey to badhye 'Majaaz'
Zamana ko aage badhana bhi hai

Tu inquilab ki aamad ka intezaar na kar
Jo ho sakey to abhi inquilab paida kar

Addressing the women of his time, he exhorted:

Tere maathe pe yeh aanchal bahut he khoob hai lekin,
Tu is aanchal se ek parham bana leti to accha tha.

Like the other progressive poets, he had deviated from the traditional Urdu poetry. A very important Urdu poet of traditional poetry Mirza Jafar Ali Khan 'Asar' Lucknawi, who was very impressed by Majaaz before he was associated with the progressive movement made a very interesting comment-a quotable quote:

"*Urdu Shairee me bhi eik Keats paida hua thaa lekin usey taraqqi pasand bhediye utha le gai*"

(A Keats was also born in Urdu poetry but he was carried away by the 'progressive' wolves).

By now he had been acknowledged as a front ranking poet of his time when only in thirties. Though he had developed a habit of heavy drinking even during his student days but a personal tragedy in his life further accentuated his problem. Majaaz was madly in love with a woman- perhaps a one sided affair, who instead of choosing a pennyless poet opted for a secured future and married another man. Majaaz was shattered. His drinking increased. He lived in New Hyderabad mohalla in Trans-Gomti area. His friends and relatives tell that he used to return to his home late at night everyday being carried by a regular rickshaw driver and slept in the outside veranda of his home, usually leaving the meal untouched. He also spent some time in the mental hospital and rehabilitation centre in Ranchi. His journey of self-destruction came to an end on 5 December 1955 when he was left alone by his other drinking partners under the sky, the first floor open space, in a tavern in the Lal Bagh area. The vender did not notice his presence, locked it and went away. Majaaz was too drunk to feel the chill and the extremely cold winter night extinguished this grand lamp of Urdu poetry:

Roen na abhi ahle nazar haal pe mere
Hona hai abhi mujhko kharaab aur ziayaada

Describing his inevitable fate he had prophetically said:

Ab iske baad subah hai aur subh-e-nau Majaaz
Hum par hai khatm shaam-e-ghareeban-e-Lucknow.

Majaaz is buried in the Nishat Ganj grave yard and perhaps he is the most visited resident of this cemetery.

Mushaira

Literally meaning a 'poetic symposium', mushaira has been an integral part of Urdu poetry and has played an important role in popularizing the Urdu poetry especially *Ghazal* among the masses. It is a special event or *mehfil* where the Urdu poets present their poetry before an audience and in turn get admiration and appreciation. Mushairas have been quite popular in North India, Hyderabad Deccan, parts of Pakistan and for that matter wherever Urdu knowing people live in the world. Many people believe that Urdu poetry by its' very nature is most appropriate for the stage. It is supposed to be recited and to be listened and admired.

Though Urdu poets began getting lot of respect and attention by the time of Nawab Shujauddaula, but by the reign of Asafuddaula almost all the important and front ranking poets had migrated from Delhi to Lucknow. Among them were such stalwarts as Meer Taqi 'Meer', and Mirza Rafi 'Sauda' who spent rest of their lives in Lucknow and buried here. They and other poets migrating from Delhi clearly demonstrated the Delhi style of poetry in their works. Later, the pure Lucknawi poets such as Naasikh and Aatish emerged with their distinct Lucknawi style.

In the initial stages the mushairas were largely confined to the palace where only the elite enjoyed access. Gradually and gradually, it came out from the confines of the *durbars* and *havelis* and established themselves where it was destined for – among the masses appreciative of poetry. The mushairas used to be held in big halls or in the open under a large *shamiana.* Usually, it began at around 7PM and continued till the dawn. It provided ample time to each poet. The usual sitting arrangement used to be such that the poets sat on both sides facing each other and the middle or intervening space remained vacant. The rest of the space in the front was occupied by the audience. It was usually carpets or white sheets of cloth over a rug on which the audience sat and the poets on carpets and rounded pillows or *gaotakiya* were placed for the poets to lean over it. A particular type of mushaira called as *tarahi mushaira* was popular in which the organizer used to give a line (*misra*) before hand and the poets were supposed to compose their *ghazals* using the same *behar* or rhythmic metre. Obviously it required a mastery over the language as well as the poetic craft. The *shama* or candle used to rotate before every poet. The poetry was not 'sung' but merely read or recited. Only a few poets used to present their poetry like a lyric. There was an elaborate and sophisticated way of expressing appreciation. The audience usually said loudly- *waah waah, subhan allah, bahut khoob* and when they wanted the poet to repeat a particular *sher*, it was *mukarrar irshaad* meaning, a repeat requested. The poet acknowledging the admiration usually said *aadaab* and *taslimaat*, *nawazish*, *zarra nawaazi* and similar other words of acknowledgement with humility. After every *mushaire* some publisher used to publish the collection of *ghazals* presented in a *mushaira.* Every poet had a committed following and they used to express their admiration for their *ustad* very loudly.

The first quarter of 20th century too, had big stalwarts such as Safi, Saaquib, Aarzoo, Azeez, Asar, Chakbast and several others. Organization of mushairas was multiplying rapidly. In late 1930s and 1940s the progressive poets emerged with a new content, diction and style. Their poetry was down to earth, tackling day to day problems tinged with political satire. Most of them used the same traditional symbols of *ghazals* but gave them different meanings. Mushairas became phenomenally popular attracting even those who were not properly trained in Urdu.

Since the 1970s or so began the trend of mixing mushaira and kavi sammelan where the Urdu and Hindi poets shared the dais with a common audience, though the exclusive mushaira and kavi sammelan continued. From this point the sitting arrangement too began undergoing changes. There was no more white sheet of cloth and carpets with rounded pillow to lean over. Both poets and audience were new seated in chairs. The venues had their own constraints. If such a literary gathering is held in an auditorium with fixed chairs and dais, one has no other option. The *wah wah, subhan allah* were now getting replaced by clapping. Hooting and catcalls by a section of the audience became an almost regular feature of the *mushaira.* Since 1990s or so a large number of madarsa students formed a big chunk of the audience and several poets, in order to get acclaim from them, began reciting religious oriented poetry. From this point several mushairas got communalized and connoisseurs of Urdu poetry and sober and serious sections of the audience almost stopped going to the mushairas. Instead, they began arranging small, private *nashist* (sitting) where their thirst for good poetry got quenched. Many good poets too enjoy reciting before this appreciative audience instead of going to mushaira while some others attend both mushairas for mass popularity and money and private *nashist* for their own satisfaction.

Unfortunately, now a day's most of the Urdu poets especially the lesser known, and middle level ones suffer from 'persecution complex' or 'victim mentality' who get maximum appreciation and clapping when they talk about the injustice and discrimination being faced by the Muslims in India and elsewhere.Moreover,several poets enjoying phenomenal popularity are more of 'performers' relying more on theatrics than quality of poetry. In this type of changed ambience, the Hindu poets feel uncomfortable and out of place. Unfortunately, the highly secular nature of the *mushairas* has been dented and diluted.

Urdu Journalism in Lucknow

The first Urdu newspaper called *Jaam Jahaan numa* was published from Calcutta in 1822 but its'editor Sada Sukh Lal was a native of Mirzapur in Uttar Pradesh. Though Lucknow may not take pride of giving birth to the first Urdu newspaper, it was more than compensated by its' other pioneering achievements. *Lucknow Akhbaar* was the first from Lucknow and began sometime in 1847. It was followed by *Avadh Akhbaar* in 1858 published by Munshi Nawal Kishore. Initially a weekly, it became a daily in 1877. Its' editorial board consisted of such illustrious persons as Pundit Ratan Nath 'Sarshaar', Abdul Haleem 'Sharar', Naubat Rai 'Nazar' and Syed Jalib Rehelvi. It continued till 1950. The legendry *Awadh Punch*, a satitical Urdu weekly began in 1877. It was edited by Munshi Sajjad Husain. It was like an Indian version of *Punch* which began in England in 1841. The brilliant satire and cartoons of Awadh Punch lost no opportunity in ridiculing the British government. The cartoons ridiculing the colonial government appeared with impunity. Mushirul Hasan's (2012) book *Wit and Humour in Colonial North India,* described in detail its' contribution and reproduced some cartoons and write ups of satire and humour so that the readers may have some idea of the way *Awadh Punch* was published and admired. Moreover, noted satirist/humourist such as Akbar Allahabadi and Ratan Nath 'Sarshaar' came into prominence by their contributions to *Avadh Punch* and *Avadh Akhbaar.*

In the pre-independence period, the daily *Tanvir,* organ of the Muslim League, enjoyed immense popularity. It was edited by a prominent leader of Muslim League Choudhry Khaliquzzaman and it unabashedly supported the demand for creation of Pakistan. In order to counter the influence of this newspaper, Indian National Congress began in 1944 an Urdu newspaper *Qaumi Aawaaz* under the inspiration of Pundit Nehru. Its' founding editor was the prominent journalist and novelist Hayat Ullah Ansari, a great patriot and nationalist. Right from the first day *Qaumi Awaaz* stood for the composite nationalism and opposed the demand for Pakistan and the 'two nation theory' propounded by the Muslim League. It maintained a high standard of journalism and refrained from yellow journalism and sensationalism. In 1970 the founding president of Muslim Majlis Dr. AJ Faridi launched a newspaper called *Qaaed* (leader). It had to close down within a decade of its' inception. When *Qaumi Awaz* ceased publication for a short period, another sober paper *Azaaim* edited by Jameel Mehdi made its debut. Previously, it was being published as a weekly. Another daily *Indinon* appeared in 1993 and continues till date but it has ceased to be a prominent daily of Lucknow. The daily *Sahaafat* began around 1990 and continues to be popular.

The first Urdu daily to have been launched by a corporate house is *Urdu Rashtriya Sahara* from the Sahara Group. It is being published from multiple cities of Uttar Pradesh and other states too. A highly circulated Urdu daily from Bombay, *Inquilab* began its' Lucknow edition in recent years and now being published in multiple editions. It has now been taken over by the *Jagran* group of newspapers.

Another prominent daily is *AvadhNaama* now being published in multiple editions. A different type of daily called *Aag* began in 2001. A unique feature of this daily is that it includes a four page Hindi supplement every day. According to official sources, more than hundred Urdu dailies are being published from Lucknow but except twenty odd dailies none may be seen on news stands.

A number of other Urdu dailes were published and closed down. Besides daily newspapers a number of weeklies and monthlies are also published and this list includes such literary magazines as *Kitaab* edited by the well known journalist Abid Suhail. Tragically, this monthly representing the best in Urdu literature had to close down because of financial problems. The Directorate of Information publishes an Urdu monthly *Naya Daur*. It represents a high level of journalism and continues to come out regularly largely because of its' financial stability.

The large number of Urdu publications is very deceptive because circulation wise these present a gloomy picture and shows the rapid decline of Urdu in Uttar Pradesh.

Munshi Newal Kisore and his Publishing House

Though the first publishing house in Lucknow was established with the blessings of Nawab Ghaziuddin Haider (1814-27) and the second one under the patronage of his son Nawab Nasiruddin Haider(1827-37) with a *lethu* press but these efforts were just not enough. The publishing was done on a limited scale. Now came 1857 revolt and the resultant destruction of Lucknow by the British administration including the printing presses. The fire of 'mutiny' was still simmering but the dust had started settling down when a young man from Aligarh-Agra region arrived in Lucknow in 1858. With lots of dreams in his eyes the enterprising young man of twenty two installed a small tredle printing machine. He was none other but Munshi Nawal Kishore, a Bharagava Brahmin and a devout Hindu subscribing to the Ballabh Cult.

Rightly described by many as William Caxton of India, in terms of his pioneering venture in printings, he founded the Newal Kishore Press and Book Depot in 1858. Establishing an 'empire of books' he became a legend in his life time. Even Mirza Ghalib was so impressed by this publishing house that he once wrote that whosoevers' collection of poetry it published became a celebrity. The collection of virtually all notable poets of Persian and Urdu were published by this press. Islamic religious literature was also published and distributed by this house including the Quran. The first four volumes of *mersias* of Meer Anees were also published by Newal Kishore Press. It hired prominent persons of Urdu literature such as Naubat Rai 'Nazar' and 'Yaas' Azeemabadi during the early years of 20th century to supervise and edit the production. Besides publishing Islamic books in Arabic, Persian and Urdu it also took up the publication of Vedas, Upanishads, Ramayana and Geeta, Purana, Mahabharat and virtually all the important books related with Hinduism.

Though Newal Kishore Press published different types of books in several languages it played a pioneering role in publishing the old Urdu classics such as *Daastaan-e-Amir Hamza* (46 volumes), *Tilism-e-Hosh ruba* (11volumes), *Alif Laila, Fasana-e-Aazaad,*and *Fasaan-e-Ajaib*. It published the total poetry (*Kulliyaat*) of more than fifty Urdu poets. Another monumental publication was more than seventy editions of *Nafeesul lughaat*, the Persian-Urdu dictionary. Among other books, it also published *Fatwa-e-Aalamigiri*, *Akbar Naama*, *Jehungir Naama* and more than hundred books on Unani system of medicine. Munshi Newal Kishore also took interest in publishing the Urdu translation of several classics of English literature too. But the most popular of his publication was the Urdu newspaper *Awadh Akhbar*.

Munshi Newal Kishore was such a visionary and had such an enterprising spirit that instead of spending large amounts of money on purchasing paper from England for large scale printing that also included stationary and books for the government agencies, he founded a paper manufacturing mill in Nishat Ganj area called Upper India Cooper Paper Mill. This paper mill used to manufacture cheap yellowish paper as well as white paper. Taking into consideration the requirement of iron for his printing press he also established 'Lucknow Iron Works'. Both these enterprises were run till 1950 by his family members (Ranjit Bhargava, 2008).

Munshi Newal Kishor passed away in 1895 but his successors kept the flag flying till the time of decline of Persian and Urdu and new technology and marketing strategies took over. His contribution to Urdu shall always be written in golden letters. Now most of the publications of Newal Kishore Press are kept in a separate section dedicated to him in Amiruddaula Public Library and listed in a separate printed catalogue courtesy the successors of this legendry personality.

Claude Martin and Walter Griffin

Among those persons who never ruled Lucknow but left a lasting mark were a French and an American-Australian. Claude Martin, the French, got sufficient time to engage in various fields- from architecture to education. Walter Griffin after designing Canberra, the capital of Australia, came to Lucknow to design the Tagore Library in now Lucknow University and had many assignments at hand but died suddenly leaving several incomplete projects.

16

Claude Martin and Walter Griffin

Among those who never ruled Lucknow but made contributions and left a mark over Lucknow, Claude Martin a French and Walter Griffin, an American-Australian deserve special mention. Even otherwise, a number of people have been contributing to the life in Lucknow in their own ways without getting a mention in the pages of history.

The French connection with Lucknow is quite old and their presence in Lucknow may be traced back to the beginning of the seventeenth century and they gave their services at the court of the Mughal rulers in a variety of ways. It is said that during the last years of the Akbar's reign, in early seventeenth century, a French trader obtained the royal permission and stayed near chowk area. He traded in horses and had achieved immense success in this field. Joining some adjacent houses he converted them into a *haveli* or palatial building. This was known as Firangi Mahal. Nobody knows whether he himself named it as such or the local people called it as, popularly speaking, *Firangi* was a generic name for all (white) Europeans. When he left Lucknow after the expiry of his residential permit, it was taken over by the government under it's control. During Aurangzeb's time, it was given to the family of the prominent Islamic scholar and sufi saint Mullah Qutubuddin Ansari. Later, it was developed as a great seat of Islamic learning by Mullah Nizamuddin, famous for his 'Dars-e-Nizami'. During this period some more houses were added to it and it became a mohalla now known as Mohalla Firangi Mahal. Though the old glory of Firangi Mahal is gone but it's historical importance remains. Jean-Marie Lafont (1997) writes "that the first 'wave' of Frenchmen apparently arrived in north India during the reign of Jahangir, in whose entourage were Doctor Bernard with his miraculous cures, and Augustin Hiriart, an architect and engineer."

Among all the Frenchmen **Claude Martin** left an important mark over Lucknow. He was (1735-1800AD) an officer in the French army, switched over to the British army and rose to the position of Major General in the British East India Company's army. That is how he appears on the scene in Lucknow in the service of Nawab Asafuddaula, Claude Martin was born in Lyon, France and was a self-made man who has left a lasting legacy in the form of his writings, buildings and the educational institutions he founded.

Claude Martin was a multifaceted personality. He was a soldier, an architect and builder, a collector and commissioner, a 'Nawab', a banker and business man, a self made surgeon, a hot air balloonist, a philanthropist and an educationist- all in one. His proximity to Asafuddaula gave him an opportunity to contribute in the making of modern Lucknow. Among the buildings bearing distinctive touch of Claude Martin are Kothi Hayaat Baksh (now Raj Bhawan, the official residence cum office of the Governor of Uttar Pradesh), Kothi Farhat Baksh, Asafi Kothi, Bibiapur and the Constantia House, a part of La Martinere College Complex.

Claude Martin earned lot of wealth but was equally interested in spending in charities for the collective good of the society. Though self educated he knew the importance of formal education. He willed a major part of his wealth to the creation of institutions of learning and that is how Lucknows' LaMartinere College was established alongwith two other colleges in Calcutta and Lyon (his native place) in France, all named similarly. La Martinere College, Lucknow has produced countless number of illustrious alumni. He is buried in the vault in the basement of Constantia. A small village on his name- Martinpurwa is still there near La Martinere College.

Walter Burley Griffin was a well known American architect whose name is closely associated with Australia because he designed the Australian capital Canberra and some other buildings. Griffin was deeply inspired by the culture and architecture of India. While working at the Greater Sydney Development Association, he won a contract to design the central library (now Tagore Library) of University of Lucknow. Although he came to India just for this job, he was virtually inundated by many offers including the Students Union Building at Lucknow University, a museum and library for Raja of Mahmudabad, a *Zenankhana* (women's quarters) for the Raja of Jahangirabad, Pioneer Press building at Vidhan Sabha Marg and several others. However, only a part of his elaborate plans could be fully executed. He spent barely two years at Lucknow and died suddenly after a gall bladder surgery.

Walter Griffin passed away in February 1937 and buried at the Christian Cemetery situated near Paper Mill Colony, Nishaat Ganj. His grave was not traceable for more than four decades. Graeme Westlake of Canberra, Australia came to Lucknow in 1988 and his quest ended successfully locating it in the cemetery where he was actually buried. Many of us were not aware of him and his architectural contribution to Lucknow till the Indian Prime minister at the G20 meeting shared his story with the heads of state of Australia and USA. Our mass media widely covered this story and Griffin is no more a stranger to the intelligentsia of Lucknow in general and students and teachers of arts and architecture in particular. Recently, a delegation of students and teachers, and experts from Australia visited Lucknow to study his contribution in this part of India.

Sub-Urban Lucknow

Because of the imposing presence of 'Lucknawi composite culture' three very important *Qasbahs* (towns) around Lucknow adopted the cultural ethos in two different ways- Kakori and Malihabad evolved along Muslim ethos while Bakshi Ka Taalaab has been predominantly a product of Hindu ethos largely because of Chandrika Devi Temple and some other places of religious importance. The Hindu advisors and ministers of the Nawabs patronized these religious centers with the encouragement of the Nawabs.

17

Sub-Urban Lucknow

The city of Lucknow is surrounded by some such *Qasbahs* and towns which have also been popular for one reason or the other. When we look at them we find that despite the aura of Lucknow culture and ethos they have been able to maintain their individuality and identity. This speaks of the strength of their cultures and value system.

Kakori

Kakori is a town and a nagar panchayat in Lucknow district. The identity of Kakori to the general public rests largely on *Kakori kebabs*, *Chikan* and *Zardozi* work, *Dussehri* mangoes, *Urdu* literature and Qadiriya Qalandari Sufi Order. Another important feature was added to its identity after 9 August, 1925 when some Indian revolutionary freedom fighters stopped the train here and looted the treasure being carried in it by the Britishers. All the revolutionaries involved in it were arrested and hanged. Now a memorial with their portraits stands on the same spot where the train was looted.

Located 13 kilometres away from Lucknow on the Lucknow-Hardoi Road, and smaller than several other adjoining towns in terms of geographical area, it is much larger in reputation in terms of literary, historical and social importance. It was considered as a leading town of Awadh alongwith Rudauli and Mehmoodabad. It occupies a central place for the two branches of Kakori Shaikh community – Alvi and Abbasi. As the very name suggest the Alvis trace their lineage to Ali, the fourth Caliph and the first Imam of the Shias. Their ancestors settled in Kakori in 16th century. The Abbasi claims their lineage to Abbas an uncle of the Prophet Muhammad and their ancestors came and settled down in Kakori in 15th century. Thus, their history in Kakori is more than five hundred years old.

The old *Hav.elis* and palatial houses remind the visitors of the grand past of the Muslim gentry. Among the famous sufis whose names still bring awe and respect are Shah Muhammad Kazim Qalandar, Shah Turab Ali Qalandar, Shah Anwar Qalandar, and Shah Habib Haider Qalandar. Their descendants have maintained their traditions. Ahmed Ibrahim Alvi (1996) bringing out some other features of Kakori writes that their hospitality is known far and wide and their feasts are recorded in history. The famous *Seekh Kebab* is now an integral part of the marriage feasts and other events in Lucknow. He tells that the famous Tunde Kababi also hails from Kakori.

The brave freedom fighters from Kakori laid down their lives in the first war of Independence in 1857 and several others were exiled to *Kaala Paani* in the Andamans jail. The literary taste of the Kakori people may be gauged from the fact that even their womenfolk have made their mark in Urdu literature and dozens of young women have been writing short stories and poetry. The *mazaars* of the Sufi saints are the centre of devotion to people of different castes and communities who not only congregate during the annual *Urs* but also on Thursdays and even any days of the week and offer prayers.

Malihabad

Malihabad is also a town and nagar panchayat of Lucknow district. It is largely known for its grand Pathans and mangoes. Considered as the 'mango belt' of north India, it is internationally known for the amazing varieties of mangoes and an amazing mango grower Padmshree Kaleemullah Khan who has created many new varieties of mangoes. Though several varieties of mangoes are grown in Malihabad, its name continues to be synonymous with Dussehri.

Its claim to fame also rests on its contribution to Urdu poetry. Faqeer Muhammad Khan 'Goya' was a famous poet and courtier of Awadh while the internationally renowned 'Josh' Malihabadi, popularly known as *Shaayer-e-Inquilab* (poet of revolution) carried the name of Malihabad to world map. Former national champion in tennis Ghous Muhammad Khan also came from Malihabad.

In recent years a controversy and debate was created by a young researcher Navras Jat Afreedi, also coming from Malihabad, who claimed that the Afridi Pathans of Malihabad have Jewish lineage and are one of the ten lost tribes of Israel. Controversies apart, the fact remain that the societal and cultural life of Malihabad carries the influence of Shaikhs, Syeds, Mughals, Kayasthas and Pathans. The finance and revenue minister of Nawab Asafuddaula, Raja Tikait Rai was a native of Mohalla Munshiganj in Malihabad. Khan Muhammad Aatif (1996) rightly opines that although Malihabad had already made its mark in Awadh but the great heights in the 'civilizational milieu' was achieved by it after the advent of Qandharis (Qandahar/Kandahar) and Afiridis. The simplicity, conviction, tribal traditions of Afghans, hospitality, refusal to obedience of any arrogant forces, protection of the week and self respect are the social-cultural traits which still characterize the Pathans of Malihabad.

Bakshi Ka Taalaab

Bakshi Ka Taalaab is an area situated at the northern side of the city of Lucknow. It derives its name from Tripuresh Chandra Bakshi, cashier of the Nawabs of Awadh. He was a devout Hindu and with the patronage of the Nawabs built a big

Shiva temple and Thakurdwara. Later, a big and beautiful pond was also created here. But the most important land mark is Chandrika Devi Temple, a 300 years old temple in Kathwara Village on the river Gomti. Mata Chandrika is no other than Durga. It is a centre of devotion for the millions of people and tourists from even far off places pay a visit to this temple.

Popularly called as BKT, it used to be a *mandi* of food grains and carpets coming from the neighbouring Sitapur district. At present the Lucknow Development Authority (LDA), in its extension scheme, has constructed the Sitapur Road Housing Colony. For the last two decades or so BKT has been developing as an 'Educational Hub'. The sprawling new campus of Lucknow University has also been established in this area and so is the Technical University. Besides, there are more than fifty Degree, Engineering and Management colleges are also now located here. Perhaps the reason for this mushrooming growth may be availability of land near the road and highway while the Lucknow-Kanpur Road and Lucknow-Faizabad Road are already saturated.

Sunni-Shia Violence

Lucknow is marked by two contrasting phenomenon- a peaceful and harmonious co-existence between Hindus and Muslims and a history of more than a century of tensions and violence between the Sunnis and the Shias. When one delves deeper into this unpleasant Sunni-Shia interface, one discovers that the religious-doctrinal differences are secondary. The primary factors are socio-economic and political. With the decline of the Shia power after 1857 and then the Zamindari Abolition after independence the Shias were economically marginalized and the majority Sunni sect rapidly climbed upward economically and politically. Their democratic assertion sometimes led to unreasonable demands vis a vis religious practices in public space and during the past 3-4 decades, the rise of radical Islamism represented by the orthodox Wahabi version of Islam further complicated the already strained ties.

18

Sunni-Shia Violence

Lucknow has had a peculiar history of social relations. On the one hand the city is known throughout the world for it's communal harmony, *Ganga-Jamuni Tehzeeb* (composite culture) nurtured by Hindus and Muslims together while on the other hand this is the only city in India that witnesses Sunni-Shia Violence, minor and major, frequently. Perhaps, this is one of the few Indian cities with a large population of Muslims where no Hindu-Muslim riot has ever occurred-not even during the frenzy of the partition days in 1947 when almost the entire north India was burning with violence but at the same time there is no other city in the country where the two main Muslim sects have so frequently clashed violently and have to spend at least some months every year in tensions and apprehensions. The Shias constitute approximately 35% of the total population of Muslims in the city. This is the largest percentage of Shias in India after Hyderabad.

No doubt there is some doctrinal disagreement and dispute between these two sects. To put very briefly, historically, the point of contention rests on the successor to Prophet Muhammed. The term 'Shia' refers to those Muslims who derive their religious code and spiritual inspiration, after Muhammed, from Muhammed's descendants- the *ahlalbait.* The majority Sunni sect accepts it from the *sahabah* (companions) of the prophet. This is the pivotal point which distinguishes, despite unanimity on all the fundamentals of Islam, the Shia from the Sunni. The Shias respect only those *sahabah* who supported and sided with Ali, Prophet's cousin and son-in-law, and then his progeny, the twelve Imams of the Shias. The Sunnis also respect Ali but did not accept his claim to be the direct successor to the Prophet but as the fourth successor and caliph.

Can this doctrinal dispute, compounded by other minor ones, how relevant this may have been, sustain a festering wound for more than a thousand years? This seems to be only an excuse for violence with some definite goals to achieve.

Let us look back briefly to identify the factors contributing to Sunni-Shia schism and conflict in Lucknow. Awadh has been under the Shia rule of the Nawabs for almost one and a half century. Locally, the Shias were politically, economically and culturally dominant. Under this cultural dominance the local Sunnis especially their lower stratum, adopted a number of cultural and religious practices of the Shias.

There has been a slow demise of Lucknows' Shias in terms of economic and political power. The first major setback they experienced was the annexation of Awadh by the Britishers in 1856 but they survived it because their *zamindari* was intact though a number of them had to pay the price for siding with the freedom fighters. The decline had begun and its pace increased with every passing decade. By the turn of the 20th century the Sunnis had caught up and raced ahead in terms of economic mobility and it was matched by further and further degeneration, stagnation and impoverishment of the Shias. Their habbit of squandering wealth on consumption, a life style not commensurate with their economic status and lavish spending on various customs especially Moharrum *azaadaari* ,also contributed to their impoverishment. At the same time the Sunnis, by sheer effort of labour, in their various occupations, crafts and business, left the Shias far behind. By 1930s or 40s most of the erstwhile affluent Shias had transferred their wealth and properties to the Rastogi money lenders. The economic marginalization of the Shias was almost complete. The zamidaari abolition proved as the proverbial last nail on the coffin.

The first sign of Sunni assertion of their power and authority was seen in 1908 when a prominent Sunni cleric raised a new religious demand and it resulted in some violent clashes. The Sunni taziadaars started going to a seperate karbala for Moharrum rituals. Not only this some Sunni Ulema and preachers declared Moharrum observance as *biddat* (innovation and sin) and an act of idolatry. This was the beginning of the end of Moharrum as a common symbol for both though even today a good number of Sunnis observe Moharrum in their own way though it is still popular among the Sunnis of the rural areas. Thus began the chain of violence- 1969,1970,1972,1974,1977 and the minor incidents continued. Post-independence era witnessed new political equations. For the Shias it was a painful period that demanded reconciliation with the changed circumstance and their marginalization from the State affairs. Their inability to create new avenues of generating wealth further accentuated their problems. It also led to 'ghettoisation' of the Shias of old Lucknow where they once dominated. Moreover, Shia-Sunni marriages, not rare till the turn of the 20th century declined sharply and today one sees hardly any such marriages arranged by the parents of the bride and the groom.

Some events which led to almost total polarization between the two sects is worth mentioning. During the early days of the freedom movement most of the Shias sided with the Congress Party while the majority of Sunnis in Lucknow were with the Muslim League like the case with several other districts. Jamiat-e-Ulema closely affiliated with the Congress Party convinced Govind Ballabh Pant, the tallest Congress leader of Uttar Pradesh at that time, to allow *Madhe Sahaaba* Procession, a demand of the Sunnis since the first decade of the 20th century, to win Sunni support and wean them away from the Muslim League. *Madhe Sahaaba* which literally means 'praise for the companions (of the Prophet)' was always an anathema for the Shias who always opposed it's recitation at public places. The demand could be seen as the democratic assertion of the new found power and authority by the majority sect. In 1939 Madhe Sahaaba procession was allowed by the provincial government on the day of Barahwafaat. The Shia protested and claimed that the previous judicial committees had already given their verdict against it. The Shias became hysterical and retaliated with a sort of civil disobedience movement in the form of *Tabarrah* agitation. Thousands of Shias of undivided India-from Punjab to Uttar Pradesh courted arrest. *Tabarrah* literally means 'disassociation' and in this case disassociation with all those personalities in Islamic history they did not like or respect. Unfortunately, these two seemingly innocuous terms were transformed into lethal weapons of provocation for both. While the *Madhe Sahaba* was not confined to merely praising certain personalities but also making unnecessary comparisons and downgrading the personalities venerated by the Shias. The same happened to the *Tabarrah* too. The simple disassociation from certain personalities degenerated into cursing them and this was also not acceptable. It is to be noted here that some of the extremist and fanatic ulema and preachers of both sides instead of dousing the fire, stoked it.

Maulana Azad was sent to Lucknow as a mutually agreed arbitrator. On his request the Shias suspended their agitation. He did his best to bring a compromise but failed. Meanwhile the Second World War broke and the Congress led ministry resigned. Minor skirmishes continued but no major riot occurred. However, the gulf continued to increase. It is to be noted here that the dispute between the two sects was confined only to allowing Madhe Sahaba processions on roads. The Azadaari or Moharrum mourning rituals and processions were not disputed by the Sunnis.

Came 1969 and Lucknow witnessed the most serious riot till date. It also heralded the entry of Jan Sangh Party, the predecessor of today's BJP. Lucknow (west) assembly constituency had the largest number of Muslim voters among the state assembly constituencies of Lucknow. Syed Ali Zaheer, a prominent Congress leader and a Shia had been winning this seat with the support of the majority of the Shia voters as well as substantial Sunni voters. In this election the Congress changed it's candidate and gave it's ticket to a highly respected Sunni scholar from Firangi Mahal and also a journalist, Mufti Raza Ansari. He lost the election against the massive wave of the rebel Congress leader Choudhry Charan Singh. All the assembly seats from Lucknow were captured by Charan Singh's party. The large section of Sunnis believed that the Shias betrayed him and this further increased the bitterness.

On May 26, 1969, the last day of mourning period for the Shias, a big mourning procession passing through a congested Sunni locality of old Lucknow was attacked and it was alleged that the processionists were also reciting *Tabarrah*. It resulted in stabbing, arson and firing. Lot of property of both sides was destroyed, some lost their lives and many got injured. The entire area remained under curfew for weeks together. This was by far the severest riot. All the processions were banned for several years and after prolonged negotiations between the representatives of both the parties an agreement was reached curtailing a number of customary processions of the Shias and permitting Madhe Sahaba procession on Barawafaat.

With the 1969 riot began the migration of a number of Shia and Sunni families to 'safer' areas exhibiting the spatial impact of the riots. This was never a mass exodus or migration neither it was organized. Silently families sold their houses and moved to the mohallas they thought safer for them. Most of the Muslim areas of old Lucknow are poverty stricken. With high density of population, rampant unemployment, lack of civic amenities, parks, recreation, sport and games, these areas serve as a tinder box always waiting for a spark.

Two factors are worth mentioning before this narration is closed. The first is the entry of BJP in the local Muslim politics. Right from the days of the Bhartiya Jan Sangh, the effort was on to split Muslim votes on a large scale to benefit it. The party decided to side with the Shias in their dispute with the Sunnis. Some Shias were also won over and shown as 'poster boys' of the party. This further alienated the Sunnis. The microscopic minority of the Shias supporting BJP try to show that the entire community supports the party to further their own, vested interests. Land mafia from both sects, the so called 'property dealers' have further vitiated the atmosphere. They have their own agenda to pursue at the cost of peace and harmony.

The anti-Shia violence going on in Pakistan, Afganistan and the Middle East also impacts the already fragile Sunni-Shia relations in the trouble spot- old Lucknow. 'Wahabism' inspired clerics and their polemics have also contributed in widening the gulf between the two sects.

Obviously, the need of the hour is devising creative interventions aimed at closing the chapter of hate and violence. There are ulema and preachers on both the sides, though only a few in number, who can play very important role in bringing about reconciliation and who are heard with respect. Let them tell their followers that they share all the fundamentals of Islam and the area of disagreement is very small and minor. Let the well intentioned NGOs tell them to focus on their economic well being and prosperity as violence not only disrupt the social fabric but also economic life. Let them develop high stakes in achieving prosperity as frequent tensions and violence are the biggest stumbling blocks in eliminating poverty and deprivations.

Shared Culture and Communal Harmony

Lucknow is known for the shared cultural space between different castes and communities popularly known as the *Ganga-Jamuni Sanskriti/Tehzeeb.* A strong tradition of accommodation, harmony and religious tolerance still continues. Undoubtedly, the credit goes to the Nawabs of Awadh who were loved and respected by the Hindus and Muslims alike. The Nawabs patronized a number of temples, fairs and festivals and participated actively in Hindu festivals too. The legacy continues. A number of Muslims continue to participate in Hindu festivals and help in the construction of temples while a number of Hindus participate in Moharrum observance and known as *Hindu Taziadaar/Azaadaar.*

19

Shared Culture and Communal Harmony

Since the days of Nawab's rule in Awadh, Lucknow has always been known for religious tolerance, communal harmony and shared culture between Hindus and Muslims. What other evidence is required to substantiate this claim than the fact that Lucknow remained calm even during the worst days of partition related violence. In a way, it was like an island. Thus, the Hindu-Muslim interface was characterized by mutual respect and tolerance. Unfortunately, this was not so in the case of Sunni-Shia relations though the fact remains that a century of conflict and violence between them was less religious and more political in nature. How did the tradition of accommodation, mutual respect and harmony between Hindus and Muslims develop? Ask any Lucknowite and you will get the same answer with little variations and the answer would be the Nawabs of Awadh. Before coming to the present scenario of harmony, let us briefly see how did the Nawab rulers achieve and perpetuated it so that it becomes deep rooted in the cultural ethos of Lucknow.

The Nawabs of Awadh patronized and participated in several Hindu festivals whole heartedly. Nawab Asafuddaula used to make elaborated arrangement for Basant festival in his durbar and also participated in the festivities outside. The Nawab along with hundreds of people indulged in kite flying- the kites and the thread both of yellow colour, and wore yellow clothes and then visited the mazaar of some sufi saint and offered mustard corns. Holi was a grand festival for them. Several of them played Holi with colours with not only his Hindu ministers and officers but also with some common people. Describing Nawab Asafuddaulas' enthusiasm in Holi, the famous Urdu poet Meer Taqi Meer says :

Holi Khelein Asafuddaula wazir,
Rang sohbat se ajab hain khurd-o-pir

(Asafuddaula plays Holi in such a way that from a child to the aged, everybody is enjoying).

Saadat Ali Khan also used to spend lakhs of rupees on arranging Holi festivities. Dussehra was also celebrated on a grand scale. A unique feature of this cultural sharing was also a strong element of commonality between Dussehra and Moharrum. Historians tell us that the tradition of Ramleela in Lucknow during the Dussehra days began in 1810AD under the patronage of Nawab Saadat Ali

A Hindu *Alam* maker from fifth generation displaying his products

Khan. Virtually all the Nawabs patronized, participated and financially assisted in the arrangement for Ramleela. The Ramleela of Aishbagh waited for the Nawab Wajid Ali Shah to begin the performance. The Nawab also participated in Deepawali and all the important buildings used to be illuminated. Krishna Janmashtami was another Hindu festival characterized by the participation of the Nawabs as well as the Muslim masses. The last ruler, Nawab Wajid Ali Shah was so deeply involved with this festival that he used to act as Krishna himself in *Raasleela*. An accomplished poet and dancer, his performance is recoded in history in minute details.

He was so much loved by the Hindus that when he was dethroned, a rumour floated that he was being exiled to London. Thousands of Hindu women with tears in their eyes raised their hands in prayers:

Hazrat Jaatein hain London
Kripa Karo Raghunandan

(O lord Rama! have mercy; Hazrat is being exiled to London).

Most of the Nawabs contributed generously not only in the construction of several temples and *ghaats* but also in their maintenance. The old Hanuman Mandir in Aliganj displays a cresent and star at the top and Yogesh Praveen, a historian-chronicler of Lucknow, says that it is perhaps the only temple in India displaying this Islamic symbol. Perhaps, it was a mark of gratitude for Begum Alia for facilitating the construction and maintenance of this temple.

Although the Hindus participated in most of the Muslim festivals, their participation in Moharrum mourning rituals need special mention. Some of the Hindu ministers of the Nawab notably Raja Jhau Lal also built an imambada for Moharrum mourning. Taziadaari was a common feature with substantial sections of the Hindus and Sunni Muslims though it enjoyed royal patronage because of the Shia Nawabs. Even some of the Hindu poets composed very impressive *Mersia* and recited it in Moharrum congregations. The most notable among them was Channu Lal 'Dilgeer' whose dirge *"Bhaiyya ko madiney me kahaan payegi zainab, ghabraegi zainab* brings tears to the mourners even today when recited in a poignant tone on *ashura* moharrum.

A strong element of syncretism may also be seen in the way a festival was celebrated and observed. Many Hindus had this tradition of relishing *Sewain* during Shravani and Anant Chaturdashi. The popular custom of preparing different varieties of *Sewain* during the Eid festival seems to have been borrowed from the local Hindus. Illumination and firework during the festival of Shab baraat has also been borrowed from the Hindus. The Shia festival of Navroz is the replica of Holi. The Shias of Iranian origin settled down in Awadh must have been fascinated by Holi festivities especially throwing colour on each other and adopted it. The Shias of Iran do not celebrate Navroz like this. If one looks closely at the Tazias of Moharrum, one finds that most of these have their domes resembling those of temples. Many people are of the view that when the Hindus had adopted the custom of *Taziadari* they must have designed the Tazias

The Muslim gentleman in front of the Durga Temple built by him recently as a gift to his Hindu neighbours

Kishnu Khalifa ka Imambada owned and maintained by a Hindu

on common temples and with the passage of time this became the universally accepted style of Tazias in Awadh. It is significant to know that the second most important centre of Shiaism and the Shias in South Asia- Hyderabad does not have Tazia as a part of Moharrum moruning but only simply Alam (the standard, flag of Imam Husain). Thus a unique cultural environment developed during the Nawabi days whose ingredients were adaptation, accommodation, sharing and tolerance.

Even today, despite substantial 'dilution' of 'Lucknowness', the traditions continue in one form or the other. During all the Tuesdays of Bada Mangal festival, a number of Muslims may be seen offering cold water and *sherbet* to the devotees on the *piau* or water stalls established by them. During the Moharrum days a number of Hindus and NGOs establish their stalls offering water to all under the scorching sun as a mark of tribute to the martyrs of Kerbala who died thirsty. A number of Muslims have been actively participating in the enactment of Ramleela and have been playing the role of different characters. The Ramleela of Bakshi Ka Taalaab had mostly Muslim actors. But Moharrum has been the highest form of composite culture in Lucknow and elsewhere. 'Mathur' Lucknavi, Sanjay Misra 'Shauq' and several other Hindu poets have been known as 'Husaini poets'. One of the signature *salaams* of 'Mathur' Lucknavi had the following lines:

Kehte hue jannnat me chaley jaaenge 'Mathur',
Shabbir ke qadmon ke nishaan dhoond rahe hain.

(I shall walk into paradise. If checked, I shall tell them that I am following the footsteps of Imam Husain).

Even today, hundreds of Hindu devotees and mourners may be seen in

Talkatora Ki Karbala on the day of *ashura*, the day of martyrdom, expressing their grief and paying tribute to Imam Husani and other martyrs of Karbala in their own way, different from the Shias. Several traditional Punjabi Mohiyaal Brahmins still participate in the Moharrum mourning and have been described as 'Husaini Brahmins'.

Imambada Kishnu Khalifa

Established in 1880 by Gaaydin Dhanuk and his son Kishnu Khalifa in a lane of Mohalla Bashirat Ganj, it has a tradition of 125 years of Moharrum observance. Here *tazia* and *alam* are installed on the seventh of Moharrum and taken in a procession on the day of *ashura* to the Talkatora Karbala for burial. The processionists walk bare footed reciting mourning poetry. Hundreds of devotees and mourners from different sections of the society visit it on all the three days for *darshan* of the *mannati tazia*, *alam* and silver *duldul* (the symbolic horse of Husain). On these days *majlis* are held addressed by various *zakir* delving on the 'tragedy of Karbala' and the message derived from it. The present custodian and legatee of this Imambada, Harish Chandra Dhanuk organized Hindu devotees of Husain into a 'Hindu Taziadaar Sevak Sangh'. His devotion to the martyrs of Karbala is seen to be believed. Though not an accomplished poet, he expresses his devotion in several poems on Imam Husain. Do not see his raw poetry but his sentiments of devotion. Some of his lines are as follows;

Gham-e-Husain ka jab jab lahoo pukarega,
Husainiyat-ki raksha me Hindu lahoo bahaega

Talwaaron ki dhaaron par Husain, Husain
Teeron ki boucharon me Husain Husain
Devta Husain, Mandir Husain

Hindu Alam makers

In a narrow by lane of Yahiya Ganj near Nakkhas,the biggest market of brass, copper and stainless steel utensil in Lucknow, Gopalji Raju and Anand Kumar with a couple of associates may be seen doing elaborate metal carving (*Naqqashi*) on the *panja* of alam, the palm shaped topmost part of the alam. Gopal ji tells that this is their fifth generation of *alam* makers and he along with his brother have been involved in this task for more than three decades. They have been carving alams on brass and copper varying between four inches to five feet and depending on the nature and sophistication of carving the price varies between ten rupees to twenty thousand rupees. They continue to do this work throughout the year but the demand for alams peak just before the beginning of Moharrum. Alams made by them have spread to different parts of India. Because of the rising cost of living they tried to deviate from this profession and opened a utensils shop and then a *Kirana* (general store) shop but incurred losses and then he realized that perhaps the *Moula* (Imam Husain) wanted them to continue with this job and that is how they continue to make alams and earn their livelihood through this art.Their relatives Om Nath and Shyam Lal also make and sell alam's panja and other items of moharrum rituals in a nearby shop but this is not their primary occupation and they also sell utensils.

'Sehri Wale Baba'. Baraati Lal Gupta

Till about 1980s or so when the present cell phone apps and other technologies were not there, small groups of people used to take round before the *Sehri* time (beginning of fast before the dawn) during the month of Ramzan. They used to recite devotional poetry with or without drums and harmonium. One Baraati Lal Gupta, popularly known as 'Sehri Wale Baba' in his locality has also been performing this job for the past three decades. Roaming from one lane to another in Dandaiyya Bazar area between 4-5 am everyday during the entire month of Ramzan, he has been singing devotional poetry for the Muslim *rozedaars* exhorting them to wake up and eat their *sehri* (meal before the commencement of fast). He has a sonorous voice and bubbling with zeal to promote Hindu-Muslim harmony and friendship. For several years nobody knew about his identity until some of his neighbours identified him.

A Muslim constructing a temple for his Hindu neighbours

During the Nawabi period a number of temples were built and maintained by the Nawabs and other Muslims and mosques and imambadas by the Hindus.The tradition still continues.One Shamim Haider alias Shammu Bhai lives in Mehdi Ganj in old Lucknow.Near his house the *charan paduka* of Ma Durga was kept on a small raised stone platform in the open.During the Navratri days every year the local Hindu women have been performing puja here.This mohalla consists of poor and lower middle class people.Shammu Bhai always felt pained to see the women performing the rituals in the open.A middle class property dealer,,he decided to construct a small temple there for the womenfolk of his neighbourhood.His family members and some Hindu friends fully cooperated in this venture and last month the Durga idol and her *charan paduka* were installed in the temple by the priests and on this occasion a grand *bhandaara* was also arranged by him.His next project is the installation of a big Hanuman idol in this temple as there is no Hanuman temple in the immediate vicinity. This created lot of goodwill but some orthodox members of his own community were not appreciative. He did not care maintaining that such people are there among all the communities.A devout Shia, he also keeps a white horse solely for the purpose of lending it free of cost during moharrum days to be used as the 'horse of Husain'. The Husainabad Trust charges a fee for lending it and many poor people may not afford it.Moreover,Shamim Haider also extends financial help to several Sunni and Hindu taziadaars to to buy a tazia or perform any mourning rituals.He is also engaged in several other philanthropic activities.

These are some of the examples of gestures of friendship and harmony and hundreds of such good deeds are scattered all around. Unfortunately, some political elements from both Hindus and Muslims have other ideas and do not feel comfortable with the harmonious social environment as it is not in conformity with their vested interest and they have been working overnight for communal polarisation.

'Others' in Lucknow

People from other districts of the state have been migrating and settling down in Lucknow but people from other states too settled here in large numbers. The Kashmiri Pundits and others started coming to Lucknow during the reign of the Nawabs and many of them served in the administration. The Bengalis in Lucknow also have a history of more than hundred years. The Punjabis (including the Sikhs) and the Sindhis came here as 'refugees' in substantial numbers in the wake of partition. All of them are now fully integrated with Lucknow. Besides them, the Oriyas live here in good number followed by the Malyalees, Marathis, Assamese, and others. Thus, Lucknow today is a cosmopolitan city with different languages and cultures co-existing in an harmonious social environment.

20

'Others' in Lucknow

The Bengalis

Coming from Sikandar Bagh Crossing (Uda Devi Chowk) towards Motimahal passing by National Botanical Garden, Carlton Hotel, Sahara Mall, National P.G. College, BSNL building and taking left from Lakshman Mela Police post trisection one will find the famous La Martiniere Girls School. Next to this 1869 structure stands another historical building known as Tara Wali Kothi ,presently housing the regional office of the State Bank of India. This Moghul Marvell was made by the eighth Nawab and the second King of Awadh Naseeruddin Haider during his regime to quench his keen interest in astronomy. He procured the astronomical instruments from England and created an observatory in Tara Wali Kothi. It is said that to look after his observatory and study the stars he invited some experts from West Bengal who are said to be the first ever Bengalis to step on Awadh soil namely Chandrashekhar Mitra, Durga Charan Bandhopadhyaya, Kali Charan Chattopadhyaya and Madho Das. Babu Kali Charan who was the chief astronomer started Kali Puja for the first time in Lucknow and ensured the regular Durga Puja celebration which introduced Lucknowites to a very important and inseparable part of Bengali culture. Gradually local people started participating in these religious festivals in several ways.

Presently having an estimated population of about two lakhs, Dakhshinaranjan Mukhopadhyaya was the first Bengali to become *taaluqdaar*. He was rewarded with Shankarpur Taluqa in 1859 for helping the Britishers during the 'Sepoy Mutiny', as the British rulers dubbed it, which was confiscated from Raja Madhodas due to his support for the revolutionaries during the first war of independence.Later in 1871 he was honoured with the title 'Raja' by the Viceroy, Lord Mayo. Among the first few very important Bengali *bhadra lok* (gentle/noble men) who came to Lucknow Dakshinaranjan babu, as he was affectionately known, contributed immensely specially in the field of education in Lucknow.

After Awadh was annexed and came under full authority of the British new avenues were opened for various occupations.Being well versed in English the Bengalis took full advantage of it and many migrated from Calcutta and settled in

Lucknow.They entered in good numbers in the departments of education, health, judiciary, municipal services etc.

During this time Kali Bari,dedicated to godess Kali was established in a lane of Ghasiyari Mandi.Kali Bari, celebrating its 150th anniversary this year, is not just a centre of religious functions and pooja offerings but has been an important epicenter for various activities which had major impact on the social, cultural and educational fabric of the city of Nawabs. In addition to Canning Collegiate primary school, Hindu Girls College initiated in the premises of Kali Bari is now known as Mahila Mahavidyalaya and now situated in Aminabad. MahaKali Pathshala which has its genesis in Kali Bari has grown into two separate educational institutions as Boys' Anglo Bengali Inter College, Sundar Bagh and Hiramati Girls' School which finally emerged as present day A.P. Sen Post Graduate College. Prelude to the organizations like Bengali Club, Young Men's Association and Friend's Gaiety were also composed in the precincts of Kali Bari. Those were the days when Durga Pooja was also performed and celebrated in the same premise along with the cultural programmes including the plays by the members of Friend's Gaiety in open space with petro max light. These performances raised keen interest among the people of Lucknow and proved to be the harbinger of the future scenario of Lucknow theatre. Founded by Raja Dakshina Ranjan Mukhopadhyaya and other Bengali *Bhadra Lok* ,Kali Bari stands tall with its testimony to the traditional, religious and equally modern approach of the Bengali community which has contributed to the Lucknow's intellectual quotient.

Durga Pooja celebration is another very important aspect of Bengali community which has gradually taken over the entire city by its festivities and colours during the last 120-30 years. The decorated *pandaals*, shops, eating joints and lively Idols of Goddess Durga's incarnation Mahishasurmardini draw massive crowds to these venues. Irrespective of cast, creed, community and religion it has become a house hold practice to visit Durga Pooja pandals, offer pooja and participate in rituals with great fervour and devotion during the festival.

Barrister A.P.Sen stepped on the Lucknows' soil in 1902 and gained popularity, fame and people's trust as a social worker and politician in a very short span of time. An ardent music lover, singer, composer and lyricist he got highly impressed with Lucknow's culture which gradually became the part of his own persona. His concern to preserve Bengali language among the Bengali Diaspora gave birth to *Uttara*, a magazine in Bengali edited by him with his assistant being Radha Kamal Mukherji and Suresh Chakraborty. He extended financial support to many educational institutions.In the meantime Gyanendra Nath Chakraborty became the first Vice- Chancellor of the Lucknow University and A.P.Sen was the member of executive committee. There were many Bengali teachers-scholars namely Radh Kumud Mukherji, DP Mukherji, Nirmal Kumar Siddhant, Charan Das Chattopaddhyaya, Avnish Chandra Chattopaddhyaya, Shachindra Nath Das Gupta, Dhirendra Nath Majumdar, Shailendra Nath Das Gupta, Narendra Sen

Gupta, Vinayendra Das Gupta, Bhupendra Nath Chattopaddhyaya.

Vishnupad Mukherji was the founder director of Central Drug Research Institute (CDRI) whereas Sunil Kumar Dutt played an important role in the establishment of Central Institute of Medicinal and Aromatic Plants (CIMAP).

One cannot imagine a Bengali house hold without musical instruments. All Bengali children are initiated into music through some musical instrument or vocal music on the occasion of Saraswati pooja on Basant panchami. Be it Rabindra Sangeet, classical vocal and instrumental music, semi classical and light music, Bengali artists are seen on every platform. Chinmoy Lahiri, Tarun Kumar Lahiri, Runa Dey, Shahana Chatterji, Divya Ranjan Chatterji affectionately known as Divyo da, Geeta Ganguly, Sujata Chakroborty, Shanta Chatterji, Sanghmitra Mukherji, Shanto Dey, Tapan Viswas and many others are famous Bengali names in the various fields of vocal music.

Apart from Literature, art, music and theatre, the Bengalis are intensely involved in sports where they have brought many laurels with hockey being the main forte where N.N. Mukhareji , Prakash Chandra Bondhopaddhyaya, Prophulla Chandra Bondhopaddhyaya and Prakash Chandra Ghosh popularly known as Habul Da were famous players of hockey. Habul Mukherji was internationally known coach and had made tireless efforts for the central stadium now famous as KD Singh Babu Stadium. He has the distinction of being coach of Indian hockey team in Olympics for 20 times out of which India won 18 times. Interestingly he never went with Indian team to any country as he was not comfortable with the idea of wearing pant shirt leaving his dhoti- kurta. Table tennis is another sport where the Bengalis have made their resonating presence through Saroj Kumar Nandi and other players. At present Arun Bannerji who lives in Lucknow is internationally known table tennis player.

The story of freedom movement of India cannot be complete without mentioning the contribution of Bengalis. Shacindra Nath Sanyal who was closely associated with the heroes of Kakori Case was wrongly implicated by the British government and sent to Andmans to serve life imprisionment. He was released in 1937 and started living in the Model House locality. He died in 1943.

The first half of 20th century can be termed as the most important period of Bengali community in Lucknow when all kinds of activities were in full bloom. Though Lucknow was already exposed to Bengali community and practices, these cultural, social and religious activities added more to the understanding and assimilation of both. Bengalis who came to Lucknow were fully conscious about their cultural and social identity with complete awareness about the responsibilities towards the city's own fabric. They were well received and welcomed with warmth and never felt that they are in some other land. Almost 150 years have gone down from their first arrival and the Bengalis have become a part and parcel of public life and Lucknow's culture. Is it possible to think of a Lucknow without Durga Pooja celebrations, Bengali Club, Saraswati Pooja and Bengali Sweets?

Kashmiri Pundits

When the Kashmiri Pundits came and settled in Awadh during the reign of Nawab Asafuddaula,it was their largest group outside Kashmir in North India. Excellent soldiers,and enjoying mastery over Persian and Urdu ,they soon became an important part of the Nawabi administration.Their cultural proximity and similarities in physical appearance with the Nawabs earned them good position in the royal court of Awadh.

Around one thousand families of Kashmiri Pundits are said to have migrated during this period and settled in various localities such as Katra Bizen Beg,Gola Ganj,Chaupatiyan,Jhawai Tola,Rani Katra and the adjoining mohallasLater many of them shifted to one moahalla and named it as Kashmiri Mohalla. Here they constructed a number of *Haveli* like large inter-connected houses to facilitate the movement of their *Purdah* observing women.Like any other diaspora group they also maintained their religious-coltural identity and had their own cooks,purohits,etc.

Kashmiri Pandits worship Lord Shiva and to practice their faith and religious belief a huge temple of Lord Shiva was erected in Rani Katra which is known as Bada Shivala. One can see the idol of their *isht devi* (most worshipped deity) Ragya Bhagwati in the same premises.

The Persian and Urdu literature was scaling new heights during the Nawabi era and almost every Kashmiri Pandit family had one or two poets. One of the most prominent among them was Daya Shankar 'Naseem' whose father came to Lucknow from Faizabad and settled in Kashmiri Mohalla. He was poet of royal court during Nawab Amjad Ali Shah's reign.

Ratan Nath Sarshar,Brij Narain Chakbast,Anand Narain Mulla have also been very famous poets and writers in Urdu.

Progressive in their approach, Kashmiri Pandits of Lucknow were ready to breathe in the wake of freedom being fully aware of the negative impact of westernization and losing their ethnic identity and hence they observed strict discipline but kept on moving with the time by introducing required modifications and changes in their way of life. On other hand they also celebrated an annual caste festival known as *Rishi Peer ka Jag* to honour a Kashmiri Pandit Saint of 17th century at Bhola Nath ki Bagia. They changed their dress pattern according to the local traditions and practices. Ladies also started wearing sarees though in a different fashion to maintain their separate identity.

Indian National Congress was founded in 1885 and gathered support from all over India. Many talented people from all walks of life joined Congress and one of them was Bishan Narain Dar who was elected president in Calcutta conference of Indian National Congress in 1911.On the insistence of Annie Besant, Pt. Bishan Narain Dar, Pt.Ram Nath Tankha, Pt. Shyam Manohar Nath, Pt.Suraj Narain Bahadur and other respectable members of the community raised the fund to open a girls' school in Kasmiri Mohalla known as Kasmiri Mohalla Girls' Inter College which was handed over to the municipal board in 1908 and still continues to serve the people.

In 1911-12 Lucknow added another feather in its cap in the form of Medical College. Taking advantage of this opportunity many Kashmiri Pandits persued the medical education to become famous doctors. Dr. Shyam Nath Chak, who was the first surgeon to perform a heart surgery in India, Dr. Tej Narain Bahadur (popularly known as T. Bahadur), Dr. Hari Nath Hukku, Dr. Kishanlal are some other names to mention. Dr. Madan Atal went to China with a delegation sent by the first prime minister of India Pt. Jawahar Lal Nehru to treat Chinese soldiers when China and Japan were at war. Dr. Dwarka Nath Kotnis was also a member of this delegation.

There is a plethora of leading Kasmiri Pandits who have not only earned goodwill, respect and prosperity for themselves but also have contributed in the overall development and growth of Lucknow from the time they came to Awadh as a small diaspora group in the hope of greener pastures.

After Independence Kashmiri Pandits carried on their legacy to enrich the city and the society. Dr. K.N. Kaul founded the National Botanical Garden, made untiring efforts to open snake house at zoological garden. First film society and the annual flower show is also his brain child. Dr. Swaroop Kumari Bakhshi's contribution in the field of education can never be forgotten. She became a member of Legislative Assembly and rose to the rank of a Cabinet minister with the education and home portfolio.

Pt. Brij Lal Chak, Dr. Moti Lal Dhar, P.P.Tikku, Kamini Tikku, Avtar Krishna Ganju, T.N. Dhar, Kum Kum Dhar (a disciple of Lachchhu Maharaj and a distinguished Kathak dancer of international repute) ,Dr. Amrit Nath Sharga, Kailash Nath Sopori, Ram Nath Kav(the founder director of RAW), Somnath Sapru, Gopal Chakbast, Uma Chakbast, Brij Krishna Gurtu, Pratap Narain Bakshi, Prakash Narain Hangal, Gopal Razdan, Prof. N.K. Zutshi, and Nupur Zutshi are some of the names whose efforts, talent and knowledge have enriched various spheres of life of Lucknow.Though many of them have left Lucknow for better opportunities,they are most conspicuous of their almost total absence in Kashmiri Mohalla.

Other Groups

Though some **Punjabis**, including the Sikhs, and **Sindhis** have always been in Lucknow for more than a hundred years but their arrival in large numbers was registered after the partition of India in 1947. Many of them came here as 'refugees' and were identified as such for 2-3 decades after which they got integrated with the rest of the population to such an extent that if they don't speak Punjabi or Sindhi, it is not easy to identify them except of course the Sikhs who stand with their separate identity because of their turban and beard. Those of the migrants of the partition days interested in business specially selling cloths and readymade garments were allotted some shops in the heart of the Aminabad market and this small market was popularly known as the 'Refugee Market' till about 1970s or so after which it was officially named as 'Mohan Market', now spread over there rows with shops on both sides. It is now perhaps, the biggest cloth market in Lucknow.

The first wave of Punjabi refugees was settled in and around Lajpat Nagar in Chowk area and Alambagh area beyond Charbagh railway station while the Sindhis were given flats in a multistoried building on the Victoria Street (now Tulsi Das Marg) in Chowk area, near the Medical College. Now both, the Punjabis and the Sindhis, are considered as prosperous communities who, with their labour and enterprise, have surpassed the local people in business and Trade. Their several festivals such as Lodi and Jhule lal related festivities are now a part of the local festivals and celebrated with enthusiasm and gusto.

Oriya, Marathi, Malyali, Assamese

Oriya, Marathi, Malyali, Assamese and others have also contributed to the mosaic of social fabric of Lucknow.

Oriya people living in Lucknow are in largest number among the communities mentioned above. The people from Orissa are Late entrants in Lucknow. The community leaders put their population between 6-7 thousands. Among the upper crust of this group are IAS and IPS officers, doctors and scientists working in several research organizations, engineers in RDSO, University teachers, bank officers etc. among others are hundreds of workers in various departments of railway and other central services.

A very interesting but significant phenomenon is the presence of around 300 plumbers in Lucknow and the majority of them coming from the district Berhampur. The plumbers of Orissa have virtually edged out the local plumbers from the markets. Go to any big construction site and you will find the majority of the plumbers from Orissa.

People form Orissa formed the 'Lucknow Oriya Samaj' in 1993 at the initiative of an imaginative and dynamic group of people who wanted to remain rooted to their culture, language and traditions. It is now a well known organization. Every year it celebrates the Utkal Diwas (Orissa Day) on 1 April in which the Governor, Chief Minister, ministers also participate. Celebrities from various spheres of life are invited and honored and people from Lucknow also get an opportunity to enjoy dance, music and other entertainments from the well known artists. The legendry Odeisi dancer Kaluchand Mahapatra has also performed on this occasion in the past. Besides this, the Oriya Samaj also celebrates Kartik Purnima, Ganesh Puja and Saraswati Puja every year. Competitions such as quiz, music, painting, elocution are also organized annually. An Oriya Food Festival has also been started in the year 2014. The annual publication of the Samaj, 'Nirmalya' is released every year on the occasion of the Orissa Day.

Like several other people from outside the Uttar Pradesh, living in Lucknow, many Oriya people to settle down in the city and become part of the local social demography. It is seen that the majority of the bureaucrats leave Lucknow after their retirement and settle in Orissa, specially in Bhubneswara but many others, mainly workers and middle level officers, prefers to make Lucknow their home.

Marathi people have also added color to the socio-cultural mosaic of Lucknow. Though only around 1500 in number, their presence is felt in felt in the city. It is said that 15-20 people from Maharashtra came to Lucknow in 1921 and made it their home. The number continued to grow with the passage of time. The legendry Bhatkhande of Bhatkaande Music College was one of the earliest entrants. By 1950s they organized themselves into a body called Maharashtra Samaj and by 1978, the Samaj has its own building called 'Maharashtra Sadan' in Katra Maqbool Ganj near the old RTO office. It also maintains a small guest house available for the guests from Maharashtra. Among the people of Maharashtra living here are doctors, University teachers, bank employees, scientist working in various research organizations and others. The Samaj organizes Ganesh Utsav, Shivaji Jayanti and Sharad Purnima as well as an annual picnic in January in which 200-300 people participate. Significantly, the majority of the Maharashtrian people living in Lucknow are Brahmins.

Among the people from the southern states who have been living in Lucknow, people from **Kerala** are most visible and organized. Their presence in Lucknow may be traced back to ore then hundred years especially in hospitals where they have been treating the patients as doctors and nurses. There used to be Sunday morning shows of Malyali films in a cinema hall before the advent of the internet. Moreover, their gatherings in substantial numbers could be seen in Churches on Sundays and other important dates in Christianity. The Malyali people in Lucknow have organized themselves into a body called 'Kelala Samajam, Lucknow'. There is also an Ayappa Temple located in Gomti Nagar area where special puja is offered on the occasion of Makar Sankrnati. A colorful procession with the traditional band in attendance is taken out from the Gomti Nagar Stadium culminating in Ayappa Temple where it is received by the office bearers of 'Lord Ayappa Service Society'. Among the people of North-East States only, **Assamese** are visible in Lucknow while some from other states specially from Manipur may also be seen in the city but not much is known about them. Many of the Lucknowites came to know of Assamese people only when they inters a glimpse of the Assamese culture this year on the occasion of Bihu Utsav in Dilkusha Garden and it was widely covered by the mass media. Though in small number the Assamese people have organized the 'Assam Association' through which they do social networking and keep in touch with each other. They are mostly scientists, engineers in RDSO, and doing miscellaneous odd jobs.

The Changing Lucknow

Lucknow has evolved from a village to a vibrant city during the past 300 years especially after Nawab Shujauddaula moved the capital of Awadh from Faizabad to Lucknow. The city witnessed the devastation and destruction by the Britishers as a retaliation against the revolt in 1857. It rose again. From the first quarter of the 20th century the transformation began in all the spheres of life. Rapid increase in population due to migration from other districts especially from eastern districts, its emergence as a hub of educational and medical facilities, diversification of economic activities and several other factors have been instrumental in bringing about this transformation. Under the impact of these and other factors the traditional culture of Lucknow has been marginalized and a new cultural ethos ,behavioural pattern and value system has emerged.

21

The Changing Lucknow

The city has been locus of all civilizations and the history reveals that the rise and fall of civilizations are integral to the rise and fall of the cities with which they are associated. Perhaps, that is why the city has attracted the attention of scholars from various disciplines. Rapid urbanization in India has led scholars to focus on cities. They have been grappling with the issue of what makes urban spaces distinctive; such a question becomes relevant in case of cities such as Lucknow- the city with lots of nostalgia and undying memories. We have to understand here that new socio-cultural spaces emerge with the advent of new technology and rapidly increasing migration. New political forces also play an important role in this change- neighbourhoods, markets, shrines etc. The gendered nature of cities and towns also invite new questions especially with reference to the importance of women in economy at macro level and division of labour at the micro, family level. In a scenario in which around 60% of the population of Lucknow city now consists of those who have come to Lucknow from outside and are not rooted here, they do not share the socio-cultural concern and nostalgia of the Lucknowites. Let us take a brief view of the many changes coming into Lucknow in view of the above mentioned questions.

The story of Lucknow evolving from a village to a city has been shrouded in mystery. A legend associates this city to the name of Lakshman, the younger brother of the mythological hero of the Hindu epic Ramayna. Historically, its origin can be traced more definitely to the medieval period and the local site seems to have been fairly occupied by the beginning of the 14th century. The town, however, grew rapidly only after the middle of the 18th century when the Nawabs of Awadh shifted their court from Faizabad to this place in 1775. Thus, the history of Lucknow as a city may not be more than a little above two hundred years. After the revolt of 1857 the British governors feared this "rebel" city for more than half a century and stayed farther away at Allahabad.

If we look at Lucknow since the first quarter of the 20th century onward the transformation of Lucknow can be well understood. Tremendous population growth may be witnessed during 1931-61. The population increased roughly 2.38 times than the previous decadel growth rate that comes around 41.2%. The shifting of capital from Allahabad to Lucknow was largely responsible for this phenomenon. The social fabric continued to be enriched by the mutual co-existence of many Hindu and Muslim castes and religious minorities. Post-independence, the period 1947-70 witnessed the influx of refugees on a large scale and migration of people from the other districts of Uttar Pradesh. This led to not only demographic but also spatial expansion of the city. Transformation of Lucknow from 1980s onwards has been radical and phenomenal. It overturned the social, economic and spatial relations of the city. Natural growth of population, immigration and diversification of economic activities played an important role in it. The period 1981-91 was a period of rapid development and again a very rapid rise in population. For the first time the governmental authorities began preparing master plans to cope with the fast pace of urbanization as the rapid urbanization is associated with spatially unplanned growth of a city, irrational land use, encroachments, slums, traffic congestions, environmental degradation, pollution-air and water both, and increased pressure on community and welfare services. Unfortunately all these aberrations are now a part of Lucknow because of lack of political will to implement the futuristic plans.

Lucknow being the only large urban centre, except of course Kanpur, amid a number of small towns makes it an attractive destination for job seekers and those needing education and medical facilities. Uttar Pradesh has witnessed rapid industrialization since the 1970s. Lucknow being the state capital became the major bureaucratic centre. Industrialists and other businessmen have to came to Lucknow to get their work, legal or illegal, done either dealing directly with the administration or through the middlemen and politicians by bribing whosoever are in a position to give the favour. This has resulted in the generation of lot of black money. Thus, large amounts of investible surplus is there to give enough boost to real estate and consumerism. This has facilitated the entry of private builders and developers-big, middle level and small, from Delhi and elsewhere. A survey carried out recently and reported in newspapers and magazines reveal that the fastest increasing prices of land and properties are now reported in Lucknow. The governmental efforts too have made it one of the top five fastest growing city in India despite the fact that during the last thirty years or so no considerably big industry has been established in Lucknow except Telco, factories such as Vikram Cotton Mill, Scooters India, UPDPL , Uptron and Eveready industries are either closed or standing on the brink of closure. Moreover, more factories from the Aishbagh, Talkatora, Nadirganj, and Amousi industrial areas are closed than those still functioning.

Of the five major areas viz. Faizabad Road, Sitapur Road, Hardoi Road, Kanpur Road and Raebarreily Road, the highest growth may be seen on Faizabad Road and Trans-Gomti area. Municipal limits of Lucknow have expanded phenomenally with sprawling suburbs. All this has resulted in concrete eating into the green. During the last thirty years or so around one hundred twenty five villages situated in and around the city has been swallowed by urbanization and these have lost their existence. The means of livelihood of these village folks have been eliminated. Once depending upon agriculture, cultivating vegetables and rearing cattle, more than two lakhs of them have lost their livelihood and have now become unskilled labour, rickshaw puller or just doing nothing. The officials looking after law and order hold these unfortunate people responsible for most of the crimes being committed in the city. They further maintain that thousands of jail inmates come from these villages.

The city has registered the presence of more than 3 lakh people from outside who come here every day to work or in search of work. A large number of them may be seen in various *mazdoor adda* (labour markets). Thousands of them work in manufacturing units, restaurants and eating places, shops and homes as domestic help while around ten thousand *pheriwala* (vendors) and vegetable sellers also come from these villages. They have to toil hard to earn livelihood. Many of them settle down in existing slums or go for new slums. These poor people have to struggle hard against eviction and illegality throughout their lives. Ironically most of these 'illegal residents' are legal voters and workers. Thus, once described as the city of government employees, teachers and lawyers, the largest number of people in todays' Lucknow are engaged in self employment.

Lucknow city is facing a crisis situation. The existing infra-structure is not able to cope with the increasing pressure of population. Though governments have been adding to the infrastructure but this is simply inadequate. Sewerage and sanitation are in bad shape. Piles and piles of garbage littered on the roadsides tell their own stories. Drainage is such that even a mild rain results in water logging in many areas, solid waste management is almost absent. But the biggest crisis pertains to availability of portable water. For lakhs of less fortunate people, it is a constant quest for water, a constant struggle for many. They have to rise easily, during unearthly hours to fetch water. There is hardly any water for animals. Groundwater level is fast receding due to blatant and unimaginative extraction through submersible pumps. Among the institutional arrangements, agencies such as Lucknow Nagar Nigam, Jal Nigam, Lucknow Development Authority, PWD, Transport Department, Power Department-all have failed in varying degrees to rise to the occasion.

II

Lucknow has been changing in some other ways too. New information technology has arrived in a big way. Hundreds of cyber cafes, business and computer centres are there even in residential areas. E-Suvidha Kendra, multi facility centres for paying bills to various departments, may be seen in different areas of the city and these remain open seven days a week for long hours. It has given big relief to the city folks especially senior citizens and women. Several new hospitals, the latest being Ram Manohar Lohia Institute of Medical Sciences have begun providing good medical facilities at affordable prices. At the same time hundreds of private hospitals and nursing homes, including some of high standards, have mushroomed giving the best of facilities to all who could afford it.

Several new hotels and restaurants have opened and some more five star hotels are under construction. Mexican, Chinese, Thai and Continental food are being served in some of these new restaurants. The taste of commoners too is changing fast. Chinese choumen and different types of noodles may be seen even on roadside *thela* and small shops. Not confined to vegetarian food, the Punjabi influence is there even in non-vegetarian food. Surprisingly the Tibetan Momo has become a big hit among the masses. For the affluent middle class and rich such international food chains as Mcdonald, Pizza Hut, and Kentucky Fried. Chicken(KFC) have arrived and their products are quite popular. In this crowd of multinational food, the arrival and the subsequent popularity of a rural food item- *Chokha-Baati* is a big surprise. Hundreds of small road side shops of *Chokah Baati* may be seen mushrooming in all corners of the city. Some relatively resourceful and comparatively bigger players have redesigned trucks, prepare the *Chokha Baati* in it and sell it, as a mobile van, in different areas by rotation. A more imaginative entrepreneur has opened a decent looking restaurant in Gomti Nagar naming it as 'Chokha-Baati Restaurant.'

Big private builders have introduced high rise multi-storeyed apartment complexes and many people prefer to move to these in view of safety and security and better civic amenities. Lucknows' skyline is changing fast. Because of the governments' apathy the traditional single screen cinema halls are dying. Several of them have remained closed for more than two decades as the administration did not allow any changes in its' use. In the face of competition from the multiplexes in malls, the government has changed its' policy and now allow the owners to demolish it and convert it into a commercial complex provided a small single screen cinema hall is also built within this complex. A beginning has already been made in one case and some other owners are also following it.

The city has now five malls and some more are in the pipeline. With a wide variety in food, clothing, shoes and other merchandise the malls are attracting large crowds. The multiplexes are an additional attraction. Parallel to this development Hazaratganj and some other markets have opened a single or multi brands show rooms of different types of merchandise especially menswear, shoes, cosmetics and perfumes. A visit to these malls and shops is revealing to any keen observer- consumer culture has arrived in Lucknow. Mushrooming growth of beauty parlours, hair stylists, gyms, health clubs and weight loss clinics tell theirown story.Weight loss clinics everywhere are preceded by the abundance of food joints especially junk food and such ads become common on TV Channels.

Khoob khao aur aaraam se pachao

(eat abundantly and digest comfortably)

Under the impact of consumerism and consumer culture, prostitution and call girl business, has been accepted a part of 'service sector' and thriving in the city along with 'phone a friend' and 'make a friend' business.Cheaper varieties of drugs are now easily available and playing havoc with the lives of poor people.

In the changing face of Lucknow, women's activism has added a new dimension. During the last 2-3 decades several women's organizations have emerged fighting for women's right and empowerment. Of these, All India Democratic Women's Association (AIDWA) affiliated with CPI (M) is most visible as it has taken this struggle to the streets and now is most visible in the public space. It has organized women, especially of the poor and the marginalized sections, as never before. At the same time eve teasing and sexual harassment of women in domestic as well as public space has increased many folds. Various surveys reveal that around 90% women have reported sexual harassment in one form or another. Eve teasing has never been a part of 'Lucknow's Culture'. Perhaps, this deviant behaviour and criminalization have, in some ways, are related with the rootless young men. The astray cases of eve teasing were always there but were negligible and never been the 'mainstream behaviour'. Those brought up in Lucknow's culture feel ashamed of this rising practice.

New parks and cycle tracks are now available for the tourists with the facility of hiring fancy bicycles with gears to take a look at heritage monuments on the heritage route with a number of crumbling monuments on sight. There are more tourists including foreign tourists and the present state government by aggressively promoting tourism hope to make Lucknow the third favoured destination of foreign tourists after Agra and Banaras. Monuments dedicated to Gautama Buddha, B.R. Ambedkar, Kashi Ram and other Dalit heroes have changed the skyline of Lucknow in several areas.

According to a popular estimate around 60% of the city's population comes from other districts out of which the overwhelming majority is from the eastern districts and other parts of Awadh. Many of them have constructed or purchased houses located in route to their native districts, so that they get public transport going into that direction from near their houses. For instance those coming from Gonda, Bahraich, Balrampur, Basti, Faizabad, Gorakhpur, Deoria, Ballia etc. settled down in Indira Nagar –Gomti Nagar area, those from Sitapur, Lakhimpur and adjoining areas live in Aliganj, Janki Puram, IIM Road etc. while the natives from Hardoi, Shahjahan Pur and adjoining districts have preferred Chowk, Malihabad Road and Thakur Ganj and living in new housing colonies.

Obviously when social demography, spatial distribution, infra-structure, politics and everything undergoes changes, the language, values, manners and etiquettes are bound to change. But the most important factor of change in the overall culture and social nuances is the decline of Urdu and the emergence of a new 'linguistic culture' based on Sanskritised Hindi. Urdu is not a language only but also a culture. Unfortunately after independence in 1947 while almost all Indian languages took their rightful place in education, administration and as the medium of mass communication, Urdu did not. Unlike most of the languages Urdu was not concentrated in any one compact geographical region or state hence failed to get political support. Urdu speakers have always been a minority of speakers everywhere. Moreover, the connection of Urdu with the employment prospects and avenues was severed as its use in administration was discontinued after independence and replaced by Hindi everywhere. Though during the last decade it was declared as second official language of Uttar Pradesh, it could not make much of a difference and it continues to slide downwards and decline. Thus, the virtual demise of Urdu is largely responsible for the decline of the traditional culture of Lucknow.

Urban Villages

An important feature of urbanization in India and elsewhere is that villages located outside the boundaries of a city get included in it over a period of time or villages get engulfed by a city. The process of urbanization in India intensified since 1950s and its pace shall further increase in years to come.

Urbanization increased manifold in Lucknow since 1970s and with the advent of the present century it has been increasing phenomenally. The rise of the local population and large scale migration of people from the other districts of Uttar Pradesh and also from other states are largely responsible for this phenomenon. The phenomenon of 'urban villages' or 'villages in the city' has mainly occurred in two ways. In villages located on the periphery of Lucknow city, initially a piece of land is sold to an individual from the city, property dealers, institutions or some government agency followed by several individuals or institutions who purchase the land cheaply but the core village settlement remains untouched and with the passage of time gets surrounded from all sides. When substantial amount of agricultural land is procured by urban people or agencies they demand urban amenities-metalled road, proper drainage, electric supply, piped water etc. With the passage of time such a region is included within the municipal limits. The other way is the large scale land acquisition by the government or semi government agencies such as Housing Boards or Development Authorities. In this process agricultural land of several adjoining villages are acquired by these agencies for developing housing colonies. Of course the land owners have been getting some compensation for the land acquired. However, the residential settlements consisting of cluster of villages or the *abaadi* areas are not acquired and remain untouched. After the housing colony is complete such residential settlements finds themselves engulfed and surrounded from all sides by modern architecture completely in contrast to the thatched or *pucca* houses.

During the last 2-3 decades around forty of such villages have been swallowed by the new housing settlements. As per the records of Zila Panchayat there are still twenty one such villages existing within the new housing colonies. Among these villages the largest one is village Anoura situated on the Lucknow-

Faizabad Road. Within the Gomti Nagar, a sprawling modern housing colony developed by the Lucknow Development Authority (LDA) the *gram panchayats* of Choti Jugoli, Badi Jugoli, Ujariyaon, Maqdoompur, Ahibarnapur and Khargapur have been in existence till 2002. In the census report of 2011, forty two villages have been mentioned engulfed by the Lucknow city. Similar village settlements may be seen within the Rajajaipuram, Indira Nagar and Jankipuram.

Rural people living within such village enclaves surrounded by urban people exhibit a unique phenomenon that may be termed as 'Rurban' and the inhabitants of these village enclaves as 'Urban Peasants'. These village enclaves and the newly emerged urban settlements impact each other in a variety of ways. For several households of such village enclaves, it has brought prosperity exhibited through architectural and economic changes. For the new urban settlers roaming stray cows, buffaloes, pigs and other animals are constant irritants. Their droppings and urine foul the streets and their presence on roads is constant threat to these 'citywalas' especially to their children but they also get the services of maids and domestic help easily and regularly.

The prosperity of the people of these enclaves gets reflected in their acquiring motor bikes or even cars and adoption of many elements of urban culture. Such village enclaves also attracts many urban workers to settle in the village providing them cheaper housing with low, affordable rents. Several such village people have constructed rooms especially for rent out. They also get easier access to better educational facilities. They also achieve occupational mobility resulting in the adoption of new occupations. Their artisans such as carpenters, blacksmiths, potters, barbers, shoemakers and repairers get new markets and increased wages and remuneration. Their life style undergoes changes. The dress pattern, language, entertainment channels and virtually the entire life style moves towards urbanity. Consumerism and 'consumer culture' make their way into their life not conducive to their economically weaker sections. It may be concluded that after becoming part of the city several of them enjoyed prosperity while others join the crowd of poor and marginalized after losing their land.

Lucknow Today : Dalit Imaginations

-Aseem Hasnain

Lucknow, the capital of Oudh, is seen as constituted of three overlapping space-time complexes in modern history. These phases pertain to Nawabi culture that flourished until 1856; the mutinous period of 1856-57 when the city rose against British excesses, but was brutally subdued; and the post Mutiny resurgent urban locale extending to the postcolonial period that aligned with the aspirations and identities of the upwardly mobile middle class. Each of these temporal phases involved architectural campaigns where monuments were erected and public spaces were manipulated in correspondence with state-society relations.

Nawabi as well as British Lucknow have been fairly well written about. Someone interested in these phases of the city will not be disappointed by the variety of texts available both descriptive, and pictorial. In comparison, discussions about urban space and built environment during the third phase of Lucknow, especially the post independence period, is almost absent from scholarship. Covering the forties to the nineties, this phase saw the rise of memorials, neighborhoods, parks, streets and buildings that commemorated first M K Gandhi, then various members of the Nehru-Gandhi family, and later icons preferred by cultural nationalist groups such as Rashtriya Swayamsewak Sangh(RSS), and socialist organizations such as the Janta Dal and Samajwadi Party. Despite this range of sponsoring organizations, the fact remains that contemporary Lucknow's parks, streets, memorials and monuments were mainly commemorative of only upper class, higher caste icons. Icons from the Dalit and indigenous traditions remained debarred from the arena of public aesthetics and imagination.

This article speaks about a fourth Lucknow, an imminently modern and contemporary city where the monopolistic sensibilities of such elite representations have been displaced, rather bulldozed, and where urban space has been sown with a new identity. This identity is that of the Dalits, or the Bahujan, as the Bahujan Samaj Party, and Mayawati like to call it. Moreover, this new aesthetic has been cast in stone, literally, and hence is here to stay despite the fact that in Indian elections antagonistic groups often alternate in capturing the state.

Bahujan Samaj Party, one of the most electorally successful Dalit parties in India, formed the government of Uttar Pradesh four times between 1995 and 2012. Mayawati, its charismatic leader, has also been the chief minister of U.P four times, and held the post for the full term between 2007 & 2012. This entire period, especially the five year period when she was the uninterrupted chief minister of U.P, was utilized to execute Mayawati's plans for transforming Lucknow's urban space. This transformation was based on the construction of a vivid Dalit imagery across the city. Between 1995 and 2012, eleven major monuments were constructed.

These monuments had incurred staggering expenses.. The locations of these monuments are spread across three zones of the city. A small number of monuments and memorials were constructed in the Hazratganj area, within the administrative and political zone where Ministers, politicians, and bureaucrats live and work. This area is also important because it is almost the border of old and new Lucknow. The second zone is the southern end of the city between the cantonment and the airport. This zone has to be crossed by anyone who flies in and out of Lucknow, as it is on the route to the airport. The third and the most important zone is Gomtinagar. An elite neighbourhood on the eastern tip of the city, it has emerged as the go-to place in Lucknow for not only the best recreational facilities, but also for living if one prefers well planned, clean, green and well serviced neighbourhoods.

Before listing and describing some of these mega monuments, let us understand the intention, and effects of these new urban spaces. These are rooted in how Kanshiram, the founder of the BSP and Mayawati's mentor, aspired to transform caste relations in India. He had famously declared that his overall plan was to destroy the monopoly of the upper castes from all spheres of life. Mayawati's monumental blitzkrieg attempted to do the same. The trend of constructing or appropriating urban space and built environment in the name of upper caste figures was broken by Mayawati when she started dotting Lucknow with small monuments, mainly on city intersections, of hitherto unknown Dalit icons such as Jhalkari Bai, and Bijli Paasi. She initiated these smaller projects from the first time she became chief minister in 1995. The effects of these smaller projects were, however, negligible, given the fact that such small-scale commemorative activities are very frequent in most parts of India, and most people don't pay much attention to such projects. These smaller projects were probably the first steps towards reimagining Lucknow, as became clear in later years.

The first notable project that Mayawati executed in Luknow's public space was the construction of the Parivartan Chowk. This was followed by the commissioning and construction of multi million mega projects such as: Buddha Vihar Shanti Upvan; Manyawar Kanshiram Memorial Samajik Parivartan Sthal; Dr. Bhimrao Ambedkar Samajik Parivastan Sthal; Manyawar Kanshiram Eco- Garden; Rashtriya Dalit Prerna Sthal; Kanshiram Bahujan Nayak Park; Ramabai Ambedkar Rally Maidan; Manyawar Kanshiram Yaadgaar Vishram Sthal; Samta Mulak Chowk; Dr. Ambedkar Chauraha; and Dr. Bhimrao Ambedkar Gomti Vihar.

These projects were mired in all sorts of controversy from the very beginning. While the main ruse was corruption, and allegations of siphoning public money in the name of mega construction projects, there was a palpable discomfort at the idea of having such huge monuments being built in the memory of icons who had remained excluded from India's public culture. Antagonistic individuals and organizations used all kinds of tactics- court petitions, stay orders, right to information requests, public interest litigation etc, to stall these projects.

Media critique of these grand projects included several substantive issues

A view of Ambedkar Park

Parivartan Chowk

such as massive original costs and budgetary spillovers; diversion of funds away from more fundamental services and schemes; suspicions over corruption and misuse of public funds; and lack of transparency over project details. But the maximum amount of attention was given to criticisms where Mayawati was compared to megalomaniacs such as Saddam Hussein and Joseph Stalin, since she was having her own statues installed. In fact, a quick reading of newspaper articles and editorials from that period suggest that the most problematic issue at that time was the fact that Mayawati was putting up huge statues of herself. Indeed it was unprecedented to have statues of a living person. Yet these critics and their arguments failed to make any impression on the projects underway. This is not surprising at all, especially in light of the fact that most mainstream media is rooted in elite sensibilities that have kept Dalit icons on the margins of the nation's public aesthetic. Mayawati's cold-shouldering of this elitist media was also no surprise given the history of her position vis a vis media, which she likes to term as Manuwadi (Brahminist), hence anti-Dalit.

Delays induced by media criticism and rival activists pushed Mayawati into a siege mentality from where she acted in unprecedented haste. Her determination to start and complete projects before rivals could stall them meant that construction often started at unconventional hours, and often took place at lightning speed. Some of the proposed sites were occupied by existing facilities that had to be shifted, and often the shifting was delayed through opposition activists. In a classic example of her haste and determination, Mayawati allegedly ordered the demolition of Lucknow's prison even before an alternative location could be found for the prison population. In another such case the design headquarters of the state irrigation department was razed to the ground overnight while irreplaceable irrigation records, furniture, fixtures and computers worth millions of rupees were still inside the building. In a third such case, a sports complex named after Dr. Ambedkar, ironically, was also demolished so that another monument in the memory of Dr. Ambedkar could be extended.

Scholars have argued that this mega architectural campaign was designed to claim the rightful place for Dalit leaders who have been kept on the margins so far. Others argue that these projects were also aimed at establishing Mayawati as the rightful heir to Phule, Ambedkar, and Kanshiram. However, what existing scholarship neglects to discuss, and this paper attempts to focus on, is the effect of these monuments on ordinary citizens of Lucknow, as well as upon visitors in the city who get to observe and experience these built environments. As a preliminary beginning, I suggest three types of, interrelated, sensory experiences that one goes through around these monuments. These three experiences pertain to location, grandeur, and content. Let us discuss these three experiences and their probable effects in the context of select monuments.

One of the earliest notable projects that Mayawati commissioned in Lucknow was a much smaller monument in the heart of the city, strategically placed on the border of old and new Lucknow. This monument, called Pariwartan Chowk ('Change' crossroads), is located on Mahatma Gandhi (MG) Marg in Hazratganj area on the banks of the river Gomti. The monument itself is a small park built as a traffic circle, with a central granite tower topped by a giant sphere. Statues of Dalit icons stand on four sides of the tower. Dr. Ambedkar's statue is on one side, while Jyotiba Phule's statues is on the other side. Its location is such that traffic going through the arterial MG Road has to circumambulate this monument, eerily reminiscence of *parikrama* (a common ritual practice in South Asian faith systems).

In fact, the location of Pariwartan Chowk is such that it disturbs vehicular traffic more than it facilitates it's passage. There was no dearth of controversies when Pariwartan Chowk was commissioned and built. One of the main criticisms for this proposed monument was that the site already had a traffic circle, and building another one next to it would create certain chaos. The second argument was on technical grounds, as the Archaeological Survey of India objected to the plan because of its proximity to a protected monument- the tomb of Saadat Ali Khan, the fifth Nawab of Lucknow, and the key architect of most Nawabi buildings in the adjoining Qaiserbagh area.

Both these objections were put aside and the new monument was constructed. The pre-existing traffic circle had the statue of Subhash Chandra Bose, a famous leader of the Indian National Movement, but an elite icon nevertheless. In this sense the new monument brought in Ambedkar and Phule as equally important figures juxtaposed against Bose. Proximity to the tomb of the fifth Nawab, and also the adjoining Begum Hazrat Mahal Park, suggests efforts at inserting Dalit icons into the founding myths of Lucknow. And indeed, when one crosses Pariwartan Chowk, one is forced to observe the tightly packed, even if confusing, symbols that are connected to Lucknow as well as with modern India.

The second group of monuments is located in southern Lucknow, between the cantonment and the airport. The same route continues to Kanpur, the neighbouring city. This location is such that all locals who fly out of Lucknow, or travel to and from Kanpur pass by them. More importantly, visitors who come to Lucknow, no matter for what purpose, pass by these monuments on their way to the main city. These visitors include journalists, foreign tourists, and people on business. This particular location is, historically, a virgin area with almost no existing monuments or symbols connected with Lucknow's past. Thus these monuments claimed new territory and appropriated it for Dalit imageries. When these monuments were built, the adjoining roads were upgraded to multi lane fast passages that allow quick connectivity between the airport and the city. While traffic passing by these monuments is at high speed and there is little chance that passengers can look at the monuments in any detail, the fact that these are huge monuments that run for hundreds of meters on each periphery means that passengers moving fast will eventually get more than a glimpse.

The third group of monuments, in Gomti Nagar, are the largest, most impressive, and most visited. These monuments have actually changed the skyline and layout of Gomti Nagar to such a degree that someone who is visiting the area after a few years will hardly believe that that this is actually Gomti Nagar. This scale has been possible because of the availability of endless tracts of land along the Gomti river. These monuments are also the most popular among visitors because of their location. Gomti Nagar hosts several of Lucknow's best shopping arcades, and movie theatres, and the construction of these monuments have complimented these attractions with spaces that add to the recreational choices of visitors. This particular set of monuments has also been the best maintained by the government, with a massive infrastructure of lighting and decorative fountains that make them major attractions. Most evenings witness thousands of visitors who come to these locations for recreational purposes but invariably engage with these Dalit imageries, even if passively.

Moving on to the experience of grandeur, one observes that most of the monuments built in this campaign are enormous in size, and high on grandeur. Most follow in the Buddhist tradition where a giant dome like *Stupa* (a Buddhist inspired dome) takes the central place in a vast open area that is full of elephant statues, myriad pillars, and metal or stone statues of Dalit icons. The outer boundaries of these memorials are laid out like the ramparts of a fort. The building material is a mix of red sand stone, granite and other stones, that together create impressions of grandeur. The combination of materials, size, and style impart a degree of unparalleled grandeur to these monuments.

The third experience comes from the content of these monuments. These monuments include a combination of symbols that draw from and point to three types of meanings- Buddhist heritage; Dalit iconography; and the Bahujan Samaj Party. Statues and murals of Gautama Buddha, as well as other figures from the *Jataka* literature adorn most of the monuments thus speaking to the religious side of the modern Indian Dalit community. Apart from Dalit sensibilities, this side of the content also appeals to the Buddhist tourists who visit Eastern Uttar Pradesh and Bihar on the Buddhist tourism circuit. In fact, visitors at these monuments often come across groups of Buddhist monks visiting from Southeast Asia. The second set of meanings are indulged through multimedia depictions of historic Dalit icons such as Jyotiba Phule, Savitribai Phule, Ramabai Ambedkar, Bhimrao Ambedkar, and others. What is notable is that these figures are, by and large, non-controversial, and barring Ambedkar, most of these figures have gradually become acceptable as social reformers by even non-Dalit communities. However, the third source of meanings are more contested, these relate directly to the BSP. This includes statues of Kanshiram, Mayawati, and the most frequently used figure of the elephant. Among these, Kanshiram was the most despised by upper caste communities for his straightforward, deemed insulting, style of communication regarding caste relations. Mayawati was probably less disliked, even if marginally, by her detractors. But the fact that her statues were part of the iconography even while she was a living person, created very negative opinion against her. However, the most controversial aspect of these monuments was the ubiquitous elephant. The elephant, being the electoral symbol of the BSP, became the most problematic of all icons used in these monuments. A walk around these monuments shows that a variety of elephants, in various forms and poses have been used, and yet it is also true that almost everyone of these monuments also includes the elephant in the exact same form that is the BSP electoral symbol. The use of public funds in constructing a public building was reason enough to exclude partisan symbols, especially electoral. Yet, the government headed by Mayawati creased over these objections and included the electoral elephant. The grimness of this situation can be gauged by the fact that the election commission of India decided to cover all these stone elephants with tarpaulin during the elections of 2012.

The content in these grand monuments is a crucial part of their appeal for visitors, not just Dalit visitors but for the wider body of people. Visitors from those communities that do not align with Dalit politics find Buddhist iconography legitimate, and acceptable, because of the historic ways in which Buddhism has been seen as a religion of peace and non-violence in India. Dalit visitors who are not directly aligned with BSP, also find the Buddhist, and moreover the traditional Dalit icons (Ambedkar and Phule) appealing. Finally, the most critical role that such content plays at the wider level is the political exposure that it provides to children and adolescents, who constitute the next generation of the citizenry, and who are yet not completely invested in asymmetric caste relations prevalent in India. For the young visitor these monuments constitute an unprecedented opportunity for knowing a hidden part of Indian history. The content in these monuments exposes them to political leaders, social reformers, and subaltern processes that have been carefully obliterated from mainstream schooling.

Thus, these recent mega monuments of Lucknow have transformed how its residents, as well as visitors, experience the city. The erstwhile city of Nawabs, is now also a city of Dalit imaginations. In fact, the location and grandeur of these projects is such that is dwarves most specimens of Nawabi architecture in Lucknow. The location, grandeur and content of these monuments ensure that a visitor to the city can never go back with memories of only a Nawabi past. What is also striking is that the same monuments that were sources of public contention a decade ago have gradually become one of the top destinations for an evening of fun.

Select Bibliography and References

Abbas,Saiyed Anwer. *Wailing Beauty. The Perishing Art of Nawabi Lucknow.*2002. AuthorLucknow.

- *Lucknow Ki Lupt Hoti Kalayein (Hindi).*2011. Hindi Vadamya Nidhi. Lucknow.

Ahmed, Aijaz. *In the Mirror of Urdu.* 1993. Indian Institute of Advanced Study. Shimla.

Ali, Naushad. '*Lucknow Ki Gayeki aur Lucknow Ka Kathak*' in Awadh Aaina-i-Ayyam me (compiled by Syed Amjad Husain): 2000. Dept. of Information and Public Relations. Lucknow.

Alvi, Ahmed Ibrahim. '*Yatarth Ke Darpan me: Kakori in Avadh Number of Naya Daur.* 2000. Dept. of Information and Public Relations. Lucknow.

Atif, Khan Muhammad. '*Sabhyta evam sanskriti ke aaeene me Malihabad*' in Avadh Special No. Naya Daur, 1996. Dept. of Information and Public Relations. Lucknow. 331

Bajpai, Ram Kishore. *Lucknow Ke Sangeetkar.*2008. Lucknow. Hindi Vadamya Nidhi.

Bakshi, Pawan. *Avadh Ke Taluqdar (Hindi).* 2009. New Delhi. Rupa Publication India Pvt Ltd.

Bandopadhya, Madhvi. *Lucknow Ka Bang Samaj. (Hindi).* 2008. Hindi Vadamya Nidhi. Lucknow.

Bhargava, Ranjit. *Munshi Nawal Kishore aur Unka Press. (Hindi).* 2008. Hindi Vadamya Nidhi. Lucknow.

Bhat, Ravi . *The Life and Times of the Nawabs of Lucknow.* 2011. Rupa Publications India Pvt. Ltd. New Delhi.

Crooke, William. *The Tribes and Castes of North-Western Proviences and Oudh.* (Vol. I &II). 1896. Office of the Superintendent of Government Printing, India. Calcutta.

Das, Neeta . *Architecture of Lucknow.* 1963. Delhi. B.R. Publishing Corporation.

Desai, Ziauddin. *Hindustan me Islami Uloom ke Marakiz (Urdu).* 1996. New Delhi. Publication Division, Government of India.

E & FCS. *Social Survey of Lucknow City.* 1952. Lucknow. Ethnographic & Folk

Culture Society.

Esposito, J.(ed.). *The Oxford Encyclopedia of the Modern Islamic World.* 1995. Oxford University Press. New York.

Farooqi, Mehmood. *'Dastangoi is a fun tradition' in Times of India.* 27 March, 2012. New Delhi.

Graff, Violette (ed.) .*Lucknow: Memories of a City.* 1997. Delhi. Oxford University Press.

Hasan, Amir. *Palace Culture of Lucknow (Reprint).* 2012. Delhi. B.R Publishing Corporation.

Husain, Mirza Jafar. *Beesvin Sadi Ke baaz Adeeb Apne Tehzeebi Pase-manzar me (Urdu).* 2004. Lucknow. Uttar Pradesh Urdu Academy.

-*Qadeem Lucknow Ki Aakhri Bahaar.* 1998. New Delhi. Qaumi Council Barai Farogh-e-Urdu Zubaan.

Hay, Sidney. *Historic Lucknow.* 2002 (Reprint of 1939). New Delhi. Rupa & Co.

Husain, Sayed Amjad. *Awadh: Aaeena-e- Ayyaam Me (Urdu).* 2000. Department of Information, U.P. Lucknow.

Hasan, Mushirul. *Wit and Humour in Colonial North India.* 2009. New Delhi. Niyogi Books.

Jafri, SZH. *Studies in the Anatomy of a Transformation: Awadh from Mughal to Colonial Rule.* 1998. New Delhi. Gyan Publishing House.

Kapoor, Pradeep. *Lucknow Ka Coffee House (Hindi).* 2012. Hindi Vadamya Nidhi. Lucknow.

Keene, H G. *A Hand Book for Visitors to Lucknow.* 1857 (Reprinted 2012). New Delhi. Asian Educational Source.

Khan, Ahmed. *Urdu Adab me Awadh.* 2010. Delhi. Kitabi Duniya.

Kumar, Hemant. *Lucknow Ka Kayastha Samaj (Hindi).* 2008. Hindi Vadamya Nidhi. Lucknow.

Lafont, Jean-Marie. *'The French in Lucknow in the Eighteenth Century'* in *Lucknow: Memories of a City (ed.) Violette Graff.* 2011. Oxford University Press. New Delhi.

Llewellyn-Jones, *Rosie. Engaging Scoundrels: True Tales of Old Lucknow.* 2014. New Delhi. Oxford University Press.

- *The last King of India* . Wajid Ali Shah. 2014.Oxford University Press.

-*Lucknow: Then and Now.* 2003. Marg Publications. Mumbai.

Mehta, Suketu . *Maximum City.* 2004. New Delhi. Penguin Books India Pvt Ltd.

Misra, PK (ed) . *Cultural Profile of Mysore City.* 1978. Anthropological Survey of

India. Calcutta.

Majumdar, Parmita. *Dynamics of Urban Development.* 2004. Delhi. Abhijeet Publications.

Misra, Amresh. *Lucknow: The Fire of Grace.* 1998. New Delhi. Harper Collins Publishers. India.

Misra, Susheela. *Musical Heritage of Lucknow.*1991.New Delhi. Harnam Publishing House.

Mohan, Surendra. *Awadh under the Nawabs.* 1997. New Delhi. Manohar Publishers & Distributers.

Nass, Peter & Ghaus Ansari (ed.). *City and Society: Studies in Urban Ethnicity, life style, and class.* 1985. Institute of Cultural and Social Studies. Leiden.

Oldenburg, Veena Talwar.(ed). *Writings on Lucknow: Shaam-e-Awadh.* 2007. Penguin Books India Pvt Ltd. New Delhi.

-*The Making of the Colonial Lucknow 1857-77.* 1985. Princeton University Press. Princeton.

Pravin, Yogesh. *Bahaar-e-Lucknow.* 2012. Lucknow. Bharat Book Centre.

-*Aapka Lucknow.* 2013. Lucknow. Bharat Book Centre.

-*Rulers of Avadh.* 2011. Delhi. BR Publishing Corporation.

Parveen, Nikhat. *Socio-Economic Condition of Awadh (1814-1856).* 2008. Lucknow. New Royal Book Company.

Qureshi, HA. *Glimpses of Deccan and Awadh (1193-1976).* 2006. Lucknow. New Royal Book Company.

Russell, R.V and Hiralal. *Tribes and Castes of the Central Provinces of India.* 1916. Macmillan. London.

Sharar, Llewellyn-Jones & Oldenburg. *The Lucknow Omnibus.* 2011. New Delhi. Oxford University Press.

Shargha, BN. *Lucknow Ke Kashmiri Pundit.* 2012. Hindi Vadamya Nidhi. Lucknow.

Siddiqi, W.H. *Lucknow: The Historic City.* 2000. Sundeep Prakashan. New Delhi.

Singh,AK *'Precarious Livlihood:A Study of Rickshaw Pullers of UP'.*2013.Lucknow. Working Papers,Giri Institute of Development Studies.

Singh, KS(ed). *People of India, Uttar Pradesh.* 2005. Manohar Publishers & Distributors. New Delhi.

Singh, Malvika (ed). *A City Between Cultures.* 2011. New Delhi. Academic Foundation.

Singh, Naresh. *Film Jagat Ko Lucknow Ka Yogdaan.* 2013. Hindi Vadamya Nidhi. Lucknow.

Speirs, Malcolm. *The Wasikadars of Awadh.* 2008. New Delhi. Rupa & Co.

Trivedi, Madhu. *The Making of the Awadh Culture.* 2010. Delhi. Primus Books.

Taqui, Roshan (ed). *Images of Lucknow.* 2005. Lucknow. New Royal Book Co.

Troll, Christian W (ed.). *Muslim Shrines in India.* 2004. New Delhi University Press.

Umar, Mohd. *Bhartiya Sanskriti ka Musalmaanon Par Prabhav(Hindi).* 1998.Publication Division, Govt of India. New Delhi.

Varshneya, Vipul. *Lucknow: A Treasure. (Year not given).* Atma Ram & Sons. Lucknow.

Verniers, Gilles. '*A Minority within a Minority: the Shias of Kashmiri Mohalla of Lucknow* in *Muslims in Indian Cities: Trajectories of Marginalization (ed.)* Laurent Gayer & Chistophe Jaffrelot: 2012. Harper Collins Publishers India. New Delhi.

Vidyarthi, L.P. *Cultural Configuration of Ranchi.* 1969. Calcutta. JN Basu & Co.

Zaidi, Asad. '*The city that chose to forget*' in The India Express, January 14, 2015, New Delhi.

1. Hamaara Lucknow Pustakmala
2. Lucknow Observer(monthly)

Annexure

Nawab Dynasty

Titular Name	**Personal Name**	**Reign**
Burhan ul Mulk Sa'adat Ali Khan Nishapuri	Mir Muhammad Amin Musawi	1722-1739
Safadarjung	Abul-Mansur Muhammad Muqim Khan	1739-1753
Shuja-ud-Daula	Jalal-ud-din Haider Abul-Mansur Khan	1753-1775
Asaf-ud-Daula	Muhammad Yahya Mirza Amani	1775-1797
Asif Jah Mirza	Wazir Ali Khan	1797-1798
Yamin-ud-Daula	Saadat Ali Khan II	1798-1814
Rafa'at-ud-DaulaPadshah-i-Awadh	Abul-Muzaffar Ghazi-ud-din Hayadar Khan	1814-1827
Nasir-ud-din Haidar Shah Jahan	Abul-Mansur Qutb-ud-din Sulaiman Jah	1827-1837
Abul Fateh Moin-ud-din	Muhammad Ali Shah	1837-1842
Najm-ud-Daula Abul-Muzaffar Musleh-ud-din	Amjad Ali Shah	1842-1847
Abul-Mansur Mirza	Wajid Ali Shah	1847-1856

Select List

Some Notable Personalities from different Spheres of Life

Poets/writers/critics (Past and Present)

Hindi

Amrit Lal Nagar
Bhagwati Charan Verma
Chandrabhushan Trivedi 'Ramai Kaka'
Kunwar Chandra Prakash Singh
Kunwar Narain
Leela Dhar Jaguri
Mishra Bandhu
Mudra Rakshas
Naresh Saxena
Raghuvir Sahai
Ram Vilas Sharma
Rameshwar Shukla Anchal
Shakeel Siddiqi
Sharda Prasad 'Bhusundi'
Shri Narain Chaturvedi
Surya Kant Tripathi 'Nirala'
Surya Prasad Tripathi 'Bheem'
Virendra Yadav
Yashpal

Urdu

Aatish
Abhishek Shukla
Anand Narain Mulla
Azeez Lucknawi
Bharat Bhushan 'Pant'
Brij Narain Chakbast
Daya Shankar 'Naseem'
Irfan Siddiqi
Josh Malihabadi
Khush Bir Singh 'Shaad'
Krishna Bihari 'Noor'
Majaaz
Manish Shukla
Masood Hasan Rizvi Adeeb

Meer Anees
Meer Taqi 'Meer'
Mirza Dabeer
Mirza Rafi 'Sauda'
Munauwar Rana
Nasikh
Nayyar Masood
Safi Lucknawi
Tariq Qamar
Waali Aaasi
Yaas Yagana Changezi

Painters and Sculptors

Asad Ali
Hariharlal 'Medh'
Madanlal Nagar
Ranvir Singh Bisht
Sanat Kumar Chaterji
Sukhvir Singh Singhal
Syed Azmat Shah
Vishwanath Mukharji
Yogendra Nath Yogi

Sculptors

Avtar Singh Panwar
Jai narain Singh
Muhammed Hanif

Musicians/Dancers

Begam Akhtar (Vocalist)
Birju Maharaj (Kathak)
Chote Munne Khan (Vocalist)
Gopinath Goswami (Violin)
Khalifa Abid Husain (Tabla)
Khalifa Ahmed Husain (Tabla)
Khalifa Munne Khan (Tabla)
Rasik Biharilal (Sarod)
Ustad Ahmed Jaan Thirkawa (Tabla)
Ustad Ilias Khan (Sitar)
Ustad Khurshid Ali Khan (Vocalist)
Ustad Rahimuddin Dagar (Vocalist)

Academicians/ Educationists/ Administrators/ Journalists

Abid Suhail (Journalism and Literature)
Birbal Sahni (Scientist)
Chelapati Rau (Journalism)
Hasan Kamaal (Journalist)
Hayat Ullah Ansari (Journalism and Literature)
Jagdish Gandhi (Educationists)
Justice Hameedullah Beg (Judiciary)
Naresh Trehan (Cardiologist)
Parveen Talha (Civil Servant)
Syed Anwer Abbas (Architecture/photography)
Veena Talwar Oldenburg (Academicians)
Vinod Mehta (Journalism)
Yogesh Praveen (Writer/Historian))

Film Makers /Theatre Personalities/Actors /Singers /Writers /Music Directors

Achla Nagar (Writer)
Agha Hashr Kashmiri (Writer)
Akhilesh Dixit (Theatre)
Anil Rastogi (Theatre)
Anoop Jalota (Singer)
Atamjit Singh (Theatre)
Atul Tewari (Writer/Actor/Director)
Begum Akhtar (Singer)
Bina Rai (Actor)
Chitra Mohan (Theatre)
Dilraj Kaur (Singer)
Hare Krishna Arora (Thratre)
Hasan Kamaal (Lyricist/Journalist)
Javed Akhtar (Writer)
Jugal Kishore (Theatre)
K P Saxena (Writer)
Kabban Mirza (Singer)
Mridula Bhardwaj (Theatre)
Muzaffar Ali (Producer/Director)
Naushaad (Music Director)
Raj Bisaria (Theatre)
Ravi Nagar (Theatre)
Sandhya Deep (Theatre)
Surya Mohan Kulshresht (Theatre)
Talat Mahmood (Singer)
Urmil Kumar Thapliyal (Theatre)

Veda Rakesh (Theatre)
Vilayat Jafri (Theatre)
Vinod Chattergi (Music Director)
Wajahat Mirza (Writer)

Sports persons

Ghaus Muhammad Khan (Tennis)
Meena Shah (Badminton)
Syed Ali (Hockey)

Business and Professionals

Asma Husain (Fashion Designer)
Shahnaaz Husain (Entrepreneur in Herbal Cosmetics)
Subrato Roy (business)

Politics

Atal Bihari Vajpayee
Begum Hamida Habibullah
Lalji Tondon
Mahabir Prasad Srivastava
Shankar Dayal Tewari
Shanksr Dayal Sharma
Sheila Kaul
Swaroop Kumari Bakshi
Syed Ali Zaheer
Triloki Singh
ZA Ahmed

Novels based on Lucknow

Hindi

Darul Shafa (Raj Krishna Misra)
Karwat
Meri Teri Uski Baat (Yashpal)
Pratham Phagun (Naresh Mehta)
Raag Darbaari (Sri Lal Shukla)
Shatranj ke Mohre
Yeh Kothe Waaliyan (Amrit Lal Nagar)

Urdu

Aabla Dil Ka (Ahsan Farooqi)
Aag ka Dariya

Chandni Begum (Qurratulain Hyder)
Dilruba
Gardish-e-Rang-e-Chaman
Mere bhi Sanamkhaane
Nayee Bastee (Masroor Jahan)
Shaam-e-Awadh
Umrao Jaan Adaa (Mirza Haadi Ruswa)

Films Based on Lucknow

Bahu Begum
Choudhvin ka Chaand
Junoon
Mere Huzoor
Paalki
Shatranj ke Khiladi
Yaa Rab

Organisations Promoting Lucknow

Passionate lovers of Lucknow have formed several organisations to promote Lucknow. Three of these- **Lucknow Connect, Lucknow Society** and **Lucknow Expressions** deserve special mention. While Lucknow connect led by its moving spirit Chandra Prakash of Universal Book Depot arranges literary and other programmes from time to time, its contribution, in collaboration with other organisations and individuals for the restoration of Hazratganj can never be forgotten. Lucknow Society led by Shamim Akhtar Aarzoo and Lucknow Expression under the stewardship of Jayant Krishan and Kanak Rekha Chauhan have been holding Lucknow Literature Festival and Lucknow Literary Carnival respectively for the past three years. These literary festivals are now rubbing shoulders with similar big events like the internationally famous Jaipur Literary festival. Lucknow Society and Lucknow Expression have been giving substantial space to Hindi and Urdu literature too. Usually organized in January-February these literary festivals have given for the first time, an opportunity to the Lucknowites to watch and interact with top literary, theatre and film personalities. All the three organisations are not for profit ones dedicated to strive for restoration of Lucknow's heritage and traditions and to educate people about Lucknow's glorious past and also help the new generations develop a sense of belonging to this fascinating city.

Lucknow Society

Lucknow Society aims to preserve, promote and resurrect the inimitable culture and heritage of the city of nawabs, revive its past magnificence as it affects a modern grace. **'Let's Unite for Culture, Knowledge, Nationalism and Objective Welfare of Society'**–each character of the christening contains the fervor of commitment to the cause. Headed by a band of zealous lucknowites, the society came into force on 25th April 2011 sanctioned under the Societies Registration Act (Act XXI of 1860). In the four years following its momentous conception, it has worked ardently as a restorative of the city's primal pride, acting as a crucial channel between governmental and non-governmental organizations, individual crusaders of its cause. Cultural pursuits have been redeemed from fading ruins of remembrance and records. Poets, writers, warriors, places, customs, the arts and a quintessential people all celebrated and deemed with dignity and respect that is their due. Raising and revealing to the youth the soul of the city, its true and inspiring legacy and the onus that rests on them to uplift and sustain its cultural and social renovation, has been one of its essential occupation. Up, Aware and rooted in its regal inheritance that is the society's goal for the city's imminent heirs.

The Society has not in only been a non-profit organization in these past years but has also acted as an extended family to the city. There have been made several efforts in making the city a better place by the Society. Be it awareness campaigns like "**Kyunki Shahar Hai Aapka**" or paying tributes to Lucknow's legends in "**Shaam-e-Adab**", LUCKNOW Society has always been paying equal consideration to the contemporary botheration as well as decrepit complications.

The "**Lucknow Literary Festival**", which has been adorned with sundry of well - known names and faces that not only grace the event with their presence but also share their experiences, their insights with young and old alike, which not only solves the purpose of making the legendry writers shine among the youngsters but also encouraging the young talent to come forward or be it bringing forward the drifting dance culture of Lucknow through "**Lucknow Dance Festival**".

Be it the initiatives like "**Let's revive**", "**Save Our Heritage**", "**Know Your City**", which are not only targeted to make the city what it used to be once but too to make the youth aware of what they have been missing for so long. The initiatives are not only in order to spread the awareness but returning the city it's timeworn glory too.

As we say the Society has always played a role of the extended family to the city, it has also given equal opportunities as well as liberty to the citizens to express their views and perspective through initiatives like "**Let's Share**" and "**Ab Isko Kya Kaha Jaaye**"where the social issues are captured and highlighted to the concerned authorities as well, in order to make them take the appropriate action; at the same time offering them equal insights of Lucknow's rich language and food culture through initiatives like "**Zabaan-e-Lucknow**" and "**Zaiqa-e-Lucknow**"

Being a family there exist no chance to obliterate the memories of the ones who made us what we are today, the legends in various fields of life. The initiatives like "**Let's Salute**" and "**Yaadein**" take us back in the dates to events and personalities associated with them. Encouraging the youth to come forward, the Society has been conducting the "**Quiz Lucknow**" strictly based on the lurking facts of the city as well as presenting the citizens with the enchanting beauty of the city through the monuments captured in the "**Right Angle**" calendar.LUCKNOW Society has also recently presented the city, a coffee table book "**Discovering Lucknow**" as well as a monthly magazine "**The Lucknow Observer**" which presents to readers with almost all aspects the city is known for.

Perpetually encouraging the new talent, the Society also conducts workshops like "**Let's Save Calligraphy**" in order to save the dying art form, which still can be seen in almost all the mausoleum and mosques of the city. Various online/offline contests like contests like "**Explore Lucknow"**: photography contest is one of its kind contest, the Society is known for its youngsters while the renowned and the legendries have been awarded with "**Pride of Lucknow Award**" and "**Wajid Ali Shah Award**" on regular basis.The Society has always been known for the way it faces the social challenges and cross every hurdle faced to achieve its goal and make the city a better place to live.

Sanatkada

Lucknow, a city known for its culture art and diversity, is a place where the present still nestles in the ambience of the past. Today a modern vibrant city whose people are known to appreciate and savour good food, language and "nawabi ada". Lucknow is a perfect place to get self help and craft groups from far flung parts of the country to showcase their products.

The idea of having such a space in Lucknow is how started Sanatkada (Sanat-Craft and Kada-Home) in 2006, where organized groups of craftspeople from Rajasthan, Gujerat, Uttranchal, Andhra Pradesh, Assam, Delhi, Madhya Pradesh, Orissa, Kashmir, Himanchal Pradesh, Bihar, Karnataka, West Bengal, and various parts of Uttar Pradesh (Bijnor, Varanasi, Bhadhoi, Farrukhabad, Chitrakoot, Lucknow, Rampur, Mathura and Noida) have directly sold their products. These groups have worked over years to revive and restore the traditional crafts of their area while providing a sustainable livelihood to the artisans. They have woven traditional skills in contemporary designs to cater to the markets in the major cities. Over the years we have organized exhibitions across the country with a view to reach out to more number of customers. Thus while being able to cater to the urban buyer it has been able to provide markets and livelihood to those making these products.

By partnering with Mahindra Group it organizes the Mahindra Sanatkada Lucknow Festival, a crafts mela (exhibition) and performing arts extravaganza at the historic and beautiful Kaiserbagh Baradari Palace in Lucknow. The first festival in February 2010 drew 100 craftsmen and over 1000 attendees.

The festival brings together four days of art, music, dance, literature, and cuisine. Artisans and master craftsmen from all over India display their work, and folk musicians and dancers perform traditional pieces. Attendees can also go on history tours, attend literature and poetry sessions, and sample a mouth-watering array of gourmet dishes. Held every February, the Mahindra Sanatkada Lucknow Festival is a celebration of India's vibrant arts, culture, and history.

The moving spirit behind Sanatkada is a dynamic and imaginative person Madhvi Kukreja and her team of associates and workers. The office cum show room is located on Jagdish Chandra Bose Marg opposite Baradari in Qaiserbagh area.

Bhartendu Academy of Dramatic Arts

Bhartendu Natya Academy came into existence as a drma institute on 2 July 1975, by the sheer effort of the legendary theatre personality Raj Bisaria.

In 1975 its name was Bhartendu Natya Kendra and the class was running at the mini Rabindralay (near Lucknow Station). At that time BNA did not have their own building; now it functions from the Bhartendu Bhawan in Gomti Nagar, Lucknow.

In 1981 the institute started providing a two-year full-time diploma course in theatre training. The institute today selects 20 candidates every year for its two-year intensive post-graduate diploma course with scholarships for the first 12 students. Raj Bisaria was the founder-director. Hindi writer Amritlal Nagar was the first nominated chairperson of the institute. Today Bhartendu Natya Academy has become the second of its kind in India after the National School of Drama, New Delhi. At the end of their course, the second-year students make a visit to the Film and Television Institute of India, Pune or Satyajit Ray Film and Television Institute, Kolkata for the basic training for film and television. This is a kind of extension program done with the financial support of Film Bandhu (a body under the Cultural Department of the U.P. Government).

Uttar Pradesh Hindi Sansthan

Uttar Pradesh holds a crucial place in the Hindi world. Moreover it has also been the work place of a number of highly talented and illustrious personalities of Hindi language and literature. For the enrichment and development of Hindi language and literature, the Government of Uttar Pradesh founded the Uttar Pradesh Hindi Sansthan in December,1976. The existing organizations of Hindi, that is, Hindi Samiti, Uttar Pradesh Hindi Grantha Academy and the administrations other projects were incorporated in it.

One of the main objectives of the Sansthan is publication of books in humanities, social sciences, Hindi language and literature, encyclopaedia etc. It has already published around 700 books in Hindi on different fields of knowledge. Besides publication, it also provides financial assistance to the aged and needy writers and poets and confers various awards with substantial amount of money every year to the scholars, writers, and poets of Hindi for their contribution. Situated in an elegant and spacious building of its own in Hazaratganj area it has a rich library, picture gallery, and auditoria for conducting various programmes.

Uttar Pradesh Urdu Academy

The Uttar Pradesh Urdu Academy was established by the Government of Uttar Pradesh in 1972 for the promotion and enrichment of Urdu language and literature. The Academy works for the benefit of the Urdu knowing public through it's schemes such as giving scholarships to students from class IV to the Ph.D level, to reprint the classical books of merit in Urdu, to publish new books to give financial assistance to the old and needy Urdu poets, writers, journalists and calligraphers to hold seminars and workshops on the current topics concerning promotion of Urdu language and literature. Besides, the Academy also organizes mushairas on the occasion of national festivals. It is now located in its own building in Gomti Nagar.

Uttar Pradesh Sanskrit Sansthanam

Established in 1976 by the Government of Uttar Pradesh for the promotion and development of Sanskrit, Pali and Prakrit, it has been functioning actively since its inception. Among it's objectives, the more important ones are publication of Hindi translation of important Sanskrit works in science and various other fields, publication of books and magazines in Sanskrit, exchange and networking with other Sanskrit organizations and helping the aged and sick Sanskrit scholars, with suitable grants.

❑❑